COMPARATIVE AND INTERNATIONAL EDUCATION SERIES

Volume 6

Vocationalizing Education

An International Perspective

COMPARATIVE AND INTERNATIONAL EDUCATION

Series Editor: PHILIP G. ALTBACH: State University of New York at Buffalo, USA

NOTICE TO READERS

Dear Reader

An invitation to Publish in and Recommend the Placing of a Standing Order to Volumes Published in this Valuable Series.

If your library is not already a standing/continuation order customer to this series, may we recommend that you place a standing/continuation order to receive immediately upon publication all new volumes. Should you find that these volumes no longer serve your needs, your order can be cancelled at any time without notice.

The Editors and the Publisher will be glad to receive suggestions or outlines of suitable titles, reviews or symposia for editorial consideration: if found acceptable, rapid publication is guaranteed.

ROBERT MAXWELL
Publisher at Pergamon Press

Vocationalizing Education

An International Perspective

Edited by

JON LAUGLO
University of London
Institute of Education

and

KEVIN LILLIS
University of London
Institute of Education

PERGAMON PRESS

OXFORD · NEW YORK · BEIJING · FRANKFURT
SÃO PAULO · SYDNEY · TOKYO · TORONTO

U.K.	Pergamon Press, Headington Hill Hall, Oxford OX3 0BW, England
U.S.A.	Pergamon Press, Maxwell House, Fairview Park, Elmsford, New York 10523, U.S.A.
PEOPLE'S REPUBLIC OF CHINA	Pergamon Press, Room 4037, Qianmen Hotel, Beijing, People's Republic of China
FEDERAL REPUBLIC OF GERMANY	Pergamon Press, Hammerweg 6, D-6242 Kronberg, Federal Republic of Germany
BRAZIL	Pergamon Editora, Rua Eça de Queiros, 346, CEP 04011, Paraiso, São Paulo, Brazil
AUSTRALIA	Pergamon Press Australia, P.O. Box 544, Potts Point, N.S.W. 2011, Australia
JAPAN	Pergamon Press, 8th Floor, Matsuoka Central Building, 1-7-1 Nishishinjuku, Shinjuku-ku, Tokyo 160, Japan
CANADA	Pergamon Press Canada, Suite No. 271, 253 College Street, Toronto, Ontario, Canada M5T 1R5

Copyright © 1988 Pergamon Books Ltd.

All Rights Reserved. No part of this publication may be reproduced, stored in a retrieval system or transmitted in any form or by any means: electronic, electrostatic, magnetic tape, mechanical, photocopying, recording or otherwise, without permission in writing from the publishers.

First edition 1988

Library of Congress Cataloging in Publication Data
Vocationalizing education.
(Comparative and international education series; v. 6)
Selected papers from a conference on the vocationalization of education which was held at the Dept. of International and Comparative Education, University of London, Institute of Education in 1986, with the Swedish International Development Authority, Stockholm as its principal sponsor.
1. Vocational education——Congresses. 2. Education——Economic aspects——Congresses. I. Lauglo, Jon. II. Lillis, Kevin. III. Sweden. Styrelsen för internationell utveckling. IV. Series.
LC1043.V63   1987   370.11'3   87-7220

British Library Cataloguing in Publication Data
Vocationalizing education: an international perspective.——
(Comparative and international educational series: v. 6).
1. Vocational education
I. Lauglo, Jon II. Lillis, Kevin M.
III. Series
370.11'3   LC1043

ISBN 0-08-035855-1 (Hardcover)
ISBN 0-08-035856-X (Flexicover)

Printed in Great Britain by A. Wheaton & Co. Ltd., Exeter

Introduction to the Series

The Comparative and International Education Series is dedicated to inquiry and analysis on educational issues in an interdisciplinary cross-national framework. As education affects larger populations and educational issues are increasingly complex and, at the same time, international in scope, this series presents research and analysis aimed at understanding contemporary educational issues. The series brings the best scholarship to topics which have direct relevance to educators, policy makers and scholars, in a format that stresses the international links among educational issues. Comparative education not only focuses on the development of educational systems and policies around the world, but also stresses the relevance of an international understanding of the particular problems and dilemmas that face educational systems in individual countries.

Interdisciplinarity is a hallmark of comparative education and this series will feature studies based on a variety of disciplinary, methodological and ideological underpinnings. Our concern is for relevance and the best in scholarship.

The series will combine careful monographic studies that will help policy makers and others obtain a needed depth for enlightened analysis with wider-ranging volumes that may be useful to educators and students in a variety of contexts. Books in the series will reflect on policy and practice in a range of educational settings from pre-primary to post-secondary. In addition, we are concerned with non-formal education and with the societal impact of educational policies and practices. In short, the scope of the Comparative and International Education Series is interdisciplinary and contemporary.

I wish to thank the assistance of a distinguished editorial advisory board including:

Professor Suma Chitnis, Tata Institute of Social Sciences, Bombay, India.
Professor Kazayuki Kitamura, Research Institute for Higher Education, Hiroshima, Japan.
Professor Gail P. Kelly, State University of New York at Buffalo, USA.
Dean Thomas La Belle, University of Pittsburgh, USA.
Dr S. Gopinathan, Institute of Education, Singapore.
Professor Guy Neave, Institute of Education, London.

PHILIP G. ALTBACH

Acknowledgements

This book is a selection from the invited contributions to a conference on the Vocationalization of Education, which was held at the Department of International and Comparative Education, University of London Institute of Education in 1986.

We are grateful to the contributors who have made this book possible, by addressing so many aspects of an internationally important policy question.

The original event which occasioned these and other contributions, received generous financial support from the Commission of the European Communities (Brussels), the International Development Research Center (Ottawa) and in particular from the Swedish International Development Authority (SIDA, Stockholm) in association with which this book is being published.

SIDA's support for this activity began with the sponsorship of an evaluation of industrial education subjects in Kenyan academic secondary schools. A contribution from that study is included in this book (the chapter by Lauglo and Närman). The main evaluation reports have appeared in SIDA's publication series Education Division documents.

We are deeply appreciative to the sponsors for their support to the conference and this publication.

JON LAUGLO AND KEVIN LILLIS
University of London Institute of Education

Contents

Introduction

CHAPTER 1

"Vocationalization" in International Perspective

JON LAUGLO and KEVIN LILLIS

University of London Institute of Education

"VOCATIONALIZATION" of secondary education is taken to mean curriculum change in a practical or vocational direction. This is an old and recurring policy theme in many countries, especially in the Third World (Lillis and Hogan, 1983; Hultin, 1987; Chisman, 1987; Gustafsson, 1987). What is remarkable in the 1980s is the prevalence of vocationalization as a trend that transcends the divide between rich and poor countries, and between different political systems (Grubb, 1985; Droogleever Fortuijn *et al.*, 1987). The range of country case studies included in this volume illustrates the international importance of the theme.

It will be argued that these policies are mainly a political response to poor articulation of schooling with the labor market. Vocationalization is intended to ease school-leavers into jobs or self-employment, under conditions of widespread youth unemployment. An important question then is how far this intention is realistic. Critics of vocationalization argue that it is not, and that educational change, at least in the short run, does not alleviate depressed economic opportunity. Vocationalization policies are nonetheless a response to economic recession. But recession means tight public finance, making it harder to meet the greater cost per student that vocationalization requires. It will also be argued that vocational and practical subjects, as "pedagogic systems," have unusually complex requirements which are not easily met, especially when they are to be established quickly and on a large scale. These equipment, materials, curriculum, support system, personnel and management requirements are especially difficult to meet in developing countries—even if finance were available and barriers related to lack of interest among pupils and parents were overcome.

Youth unemployment may provide the political momentum behind the vocationalization trend, but there are long-standing justifications for "practical subjects" according to certain internationally influential concepts of general education which are related to political ideologies. "Educators" tend to stress these concepts more, whilst "trainers" and politicians tend to stress labor market relevance, sometimes leading to ambiguities within the curriculum.

3

Concepts of General Education

Pragmatism

Pragmatist epistemology underlies ideas which hold that learning should be directly relevant for the active interests and concerns which pupils have—or will face—in their out-of-school life: in their private lives and in their future roles as workers and citizens. There is a stress of "relevance" for out-of-school application. There is a rejection of the view that curriculum should be justified by reference to intrinsically worthwhile structures of knowledge. Pragmatism rejects dualism between "pure" and "applied" knowledge. Pragmatists argue that learning occurs best when arising out of application to "real-life" problems, and when it is derived from sensory experience. Further, they stress the importance of broad human development, including psycho-motor and aesthetic abilities.

Pragmatism provides varied justification for vocationalization. On the one hand, it implies that problems of finding and preparing for an occupation should be addressed by the school. Similarly, the uses that pupils may have for using tools and practical techniques in their private life should be included. But there is also support for the aesthetic side of practical subjects, and a general emphasis on a practical approach in the teaching of any subject.

There is within the pragmatist perspective tension between a "hard" emphasis on the teaching of highly specified useful skills (e.g., behavioral objectives), and a "soft" emphasis on development of such highly generalized processes as "creativity" or "ability to work independently" (Lauglo, 1983). These contrasting emphases may be reflected in the pedagogy of different practical subjects. One can expect that the "hard" emphasis will prevail when practical subjects are justified by relevance for jobs in a depressed labor market ("employable skills"), when they are taught by poorly qualified teachers (cf. Beeby, 1966), or more generally when a highly didactic educational culture prevails in an education system, with detailed syllabuses imposed on schools (cf. Davies, 1985; Lauglo, 1985a, Chapter 9; Lillis, 1985).

Curriculum thought in the United States has been profoundly influenced by pragmatism and its emphasis on the importance of "useful" learning. Not only the American pragmatist philosophy of education—with Dewey as the main exponent—but also the utilitarian strain in American culture in general, along with populist scepticism of "academic" high culture, has reinforced the view that education should be as directly useful as possible.

Mass secondary education reduces the dominance of university preparation in curriculum development, leaving more scope for preparation for work, citizenship and for the concerns of private life. Thus, when secondary education assumes a mass character, a pragmatist view of curriculum is strengthened. In the United States, the inclusion of such subjects as industrial arts, domestic science and business subjects in the high school curriculum reflect both pragmatist educational theory and the mass character of the high school. Wilms argues that vocationalism is also a reflection of the American ideology of "self-improvement"—stressing social ascent by means of education.

Recent trends in the United States seem to agree with the "hard" variety of pragmatist education: "back to basics" plus "employable skills." Similar trends can be detected in the mass secondary education systems of Western Europe (cf. this volume, Chapter 9). In general, it seems as if it is the hard variety of pragmatism—which could be labeled "austere utilitarianism"—which gains ground during economic depression.

Polytechnical Education

Support for practical subjects is found in the socialist concept of polytechnical education which is rooted in Marxist epistemology. There are some overlaps with pragmatism. One is rejection of dualism between "theory" and "practice" (or "pure" and "applied" knowledge), and of the educational superiority of the former. The notion of Praxis is central to Marxist epistemology. Man learns by acting on natural phenomena, transforming them while experiencing their influence. This experience is also the criterion of truth. Therefore, curriculum should seek to integrate "theory" and "practice." But whilst pragmatism stresses the value of "experience" and "activity" more generally, Marxism holds up the educative value of productive work in particular. "Education with production" is an idea which has been a recurring theme in socialist rhetoric and policy. It has taken different forms and been given different emphasis at different times, and in different countries.

In its most "romantic," post-revolutionary vision, "education with production" has meant that students should participate in productive work outside the school and learn directly from workers and peasants. In China, during the Cultural Revolution, such ideas prevailed. Further, the goal has been that real-life problems of production should be the starting point of the teaching of science. Thus the original ideal has been to break down the institutional boundaries between education and productive work. The most extremely romantic idea within this tradition would be that of Shul'gin in the early years after the Russian Revolution: "the withering away of the school." The current interest in education with production in Zimbabwe (cf. this volume, Chapter 13) is a less extreme example of this post-revolutionary socialist pattern in education policy. Nevertheless, the trend in socialist countries has everywhere increasingly been to recognize the need for institutional boundaries between different school subjects and between education and productive work. Specially trained teachers are needed—also in vocational subjects—and the natural flow of productive process does not easily fit pedagogic needs, as Price (1974) has noted in a study of productive work in the curriculum of Chinese and Soviet secondary schools, so long as the aim is not only to teach well-defined and stable technique but also a grasp of underlying general processes and related bodies of knowledge.

Hence "learning about production" has become a distinct school subject, and natural science is taught as an academic subject with a structure and sequence of concepts that are quite independent from local production. The more clearly "polytechnical" elements of the curriculum (learning about production and labor training) have in Eastern Europe become established in "polytechnical centers" which may be lodged within local industry but which still remain separate from the normal production organization of the firm—a system pioneered in East Germany (Siebert-Klein, 1980). In short, pedagogic and organizational imperatives of schools imply institutional boundaries also when integration is the professed ideal. O'Dell's chapter in this volume (11) on recent Soviet vocationalization trends shows such institutionalization in spite of an educational ideology which in its origins militated sharply against it. What remains is support for work-related practical skills as a worthwhile part of general education and an ideology that stresses the economic and political importance of work—especially manual labor.

After socialist regimes have gained power, they have attached great importance to political socialization—especially of pupils in select schools who potentially are part of the country's future elite. One measure has been to include political views (or proletarian origin) among the selection criteria. Another measure is to introduce some form of national service or participation in production in order to instil respect for labor. This theme of practical work as a means of teaching values is one that polytechnical education shares with populist ideas. It has therefore been salient in those socialist countries which for reasons of colonial domination have had an unusually sharp cultural divide between the elite and the populace.

Populism

Populism refers to movements or sentiments that celebrate the culture and good sense of ordinary people and their political and economic rights. Further, populism is defined by its anti-elitist and anti-bureaucratic character, rather than by any single ideology or philosophical expression. Populism has often been a predominantly rural phenomenon, directed against the economic, cultural and political dominance of an urban elite or against an "alien" rural aristocracy. It may also be seen as a reaction against industrialism and its associated urban-centered development strategy (Kitching, 1982). In this regard, Nyerere and Mao are within the populist tradition, as are 19th-century European anarchist philosophers.

Populism tends to define "the people" in broad and communal terms and to de-emphasize conflicting group interests within "the common folk." Thus, a local "organic" community is assumed, pitted against an oppressive and often culturally alien upper class and its local representatives. Among the diverse manifestations of populism are: cooperative movements designed to replace exploitative "middle men," movements seeking to establish a national language based on the vernacular, "Low-church" religious revivals, and a wide range of political movements that have sought to make political institutions more broadly, more locally and more directly accountable to the populace. Nevertheless, charismatic leadership has sometimes led to strong central direction within populist movements. The profoundly democratic Danish folk high school movement is part of the populist tradition. But Fascism can also be seen as populist in character.

Hard, physical toil is an important basis for identification as "common folk." Populism typically celebrates the importance of work as a source of moral fiber, self-reliance and civic virtue. Productive physical work is by this perspective educational in that it develops valued personal qualities. Populism may be sceptical of formal schooling on the grounds that it unduly distances the young from their cultural origins, or because school removes a person from the hurly-burly of "real-life" situations in which true character is formed. Indeed, populist ideas have usually been invoked to support anti-intellectualism—whether Mid-Western McCarthyism or Mao's Cultural Revolution.

Local, popular control of education is a typical populist demand. Schools are accepted when their teaching accords with the high culture of ordinary folk and when they otherwise reinforce pupils' identification with their cultural origins. Within school, populist values can lend support to the teaching of the design and tools of folk crafts. Arguably, the teaching of woodwork and textile craft in the Scandinavian primary schools developed historically as an expression of such sentiments. As legacy today is a strong concern with "creative activities" in subjects which are now more widely defined (cf. this volume, Chapter 10).

Populists view secondary schools with suspicion because of their role in the transmission of elitist culture, but at the same time there is the concern to ensure that secondary pupils identify with "the people." Productive work may be introduced for this end. A further implication of a populist stance is that secondary education should look to the needs of those who will leave school and "return to the community," and not let the requirements of higher stages of schooling unduly dominate the curriculum further down the ladder. This gives support for subjects purporting to be directly relevant to work, home and community life—including practical subjects.

Throughout the Third World, there is the legacy of independence movements with a populist ideology. Yet another legacy of colonialism is a sharp cultural divide between the elite and "the people." Along with various "national service" schemes, there are examples of "practical subjects" or "practical work" which are intended to combat elitism. Education for self-reliance in Tanzania (cf. this volume, Chapter 16) is one such example, rooted in a combination of socialist and populist ideas. In this case, the egalitarian goal is not primarily that of equal access to secondary education for persons from different socio-economic backgrounds (cf. this volume, Chapter 15)—or more likely in Tanzania, equal access for different ethnic/ regional groups—it is rather that of reducing the cultural gap between ordinary people and the elite, whatever its origins.

The implications of pragmatism, of polytechnical education and of populism overlap considerably though numerous conditions constrain their implementation. The current wave of interest in vocationalization is not rooted in ideological revival but in political and economic conditions. But the ideas discussed above matter as long-standing educational justifications for these policies. They are ideas which are "actualized" by political and economic circumstance.

It is also important that each superpower—the USSR and the USA—is the "home base" of a supportive ideology for vocationalization, polytechnical education and pragmatism respectively. Thus the international networks of influence centered on each of these superpowers carry assumptions and ideals about education which are supportive of the present trend. Conversely, the ideals associated with a purely academic secondary school curriculum have historically been associated with powers whose influence has faded: Britain, France and Germany. One of the reasons why vocationalization is a policy issue that refuses to die (see this volume, Chapter 2) is that it is far more than a hoped-for remedy for youth unemployment: it is strongly related to internationally influential political ideologies and educational ideals.

Program Goals and Outcomes

Psacharopoulos reviewed the declared aims of World Bank financed "curriculum diversification" (vocationalization) in a number of countries. He concluded that "relevance for the world of work" and "equity considerations" are the common aims. The chapters in this volume by Wright, Saunders, Marklund, Gallart, and Chin-Aleong (Chapters 7, 9, 10, 12 and 17, respectively) all reveal goals of these types, though Marklund notes that the "means and ends" of vocationalization are related to the specific level at which a program takes place.

Labor Market Relevance

Vocationalization policies are a quest for greater labor market relevance of education: for better articulation between the content of schooling and subsequent application of acquired skills, attitudes and knowledge in the world of work, both in obtaining a livelihood and in becoming more productive in the work obtained. The programs examined in this volume show a spectrum of such "economic relevance" goals: pre-vocational education (preparation for vocational training), skills training, preparing for direct entry to jobs, diminishing the pressure on higher education by making secondary education more "terminal," instilling more favorable attitudes to technical and practical work and remedying youth unemployment.

Most of the chapters identify the overt political rhetoric behind the program goals, revealing considerable commonality of intentions across different economic and ideological contexts. Bacchus traces the political origins of vocationalization within the colonized Caribbean—and by inference, many other less developed countries—as aimed at preparing pupils to be economically productive within the socio-economic context from which they come. Behind this rationale lie strong political motivations to use vocationalized programs as a means of lowering occupational aspirations to more "realistic" levels as well as to meet lower-level manpower needs. Bacchus implies that this motivation has shifted little over time, from colonial rule to indigenous political leadership after independence. Contemporary programs remain essentially political responses to the harsh labor market contexts in which school-leavers are unable to find jobs. The hope is that teaching more specific vocational skills will alleviate this problem. This quest for the greater economic relevance of education by stressing more job-specific skills may be inspired by a human capital approach to education, but it should be noted that human capital theory as applied in rate-of-return analysis can also be applied in criticism of vocationalization (cf. this volume, Chapter 15).

When general education aims are officially invoked, labor-market relevance will still be the hidden agenda of vocationalization so long as the context is one of widespread school-leaver unemployment. There are some ironies in this situation. During the years of rapid economic growth and enrollment expansion in the 1960s, when school-leavers were easily absorbed into the labor market in most countries, there was an international trend in favor of general education and of a more "general" kind of vocational training—at least in the OECD countries. The argument then was that rapid technological development and economic growth required a labor force with a better general education so that people would become better able to cope with changing technology and types of work.

There was emphasis on language, mathematics, natural science, social science and on developing highly generalized mental processes—such as the elusive "learning to learn." General education gained support from this view. In some countries one saw shifts in policy for vocational education, making it more school-based and more like general education: more scope for general education subjects, and a broader concept of vocational preparation. The Swedish system (cf. this volume, Chapter 10) is the result of strong shifts in this direction. More weakly expressed trends occurred in other OECD countries. Gallart points to similar developments in Argentina. The academic drift of technical secondary schools in Kenya (Lauglo, 1985b) is another case of a shift from vocational "training" to "vocational education."

The argument at that time was that when it is difficult to predict the exact vocational skills which a person will require in the future, one should stress education rather than training. But a loose association between curriculum content and subsequent work does not only occur under conditions of rapid economic growth and technological change. It is equally true in a depressed economy with a high rate of unemployment, that acquired specialist skills which relate to particular occupations may not be put to use in those occupations because of constricted opportunity.

Secondary school output has in recent years grown much faster than employment opportunity. Policymakers therefore need to address the problems of slow growth and youth unemployment. These imperatives shape educational policy, regardless of whether the problems can be remedied by educational means. Vocationalization has political appeal as an educational response to economic problems. In these circumstances, parents and pupils will themselves become more attracted both to vocational training and to "vocationalized" elements in general education, because such education holds out the hope—realistic or not—of competitive advantage in access to work. The hope that skills acquired will lead to the types of work for which they are earmarked shapes both the policy rhetoric and the nature of "social demand" for education.

Vocationalization of mainstream, general secondary schooling, rather than more specialized and institutionally separate vocational training, is at the center of policy attention because policy is not responding to shortages of trained persons but to unemployment among those leaving the mainstream of the education system. Hence the thrust of vocationalization policies is to graft vocational elements onto a curriculum that remains predominantly academic, without shunting students away from the path to higher education. Vocational elements which are supplementary to a mainly academic course cannot provide training in depth. The term "pre-vocational" is used about such subjects. Whilst broadly related to a "family of occupations," pre-vocational education does not provide sufficient training for direct entry to the occupations concerned, but is rather a form of "familiarization" which would be useful in subsequent training and for making more informed choice about training. A term that is often used is that the goal is to make students more "trainable." This concept has some weaknesses. In a depressed labor market, access to more specialized training (especially apprenticeships) will be constricted. Therefore, pre-vocational education may not lead to any related vocational training.

Further, the aim of informing "choice of career" will be somewhat misplaced because the problem facing prospective school-leavers is simply to find a source of livelihood, not so much to choose one that is congenial with their own interests.

An important question in assessing the economic relevance of vocationalized education is what employers in fact are looking for when hiring school-leavers. Oxenham's chapter (4), mainly drawing on research in certain developing countries, argues that there is no neat universal explanation of what employers want from school; that in Britain too, there may be no coherent employers' view, and that there is in any case no firm connection between scholastic qualification and job function. His inference is that vocational training is best left to the employers themselves, and that schools should concentrate on improving what is their distinct role: general education. Wilms, writing on the United States (Chapter 5), similarly argues that employers "tended to favor applicants with academic rather than vocational educational backgrounds; they place premium not on technical skills but on good work habits and attitudes."

Noah and Eckstein's study of Britain, France and Germany (Chapter 3) reaches a similar conclusion about mainstream schools. The demand from employers is not exactly for pre-vocational courses relating to specific occupations or families of occupations. Rather, the emphasis is on better teaching of basic communication and computation skills, and a more practical approach to teaching such skills so that greater attention is paid to their application in work situations. Though stressing general education, this is nonetheless a utilitarian or "hard pragmatist" view. A depressed labor market places employers in a position of advantage *vis-à-vis* schools, enabling the former to espouse with greater force their distinctive perspective on general education. Thus, Noah and Eckstein noted that employers would like schools to be managed more "efficiently" (i.e., more in keeping with business notions of good management), and that schools should teach more general knowledge about the "world of work" and its requirements. What employers want from general secondary schools is that schools should define their work so that it better corresponds with the values and interests of the "buyers of labor": socializing youth into conscientious employees with appreciation of the "needs of industry," and with good and practically-oriented basic communication and computation skills. However, employers seemingly do not wish schools to place greater emphasis on the specific skills associated with particular occupations, whether pre-vocational or vocational training. One reason is that employers often doubt that schools can do this properly. It is often reported that employers are sceptical of training that is solely school-based.

In a depressed labour market, the job seekers and the institutions educating them have to adapt to the values and interests of employers. On the other hand, in a buoyant labour market, it is employers who face the need to pay greater attention to the concerns for personal fulfilment which job-seekers then can afford to have. In Western industrialized countries, at least, there has been a profound shift in the salient themes in public debate about education since the late 1960s. Then, strong allegations were made that both schools and work organizations have alienating consequences for human fulfilment. Specifically, the claim was that schools in their organization, content and selection function are too closely geared to the requirements of business and industry. It was argued that education must become more relevant for social criticism and for the self-realization of learners. Today, the prevailing concerns in educational debate are different and in some respects the opposite: how to meet the requirements of the work place in order to ease access to scarce employment. Further, there is a tendency to blame the schools for the present economic ills—or at least to view curriculum change as a means to make the future work-force more employable and productive.

Do pre-vocational and vocational courses at secondary level provide young people with an advantage in the labor market? The studies of "employers' views" cannot answer this question adequately, for hiring practices may also be governed by other considerations than school credentials and the views that employers have of them. One must examine the patterns of labor market absorption of young people exposed to different types of school or curricula. Tracer study findings on these issues are rare. One would expect that training in depth gives an advantage for available jobs which clearly require such training. But it depends not only on the work-relevance of training. It also depends on the balance between demand and supply of persons with a given type of training. Chin-Aleong's chapter (17) on Trinidad and Tobago shows that in the context of a booming economy, "specialized craft students" found jobs more quickly and earned better salaries than did "academic students" or those with "pre-technician" courses akin to pre-vocational education. Similarly, Gallart notes that technical school graduates in Argentina who entered the labor market at a time of good employment prospects evince high rates of labor force participation and that only ¼ of them after 11–12 years were in "occupations that had nothing to do with the training they had received." But we do not know whether such school-based training in depth is a general asset for access to jobs in a depressed economy. On the one hand, depth of training should give advantage for directly related jobs. But its value for access to other types of work could be inferior to a broader preparation with more general education elements (such as pre-vocational education) unless "training in depth" is perceived by employers to convey valuable transferable attitudes and skills.

The other tracer studies reported in this volume concern pre-vocational education. Psacharopoulos's research in Colombia and Tanzania showed no labor advantage of graduates from such vocationalized courses, neither in terms of success in finding employment nor pay levels when employed. Närman's findings from Kenya, reported in the chapter by Lauglo and Närman, are similar: school-leavers with greater exposure to the "industrial education" subjects were no more successful than others in finding employment. When employment was obtained it rarely had any direct relationship to the pre-vocational component in their secondary school background. Thus, the findings indicate that the kind of vocationalization which is only a supplement to a mainly academic curriculum is no remedy for youth unemployment.

There is, however, good reason to eschew cavalier generalizations about the lack of labor market benefits of vocationalization. One needs to distinguish between and examine separately pre-vocational education, and the different forms of vocational training. Whilst it seems true that curriculum reform creates neither jobs nor opportunities for self-employment, at least not in the short run, it is equally true that even a depressed labor market is not uniformly bleak. Shortages and surpluses of skilled labor will often coexist, but relate to different occupations or localities. Training programs may have little effect on the overall scale of unemployment, but small-scale vocational training can still prepare for those pockets of opportunity which do exist even in a depressed labor market.

Training programs developed in response to such "pockets of opportunity" require careful monitoring. There is the need to adapt to labor market change. Yesterday's shortage is often tomorrow's surplus. Programs purporting to prepare for specific occupations and/or further vocational training should therefore have built-in procedures for monitoring what happens to the trainees after training. Such procedures are rare.

The Kenyan findings also showed that doing well across all school subjects—even the fact of passing rather than failing—gave no advantage in the search for jobs during the first year after junior secondary school. This raises general questions about the role of school in selection to jobs. One suspects that when faced with an abundant supply of school-leavers for the few jobs available, employers resort more to other criteria than credentials from school. It is likely that personal connections through kinship networks, home district and other sources of prior acquaintance become increasingly important instead. This hypothesis contrasts with both "functionalist" and "social reproduction" perspectives on schooling. Both perspectives stress the selection function of schools for the occupational structure and its associated social hierarchy. A depressed labor market may erode the importance of that selection function, rather than leading to selection by ever finer gradations of credentials.

Vocationalization policies may aim to discourage unrealistic ambitions for further academic study, when selection to such study is becoming increasingly competitive, and to teach attitudes conducive to work-place discipline. A recurring theme in policy debate in developing countries is that students harbor "unrealistic" ambitions for further academic study and eventual entry to white-collar jobs. Bacchus refers to this concern in both colonial and post-independence educational policy. Gustafsson notes how this theme came out of a 1976 conference of African Ministers of Education: "breaking down the barriers of prejudice which exist between manual and intellectual labor . . . ". Psacharopoulos similarly refers to "the allegation that a system of academically oriented education instils attitudes in most students towards white-collar occupations in the urban-modern wage economy and not towards manual occupations and skills that are in short supply". O'Dell notes a strong present stress in Soviet policies on inculcating "the desired attitudes towards both work and society" as part of "labor training" in the schools.

What in socialist countries is assumed to be unconditionally desirable, that schools should transmit attitudes to work and types of work which accord with the "demands of industry," is in capitalist countries more problematic, from the point of view of socialist critics of capitalism as well as liberals concerned with general education. Hence, one concern in debate about the British vocationalization policies that are described in Murray Saunders' chapter (9), is the fear that the Technical and Vocational Education Initiative (TVEI) program is too "employer-orientated" and insufficiently attentive to the interests and wider educational needs of the students concerned. A recent book edited by Dale (1985) gives a broad survey of the wider issues related to current British policies.

In general, a main critique of education under capitalism has been that it teaches attitudes which correspond too closely to the social control requirements of industrial capitalism. At the same time, employers complain that the attitudes acquired in school are insufficiently supportive of industry and work-place requirements. Recent revisions of neo-Marxist critique (Carnoy and Levin, 1985) have come a bit closer to the liberal argument that education can and should be relatively autonomous of economic and political control imperatives. Nevertheless, there is at present a policy trend, in socialist and capitalist countries, in industrialized countries and developing countries alike, that emphasizes the desirability of teaching attitudes which are in keeping with economic realities and requirements.

Is vocationalization of curriculum content an effective means of teaching such attitudes? Effects on initiative, perseverance, docility *vis-à-vis* superiors, and habits of hard work are difficult to gauge. Occupational aspirations can be researched more readily. Critics of vocationalization (Foster, 1965) have argued that such aspirations or occupational preferences are shaped by structures of opportunity, not by curriculum. Therefore, exhortation or exposure to practical subjects will not make students interested in manual work so long as white collar jobs hold out the prospect of superior economic rewards. But high rates of unemployment and shrinking chances of promotion to higher stages of education may make vocationally-orientated courses and the types of occupation for which purportedly they are a preparation seem more attractive. Under such circumstances, it is more reasonable to expect attitudes to be affected by exposure to practical subjects in school. In other words, aspiration effects may result from interaction of opportunity structure after school and exposure to vocationally-orientated curriculum elements.

Wright concludes that business subjects are popular options in Sierra Leone secondary schools, that technical subjects (wood- and metalwork) were at least "not rejected," and that in general it is simply not true that students have a negative attitude to these subjects. Similar findings are reported by Lauglo and Närman from junior secondary schools in Kenya: woodwork, metalwork, electrical technology and power mechanics are popular subjects attracting students of good academic caliber. The Kenyan findings also show that exposure to these subjects increases students' interests in related "practical/technical" work. But equally important, there is no dearth of interest in such work in the first place. It is likely that in a depressed labor market for school-leavers, it is a misplaced policy concern to teach "appropriate" occupational attitudes. The Kenyan findings suggest that the problem is not lack of interest in vocationalized courses—at least not when their inclusion does not jeopardize prospects of further academic schooling—rather, the problem may be that not only students, but also parents and especially policymakers have unrealistic hopes about labor market advantages accruing to such courses.

Egalitarian Aims

Egalitarian values are also invoked in support of vocationalization. O'Dell points to the importance of such values for Soviet policies in the context of a system for which polytechnical education is the national educational ideology. Gustafsson traces similar influences in Zimbabwe. Wilms argues that "equality of educational opportunity" has historically been a major rationale for vocationalization in the US education system, as expressed in the aim of extending opportunity for basic industrial training to all pupils.

But egalitarian considerations can lead to different diagnoses about the merits of vocationalization. On the one hand, egalitarian values can justify curricula which would include practical subjects for all pupils, e.g., to reduce the sharpness of distinction between "theoretical" and "practical" knowledge and by extension the status gap between manual and non-manual work. These values will also favor the idea of using schools in order to make opportunities for vocational training more widely available than what on-the-job training will achieve. On the other hand, curricula that create within the same school a distinction between academic and vocationalized tracks run the risk of curtailing prospects of further promotion along the academic ladder for those in the vocationalized tracks, unless the vocationalized components are but a minor adjunct to an academic curriculum. Thus, vocationalization may conflict with egalitarian values when it creates, within the same type of school, curricula of different status. The vocationalized variety can then become a second class alternative which serves to discourage academic ambition without offering much real labor market advantage.

It should be recalled that in the 1960s, the thrust of Western European comprehensive school policies was to postpone the point of sharp division between curricula along the path to higher education, and curricula outside that path. Present vocationalization policies can be construed as a retrograde step according to the egalitarian perspective which then prevailed. A depressed labor market for secondary school graduates has shifted the object for egalitarian educational policies so that more attention is now given to the scarce opportunities for those who will not continue on the academic ladder. Thus, equity considerations can be invoked to justify more attention in the curriculum to the needs of those who will leave school to look for work. But considerations of social justice have also been prominent in policies seeking to reduce dualism within the secondary system between "practical" and "academic" curricula and types of school.

"Equity of educational opportunity" is a narrow concept in terms of current international debate about education and social inequality. A wider view of the role that schooling plays in reproducing inequality in society would also include analysis of how far vocationalization policies reinforce the legitimacy of hierarchical relations between social classes, genders or ethnic groups in terms of power or economic resources. The previous section discussed the view that vocationalization is part of a shift in control over school content in favor of employers. It can be argued that in both socialist and capitalist countries, current vocationalization policies are part of a trend of austere utilitarianism, and that it has an ambience of accepting and adapting to hierarchy and authority rather than questioning it. Vocationalization can thus be seen as part of a wider pattern of austere social values: of discipline, fitting in and making young people buckle down early to the private imperatives of earning a living.

The notion that vocationalization can serve social discipline is not new. Georg Kerschensteiner, through his writing and work, influenced the development of vocational education in Germany and subsequently in other countries emulating the German model of apprenticeship and part-time vocational schooling. In addition to trade efficiency, he stressed moral and civic goals: conscientiousness, industry, perseverance, responsibility, self-restraint, devotion to an active life and the importance of a person's duty to the state. In some countries, social control goals behind vocationalization policies may be quite manifest. These goals gain salience due to political unrest among unemployed graduates and school-leavers, or because those who frame educational policy worry about other forms of alienation among youth—such as delinquency, drugtaking or involvement in pop culture. Whether vocationalization in fact serves goals of social discipline remains an open question. Also, whether social discipline is antithetical to egalitarian values depends crucially on how far the established social order is perceived to be fundamentally oppressive—or conducive—to social justice. Thus, the equity considerations will in this regard depend on the political diagnosis that observers make of a given society.

The Formulation of Policy

Several chapters in this volume discuss the nature of policy formulation. Neave (6) seeks to establish how, within the Commission for European Communities, specific policies towards vocational education and training have evolved. He traces the dual origins of Community policies in separate administrative and juridical bases. On the one hand, there is vocational training *per se* which becomes a Commission concern as an instrument for encouraging mobility of labor among the then six member states. On the other hand, there is vocationalization as part of the cultural sphere of "education." Neave points to tensions between the two Commission Directorates concerned, as to the definitions of vocationalization and the role that the two Directorates should play. Those with responsibility for vocational training sought to extend elements into compulsory education in order to strengthen vocational training. Those working within "education" sought to strengthen within the vocational training system those elements of general education which might serve a remedial function for groups at risk. Neave's analysis is also useful for understanding of national policy-making. Different ministries will simultaneously be involved in vocationalization policies, with different connections with outside interest groups, different views of content and appropriate organization of provisions, and competing in their claims for jurisdiction and resources within the constraints of their legally defined scope. Coherent and speedy policy formulation is thus rendered more difficult. As Saunders points out, in the case of those special programs within secondary schools in the United Kingdom which are funded by the Manpower Services Commission outside the normal channels of finance and accountability of the education service, such programs may appear as well-resourced "enclaves" in the schools. This separateness reflects their separate channels of funding and accountability. Lack of integration locally will mirror lack of integration at the national level.

Neave describes how the main concerns behind the Commission's vocationalization policies have shifted over time, as problems of low economic growth and high youth unemployment have persisted longer than projected. At first, policies were directed to established patterns of vocational training and defined youth unemployment as "short term." Later policies were extended to also include compulsory education and universities, based on the view that a more comprehensive and long-term response was needed to "ensure the industrial renewal of Europe."

Similar shifts in policy occur in national systems, as the persistent severity of youth unemployment receives greater political recognition, and as established training provisions supplemented by unemployment palliatives are recognized to be inadequate. Politicians then face the need to propose more radical solutions—and the need to profess the belief that the solutions will work.

In developing countries, where problems of youth unemployment and low economic growth are far more severe than in member countries of the EEC, external agencies play an important part in policy formulation, through conditions for grants and loans, and sometimes through high-level policy advisers. Wright's chapter reveals the plurality of pressures on the Sierra Leone government for "curriculum diversification" policies which until recently were forcefully espoused by the World Bank. Through external pressure, many countries have been induced to launch vocationalization policies and have endeavored to build internal acceptance for these policies, often with little support from the concerned institutions and clienteles. But agency policies may be reversed and leave governments without further support for policies which were externally induced in the first place. Wright reasons that disappointing results from evaluations which seek to gauge costs and the intended benefits are insufficient grounds for abandoning policies. A project may be inadequately implemented, and a government may have other rationales for continuing policies, apart from those addressed in externally conducted evaluations. (See also Cooksey and Ishumi's (1986) discussion on policies in Tanzania.)

The implementation problems which evaluations by aid agencies reveal, can be due to the tensions created by pressure from the agency to begin with, and such programs are rarely implemented: "It could be argued that high priority on diversification was not really a matter of Government preference but much more an offer that the Government was constrained to accept." Wright suggests that funding agencies and recipient countries sometimes operate at "cross-purposes over policy, with bizarre and distorting consequences for the implementation of such policies." Often, the application of an input-output evaluation paradigm is inappropriate since it assumes that a project has been implemented when in fact it has not, and it is the process of implementation itself which then is in need of evaluation.

Industrialized countries are not subject to such external pressures on educational policy. But within countries, the autonomy that regions, localities or institutions may have legally, can be constrained and manipulated by external pressures from outside interest groups or higher authorities in a manner which bears some similarity to relations between a country and an aid agency. Wilms reveals how a confluence of political and commercial interests may exert pressures on local school districts in the United States, and he identifies the pipelines through which funds travel from Congress to schoolhouse in support of vocationalization.

Vocationalization projects and programs are not unique in being subject to competing jurisdictional claims between different governmental agencies, in evolving with shifting priorities in response to changing economic contexts or in resulting from external pressures. But they are in many other respects more complex in their management requirements than conventional "academic" school subjects. The complexities arising out of the mode of policy formulation are therefore important as an additional problem to overcome in their implementation.

The Variety of Programs

There is variation among countries in the form that vocationalization takes in the schools. There is debate about how far general secondary education should have a compulsory or voluntary pre-vocational adjunct, and about whether vocational education should be lodged in mainstream secondary schools, in separate institutions, or mainly be offered in the form of apprenticeships and other employment-based provisions. The main concern in this book is with mainstream secondary schools, not with employment-based or separately institutionalized vocational schooling. In mainstream secondary schools, it is usually pre-vocational education which is at issue.

The distinctive features of pre-vocational education are that it is combined with general education in such a way that a student does not forfeit the possibility of continuing to higher education in areas unrelated to the pre-vocational speciality. Further, it does not purport to be a complete training for entry to the occupations concerned, but is conceptualized as a preparation for such training. As noted earlier, the viability of this concept therefore depends on how far such opportunities for further training are available, and whether pupils who are enrolled in pre-vocational curricula make use of these training opportunities.

Since school-based vocational training also tends to require further training on the job, the distinction between pre-vocational and vocational education is not clear-cut. Further, notwithstanding the view that pre-vocational education is not a complete vocational training, these programs are usually espoused politically as a remedy for youth unemployment, which implies the expectation that pre-vocational education—like vocational training—will give direct advantage in access to work in the area of specialization. There is often considerable ambiguity about the goals of pre-vocational education. One can find varying perceptions and expectations among different concerned parties in the same education system, from those who see it as a widening of general education, and those who view it as a broad familiarization and preparation for further training, to those who see it in effect as preparation for work.

Pre-vocational provisions vary in degree of exposure and in organization. Psacharopoulos notes how in Colombia's multi-track system of "diversified education" students rotate throughout vocational options, then focus on one and finally specialize in a particular skill, all the while taking academic course work along with their vocational studies. In Tanzania's "uni-track diversified system" students are restricted to one vocational topic in a specialized physical setting; the pre-vocational program takes place during the first four years of secondary school alongside the standard academic material. There may be differences within national systems, as exemplified in Wright's chapter on Sierra Leone, as to depth of specialization and whether a pre-vocational subject is compulsory or not. Or, as in the case of Kenya (Lauglo and Närman, Chapter 14), the pre-vocational industrial education subjects exist as relatively high status options available in a small number of schools. But there are also in Kenya "technical secondary schools" which provide for some greater degree of exposure to technical subjects but still only one-third of the pupils' timetable and without foreclosing opportunity for further academic education (Lauglo, 1985b). This variant could be seen as another form of pre-vocational education within the same country.

The technical secondary schools were, however, originally clearly defined as vocational training ("trade schools"). These schools underwent "academic drift" at the expense of depth of vocational training, in response to demands from their clientele for an education which did not foreclose opportunities for further academic study. Thus, Kenya has evinced curriculum convergence between previously much more sharply distinct academic and vocational education after primary school. At present, Kenyan policy is to return to training in much greater vocational depth in the technical secondary schools.

Gallart examines both of these trends—vocationalization of secondary education and what she terms "secondarization of vocational education"—the former in Brazil and the latter in Argentina, and the processes of change involved. It is interesting to note that linking vocational training with the (higher status) mainstream secondary system was politically easier to implement, whilst the vocationalization of academic schools ran into opposition from their clientele.

One may speculate that different forces lie behind vocationalization and secondarization. Whilst the former is a response to a depressed labor market, the latter may be a response to a shortage of manpower and to economic growth. Whilst the former seeks to socialize youth to the requirements of the world of work, the latter seeks to free vocational training from excessive dependence on "what employers want" and to offer broader training. In terms of status aspirations of youth, the former may be seen as a means of discouragement while the latter is a response to demands for greater status through linkage with academic education. In the former case, general education shifts towards vocational training. In the latter case, vocational training shifts towards general education. The suggested underlying condition is whether the labor market is a "buyer's" or a "seller's" market.

The diversity of vocationalization programs and of the labor market contexts in which these programs operate, argues against sweeping generalizations about their status in the eyes of their clientele, or about their articulation with the labor market. Whilst vocationalization has suffered from low status in Brazil (see this volume, Chapter 12), it is apparently now popular in Kenya and Sierra Leone (Chapters 7 and 14). Acceptance by the clientele can be expected to depend on a variety of conditions, including perceptions of opportunity after school and whether vocationalization forecloses opportunity for further academic study.

Implementation Issues

Among the common constraints on implementation are: lack of clarity of curriculum, problems in assessment, shortage of teachers, lack of status or attractiveness to students and their families, high costs, and demanding management requirements for establishing such subjects and meeting their logistics needs for materials, maintenance and repair of equipment.

Pre-vocational subjects often lack clarity in curriculum definition. One reason is tension between general education considerations and those that relate to basic vocational education. Even when the official stress is firmly on general education, the link between the high aims and curriculum content is often unclear. The aims will often stress process and development of generalized abilities, whilst the content will tend to stress accuracy in carrying out well defined tasks using specified techniques. Even if not declared to be pre-vocational, a practical subject—more so than a "book subject"— will be fraught with expectations of usefulness for work. If the goal is pre-vocational, then the question is what skills and techniques to include. There can be confusion about how far the content is vocational, i.e., actually transmitting the necessary entrance skills for specific occupations. Pre-vocational means preparatory for vocational training. But rarely is it clear what types of further training it is that pre-vocational courses will give access to. Since pre-vocational subjects are but an adjunct to an academic curriculum, the time available will be limited and will constrict the range of skills that can be covered. Equipment requirements are a further constraint on the range of skills and materials, especially in developing countries.

In practice pre-vocational subjects have in many countries become rather traditionally defined, i.e., woodwork, cookery, agriculture or commerce— with hazy links of content to vocational training after school and without conferring clear advantage in selection to such training. In terms of government policy, such subjects may be a response to youth unemployment. Yet the high aims of a subject may stress familiarity with tools and "technology" as valued parts of a well-rounded education. It may be seen as a dead end by those in the know, as preparatory neither for further academic study nor for training for employment opportunity; and yet others more remote from the subject and its context may think it is vocational training.

Theory can be more cheaply and reliably assessed than practical skill. When there is intensely competitive selection from one stage of schooling to the next and when teachers are poorly trained in internal assessment, there is a tendency for the theory aspect of practical subjects to dominate unduly in assessment of pupils. When equipment and materials are lacking or unevenly provided, there can be pressures to only assess the theory aspect. When practical skills are assessed, external examination is a force for standardization, reinforcing a pedagogy that leaves little scope for problem-solving skills or creative design. Thus, external examination of practical subjects constrain efforts to emphasize process skills rather than precise execution of standardized tasks.

Shortage of competent teachers is a constraint on implementation. Suitable candidates for teacher training, with sufficient and relevant prior experience, are hard to recruit. This problem is exacerbated when the tools, techniques and materials to be taught are set apart from the material culture that prospective teachers acquire informally through everyday life. When trained, the good teachers will tend to find better-paid work outside of teaching, in the very sector for which they prepare their own trainees. In general, when the demand for the teachers' own trainees is buoyant, vocational teachers will more easily find better-paid opportunities outside teaching. Conversely, when trainees have problems finding jobs in their speciality, the incentive for teachers to leave will be less. Thus, one of the conditions which can help establish vocational training as a viable and school-based pedagogic system is better satisfied when the external effectiveness of such training becomes more problematic. For pre-vocational subjects, and for practical subjects further remote from direct work application, the problem of good teachers being lured away into alternative work will be less pressing. Even so, shortages are common when provisions expand. The skills required are also so distinct from the general "academic background" which teachers of other school subjects have, that most practical subjects cannot easily be covered by teachers who are not trained in the subjects.

Practical subjects often suffer from low status, recruiting students who take such subjects as a second choice to academic and more prestigious courses or options for which they have failed to qualify. Morale can be low, among students and teachers alike. Or so we are frequently told. But as noted earlier, there is no iron law by which practical subjects are doomed to suffer from low attraction to students, nor are students attracted to such subjects necessarily academic rejects. Chapters 7 and 14 show this to be true. As noted earlier, popularity will be tied to the perception that students and their guardians have of the links between such subjects and subsequent opportunities for training and work. A subject's status will also depend on how far it is in other respects staffed and equipped to function adequately as a pedagogic system.

Practical subjects have high unit costs, though available data render subject cost calculations difficult. This is discussed in some detail in Chapter 8. The high cost is also stressed in Chapters 3, 7, 10, 12, 15 and 17. The development costs are often much greater than for academic subjects, especially so for practical subjects requiring separate workshop facilities. Recurrent costs are greatly affected by class size. Very often, practical subjects are taught to groups half the size of a normal academic class. This doubles the unit teaching costs, and teaching salaries are the dominant component of recurrent expenditure everywhere. Further, supplies and materials are typically much more costly for practical subjects than for those other school subjects which require only books and writing materials. Even when precise estimates cannot be made, it is evident that practical subjects very often are more than twice as expensive as other subjects, per student period.

This high cost is a major constraint on implementation. It becomes more important as a constraint when policies favoring the expansion of such subjects are rooted in the same conditions which make it harder to meet their financial requirement: slow economic growth. At the same time, the great resource needs create more exacting requirements as to external effectiveness. Attempts to express this in the form of cost-benefit analysis invariably have shown, as Bacchus notes, that: "in economic terms these higher costs do not seem to be compensated for by a higher rate of return." Psacharopoulos' research strongly supports this conclusion.

Apart from finance, it can be argued that practical subjects—depending on their requirements for special equipment and materials—are unusually complex pedagogic systems to establish and service. Specialized facilities with equipment, tools, and stock of materials are not only expensive, they need to be established and maintained. The setting up before teaching and the putting back into order after teaching, requires more time than in subjects which can be taught with pen and paper as minimum technology. In general, the logistics requirements are usually very demanding, requiring greater management skills from teachers and headteachers. There is also a need for external support systems to provide repair, maintenance and supplies. This is especially true for workshop subjects which require power-driven equipment. It is less true for subjects requiring only handtools.

There are some dilemmas in implementation. The type of "humble technology" vocationalization which may be cheap and have simple logistics requirements, e.g., agriculture with handtools (provided land is available) may meet lack of student interest. Conversely, electronics would be prohibitively expensive in most countries but likely to have high status. Accountancy stands out as the one subject which has cheap and simple technology at the same time as it gains from perceived association with attractive life-chances in the modern economic sector. It is therefore more easily implemented on a large scale throughout an education system, than are the equipment-intensive subjects, or subjects suffering from association with low status work.

The constraints discussed above are such that even when finance is available and the commitment to implementation is strong, vocationalization on a large scale and at a fast pace is unlikely to succeed. Successful implementation requires concentration of resources in depth. Such concentration is possible when specialized vocational training institutions are established. But it is usually beyond the capacity of an education system, notably so in developing countries, when the attempt is to vocationalize the curriculum throughout an entire stage of secondary schooling. The daunting problems of "system-wide" vocationalization are compounded when the policy is to implement rapidly. Yet, when policy seeks to address the important concern of school-leaver unemployment, there are political pressures for rapid and large-scale implementation.

Concluding Remarks

It is not novel or remarkable that governments provide vocational training in specialized institutions in order to meet manpower needs. Such training will usually have high unit costs. The complexity of setting it up and servicing it requires the concentration of resources. Specialized institutions make such concentrating possible. The types of occupation prepared for by such training will vary greatly. It is difficult to generalize about the labor market take-up of trainees.

However, what is at issue in the present policy trend is the vocationalization of mainstream secondary education. Here it usually means pre-vocational courses, or other forms of "familiarization" and basic skills training which are so placed in the larger school curriculum that a student will not forfeit the opportunity for further academic education. We have pointed to the strong political concerns behind these policies. Influential educational and political ideologies or sentiments are also invocable in support of these policies. Thus, regardless of how affordable such policies are, how easily they can be implemented, and regardless of whether they provide remedy for the problems they are meant to address, the policies are rooted in strong political, ideological and educational considerations. This is, as Bacchus notes, the reason why the "vocationalism debate" has such a long history and refuses to go away, though the same arguments tend to recur.

The contributions to this volume, and research and experience elsewhere, suggest three main lessons for attempts to inject vocationalized curriculum components across an entire stage of previously general education:

(1) It can be justified as a valued extension of general education, but should not be seen as a remedy for school-leaver unemployment.
(2) It is very expensive.
(3) There are numerous constraints which argue against rapid large-scale implementation.

Both Marxist and structural-functional analysis of modern society stress the importance of the selection function that schools have for the economy. Human capital theory similarly stresses the role of the schools in making people more economically productive. These theoretical perspectives all serve to focus attention on the functional correspondence between "output from schools" and "economic needs", whether such correspondence is noted with approval or not. It is interesting to note that vocationalization policies are typically prompted by the lack of such functional correspondence. They are attempts to create a better match by targeting the content of schooling more on specific occupations. But in a depressed labor market, the lack of correspondence is mainly due to a shortage of employment opportunity, not of job applicants with some exposure to skills which are relevant for occupations or for vocational training.

It is possible that schools become less important for selection to occupations in a depressed labor market, because applicants with minimally adequate qualifications are then usually plentiful. Particularistic criteria can then become more important for access to jobs. Both tracer studies of school-leavers and research on what criteria employers use when recruiting and promoting staff, are needed to show how far these speculations are valid. If, as we have argued, vocationalization policies are mainly a political response to poor articulation between school and the world of work, then it is important to assess empirically the effect of these policies on that articulation. Such studies are unfortunately rather rare. We hope that the present volume will help to stimulate interest in such research.

References*

Beeby, C. E. (1966) *The quality of education in developing countries*. Cambridge, Mass.: Harvard University Press.

Carnoy, M. and Levin, H. (1985) *Schooling and work in the democratic state*. Stanford: Stanford University Press.

Chisman, D. (1987) *Practical Secondary Education. Planning for Cost-Effectiveness in Less Developed Countries*. London: Commonwealth Secretariat.

* In addition to papers included in this volume.

Cooksey, B. and Ishumi A. (1986) *A critical review of policy and practice in Tanzanian Secondary education since 1967*. Mimeo, University of Dar es Salaam.

Dale, R. (Ed.) (1985) *Education, training and employment: Towards a new vocationalism?* Oxford: Pergamon Press in Association with the Open University.

Davies, M. (1985) How is "industrial education" taught? Does the way it is taught promote its objectives? In C. Cumming, M. Davies, K. Lillis and B. Nyagah (Eds.), *Practical subjects in Kenyan academic secondary schools: Background papers*. Stockholm: Swedish International Development Agency, Education Division Documents, No. 22.

Droogleever Fortuijn, E., W. Hoppers and M. Morgan (Eds.) (1987), *Paving Pathways to Work. Comparative Perspectives on the Transition from School to Work*. The Hague: Centre for the Study of Education in Developing Countries.

Foster, P. J. (1965) The vocational school fallacy in development planning. In C. A. Anderson and M. J. Bowman (Eds.), *Education and economic development*. Chicago: Aldine.

Grubb, W. N. (1985) The convergence of educational systems and the role of vocationalism. *Comparative education review*, **29** (4).

Gustafsson, I. (1987) *Schools and the Transformation of Work: A Comparative Study of Four Productive Work Programmes in Southern Africa*. Stockholm: Institute of International Education, University of Stockholm.

Hultin, M. (1987) *Vocational Education in Developing Countries*. Stockholm: Swedish International Development Authority. Education Division Documents. No. 34.

Kitching, G. (1982) *Development and underdevelopment in historical perspective: Populism, nationalism and industrialization*. London: Methuen.

Lauglo, J. (1983) Concepts of "general education" and "vocational education" curricula for post-compulsory schooling in Western industrialised countries: When shall the twain meet? *Comparative education*, **19** (3).

Lauglo, J. (1985a) *Practical subjects in Kenyan academic secondary schools: General Report*. Stockholm: Swedish International Development Agency, Education Division Documents, No. 20.

Lauglo, J. (1985b) *Technical secondary schools in Kenya: An assessment*. Stockholm: Swedish International Development Agency, Education Division Documents, No. 26.

Lillis, K. M. (1985) Processes of secondary curriculum innovation in Kenya. *Comparative Education Review*, **29** (1).

Lillis, K. M. and Hogan, D. (1983) Dilemmas of diversification: Problems associated with vocational education in developing countries. *Comparative Education*, **19**.

Price, R. G. (1974) Labour and education in Russia and China. *Comparative Education*, **10**.

Siebert-Klein, M. (1980) *The challenge of communist education: A look at the German Democratic Republic*. New York: Columbia University Press/East European Monographs.

PART 1
Goals and Justifications

Introductory Note

THIS section deals with views and expectations relating to the purposes of vocationalization. As shown in these chapters, the goals and rationales of vocationalization often relate to a blend of considerations about ideals of general education, political ideologies and economic relevance.

Bacchus refers to the drives made during the colonial and post-colonial periods to provide pupils with specific skills and attitudes in order to influence their occupational choices away from white-collar jobs. He argues that the dominant "academic" Western model of education when introduced to developing countries was at that time in fact "vocational" in that it did give access to jobs. The attempts to introduce more explicitly vocational subjects, such as agriculture, have been underpinned by political, social and economic motivations. Bacchus accepts the main reasoning behind vocationalization policies, that "if students were provided with some kind of useful practical or vocational skills relevant to the needs of society, they would be better equipped to contribute to its economic development", yet he concedes that the outcomes of vocationalization efforts have been disappointing. The reason for failure, according to Bacchus, lies in an inappropriate development strategy.

It is widely assumed that school-leavers would become employed more easily if schools could equip them with skills which are more specifically vocational than the types of knowledge associated with general education. To what extent do employers want schools to undertake vocational training?

The chapter by Noah and Eckstein is based on an empirical investigation into the involvement of business and industry with the education and training of youth in Britain, France and the Federal Republic of Germany. A substantial part of the chapter concerns criticism of schools made by spokespersons for business and industry, such as that schools are too academic and biased against children with practical talents, or that employers want schools to generate qualities which are valuable for work and training. But what is stressed is personal qualities which are essentially noncognitive, appreciation of the world of work and its requirements, and basic communication skills. To this end, employers seek a closer relationship between classroom learning and the world of work, and reforms in teacher education. This chapter also deals with the nature and locus of programs in the three countries, discussing the agencies involved and the modes of transition that operate between the programs.

Oxenham asks, with special reference to developing countries: what do employers want from education? His conclusion closely parallels that of Noah and Eckstein: employers are seeking a range of noncognitive outcomes from schools, in addition to communication skills, rather than skills which are geared more specifically to particular occupations. Moreover, Oxenham stresses the imprecise nature of relations between schools and work. The connections between education, employment and salaries appear imprecise, even arbitrary. He argues that no broad agreement exists between employing organizations as to what levels and performances of education are required for specific jobs or groups of jobs. Within different contexts, the same types of job calls for different levels and types of schooling. In terms of qualifications generally, employers prefer the "more educated." Oxenham concludes with the belief that selection and training for jobs should be arranged not by the schools but by the employers themselves.

Vocationalization policies are often rooted in prevailing ideologies in society. Wilms' chapter on the United States discusses the rationales surrounding the development of school-based vocational education. There is the influence of the "American Dream": from rags to riches by dint of hard work, initiative and pluck. Wilms argues that vocational education was seen as an equalizer of opportunity and a source of human dignity for industrial workers. He then reviews findings from empirical research and concludes that the outcomes of vocational education in schools do not accord with these lofty aims, notably that it fails to improve the students' chance of success in the labor market. In these conditions, Wilms argues that vocationalization policies are sustained by ideological continuity, by the vested interests in the extra finance brought by these programs and because vocational subjects serve as a convenient repository for students who are academic failures and who come disproportionately from a low-income, ethnic minority background.

Chapters in other parts of the volume include some discussion of socialist ideological support for vocationalization: King on Tanzania, Gustafsson on Zimbabwe and O'Dell on the USSR.

THE EDITORS

CHAPTER 2

The Political Context of Vocationalization of Education in the Developing Countries

KAZIM BACCHUS

University of Alberta at Edmonton

THIS chapter focuses on the vocationalization of education in the economically less developed countries, (LDCs) and suggests that whilst, in this educational area, there might be some apparent similarities with the economically more developed ones, (MDCs), there are also important differences between them that arise largely from their social and economic structures and the resulting differences in demand for skilled manpower. The role of the LDCs is as "price-takers" rather than as "price-makers" on the world market; the development strategies which they use often occur without full recognition of their own realities and resource limitations. As a result, the problems arising from the efforts by these countries to vocationalize their school curricula are, in many ways, qualitatively different; this whole educational strategy is usually much more problematic for them than for the MDCs. However, it is not unlikely that with the declining youth labor market in the MDCs some of these differences may become less marked. Also amongst the developing countries themselves there are often substantial differences in their demand for skilled manpower which make any kind of overall generalization on this issue even more difficult. However, there are enough commonalities among them to make the following observations widely applicable within LDCs.

Towards a Definition of the term "Vocationalization"

In discussing the issue of vocationalizing education we are faced with the question of definition. The term "vocationalization" refers to efforts by schools to include in their curriculum those "practical" subjects which are likely to generate among the students some basic knowledge, skills and dispositions that might prepare them to think of becoming skilled workers or to enter other manual occupations. The inclusion of practical or industrial arts subjects especially in the curriculum of secondary schools, as part of a program of general education is here considered an essential element in the

31

vocationalizing of education. In most developing countries which have limited secondary educational facilities pupils ordinarily receive only a few years of elementary or primary education. So the vocationalizing of the school curriculum is often attempted even at the primary or senior primary grades. With increases in secondary school enrolment in the LDCs over the past two decades the vocationalizing of the curriculum is gradually penetrating this level also. Here, the main objective is to influence the occupational choices of pupils away from white-collar jobs to which they have traditionally aspired and make them somewhat better prepared to work in other types of occupation.

Since Western schooling was introduced in most developing countries, it has always had a strong vocational focus. It was essentially geared towards preparing individuals for jobs in the emerging European or expatriate dominated sectors of these economies. Traditional knowledge and culture came to be de-emphasized by schools offering Western-type education which was considered necessary to equip students eventually to become clerks and junior functionaries, either in government departments or in the private sector, teachers, preachers, catechists and later even priests. For such jobs an "academic" education which stressed reading and writing skills and some general knowledge was considered necessary and this was the kind of "vocational instruction" that the primary schools offered. Later, as the number of "educated" individuals outstripped the demand for these white collar jobs in the LDCs, attention became focused on gearing the curriculum to prepare students to occupy such roles as farmers and farmers' wives, especially within rural communities. In this changing context "practical subjects" began to be taught as part of the program of vocationalizing the curriculum of these schools. The hope was that the training which they would provide would better equip the students with the kind of skills and attitudes that would encourage them to seek manual rather than just white-collar occupations.

The Controversy of the 1960s

On reading or re-reading the literature on education in the developing countries one would have thought that, after the controversy over vocationalizing the school curriculum that raged in the 1960s between advocates of this approach such as Balogh (1962 a,b) and Dumont (1962) who saw it as the solution to the educational problems of the LDCs, and those in opposition to it, such as Foster and others, the issue was dead and buried. But the issue is still very much with us. Incidentally the "death sentence" on vocationalization of the curriculum was pronounced mainly by First-World scholars with some support from their intellectual compradors and former students from the developing countries. It was based on the "research evidence" that existed at the time and which has continued to be supported by results from subsequent studies.

The Issue has Refused to Stay "Buried"

Judging from some of the educational developments that have continued to take place in the LDCs, it seems that this issue has never been entirely abandoned by educational policymakers, even though, through the advice offered by influential foreign education experts, including those from the international agencies, it might at times have been placed on the back burner. But even then, despite the available evidence, many LDCs never fully abandoned their efforts to diversify the curriculum, increasingly at the secondary level, by adding practical, pre-vocational or even vocational subjects to it. One outcome of these efforts has been the fifty or more educational projects with vocational education components, for which the World Bank or other international agencies have lent or donated funds to the developing countries during the recent past.

Vocationalizing the Curriculum has Deep Historical Roots in many LDCs

The faith in the vocationalization of the curriculum as a means of improving the contribution which education can make to the development process has deep historical roots and has continued to persist despite the fact that traditionally these practical subjects have had little or no appeal to the students or their parents in the LDCs. However, in the present situation of increasing unemployment amongst school-leavers, this attitude might be changing.

In the former West Indian colonies the controversy over vocationalizing the curriculum, even of primary schools, initially emerged when the first formal attempts began to be made in the 1830s to provide education for the masses. For example, in 1835 the *Kingston Chronicle*, in commenting on the curriculum that the schools in Jamaica then offered, suggested that:

> Instead of being taught the mechanical arts, the use of the plough and harrow, the plane and the adze, the awl or needle . . . instead of practical industry the children are [first] taught to *read* the Bible and sing hymns. They all begin at the wrong end. They attempt to finish the superstructure before they have laid the foundations. (*Kingston Chronicle*, 1835)

An interesting point in this comment, and one that continues to be made, is that the basic purpose of education should be to prepare individuals to be economically productive in the socio-economic context in which they live. In the West Indies the teaching of practical skills was, therefore, regarded as necessary as a foundation stone for such a life. Other subjects—in this case even reading—which were offered for enjoyment and for the spiritual elevation of the pupils, were seen as part of the superstructure rather than the infrastructure of the educational program and were considered by the then dominant planter group to be of secondary importance.

These and other similar criticisms of the current educational practices offered in the West Indies led the British Government to ask its then eminent educator, Sir James Kay Shuttleworth, to draw up an appropriate educational program for the masses in the colonies. The outcome was a memorandum (CO 318/138,1847) giving practical suggestions for organizing "day schools of industry" as part of the system of education for "the Colored Races of the Empire" and this became the British Government's first officially adopted colonial educational policy. It emphasized the "practical" side of the curriculum and proposed an educational program which was to combine "intellectual and industrial training," one in which "instruction was interwoven with labor" because it was considered that only through this approach to education would "the native labor of the West Indian colonies be made generally available for the cultivation of the soil" (CO 318/138, 1847)

About six decades later, i.e., by the turn of the century the then Secretary of State for the Colonies, Joseph Chamberlain, came up with the most comprehensive program ever put forward anywhere even up to today, for vocationalizing the curriculum of the schools in the region. Starting from the assumption that the West Indies were and must remain agricultural colonies, it was argued that

> it would be deplorable, if the effect of an improved system of education were to be to inspire in the rising generation a certain disgust with the agricultural pursuits in which the children's parents have been engaged and [create] a desire to earn a living only by means of clerical employment. That this is a danger [with the present educational system] cannot be denied. (Government of Trinidad, 1903)

The major objective of this new program was again to fit children for the "practical work of life" and for this reason schools were to offer a "sound industrial instruction" aimed at the training of the "hand and eye" in subjects relating to agriculture and agricultural pursuits and farm life. As a guide the Colonial Office even sent out to each Governor of the various West Indian territories a pamphlet which comprehensively described what was then considered the most modern approach at integrating "industrial" and "intellectual" activities, especially in schools in the rural areas. It was the curriculum content and instructional strategy then used in the rural schools in France (CO 854/35, 1899).

This view that a major concern of schools in the colonies should be to teach practical subjects was also reflected in the first statement on Educational Policy for British Tropical Africa issued in 1925, and Lord Hailey was still suggesting a few years later that "simple village craft" should be a key element in the instructional program of African schools—with boys being given enough skills and knowledge about construction to build their own homes on the model of those which were to be found in the villages. In many other developing countries this policy of providing pupils with the kinds of vocational skill that would increase their economic contribution to their societies was generally accepted. Even idealists like Gandhi with his proposal for "basic schools" and ideologues like Mao Zedong with his "half day–half work schools" supported the general idea that schools should attempt to pass on to their students the kinds of practical skills and inculcate in them those attitudes which would better prepare them for the kind of economic existence which these societies offered. Vocationalizing the curriculum was, therefore, a policy which was actively pursued both by the colonial rulers and the indigenous leaders of these countries and this has continued even after their countries have achieved independence.

Political Motivation an Insufficient Explanation of Recurrent Efforts to Vocationalizing Education

There is no doubt that these attempts at providing "industrial" or practical training or at vocationalizing the curriculum of schools had, at their roots, a strong political motivation. They represented an important part of the effort of the colonizers and later, the indigenous leaders, to use the instructional programs of the schools as a mechanism of social control—a means of lowering the occupational aspirations of the youngsters in these societies to a more "realistic" level. It was also hoped that this "practical" education which was offered to the children of the masses would better prepare them to serve as a source of cheap labor for the expatriate firms operating in these countries. In situations where there was a resident white population or where the society was rigidly stratified the provision of this type of education was also partly an attempt to prevent the children of the masses from interfering with the "exclusive right" of the dominant groups to the higher level jobs in the society. Even more recently, Lauglo's (1985) study of "Practical Subjects in Kenyan Academic Secondary Schools" indicates that the efforts at curriculum diversification had not been so much an attempt to meet certain projected manpower needs as an essentially political response to a situation in which the school-leavers from the regular academic programs of the schools were increasingly having difficulties in finding jobs.

The Logic Behind the Argument for Vocationalizing Education

One acknowledges the importance of political considerations in these efforts at vocationalizing the curriculum of schools in the LDCs. But to see them *simply* as attempts by the dominant groups to reproduce the existing social order and maintain social control over the masses by moderating or reducing their "unrealistic" levels of aspiration would be too limited an explanation of why these attempts continue. Social control considerations are not the only explanation of why political leaders, including those in the developing countries, seek educational change.

If one tries to ascertain why there is continuing faith in vocationalization among key educational policymakers in the LDCs, one sees that there are some eminently logical and reasonable arguments which are either formally put forward or implicitly accepted for such programs.

First policymakers still tend to believe that one of the major functions of schooling is the development, among the young, of appropriate skills and attitudes, or competencies and commitments, that are needed to make the economic system of society function more efficiently. This is an assumption that has dominated, and still continues to dominate, much of the thinking about the content of education, from the days of the apocryphal New-Fist Hammer-Maker in the Saber Tooth Curriculum to the human capital theorists who argue that the major contribution of education to economic development has been through its qualitative improvements of the man-power resources of a society.

Educational policymakers seem to take it as axiomatic that if individuals in a society have the "appropriate" skills, they will be more productive than those without such skills. Following this line of argument they have made what seems to be a reasonable conclusion—that if students at school were provided with some useful, practical or vocational skills relevant to the needs of that society, they would be better equipped to contribute to its economic development. As they looked around their existing school systems they saw that the type of education which students were receiving was "too academic," leading them to aspire to white collar jobs which were becoming relatively more difficult to obtain. Therefore, they felt that if schools could provide students with, or introduce them to, other more useful skills this would widen their range of occupational choices, make their aspirations more "realistic" and increase the possibility that such education/training would better prepare them to meet existing manpower shortages in these societies.

Further, the skills and attitudes that such individuals would develop were likely to make them keener to enter the labor force even earlier and hence decrease the demand for more schooling—and it is such demand which has been rising faster than many countries can afford. This kind of preparation would also, it was believed, help those who still could not find wage employment to create jobs of their own and thus become self-employed. So within this context it was felt that a more effective educational policy would be for schools to attempt to provide students with relevant practical or vocational training. This seems to be a reasonable assumption and it is difficult to fault the logic of the argument. It is this kind of reasoning which largely explains why educational policymakers in the LDCs keep returning to this solution. These attempts are usually revived whenever the authorities consider that there are too many school graduates unable to find the white-collar jobs for which they are looking. In fact, such efforts have been intensified more recently in many other developing countries where the output from their school systems, especially at the secondary level and above, has been increasing faster than jobs in the modern sector. It has, of course, been the modern sector where "educated individuals" in these societies have traditionally looked for employment.

Logic Versus Reality

Despite the logic of the argument and the continuing efforts by educational policymakers to implement such policies the available research evidence has indicated that, in the real life of most developing countries, the outcomes have not matched expectations. First, the cost of providing vocational education is substantially higher than that of traditional literary instruction and, in economic terms, these higher costs do not seem to be compensated for by a high return. Psacharopoulos and Loxley (1985) suggest that in Colombia the social return on the diversified curriculum is no higher than for the regular schools, despite the higher rate of capital investment, while in Tanzania the return might even have been somewhat lower. Second, among those who have taken pre-vocational subjects as part of their educational program, there does not seem to be any marked shift in their occupational choices. Nor has their exposure to such subjects reduced their desire to proceed further up the educational ladder. Third, when such students enter the work force their employers do not financially compensate them for this more expensive and assumedly more relevant type of education; in fact, those from the academic tracks are often better rewarded, in terms of salaries.

Faced with this evidence the development of a rational educational policy would seem to suggest a withdrawal from such efforts at introducing practical subjects into the curricula of primary and secondary schools. Such a strategy would be particularly appropriate for countries where universalization of primary education has not yet been achieved. The argument that can be forwarded in such a situation is, rather than the Government increasing the unit cost of education by attempting to vocationalize the curriculum, it would make much more economic sense to use these additional funds to universalize primary education. The latter is seen to produce a greater rate of return on investment than educational programs aimed at diversifying the curriculum of the existing schools through the introduction of practical subjects.

Are Intervening Variables Affecting the Rate of Return on Efforts at Vocationalizing Education?

But whilst the research evidence suggests that this seems to be the obvious policy direction which the LDCs should follow, the question of vocationalizing the curriculum cannot be dismissed so lightly especially since, as the historical evidence indicates, this policy has refused to stay buried. In such a situation in which the available research evidence seems to go against the logic of an argument we need to look again at the assumptions underlying the proposition itself to see if these can be faulted. If they cannot be, then we have to examine the context in which the evidence arises since there might be important intervening variables that are responsible for the kinds of result being thrown up and which might be distorting the expected relationships—in this case, that between the practical skills provided in the secondary or even the primary schools and the "productivity" of the individuals who have acquired such skills.

Let us examine the assumptions which underlie the seemingly logical conclusion, i.e., with vocationalization of education we should be able to increase the range of relevant skills which school-leavers have and this should improve the productivity of their education. The first assumption is that the skills which schools try to pass on through vocationalization of their curriculum are those which are likely to be more relevant to the needs of society and, therefore, the individuals who possess such skills should contribute more to development than those without them. The second assumption is that the type of education that transmits these "relevant" skills and knowledge, is also likely, in economic terms, to yield a greater individual and social rate of return than an education which does not. In other words industrial arts or vocational education programs which aim at providing individuals with skills relevant to the development needs of the society are likely to be more economically valuable both to the individual and to the society than an education which does not transmit such skills.

If one accepts the argument about the greater relevance of the education, it seems difficult to refute either of these assumptions on which the case for vocationalizing the curriculum is often built and which many educational policymakers treat as axiomatic. True, it might be argued that schools have not been very effective in passing on these skills or that formal educational institutions, as they now operate, are not the best means of achieving the task or even that the skills which schools have tried to pass on in these practical subjects were not really relevant to the needs of the society; but with these issues there is a shift from policy considerations about vocationalizing the curriculum to one of dealing with policy implementation, i.e., we are now questioning the instructional strategies that are being used and the selection of curriculum content—*what types of skill* should be taught and *how* they should be taught in order to increase their effectiveness.

But while the assumptions underlying the efforts to vocationalize the curriculum might seem reasonable, the evidence, as indicated previously, continues to show that the outcomes are not those which one would normally expect, given these assumptions. So it is not enough to say that vocationalizing the curriculum does not work—we need to go beyond this and see whether there are other variables which are operating within the particular socio-economic context of these societies which might be interfering with the expected relationship. And for this we have to look at the nature of the socio-economic structures of the developing countries and the kind of development strategies which they are pursuing.

Failure of Efforts at Vocationalizing Education Results from Inappropriate Development Strategies

The substantive point in this chapter is that the factors which militate against the effectiveness of vocationalization programs might be due largely to the failure of countries to grapple effectively with the basic problems of their underdevelopment rather than the inherent futility of this policy. Thus, in many LDCs the number of individuals who live below the poverty line seems to be steadily increasing. It is estimated that about 1 billion persons in these countries are now living at a sub-marginal level of existence; 500 million are said to be directly suffering from malnutrition; 40,000 children under five die every day from preventable causes, such as hunger, thirst and illness.

What has the failure of the LDCs to grapple effectively with their development problems to do with the negative rate of return on programs directed at vocationalizing education? The answer could be that it is the development strategies used by these countries which have largely produced both results.

To illustrate the point it is useful to present a brief review of the economic history of the LDCs as it pertains to vocationalizing education. First, the metropolitan colonial powers began their colonization by introducing into these countries a new range of economic activity, whether this was the commercialization of some agricultural crop for export, the establishment of mining ventures in areas with valuable mineral resources or some other activity which suited the interests of the colonizers. For their operation such ventures often needed manpower with a certain amount of Western education.

Second, it was not only literacy and numeracy skills which were required from these workers but their loyalty also. This was because, in a society ruled by a foreign power, with little consensus or participation of the masses in their own governance, it was necessary to produce a local group of "comprador elites," especially among those holding administrative and supervisory positions. To do this it was considered valuable to develop in them some vested interest in the existing arrangement and a sense of loyalty to the dominant group. Partly for this reason those who were employed in white-collar jobs in the expatriate dominated sector of the economy, including the public sector, were comparatively well rewarded. So the rate of return on their investment in education was relatively very high and their income levels, low as they might have been, were nevertheless substantially above those working in the traditional sector.

This helped to fuel the demand for the type of education which would qualify individuals to enter into the supervisory positions that gradually became open to them. The education that was most helpful for this purpose was of an academic rather than a technical or "practical" nature. This marked the beginning of the differential rate of return in favor of academic education. It also indicates why an academic education was primarily "vocational" in these countries.

Another outcome of this early wage policy was that it laid the foundation of a dualistic income structure between those employed in the "modern" sector as against those earning their living in the traditional sector—a structural feature which still characterizes the economies of most developing countries. Even with independence there has been little or no erosion in this dualistic income structure even though the supply of individuals with the necessary skills to undertake these jobs has increased—in some cases to the point of a substantial number of "educated unemployed." Their wage levels have not been very responsive to the increased supply of skills, a phenomenon which economists like Arthur Lewis (1954) and others once assumed would almost automatically happen. One reason for the stickiness of wages of those in the modern sector, especially those in supervisory and senior administrative positions, has been the powerful influence which they exert on the political leadership, especially through their well-organized professional associations or trade-union groups. In contrast, those who earn their living in the traditional sector of the economy are relatively unorganized and thus tend to have less influence on the political decision-makers with the result that, in some countries, the observed inequalities between these groups have even been increasing.

Further, the development strategies pursued by most countries even after independence contributed to the strengthening of their colonial socio-economic structures. The policies resulted in the demand for skilled laborers increasing much more slowly than the demand for others with an academic education, partly due to the rapid expansion of the public sector. In other words, they helped retain or increase the existing dualism in income structure, making white-collar modern sector jobs for which an academic education is still often considered very desirable, even more attractive.

This modern sector, import-substitutive and export-oriented development strategy has often only marginally helped to improve the quality of life of those not employed in the traditional or subsistence sector. Whenever an additional demand for educated manpower has been created it has tended to be essentially for individuals with supervisory rather than technical skills and this has reinforced the income superiority of those with an academic education.

Even when formal skill training has been provided, it has often been inappropriate, both in terms of techniques taught and the cost of the skills acquired, for those in the traditional sector. Most of those outside the modern sector cannot afford the services of say the carpenters who were trained in the new technical institutes or the well-trained nurses/midwives. This is one reason why, in most developing countries, about 80 percent of the doctors live in the urban centers servicing the needs of the 20 percent of the population who live there because they are more likely to be able to afford the cost of their services as compared with those who live in the rural areas. Therefore, when those in the heavily populated traditional and rural sector build their houses they try to seek the services of village carpenters who usually have had no formal training, who cannot read a blueprint but who might be willing to barter part of their services for some of the crops which the farmer produces—that is, providing the farmer does not try to build his own home with the help of the extended family. In other words, because of the cost factor, the demand for formally trained skilled individuals outside the small modern sector is very limited.

Many of the import-substitutive industries which are involved in assembling videos or television sets or bottling imported strawberry jam into small containers or mixing the imported ingredients of paints, do not have much spill-over benefit, in terms of the demand for skilled manpower. These "screwdriver" industries often require very few individuals with formal technical/vocational skills, beyond that which can be acquired on the job. The demand for labor has been for individuals who would supervise production and for sales representatives—again, jobs for which technical/ vocational education is usually not necessary.

The import substitution policy also creates a continuing divergence between domestic production and domestic consumption, with the components of the products that are to be assembled locally, being nearly all imported. Local consumption of the finished products also tends to increase and even those with lower incomes spend more of their limited resources on such commodities, even if they are just cigarettes and beer. This in turn has contributed to the worsening of the foreign exchange situation in these countries.

Finally, these new economic enterprises usually have little or no backward linkages to the rest of the economy and produce limited local spill-over benefit, especially to those in the traditional sector. The links which exist are normally with the MDCs, from where the elements which enter the production process are imported. Also the often artificially high rate of exchange of local as against foreign currency tends to make imported commodities artificially cheaper on the local market and penalizes the farmers whose crops attract foreign exchange. This again leads to the increased attractiveness of the modern sector with its greater demand for individuals with an academic education.

In the plantation and mineral enclaves engaged in production for export, the situation is not much different. In fact, as happened in the case of the Green Revolution the larger farmers are often able to buy out the land owned by smaller farmers, increasing their production for export and marginalizing a larger proportion of those already at or below the subsistence level. A somewhat similar point was made by Beckford (1972) who suggested that the plantation system was largely responsible for the underdevelopment and persistent poverty in the peasant sector of plantation societies.

It is obvious that a change is needed in the development strategy if some of these problems are to be overcome and if vocational skills are to contribute to an increase in the productivity of these societies. The new strategy would have to be one which de-emphasizes the externally oriented development that has been pursued so far by many LDCs and which has been so strongly supported by the IMF. Instead, these countries need to focus on a more autocentric development strategy which is likely to produce more balanced development. Such an approach will strengthen the economic linkages between the two sectors of the economy—the traditional and the modern— to the benefit of both.

This is not to suggest that production for export should be eliminated. In fact, some developing countries have done well economically by pursuing such a strategy. But this is unlikely to be effective for more than a very limited number of countries. Most of them would therefore need to balance their production for export against a more determined attempt to increase domestic production for local consumption. As part of this strategy, efforts would also need to be made to reduce the marked income differentials and the inequalities in the distribution of facilities such as education and health services that now exist between the two sectors of these societies. For example, the farmers in these countries have, for far too long, subsidized the increase in standard of living that has been occurring among some of the urban dwellers and others employed in the modern sector.

Conclusion

The export-oriented development strategy which has been pursued by many developing countries has created little new employment opportunity for workers with a higher level of vocational or technical skill than those which could be easily acquired on the job. If the production process is not automated it is usually of the type that needs only "screwdriver technology," in such a situation it is not surprising that only a restricted amount of development has taken place in most of these countries, even though growth rates were sometimes quite respectable. With the failure of the current development strategies to do much to improve the standard and quality of life in the traditional sector, it is not surprising that the political leaders and their key policymakers continue to think that some changes in the curriculum content of schools, such as diversification, the linking of practical work with academic studies or providing work experiences as part of general education, would help to solve their unemployment problems.

In fact, whenever an economic crisis or major economic problem arises in these countries, such as the current increase in the numbers of "educated unemployed," the policymakers resurrect such solutions as vocationalizing the school curriculum. This continues despite the fact that the available research evidence indicates that manipulation of school variables, whether by modifying the curriculum or developing new educational programs, will not by itself help to overcome the problems of underdevelopment or unemployment. It can be argued that continuing concern with issues such as the vocationalization of the curriculum only draws attention and efforts away from the more important and burning issue of developing strategies that might produce more effective development.

It is only after a country comes up with an appropriate development strategy that educational change, such as the introduction of vocational or pre-vocational subjects, might increase the contribution of education towards raising general productivity. In such a changed context education might help with efforts to grapple with problems of underdevelopment, especially in the traditional sector and the seemingly intractable problem of unemployment which results from it. But this requires the kind of development strategy and the political will and determination to implement it, which most political leaders in the LDCs have not been prepared to demonstrate, at least up to this point of time.

One needs to recognize that these efforts are greatly affected by the attitudes and practices of the economically more developed countries. But it is insufficient for Third World leaders to be passive in such a situation and simply wait until the MDCs realize the need to respond more positively to the demands of the LDCs for a new international economic order. The crux of the argument in this chapter is simply that any educational strategy, such as the inclusion of practical/vocational subjects in the curriculum of schools in the LDCs, can only be *made* effective if it is an integral part of an overall development strategy pursued by these countries. Therefore, to say that vocational education is or is not a useful educational approach is in itself meaningless, despite the research results that now exist.

References

Balogh, T (1962a) Catastrophe in Africa. *Times Educational Supplement*, 5 Jan., p.8.

Balogh, T. (1962b) What schools for Africa. *New Statesman and Nation*, 3 Mar. p.412.

Beckford, G. L. (1972) *Persistent Poverty*. London: Oxford University Press.

CO 318/138 (1847) *A Brief Practical Suggestion of the Mode of Organising and Coordinating Schools of Industry . . . as part of a System of Education for the Coloured Races of the British Colonies*, prepared by J. Kay Shuttleworth, 6 Jan. 1847.

CO 854/35 (1899) Circular from Mr Chamberlain, Secretary of State for the Colonies to the Governors of the West Indian Colonies, 11 March 1899.

Dumont, R (1962) *False Start in Africa*. New York: Praeger.

Government of Trinidad (1903) *Report of the Inspector of Schools*. Port of Spain, Trinidad.

Kingston Chronicle,1835, quoted in Burke, M. (1965)*The history of the Wesleyan/Methodist contribution to education in Jamaica in the nineteenth century*. M.A. thesis, University of London.

Lauglo, J. (1985) *Practical subjects in Kenyan academic secondary schools*. Stockholm: SIDA, Educational Division Documents, No.20.

Lewis, A. (1954) Economic development with unlimited supplies of labour. *Manchester school of economic and social studies*, 131–191.

Psacharopoulos, G. and Loxley, W. (1985) *Diversified secondary education and development*. Baltimore: Johns Hopkins University Press.

CHAPTER 3

Business and Industry Involvement with Education in Britain, France and Germany

HAROLD J. NOAH

Teachers College, Columbia University

MAX A. ECKSTEIN

Queens College, City University of New York

THIS chapter examines the involvement of business and industry with the education and training of young people aged 14–18 (middle and upper secondary level) in three industrialized countries: Britain, France and the Federal Republic of Germany. It is concerned with the two broad categories of this involvement: what employers and their associations say about the schools, and how they actually participate in education and training.

Business/Industry Criticisms

Employers have been complaining about deficiencies of formal schooling ever since the establishment of national systems of education. Their criticisms of the schools continue unabated, and are directed at both the schools' curricula and at their organization and management practices.

With respect to the curriculum, in Britain, France and Germany, as in the United States, the most frequent criticism voiced is that schools provide an inadequate and inappropriate preparation for entry into work. Thus, a memorandum submitted by the British Manpower Services Commission to a House of Commons committee observed:

> There are a number of common specific points raised by employers in criticism of school curricula. A frequently heard concern is that the standard of school leavers' literacy and numeracy is well below what it

* This chapter is a shortened version of a project report funded by the Exxon Education Foundation, through the Institute of Philosophy and Politics of Education and the Center for Education and the American Economy, Teachers College, Columbia University, New York, NY 10027. A copy of the full version may be obtained by writing to the Institute.

Support from the Spencer Foundation and the research assistance of Peter Fan and June Williams are also acknowleged.

should be. When pressed to be more specific about standards of literacy, employers point to illegible writing, limitations of vocabulary, weakness of grammar and syntax and poor presentation. Lack of facility in mathematical skills means that many school leavers are unable to cope with craft training without remedial education and this gives widespread cause for concern. (Great Britain, House of Commons, 1983, p. 361, para. 3.9)

The Association of British Chambers of Commerce has also complained that employers remain unconvinced that the schools are equipping their leavers with the sort of numeracy needed in the work-place. They fault the schools for giving too little attention to equipping students for group work and deplore "the stranglehold which academic selection for universities has on the schools' ability to provide either a broadly-based, relevant or practical education for high attainers" (Association of British Chambers of Commerce, 1984, paras. 15, 16).

Similarly, in France:

Employers do not mince their words when criticizing the training of young workers and employees, especially those graduating from the *Lycées d'Enseignement Professionel* (LEPs): absence of necessary workskills; lack of practical training; ignorance of working conditions, limits and norms characteristic of the enterprise. (Cans and Coutty, 1982, p. 10)

German employers offer parallel criticisms of their educational system. It is alleged that the recent reforms intended to improve access to middle and upper secondary education have increased the emphasis on general academic schooling to the neglect of preparation for work; and that the needs of employers and the demands of the work-place are ignored and vocational schooling is disparaged (Goebel, 1984, p. 71).

Citing the results of a survey of British employers, Jamieson and Lightfoot report:

the vast majority [of local industrialists] had particular grievances about the [educational] system which they felt should be redressed. Three of the most common criticisms of the school system were, in rough order of importance: pupil attitudes towards work (including attitudes towards the disciplines of work of any kind as well as specific attitudes towards industry); the maths problem; the literacy and communications problems. (Jamieson and Lightfoot, 1982, p. 105)

It is argued that attempts to improve the school system may have made important things worse. Business interests in Germany claim that reforms in both the organization and content of secondary schooling have led to a deterioration in general education (Goebel, 1984, p. 34).

The British Chamber of Commerce and Industry makes the following summary criticisms:

> the education system has not hitherto proved flexible enough in adapting to the changing needs of the community which it serves . . . There is too much choice in the curriculum of most secondary schools. (Association of British Chambers of Commerce, 1984)

In apparent paradox, employers fault the schools for being too academic while at the same time failing to equip young people with adequate basic educational skills. In addition, it is alleged, students lack the skills of cooperation and communication needed for successful work in a business environment. Making a more ideological point, British employers especially have complained that schools do not inculcate in school-leavers positive attitudes toward business/industry, but instead even promote negative attitudes to authority, entrepreneurial activity and the fundamental concept of a market-driven, profit-oriented economic system (Confederation of British Industry, 1984).

In a memorandum submitted by the Confederation of British Industry to a House of Commons Education, Science and Arts Subcommittee in 1981, similar views were expressed:

> Employers therefore strongly support the case for vocational elements within the school curriculum particularly in the later years of compulsory education. By this we do not mean specific vocational courses as an entry into particular trades or occupations, but a general vocational approach leading to an orientation across the whole of school life which encourages the development of attitudes, skills and knowledge of relevance to adult society . . .
>
> We believe that young people should leave school with an adequate understanding of how wealth is created in our society and an appropriate evaluation of the essential role of industry and commerce. (Confederation of British Industry, 1981, p. 117)

In similar vein, a French employers' group (the *Chambres de Commerce et d'Industrie*) complains of the "excessive segregation between the world of the schools and the outside world" (*Mission Education-Entreprises*, 1985, p. 2).

Part of the problem, observes Otto Esser, President of the Confederation of German Employers, has to do with the way school textbooks portray the economic aspects of society:

It would not be right to present an idealized version lest cynicism immediately overtake the new entrant into the workforce. But it is equally untrue and irresponsible to show it only as negative and marked by conflict. (Cited in Goebel, 1980, p. 332)

A second set of criticisms refers to employers' concerns about the operation and governance of the educational system. They allege persistent wasteful practices that lead to high costs per unit of "output," for example the proliferation of elective subjects and courses. As far as the external efficiency of the school system is concerned, employers everywhere complain about a lack of response to the changing needs of the work-place. Plans for school reforms completely omit consideration of market mechanisms (Goebel *et al.*, 1984, p. 71). Where the schools provide skill-specific training, waste is said to occur because the training tends to be extremely expensive and the skills provided too often do not conform well to those needed in the work-place. French employers' criticisms are particularly pointed (Cans and Coutty, 1982, p. 14).

Moreover, and notably in Britain, employers state that the credentials gained through schooling are poor predictors of an employee's eventual performance, and that where new credentials have been introduced during recent years they are difficult to understand.

In England, France, and Germany, employers point to what they consider to be excessive red tape and government interference in both school-based and out-of-school vocational training. Efforts to improve education by more planning have resulted in inefficiency and bureaucratization. At the same time, they view the schools as insular, dominated by educational professionals who pay too little regard to the realities of economic life and business people's advice. According to one German industrialist, this is a result of the poor education of teachers who are all too often unable to relate their teaching to practical experience and reality (Goebel *et al.*, 1984, pp. 31–32).

Business/Industry Recommendations

Business/industry involvement with education goes far beyond voicing complaints, and extends to making both general and specific recommendations for change. In spite of significant differences among the three countries in educational goals, structures and processes, there is remarkable similarity of view expressed by employers and their organizations in Britain, France and Germany, regarding what needs to be done in the realm of secondary education.

Business people wish to see the distance between the world of work and the world of the schools sharply diminished, and to that end they propose changes in school curriculum, in teacher training and in-service education, and in the management and structure of the school system.

As noted in many citations above, a major charge made against the secondary school curriculum is that it has been too academic, and is biased against the child with practical talents. British, French and German employers are united in their specification of the qualities they desire to see in the young people they hire:

> The qualities which employers want in school leavers are qualities which are equally valuable to those looking for work, the self employed or those training or re-training. They are: the ability to learn; the ability to get on well with other people; the ability to communicate; reliability; basic literacy and numeracy; and an understanding of how the community's wealth is created. (Association of British Chambers of Commerce, 1984, Recommendation 16)

In the hope of promoting the acquisition of such skills, business/industry recommends that it be afforded a much greater opportunity than at present to influence the content, pacing and balance of the curriculum. It argues that its influence should be used to insure that preparation for work be made an organic element of the secondary school curriculum, and not just a mere "add-on" subject (Association of British Chambers of Commerce, 1984, Recommendation 8). German industry in particular recommends that the upper grades of the secondary schools move away from their single-minded concentration on preparing young people for university entrance and that throughout the school system the emphasis on academic material be tempered by giving more attention to music, art and sport. French employers make explicit recommendations for a more desirable pedagogy in French schools: young people should have the experience of carrying out their own research projects and of working together in small groups. (*Charte des Apprentissages Professionels*, 1984, pp. 6, 23).

In England and Germany especially, business/industry wants a curriculum that adapts much more readily than at present to the changing needs of the economy. The key to greater flexibility, they suggest, is to adopt in education the market principles guiding the business world:

> Curriculum policy should be customer oriented instead of producer oriented. It should begin with an audit of the skill requirements which people need in their normal daily life, including their working life, followed by the matching of these requirements against what the schools are providing. (Association of British Chambers of Commerce, 1984, Recommendation 5)

Business/industry wants a good deal more knowledge of economic and business affairs incorporated in the general education curriculum, and it recommends that school subject-matter be conveyed using less abstraction and more practical applications of language, mathematics, the natural sciences and the arts. The curriculum should provide for visits to enterprises on a regular basis in the early years of schooling, and for opportunities for older children to spend periods engaged in practical work in enterprises (Letter of response, Conseil National du Patronat Français, in *Mission Education-Entreprises*, 1985, p. 152; Goebel *et al.*, 1984, p. 46). By the same token:

> Teachers with no experience of business should be encouraged to seek it. The value of such experience should be reflected in salary and career progress. (Association of British Chambers of Commerce, 1984)

The counterpart French organization recommends, specifically, that regional inspectors and teachers of geography and history should be taught the real facts about the economy, that teachers should have the opportunity to acquire continuing education through meeting business people and through visiting firms in, for example, summer courses (Assemblée Permanente des Chambres de Commerce et d'Industrie, n.d., p. 2).

In like manner, the *Institut der Deutschen Wirtschaft* (the Institute of the German Economy) wishes to encourage business to provide teachers with economic education and experience in the business/industry world, in both their initial and in-service training (Goebel, 1980, pp. 333–335). In the view of Paul Schnittker, President of German Handicrafts, *Arbeitslehre* (familiarization with the working world) should be a compulsory subject for all teachers undergoing their training ("Technical change triggers new discussion on education content," 1984, p. 90).

Business/industry organizations urge their members to sponsor partnerships with individual schools and groups of schools, to make available to the teachers more printed information about themselves and about the world of work, and to be as explicit as possible about the specific educational characteristics they would like to see in the young people they hire. All of this should be aimed at helping teachers overcome ignorance about and prejudice against the business world, to reduce the chance that they will impart to their students negative attitudes toward business, either consciously or unconsciously.

Business/industry recommends a sharp improvement in the management of schools, to help them become more effective users of society's resources. School administration should learn from business practice. The Institute of Directors in Britain wants at least one member of each maintained school's governing board to be appointed specifically as a representative of employers (*Times Educational Supplement*, 12 October, 1984). As in the commercial world, so in the world of education, argues the Institute of the German Economy, competition will tie education more closely to the changing demands of the market-place, thus improving quality (Goebel *et al.*, 1980, pp. 32–33). As in the commercial world, too, teachers (as producers) should have clear, agreed, and regularly monitored objectives in mind, and should be held accountable for their performance (Association of British Chambers of Commerce, 1984). The strong State monopoly of educational provision should be tempered by strengthening non-State (private, foundation, business/industry) institutions and arrangements in education. Personnel coming from business and industry should be permitted to serve in the schools (Assemblée Permanente des Chambres de Commerce et d'Industrie, n.d., p. 2, Propositions 8–9). Wherever possible, business initiatives should be supported by tax relief, or subsidies.

Business/industry makes specific recommendations for changing the structure of the school system and rationalizing the articulation of its several levels and institutions. The recommendations differ in detail among the three countries, as each has its own established pattern of institutions. But across the three countries the general tenor of the recommendations is the same: the position and prestige of those parts of the system providing vocational training and direct preparation for work need to be enhanced *vis-à-vis* the more purely academic parts; the prestige of vocational credentials should be raised; and opportunities for students to move from one part of the system to another should be improved. British employers would like to see a reformed system of credentials, that would go far beyond a simple recitation of academic achievements, to include a student profile. They ask also for greater uniformity and systematization of what appears to them as a "bewildering array of courses, course providers, and methods of assessment" (Association of British Chambers of Commerce, 1984).

There is widespread agreement that partnerships between enterprises and the schools should be formed, and where they exist, they should be strengthened, so that the abyss separating the world of the school from the world of work is closed. Too much preparation for work continues to be located in schools, and more should be done within enterprises.

The German dual system of vocational education, in particular the reliance on apprenticeships, finds strong support among employers, although it receives criticism from school people. Approving the example of their German counterparts, French and British employers generally recommend moving vocational education closer to the German system, but, as in Germany, they too face opposition from many spokespersons of school-based interests.

In making recommendations for desirable changes in the schools, business/industry spokespersons are wary of the schools taking over training functions that they believe are best left to business initiative. They also warn against government control of training given within firms, and (in France, at least) they do not view government subsidies to training as justification for detailed governmental regulation of their apprenticeship programs.

The general stance taken by business/industry toward the conditions for partnership with government and the schools is that they should be given a freer hand, with less red tape associated with getting involved with education, and with less concentration upon detailed accountability. This attitude is taken in the name of facilitating pragmatic experimentation, quick response to perceived needs, and the capacity to change direction quickly as some things are seen to work and others not (Confederation of British Industry, 1981, p. 117; Jamieson and Lightfoot, 1982, p. 106).

Although the recommendations made in the three countries are remarkably similar, both in premises and in specifics, the posture taken by business/industry toward its "educational responsibilities" varies. In France, business organizations tend to defer more to the education authorities and the teaching profession than in the other two countries, although their claims to a voice in educational policy are growing. In Germany, where business/industry involvement in training policies is long-standing, there is no hesitation on the part of business organizations in making recommendations for far-reaching change. In Britain, business organizations, taking a relatively new stand, assert the necessity for business to get involved in setting policies for education, and even business/industry's positive right to do so. They point out that not only does the world of work have a *special* claim to be heard, but that education and business are mutually dependent, have common interests and many common purposes, and must therefore cooperate as partners (Association of British Chambers of Commerce, 1984).

Business/Industry Participation

Business/industry has become involved with the education of young people beyond simply offering criticisms and making recommendations for change. Since roughly 1975 their active participation has been stimulated by a number of increasingly important factors. The downturn in economic growth and a sharpening of economic competition among nations, combined with increasing numbers of young people in the age-groups leaving school, resulted in rapidly rising youth unemployment rates. These reached quite unprecedented levels in France, for example, where the percentage of unemployed males aged 15–19 increased from about 5 to over 20 percent in the period from 1974 to 1982, and in the UK, from a similar level to nearly 30 percent (OECD, 1984:2, p. 26). In Germany, however, the rise was much smaller, from close to 2.5 percent to about 7 percent. These figures were interpreted as demonstrating the extent to which the existing structures and content of secondary schooling had become outdated, despite the prolongation of schooling for many. Moreover, technical progress had apparently eliminated many low-skilled entry level jobs formerly available to school-leavers, creating a problem which had every prospect of worsening in the future. Thus there was a widespread feeling that even when economic growth rates improved, and the size of the entry level age groups fell, a severe problem of adequate education and training of the young labor force would remain.

The result has been a new focus in all three countries on the requirements of so-called "transition education," in which business/industry would play a larger role than ever before, not only in its more usual training function but especially in an increasing contribution to general education. This has called for changes in the legislative and regulatory frameworks for education and training, for changes in financial arrangements, for novel institutional functions and provisions, and for greater acceptance of business/industry as a full partner in a total national education and training enterprise.

The following three sections are devoted to the context and the experience of each of the three countries, as business/industry participates in activities aimed at a more directly work-relevant education. These endeavors take a variety of forms, among which are: providing an increasing number of teachers and students with opportunities to observe life in the work place and gain practical experience; twinning and partnership arrangements to improve communication and cooperative work ties between the world of learning and the world of earning; providing schools with material and human resources, and opportunities to collaborate directly with business/industry; and sponsoring many kinds of activities, local and national, designed to encourage the development of work-related skills, an appreciation of the importance of efficiency in production, and a more positive attitude toward business/industry.

1. Britain

The distinction between educational and vocational training has been quite sharp in Britain, where vocational training has been regarded as a substantially inferior preparation to academic education. Until the passage of the Industrial Training Act of 1964 the principle of non-intervention by the State in job-training had for the most part prevailed, and business/industry was considered to have sole responsibility for preparing its own workforce. The State had assumed responsibility for providing general education, and there was little expectation that commerce and industry had any part to play, except with respect to particular craft and technical qualifications. General education remained predominantly within the jurisdiction of the local education authorities (LEAs), who guarded their prerogatives quite jealously, and who were unaccustomed to accept advice from non-professionals concerning the educational system they provided.

The 1964 legislation marked a new view of the role of employers in the education and training of young people. Since that date, legislation (for the most part permissive, and intended to encourage activities at regional and local levels) has increasingly drawn the State into the training field, while growing business concern about the quality and structure of schooling has led to greater involvement of employers and unions with schooling.

The contemporary role of British employers has been summed up in the following terms:

> Business and industry take an active part in secondary education by supporting such initiatives as the Technical Education Initiative of the Manpower Services Commission, the School Curriculum Industry Project, Understanding British Industry and in a number of school company links. (Confederation of British Industry, private communication, 2 Feb. 1985)

Employers may also exercise advisory powers, both regionally and nationally, with respect to the general education provided in LEA schools.

Apprenticeships and other types of in-company training continue to be entirely in the hands of employers' associations and trade unions, though the State, through regional Industrial Training Boards (ITBs), has played a growing part in expanding provisions for apprenticeships.

Employers (and trade unions) are represented on the numerous examination boards that award credentials in craft and technical areas. These boards are important in Britain, because their examinations serve a coordinating role in the extremely diverse system of further education and training. The examination boards in the vocational training areas have a decisive influence over the curricula of the colleges and schools preparing students for business/industry, which in turn gives ready recognition to the credentials awarded by the examining authorities. The most notable of these are: the Royal Society for the Encouragement of Arts, Manufactures and Commerce (RSA), an independent body founded in 1774, now primarily concerned with secretarial, commercial, and public administration occupations: the City and Guilds of London Institute (CGLI), the largest such examining body, with between 400,000 and 500,000 candidates a year in the manual trades and other basic skill areas; the Technician Education Council, which since 1973 has progressively assumed responsibility for the establishment of curricula and examinations for middle-level qualifications from CGLI; and the Business Education Council, established in 1974, to develop curricula and qualifications below the university level for clerical, commercial, and administrative occupations (CEDEFOP, 1984, p. 453).

Beginning in 1964, the introduction of a levy/grant system placed pressure on employers to increase the quantity of vocational training they provided. A tax of up to 1 percent of the payroll was imposed on (larger) companies that did not have their own training schemes, and the proceeds were used to compensate companies offering training. New bodies, called Industrial Training Boards (ITBs) were established to administer the levy/grant program. Companies thus paid the costs of on-the-job training, while the LEAs continued to cover the costs of general education.

Anecdotal evidence indicates that company expenditure on ET [education and training] in the UK declined considerably in 1981 and 1982 and began to recover somewhat in mid-1983 . . . a first British priority is to get better value for money . . . Without the wealth, size and "frontier" tradition of the US, Britain may not be able to afford a process in which each company decides not only what ET it wants internally but also what it wants the public education service to supply and in which each company also has the capacity to negotiate for what it wants with the appropriate public authorities. (National Economic Development Council, 1984, p. 90)

In 1973, the Employment and Training Act established an independent Manpower Services Commission (MSC), charged with responsibility for developing a national training effort. The Act was partly a response to complaints from smaller employers that they derived little or no benefit from the levy/grant system. Since 1973, the Manpower Services Commission has increased so rapidly that it has been termed "Britain's fastest growing quango." ITB activities have been increasingly taken over by the MSC, and it is expected that training through ITBs will cover no more than about 25 percent of the youth labor force, predominantly in construction and engineering. For the rest, MSC has administered a changing menu of work-subsidy and youth training programs involving employers. The most important date from September 1983, with the establishment of the Youth Training Scheme (YTS) and the Technical and Vocational Education Initiative (TVEI).

YTS is directed at the post-16 age group, to guarantee a 12-month training period for unemployed school-leavers. MSC is currently proposing extension to two-year programs. Training takes place either in firms (who receive public funds amounting to about $3000 per training place), or in a variety of off-the-job training establishments run by local authorities. The YTS has incorporated three or four prior government initiatives that encouraged employers to give school-leavers work experience or training, or both, although YTS' target of providing 400,000 training places has not yet been completely met.

The Technical and Vocational Education Initiative (TVEI) promotes technically-oriented and vocationally-relevant courses for the 14–18 age group in schools and colleges. Pilot courses were instituted in 14 LEAs in 1983, and the activity was extended to a further 45 LEAs the following year. By September 1984 the program enrolled 16,000 students. Courses are intended to provide general as well as technical education, vocational preparation and work experience for young persons of all levels of ability, including senior grade students in academic secondary education (sixth-formers). The courses are intended to be attractive to those students in the post-compulsory grades who do not intend to proceed to higher education, and thus to help widen curriculum and career choices. In this connection, the new Certificate of Pre-Vocational Education (CPVE) should be noted. Its introduction was strongly supported by both the Confederation of British Industry and the Trades Union Congress (TUC), and it was designed especially for those sixth-formers who may not wish to sit for the Advanced Level (academic) examinations.

Funding levels for these programs were as follows (£1 = $1.35, approximately):

Industrial Training Boards, 1981–82	£117 million
Youth Training Scheme, 1983–84	£845 million
Technical Vocational Training Initiative, 1983–84	£ 7 million

(MSC, *Annual Report 82/83*, cited in Ryan, 1984, p. 33).

Summary

Two main characteristics distinguish business/industry involvement in the education and training of young people in Britain: active encouragement of local firms' participation by the national voluntary organizations of employers and local collaboration of individual firms with schools and LEAs.

Legislation and initiatives of government agencies have been important in setting out the guidelines for these activities, revising the organizational frameworks necessary, and providing financial incentives for companies to increase job training opportunities.

In the course of developments over the past decade, the traditional separation of academic general education from vocational training has narrowed. Business/industry has contributed to new thinking and practice in general education, has expanded its training activities, and has participated in revisions of examinations and proposals to introduce new credentials and new forms of assessment.

Business/industry involvement over all aspects of education and training is of recent date, and has been growing rapidly. The series of new initiatives and the blurring of the distinctions between academic and vocational education has led to anxiety over what is regarded as vocationalization of the school curriculum, and rising tension between the Manpower Services Commission and the Department of Education and Science. As a memorandum submitted to a House of Commons committee by Imperial Chemical Industries noted: "the national organizational relationships between MSC and DES undoubtedly have within them the potential to generate unsatisfactory local competition which can only in the end act to the disadvantage of the young people themselves" (Great Britain, House of Commons, 1983, p. 218).

2. France

In France most pre-service vocational training is undertaken full-time in the schools as part of general education. Moreover, as a consequence of the Haby Reforms of 1975, all 12–16-year-old students receive an introduction to manual and technical subjects, as part of a common, comprehensive curriculum at the lower secondary stage.

For most pre-vocational training, the Ministry of Education promulgates curricula, sets standards, and provides staff, finance and facilities. However, for the purposes of academic organization and educational provision, France is divided into 25 so-called *académies*. Nineteen *commissions professionelles consultatives* (CPC) (vocational consultative commissions), one for each major economic sector, advise the Minister on such matters as the establishment of training courses and diplomas, curricula and the number of training places to be financed. The membership of the CPCs is representative of the major interested parties: government, employers, chambers of commerce and trades, workers, teachers, parents and experts (*Le Monde de l'Education*, May 1982, p. 17).

Firms have only recently begun to play an active and direct role in pre-service training; previously, business/industry involvement was virtually entirely confined to contractually-based apprenticeships. Employers influence initial vocational preparation in the schools through local arrangements and are involved nationally with the school system through participation in the councils that govern the *lycées techniques* (technical *lycées*), and on the examination boards of the *LEPs* (vocational education *lycées*). Representatives of the skilled trades sit with education officials and teachers on boards of examiners. They will often participate in instruction in the vocational schools, and help define the curricula and examination regulations (T. Malan, private communication, April 1985).

Business/industry is formally involved in educational matters through national organizations of employers, workers and the specialized trade- and craft-based chambers. In each of the 25 *académies*, a Ministry of Education nominee is responsible for coordinating all in-service training activities. This official presides over the regional center for the training of advisers working with firms to establish their in-service training needs, and with schools, *collèges* and *lycées* to establish the arrangements to meet those needs. Instructional staff who provide in-service training receive supplemental pay financed from the proceeds of a payroll tax. Business/industry in France has been acknowledged as a "social partner" (together with unions) of the public authorities for the continuing education of school-leavers and young workers. This is organized within a legislative framework established in 1970–71 (the National Inter-Trade Agreement of 9 July 1970, for vocational and continuing education, signed by employers' and employees' organizations: and the Law of 16 July 1971, for continuing vocational education).

VE—C

However, this legislation was passed during a period of vigorous economic expansion and shortages of skilled labor, circumstances that have since changed.

The major national organizations of employers involved with educational policy are the *Confédération Générale des Petites et Moyennes Entreprises* (Confederation of Small and Middle-Sized Enterprises) and the *Conseil National du Patronat Français* (National Council of French Employers). In addition, there are three national chambers which include employer members and which discharge important education and training functions for companies: the *Chambres de Commerce et d'Industrie* (Chambers of Commerce and Industry), the *Chambres de Métiers* (Chambers of Manual Crafts) and the *Chambres d'Agriculture* (Chambers of Agriculture). These chambers provide an organizational framework for employer participation in training, establishing training facilities, supplying instructional staff and setting standards for qualification in their respective occupations.

The appointment of the Bloch Commission in October 1984 underscored French governmental interest in promoting closer collaboration between education and business/industry, with the aim of improving both sectors of society. The Commission included education system administrators, higher education officers, and representatives of business organizations and trade unions. They were charged with the task of reviewing conditions and making recommendations regarding overall educational policy and practice, and they were also asked to consider specific ways in which regional and local initiatives might be promoted, particularly in the form of joint school-enterprise consultation and activities. The eventual report, entitled *Mission Education-Entreprises: Rapport et Recommandations*, May 1985, set out a program for tying education and the economic sector more closely together. Representatives of the national employers' organizations cited above participated in formulating the report and in the public discussions that took place after its appearance. An important outcome of the Bloch Commission's work has been the legitimation of participation by associations of employers and organized labor in the policy and practice of general education and vocational training.

The major source of funds for full-time apprenticeship education is the payroll tax levied on most firms (Centre International d'Etudes Pedagogiques, 1984, p. 24). Since 1925, a *taxe d'apprentissage*, amounting now to just over one-half of one percent of their payroll, has been levied on French employers, who have the option of paying the proceeds directly to a secondary or higher education institution of their choice, rather than to the Paris Treasury. In 1971, a further tax, the *taxe de formation continue* (continued training tax) was introduced. This tax amounts to 1.1 percent (minimum) of payroll. It is payable by firms employing 10 or more workers, and the proceeds are used to support both general and vocational recurrent education, either in courses run by the firms themselves, or in those given in other establishments. In 1982 for firms in France as a whole, the training tax contribution amounted to 1.96 percent of payroll, substantially more than the compulsory minimum (CEDEFOP, 1984, p. 222). It is estimated that in 1981–82 about 6.5 percent of the working population (1.5 million out of a total of 23 million) participated in the in-service training organized and provided at *lycées* and *collèges*, and financed by these levies.

In addition to formal financial involvement of employers with education, their national organizations have undertaken campaigns of information and consciousness-raising, to alert the general public about the importance of the business world, and to try to correct what it considers to be ignorance or misunderstanding among members of the general public. In 1984, an inventory of Chamber of Commerce and Industry activities along these lines identified a wide range of such public relations initiatives.

Government efforts to involve individual firms and organizations in a variety of educational activities as "social partners" has been a progressive development for about two decades. The Chairman of the National Chambers of Commerce and Industry has observed:

> The extremely positive results (from these partnerships) have for some years now resulted in public authorities increasing the number of programs that bring the schools closer to the economy: educational programs, internships for teachers. These have led today to . . . twinning of *lycées* and *collèges* with enterprises. (*Assemblée Permanente des Chambres de Commerce et d'Industrie*, n.d., p. 1)

Encouragement of local and regional collaboration between schools and business/industry is a distinguishing feature of these initiatives, which have different emphases: the provision of opportunities for work experience; the joining of business/industry and the schools for collaborative research and design in development and/or training; the involvement of firms in providing schools with materials and equipment; facilitating the membership of business/industry personnel on the schools' examination boards and informational and consciousness-raising activities, mostly directed at young people.

Summary

France has had a strongly developed system of vocational training in the regular school system, alongside a relatively limited system of apprenticeship training. On the initiative of the Ministry of Education, employers' groups were involved in establishing the curricular outlines and content of this vocational preparation, but they were excluded from participation in school-based training as well as from involvement in academic education in the schools.

This exclusionary policy has been greatly modified in recent years, with a good deal of central government encouragement for business/industry to offer teachers and students information, counseling, work experience, tools, materials and opportunities for collaboration on specific production projects.

Other changes proposed to encourage business/industry participation in education and training have focused on simplifying the financial arrangements for reimbursing firms providing such facilities, and on adapting the content and organization of training programs to the needs of small and medium-sized firms.

It is commonly assumed that the French administrative style calls for central control of every detail of local operations, in the interest of insuring uniformity and equality across the entire country. However true this may be of school organization (and there are some doubts that it is indeed the case), it is decidedly not true with respect to involving employers with the school system and with training. Instead of detailed direction from the center, the central authorities and the national organizations have chosen recently to promulgate general frameworks of law and encouragement, leaving the regional and local organizations to determine the extent and the form of their activities in detail. As a consequence, there are substantial differences in employers' involvement to be observed, both among the various geographical regions of France and, within the regions, from one economic sector to another.

3. Germany

In Germany, business/industry prepares nearly 70 percent of young people of secondary school age for employment. This dominant business/industry role is accomplished within the "dual system," which provides for a division of responsibilities between the employers and government authorities. A further distinguishing mark of the German system is the decentralization of authority over school-based education and training to the ll German *Länder*.

However, the general guidelines and specific content of training for each of the 439 occupations officially recognized (1983) are determined by Federal government agencies, employers and trade unions. Much of this is in the form of apprenticeship training, which takes place within firms, but with provision for apprentices to be released from work for one to one-and-a-half days a week to continue their general education in vocational schools. The programs provided and implemented by individual companies are supervised by regional organizations with responsibility for maintaining standards and ensuring that Federal regulations are carried out. In this manner, vocational education is dominated by the firms and the associations of members of the major occupations. On the other hand, general education, whether full-time, or as a part-time component of vocational training, is determined by the *Länder*, with little direct input from either Federal authorities or business/industry.

The chambers of commerce and industry, crafts and professions (*Kammern*) are provided for by law in each *Land* and they are charged with providing and administering many types of programs (including education and training programs) in their respective economic sectors. Individuals (firms and masters) are legally required to be members. The functions of the *Kammern* include appointing the boards to examine apprentices at the end of their training, with the boards' membership drawn from among employers, trade union representatives and vocational school teachers. The *Kammern* thus exercise important influence over the implementation of vocational education, whether undertaken in the work-place or in vocational schools.

To the extent that employers dominate the training process and bear most of the immediate responsibility for training, "the apprentices are thus primarily under the authority and control of the firms which give them their practical training" (Max Planck Institute for Human Development and Education, 1983, pp. 242–243). Though largely of a practical nature, this training may also include classroom instruction in vocational material and (occasionally) elements of further general education. As noted above, the *Land* education authorities provide in-school general and vocational education to apprentices on release time. In-school training is shared fairly evenly between further general education and theoretical aspects of the occupation. It is mostly classroom-based, but may include opportunities for practice in school workshops.

Virtually all the costs of in-company training are borne by the employers, while the *Land* authorities bear the costs of in-school education. It has been estimated that the total costs of vocational training (including in-company and in-school training) are shared in the ratio of approximately 40 percent (*Länder*) and 60 percent (employers) (Tanguy and Kieffer, 1982, p. 71). The average annual expenditure (1980) per apprentice across all occupations amounted to some DM17,000 (approximately $5600), of which trainees' allowances ("wages") averaged $1960, and the value of apprentices' output equalled $2240. Net "instructional costs" thus amounted to about $1400 per apprentice per annum (National Economic Development Council, 1984, pp. 16–17). Gross costs of initial vocational and educational training in 1980 amounted to 1.68 percent of Germany's GNP, a major commitment of the nation's resources.

A number of full-time vocational schools also prepare a relatively few students for entry into apprenticeship programs. Other full-time schools extend the training given in firms, and/or provide training not otherwise available in release-time schools, or apprenticeships (Max Planck Institute for Human Development and Education, 1983, pp. 249–250). Although business/industry exercises the preponderate authority in its part of the dual system, it has little or no role in the other (school-based) segment of the dual system.

No doubt because employers in Germany are so heavily committed to the vocational education and training of young people in their transition from school to fully qualified employment, business/industry tends to play a sharply diminished role *vis-à-vis* the general education schools. This is reflected in the rarity of formal partnership activity and specific twinning arrangements linking firms with schools. However, business/industry activity outside the dual system is not entirely absent. For example, work experience opportunities are provided for *Hauptschule* teachers and school-children; there are some opportunities for immigrant youth to gain more knowledge of employment conditions and possibilities; business/industry provides information and instructional materials and resources to the schools; there are a few special programs for the technical training of young women, and there is significant growth in the establishment of training consortia among groups of firms.

Summary

The long-standing and highly regulated participation of business/industry in training is an outstanding feature of the German system. It is characterized by clear definition of roles and responsibilities by the national government, specification of training content and standards by federal agencies (with business/industry participation), provision by employers, and supervision, evaluation and enforcement of regulations by regional and local employer-and-worker boards. The system reaches the majority of youth and enjoys high status. It exemplifies the adaptation of a traditional apprenticeship system to the requirements of a contemporary economy.

However, this intensive involvement of business/industry in work-related training is not matched with respect to school-based education and training, though a few isolated examples of firms' involvement can be identified. In any event, the contrast between the elaborate organization of the dual system and the reliance upon individual and local initiatives with respect to the secondary schools is marked.

Comparative Discussion and Findings

While collaboration between business/industry and the schools is widely supported rhetorically, it has not proved to be easy to install and maintain in practice. By tradition, business/industry has been excluded from direct participation in general education in the secondary schools, and the schools continue to maintain a certain degree of defensiveness against what they view as "outside interference" in their work. At the same time, business/

industry continues to feel that it has a special expertise and interest in vocational training, and should be its main provider.

This exclusion of business/industry from general education has been modified somewhat in recent years, as schools have recognized that they need to improve collaboration with the world of work. It is increasingly conceded that educators need to become better informed about employers' wishes; that, as education becomes more costly, it can profit from the material and political support the business sector can provide; and that the schools need access to the workplace in order to bring a greater degree of realism and sense of immediacy to their curricula. Also, as the general education component in vocational education curricula has grown, the distinction between general and vocational education has become less well defined. Finally, as secondary schooling has become less exclusively a preparation for university entrance, its significance for the economic welfare of the nation has been enhanced, and business/industry's role as a "social partner" in the definition of secondary schooling has become more legitimized. In all three nations, the new conditions of transition have brought with them additional pressures for business/industry to become involved, and an increased willingness on the part of business/industry to do so.

Tensions and pressures

In Britain, as the jurisdictional boundaries between the educational authorities' schools and the employers' training arrangements have blurred, uncertainties about the eventual limits of change have grown. This is evidenced in fears that current plans of the politically and financially well-supported Manpower Services Commission to extend the Youth Training Scheme from a one-year to a two-year program of employment, education and training will undercut the Department of Education and Science, which is also trying to make school curricula more relevant to employment and more attractive to young people. The British worry especially about what they see as an undue vocationalization of the school curriculum. In France, too, the government is concerned that new transition programs might empty the LEPs and, as it is committed to maintaining a variety of educational and training arrangements (traditional *lycées*, LEPs, apprenticeships and apprenticeship centers), it has tried to move forward on a broad front, first providing financial and political support to the LEPs, then to apprenticeship arrangements, then to the traditional *lycées*, all the while encouraging extension of business/industry involvement in schooling.

Germany's long-standing practice of having employers participate in the transition of youngsters from school to work, via the offer and operation of formal apprenticeships, has meant that Germany has not had so far to go as the other two countries in expanding the involvement of employers. Consequently, Germany has not experienced the wrenching adjustments that the introduction of new transition arrangements has brought about in England, and even to some extent in France.

Indeed, in Germany, if there has been change in the demarcation of responsibilities for transition education, it has been in a direction opposite from that of Britain and France. The tendency in Germany, especially under Social Democratic governments, had been to strengthen the school-based modes of training while faulting the traditional apprenticeship arrangements on at least three grounds. Specifically, the dual system has been charged with being overly and narrowly craft-based, and for that reason unresponsive to the needs of modern technologically-advanced industry; crudely exploitative of the cheap labor of young apprentices, in the interest of higher profits, and inherently incapable of meeting the quantitative demand for training places. However, attacks on the dual system along these lines have not gone unanswered (Lutz, 1981, p. 85), and the return to power of a Christian Democratic government at the Federal level has encouraged business/industry organizations to become more active than ever in support of a continued, and even expanded, role for employers in both defining the content of education and in providing young people with opportunities for the transition to work.

In France there has been a fairly clear and highly developed school-based system for equipping young people with academic and vocational knowledge; and in Germany the dual system also has been very clearly defined across all the *Länder*. Because of the absence of a uniform, central direction of their system of schooling and transition, the British may well have experienced unusual tension and difficulty in the process of adjusting the connections among schooling, training and work. The British had left school matters largely in the hands of local authorities, and training matters in the hands of professional and industrial organizations. The result has been a hodge-podge of *ad hoc* arrangements, satisfactory-to-excellent in some areas (for example, advanced skill training of a relatively few young people), but only fair-to-poor for the majority entering lower skilled employment.

As concerns the impact of changes in transition education on administrative arrangements for providing education and training to young persons, Germany had a relatively easy task, given its long tradition of business/industry involvement. Britain, on the other hand, has had to create new mechanisms for incorporating business/industry organizations in educational planning and practice. In a somewhat startling paradox, the poor economic record of Britain in the past decade has led a Conservative government, inclined towards a *laissez-faire* rhetoric on most social and economic matters, to adopt an interventionist tone in educational policy, with the goal of providing radically altered transition arrangements for young people into work. Alongside an official policy of encouraging collaboration between firms and education authorities at the local level, the central government's Manpower Services Commission has become the chosen instrument for defining and executing education and training policy. The justification for this accretion of responsibility on a national scale has been largely in terms of the MSC's (alleged) keener appreciation of the skill requirements of the British economy as a whole, and of business/industry in particular.

While the British have been moving quite rapidly away from their traditional mode of decentralization, in France more responsibility for both the organization and funding of programs of transition education has been recently assigned to the localities, perhaps as a reaction to the traditional practice of initiative and control from the center (Jallade, 1985, pp. 178–179).

The state of the economy

Apart from adjustments in the traditional machinery of government and the financial arrangements governing firms' training efforts, economic conditions are likely to be a crucial factor shaping the nature and extent of business/industry participation in education and training. All three countries have experienced economic recession—France and Britain quite severely, and Germany noticeably, but more moderately.

The effect of economic downturn on business/industry efforts in education and training is likely to be somewhat ambiguous. Faced with a relatively abundant labor supply, firms will tend to curtail training, because they do not need to offer training opportunities as an additional recruitment incentive. They also have an incentive to call for more vocational training in the schools, in order to shift training costs to the public purse. But, working in the opposite direction, a slacker labor market implies less labor mobility. This means that firms do not have to fear quite as much the loss of newly-trained labor to competitors, thus giving them some incentive to maintain their training efforts.

In contrast to these ambiguities, government policies in all three countries have been strongly directed at promoting more business/industry involvement in education and training. This seems to have been prompted by two considerations. First, governments in Britain and France have now accepted the responsibility (long recognized in Germany) for providing a systematic, national approach to preparing young people for entry into work. Second, each nation views itself as being in severe economic competition with other industrialized and trading nations, and believes that success in that competition will depend importantly on the skills and adaptability of the labor force. Both considerations have argued strongly in favor of an enhanced role for business/industry in education and training. Thus, Britain, with the poorest economic record of the three, has witnessed the most change in government activity aimed at increasing such involvement; Germany, with

66   *Harold J. Noah and Max A. Eckstein*

the best economic and employment record (and also the most business/
industry involvement already), has seen the least. France lies somewhere
between these two extremes.

Findings and Conclusion

The major findings of the present study may be summarized as follows:

- Employers in all three nations make similar criticisms of the schools.
  These include: lack of connection of school curricula with the world of
  work, the schools' preoccupation with academic study and credentials,
  inadequacy of basic skill training, and the consequent unpreparedness of
  school-leavers for work.
- Their recommendations for change, aimed at repairing these deficiencies, are also very similar. They want a more "practical" curriculum,
  greater knowledge and appreciation of the world of work on the part of
  both teachers and students and more efficient management of the
  schools.
- Business/industry participation is organized in substantially different
  ways in each of the three countries, though specific types of activities tend
  to be repeated.
- The three nations represent three different models of transition
  education and training: school-based (France), firm-based (Germany)
  and a mixed model (England).
- There is considerable variation in the extent to which business/industry is
  involved in secondary transition education, from extensive (in Germany)
  to relatively low (France).
- In Germany, there has been little change over the last few years in either
  the extent or the structure of business/industry involvement in education
  and training. This is in sharp contrast to both France and Britain (the
  latter, particularly), where the trend of government policies has made
  remarkable shifts. These shifts have, in turn, produced substantial tension between the traditional authorities governing education and the
  newly created ones.
- In Germany, employers bear a large proportion of the costs of training,
  recouping much of this by utilizing the relatively cheap labor of apprentices; in Britain, the wage costs of trainees are rather high for employers,
  and government tries to reduce these by offering employment and
  training subsidies. In France, too, the combination of a secondary
  school-based vocational and technical training and a payroll training tax
  implies that a large fraction of total education and training costs are
  covered either directly or indirectly by public funds.
- There is no evidence from these three cases that any particular mode of
  financing (by State, employer or trainee) or administration (local or

central) is to be preferred as a way of involving business/industry, though presumably the greater the reliance on public funding, the greater the risk that changes in government budget priorities will adversely affect business/industry involvement in the future.

- Business/industry continues to have an important if not dominant role in vocational training. In spite of the sizable increase in business/industry interest in secondary education, the base from which it began was extremely small, and its involvement, therefore, remains limited and sporadic, especially as regards the general education system.
- If business/industry involvement in general education is to be successful, and even expand, careful attention has to be given to establishing the conditions and appropriate institutional arrangements for collaboration between business/industry and the schools. Some progress toward this in France and Britain is noted; in Germany the dual system has for long provided these conditions for vocational and technical training, though relatively little has been done to expand collaboration with respect to general education.

In Britain, business/industry involvement with education is shaped primarily by the national voluntary organizations of business and by local initiatives, nowadays with substantial governmental encouragement. The result has been an assortment of *ad hoc* arrangements, hardly amounting to a system of transition education and business/industry involvement in general education, though there is a good deal of agreement that it is precisely such a system that is needed. In France, government encouragement (and rhetoric) for business/industry to get involved is also quite strong, but the major locus of change remains the schools, with relatively little willingness to accord business/industry more than a supplementary specialized role in preparing young people for work. In Germany, not only is there little substantial change to be seen in the traditional ways of involving business/industry with the education and training of youth, but even the governmental rhetoric is muted. By and large, Germany is satisfied not only that it has come a long way in involving business/industry in the preparation of young people for work (certainly much further than all of the European countries, other than perhaps Austria and Switzerland), but that the nation has already encompassed the changes that both the British and the French are seeking to make. Under the circumstances, it is not surprising that both Britain and France look to Germany as a model of transition to work in which they find much to admire. However, a common set of challenges has produced noticeably different responses in each country, and it is likely that each nation's institutions will continue to respond in its own characteristic way.

68   *Harold J. Noah and Max A. Eckstein*

References

Assemblée Permanente des Chambres de Commerce et d'Industrie (n.d.1) Allocution de M. le President Netter . . . Press release. Paris. (Mimeo).

Assemblée Permanente des Chambres de Commerce et d'Industrie (n.d.2) Mission "Education-Entreprises": Conclusions du groupe de travail sur le thème "L'information économique aux divers niveaux de l'enseignement". Paris. (Mimeo.)

Association of British Chambers of Commerce (1984) Business and the school curriculum. London: Association of British Chambers of Commerce.

Cans, R. and Coutty, M. (1982) S'adapter à la réalité du travail. *Le Monde de l'Education*, May.

CEDEFOP (1984) *Vocational training systems in the Member States of the European Community*. Luxembourg: Office for Official Publications of the European Communities.

Centre International d'Etudes Pedagogiques (1984) An outline of the French education system, Sept. Sèvres: CIEP. (Mimeo.)

Charte des apprentissages professionels (1984) Paris: Assemblée Permanente des Chambres de Commerce et d'Industrie.

Confederation of British Industry (1981) Memorandum, Great Britain, House of Commons, Education, Science and Arts Committee (session 1981–82) *The secondary school curriculum and examinations: with special reference to the 14 to 16 year old age group*, Vol.II.

Confederation of British Industry (1984) Memorandum, House of Lords Sub-Committee C (Education, Employment and Social Affairs). London: CBI, v.28. (Mimeo.)

Confederation of British Industry (1985) Private communication, Feb.

Goebel, U. (1980) Wirtschaft als Partner der Schule. In U. Goebel and W. Schlaffke (Eds), *Berichte zur Bildungspolitik 1980/81 des Instituts der deutschen Wirtschaft*. Köln: Deutscher Instituts-Verlag.

Goebel, U. (1984) Das Bildungskonzept der neunziger Jahre—Plaedoyer für ein begabungsorientiertes, flexibles und effizientes Bildungssytem. In U. Goebel and W. Schlaffke (Eds), *Berichte zur Bildungspolitik 1984/85 des Instituts der deutschen Wirtschaft*. Köln: Deutscher Instituts-Verlag.

Great Britain, House of Commons (1983) Education, Science and Arts Committee (session 1982–83) *Education and Training, 14–19 year olds. Minutes of Evidence together with Appendices*. London: HMSO.

Jallade, J.-P. (1985) The transition from school to work revisited. *European journal of education*, 20 (2–3).

Jamieson, I. and Lightfoot, M. (1982) *Schools and industry*. London: Methuen.

Le Monde de l'Education (April 1982, May 1982, Sept. 1983, Feb. 1984).

Lutz, B. (1981) Education and employment: Contrasting evidence from France and the Federal Republic of Germany. *European journal of education*, 16 (1).

Malan, T. (1985) Private communication, April.

Max Planck Institute for Human Development and Education (1983) *Between elite and mass education*. Albany: State University of New York Press.

Mission Education-Entreprises (1985) *Rapport et recommandations*. Paris.

National Economic Development Council (1984) *Competence and competition: Training and education in the Federal Republic of Germany, the United States, and Japan*. London: National Economic Development Office.

OECD (1984:2) *Youth unemployment in France: Recent strategies*. Paris: Organisation for Economic Co-operation and Development.

Ryan, P. (1984) The New Training Initiative after two years. *Lloyds Bank review*, 152.

Tanguy, L. and Kieffer, A. (1982) *L'école et l'entreprise: l'expérience des deux Allemagne*. Paris: La Documentation française.

"Technical change triggers new discussion on education content" (1984) *Bildung und Wissenschaft*, 5/6.

Times Educational Supplement (12 Oct. 1984; 3 Jan. 1986).

CHAPTER 4

What do Employers Want from Education?

JOHN OXENHAM

University of Sussex

LET me start with three very recent, up-to-date quotations, one from employers, the second from an intermediary between employers and job-seekers, the third from manpower planning. Then let a fourth, rather older one, from an academic observer follow.

> In selecting candidates, employers are placing more and more empha-
> sis on personal qualities, which cannot be taken for granted even in
> applicants with very good academic qualifications. The ability to
> communicate, both orally and in writing, together with good
> motivation, potential leadership qualities, breadth of outlook and a
> positive attitude to change, are obvious requirements alongside
> numeracy and specialist skills.
>
> > (Confederation of British Industry in its response to the British
> > Government's Green Paper on higher education, 1986)

> It is not sufficiently understood that less than 40 percent of the total
> demand is for the highly specialized, while the biggest single demand is
> for graduates of any discipline.
>
> There always has been and no doubt always will be a huge demand
> for broadly based first-degree candidates who are recruited for their
> trained minds, problem-solving capacities, their social skills and their
> mobility. Industrial and commercial recruiters find that arts and social
> science graduates meet these requirements and are easily trained in
> new skills.
>
> > (Senior Careers Adviser, Saint Andrew's University,
> > Scotland, 1986)

> What is probably more remarkable still is the change that has come
> over the [manpower] forecasters themselves, . . . they now reject the

The material for this chapter has been drawn mainly from research done between 1974 and
1981. It is discussed in full in Oxenham (1984). Germane research by others between 1981 and
1986 has tended to confirm the conclusions.

idea of comparing manpower needs and availability as a means of providing guidance to the training system.

(Jean-Jacques Paul, 1985)

In a free market the salaries of technicians would rise relatively to those of skilless and mediocre graduates in arts, but since the government, the principal buyer, bases relative salaries on tradition rather than on scarcity, the market situation cannot right itself.

(W. Arthur Lewis, 1977)

The implied drift of all four quotations is that the relationships between education, employment and salaries are broad, imprecise, even arbitrary. We might infer that educators would be imprudent to worry much about what employers wanted from education. They would be wiser to worry more about good teaching, good learning and helping people to develop all the abilities they possibly can. The evidence to be discussed here will confirm the good sense of that view.

Working Terms

Four definitions are required.

First, *employers* are not individual men and women. Rather, they are employing organizations, like government civil services and commercial or industrial corporations. This sort of employer tends to account for the bulk of waged or salaried employment in most economies. Such employers also tend to set the standards for wage rates, employment conditions and the educational qualifications required for them. When an *employer* is mentioned in the singular, the pronoun *it* will be used, rather than *she* or *he*.

Qualification can mean the licence for a specialized set of skills, like those of a computer programmer or a water engineer. It can also mean something of general application or of no obvious application at all. Reasoning ability, literacy and numeracy are examples of skills with general application. Attainments in ancient Latin, Greek or Sanskrit are clear examples of qualifications with few obvious applications. It is the case that in most countries, most young people leave school with general qualifications—certificates of primary or secondary schooling. So, for this chapter, *qualification* will always mean general qualifications.

Recruiting and *selecting* are two steps that employers usually take before employing people. They first delimit a pool of potential employees within the total labor force, then from that pool identify the people who appear to fall least short of their requirements. The preliminary delimitation is *recruiting*, the second is *selection*.

Employees can include the whole range of people paid by a particular employer. However, as the interest of this chapter is what employers seek in the educated and as educational qualifications count most heavily with those who have no work experience to offer, *employees* here will indicate young people with general qualifications who are just starting to earn their own livings in salaried employment with large organizations, most probably in what are called "white-collar" jobs.

Differences and Inequalities

Selecting between people means that employers accept pragmatically that there are *differences* between people. They also accept that there are *inequalities* between people: some electricians are neater and more meticulous than others. We shall be asking here what differences do different levels of general qualifications make to the qualities, skills and knowledge that are sought by employing organizations? For example, in Mexico there is a three-year difference in schooling between *secundaria* (a 9-year qualification) and *preparatoria* (12 years). In what ways does the difference affect whatever is sought in the generally qualified? Then, within a level, what does inequality of performance signify for the employer? For example, in Sri Lanka in 1975–1977, the Government valued a *distinction* at "O" level 50 percent higher than a *credit* and 87.5 percent higher than a *pass* (Deraniyagala *et al.*, 1978). How are inequalities in scholastic performance interpreted in recruiting and selecting employees?

We should note here a universal assumption and practice. Increased schooling is believed to increase suitability for more responsible and demanding work (and, of course, higher salaries). Similarly, better performance within a level tends to provide an edge of advantage over inferior performance—all else being equal. Varying historical experience and varying political regimes make no difference to this central belief. We would be justified then in believing it was well, even incontrovertibly, founded. We could expect that there would be close agreement between employing organizations on what levels and performances of education would be required for given jobs or groups of jobs.

Consistencies Between Countries

Let us test whether that agreement actually exists, first between employers in different countries, then between those in a single country. Since primary schooling—of between five and eight years, depending on the country—and middle schooling of between eight and 10 years have almost universally ceased to count as qualifications for jobs—and in some countries even for training—a convenient starting point is the general secondary school course. "O" levels in Britain and most of the States it influenced; the Baccalaureat in States influenced by France; "high school" in States adopting the North American pattern, and *preparatoria* in States like Mexico, are now the minimum qualifications required for most clerical or junior white-collar jobs. The content of such work does not appear to differ much from country to country. We might expect then that the same level or quantity of schooling would be required for it.

But *level* turns out not to mean the same as *quantity*. In Sri Lanka (in 1976), "O" levels took 10 years to achieve; in India and Kenya, they took 11. The Baccalaureat, high school and *preparatoria* all represent 12 years of school. (Indeed, parenthetically, Zambia's Junior Secondary Certificate, Cameroon's *Probatoire* pre-secondary exam and Ghana's Middle School Leaving Certificate needed as much time as Sri Lanka's "O" levels, but gave access to lower level jobs, such as clerical assistants.) True, the largest difference is only two years. Yet, think what those two years imply in countries where universal primary education has not been achieved and where secondary education is still the privilege of a minority. In many countries, a secondary school place costs as much as 10 primary school places. If it takes the secondary schools 12 years to achieve what similar schools elsewhere achieve in 10 years, then each unnecessary year spent in schools by a secondary pupil is, in effect, depriving 10 younger children of educational opportunity. Even if a secondary place costs only two or three primary places, the unnecessary equity caused would still be deplorable. At the very least, there could be a misallocation of resources dealing over-education to some, and under-education to others and depriving yet others of any education at all. We could discuss possible explanations for these discrepancies, but, as far as I know, we do not have the evidence to assess which would be the most accurate.

A refinement in this inconsistency appears between States which operate centralized examination systems, on the one hand, and those which, on the other, allow each school to graduate its own students within broad guidelines. Within the second group, such latitude occurs that exact comparisons between schools and particular subjects are almost impossible. For the first group, such comparisons can be—and are—easily made between schools, subjects and, most critically, between individual pupils. A consequence is that, in the second group, employers set qualifications simply in terms of level of schooling, whereas those where centralized examinations are organized, are much more specific in their requirements. The Sri Lanka government, for example, required clerks to have achieved a minimum of six "O" levels, of which four had to be credits—at least 50 percent marks—of which one had to be mathematics and another had to be Sinhala, Tamil or English and achieved in no more than *two* attempts. The Gambian Civil Service was less exacting in one way but more so in another. It demanded only four "O" levels with only pass marks, if mathematics and English were included, but it required all four to be achieved in *one* sitting. If mathematics were failed, then five "O" levels were required instead, again only with pass marks and again at only *one* sitting. The Kenyan Civil service was more exacting, but also more elaborately flexible. It asked for six East African Certificate of Education passes with two credits; five East African Certificate of Education passes with two credits (*sic*, but three credits were probably intended); the East African Certificate of Education with four credits, or the General Certificate of Education with four "O" levels. The Gambia and Kenya Governments judged that four "O" levels were sufficient for clerical officers. The Ghana Government, however, even though it shared the same examination board with Gambia—the West African Examinations Council—took the view that its clerical work needed five "O" level passes, including English (JASPA, 1982).

These variations and trade-offs in educational attainment are puzzling to square with the idea of the relatively homogeneous set of functions performed by clerical workers. Perhaps then there is only a loose and variable fit between jobs and education. How loose and how variable is an important issue, if not for efficiency and productivity in jobs, at least for the volume and allocation of resources for education.

More open inconsistency is found when the same job title calls for different levels of education, directly indicating requirements for a different amount of schooling. Managers in the Philippines are expected to have university degrees, which entail at least 16 years of schooling. In neighboring Indonesia, the average manager in the late 1970s had been in school for less than 12 years. The import of this difference of four years is emphasized by recalling that most people in most developing countries still achieve only five or six years of school in all. Consider also that a university place can cost anything between 20 and 200 primary school places, depending on the country. If it really is the case that managers can manage with only 12 years of education, what is the sense of forgoing literally thousands of primary places for the sake of having university graduates as managers? There are several issues latent in this question: they will be taken up, as this chapter proceeds.

Consistencies Within Countries

Inconsistencies between employers in different countries might not seem so telling. More significant perhaps are the inconsistencies between employers of a single country or even within a single employer. In the 1970s in Sri Lanka groups of clerks could be found doing the same job under a single supervisor. Within a single group education could range from eight to fifteen years (the mean difference was two to three years). Similarly, wide differences could be found among managers in a single organization. Corresponding examples could be quoted from Ghana and Mexico and probably any country one could care to name.

Conversely, people of equal educational attainment could be found spread through a number of jobs within a single hierarchy. University graduates could be found as clerks, executives and managers within one employer and so could secondary-school-leavers.

Concomitant with the diffusion of qualifications along the job-band is the escalation of qualifications for particular jobs. The process seems universal: employers everywhere require higher and higher general qualifications for jobs which seem to change little. We shall return to the point later.

The inconsistency between jobs and qualifications was highlighted by Hallak and Caillods (1980), who suggested that qualifications depended less upon the nature of jobs and more upon the nature of the employer. Economic sector, ownership, size, degree of modernity and location affected the qualifications that an employer required, even though the jobs to be done were much the same. The impression is that setting qualifications is less a matter of systematic evaluation and more a function of circumstance and possibly arbitrary decision. More strongly, it suggests that employers do not know what they want in the way of education, but simply take what is on offer at prices they can afford.

Determining Qualifications

So, how do employers decide what qualifications they need for particular jobs? A naïvely technocratic view might suppose that the following stages would be undertaken:
1. analyse the job into its component functions;
2. test what levels of general schooling and special training are required to cope with the functions;
3. assess what other qualities are needed for the smooth execution of the job within the environment and ethic of the organization;
4. assess whether further schooling or other qualities might be required for promotion, if promotion and a career were part of normal employment;
5. recruit and select according to the findings.

The technocrat would be disappointed, however. Most employers are much less systematic. Even among the 17 government civil services looked at, only one, Liberia, appeared to have actually undertaken such an exercise comprehensively and that only in 1978! Of 26 private employers in Mexico, only six had introduced some form of job evaluation. Perhaps, surprisingly, educational qualifications were their last consideration, after they had fixed the salary applicable: what sort of education would such a salary attract at the time? Education, then, was determined not by the needs of the job, but by the "market" and the going rate. Did the employers want or really expect anything from education?

In contrast, most civil services calibrate their salaries less by what the job involves and more by the qualifications of their staff. Thus clerical officers in Kenya with "O" levels are paid more than those without "O" levels but promoted for good performance; clerical officers who have failed their "A" levels are paid more than those with "O" levels, and those who have passed their "A" levels are paid more than the rest. The important feature to keep in mind is that the promotees, "O" level leavers and "A" level leavers would all be in the same job group, with the same title and identical functions. But by sole virtue of educational qualifications, the "A" level leavers would enjoy a 38 percent salary advantage (1979 scales) over the promotee. Yet in 1972 a Government commission had advocated the principle of paying by job requirements not by qualifications. Kenya's Civil Service was of course not unique in this approach to education, jobs and salaries (see especially JASPA, 1981).

In between these two poles are the bulk of employers, who appear not to have any well-tested means of relating educational qualifications to job functions. Instead, the impression is that the process of determining educational requirements is very particularistic: each employer has its own rules of thumb. This leads, as would be expected, to a lot of disagreement between employers. Indeed, a study of British employers by Brunel University in 1984 concluded that there was nothing that could be called "an employers view" (Kogan, 1984).

The disagreement in itself suggests that employers cannot agree on what they want from education because they really do not know what they actually get from education. Only one exception was encountered. An Anglo-American multinational, uncertain whether to aim for an all-university-graduate managerial cadre, tested some of its British managers to see whether university graduates (17 years of school or more) showed any distinct managerial superiorities over colleagues with only "A" level schooling (14 years)—and found they did not. That is, the employer did not know previously what it was getting from the extra schooling of some of its managers and, after testing, knew that it was getting virtually nothing.

Preferring the More Educated

Nonetheless, employers tend—with many exceptions—to prefer applicants with more schooling, whether or not they need them. Perhaps the more schooled are thought to do jobs better? Again, the employers do not permit a single or simple answer: they disagree among themselves in numerous countries—Mexico, Ghana, Kenya, India, Zambia, Indonesia, Panama (see especially Oxenham, 1984, pp. 63–66).

Despite a bias towards the more schooled, however, employers do seem to be nervous about hiring the over-schooled or over-qualified. The main reason is not that such people get bored, but rather that they demand promotion too quickly and too impatiently.

The combination of the preference with the nervousness means that, even as the average level of qualification set for a job is edged upward, employers tend not to bid too far ahead of it. In this way they can dampen undue expectations based solely on educational differences.

Superior Social Skills

An example from Sri Lanka illustrates that, for a number of employers, having more schooling is associated with superior social skills. "Good all rounders" from "first rate" schools were what 10 private employers sought. Such boys and girls were "usually from families who have influence in society, and their school friends are also going to have influence in society. So they are going to be useful to the organization. And also they can hold their own, when they go out to meet members of the public. They know how to mix with proper people" (Deraniyagala *et al.*, 1978. p. 38). Similar examples could easily be given for numerous other countries. They show the influence more of social class than of schooling as such, (both are part of education), but help explain the upward drift of qualifications.

Discrimination against rather than in favor of particular social classes was shown by an employer in Mexico. It had previously relied on the education system to sift out the classes with "no culture." The spread of education and the invasion of the universities by the less cultured classes meant that people now possessed technical knowledge, but still lacked culture (Brooke *et al.*, 1978). The employer seemed to imply that what the school as such offered was not really what employers sought: social skills, not a speciality of the school system as a whole, outweighed the cognitive attainments, which are the school system's purview, at least for this employer.

Moral Obligation

An additional element of explanation came from the moral obligation employers felt towards the longer schooled. A civil servant in Ghana could defend the preference by pointing out, "These people have been weeping over their exams, not just doing ordinary jobs. They deserve more." A private paper company in Mexico justified raising its qualifications with the protest: "doctors are now selling medicines—so we cannot go on filling the company with people of secondary education."

Escalating Qualifications

The tendency to prefer the more schooled accords, of course, with observations that the educational qualifications of those holding jobs seem to be influenced more by the supply of qualifications than by the needs of jobs (OECD, 1970; Psacharopoulos and Sanyal, 1981).

We may state the consequence a little more formally.

Since Factor (1)	there is no well-based link between jobs and qualifications;
Factor (2)	there is nonetheless an informal, relatively unargued, preference for those with more rather than less schooling;
Factor (3)	the supply of people with qualifications has been rising fast at all levels (across the world, primary school enrollments have been rising at more than 5 percent per annum, secondary at 8–10 percent per annum and tertiary at 12–15 percent per annum);
Factor (4)	the supply of people with qualifications has been rising faster than the supply of jobs previously equated with those qualifications;
Then Consequence (1)	people with "higher" qualifications will resign themselves to seeking, competing for and settling into "lower" jobs;
Consequence (2)	employers will begin admitting people with "higher" qualifications to the "lower" jobs (and even pay them an "educational premium");
Consequence (3)	the average qualification of the people in a given job will begin to rise, as those with "higher" qualifications become more numerous and even a majority.
Consequence (4)	employers will feel forced to abandon the "lower" qualification and require a "higher" one from future applicants, *whether or not the job-contract has changed.*

And so it has been found in virtually every country examined, industrialized or developing (see Oxenham, 1984, 76 *et seq.*).

Conclusions

The overwhelming impression from the evidence surveyed is that there is no neat and universal explanation of what employers want from school and university education. Still less is there any firm connection between scholastic qualifications and job functions. Any expectation of consistency within large organizations which try to be rational is disappointed.

The almost universal absence of systematic matching makes it more appropriate to think in terms of a theory composed of unexamined assumptions, rules of thumb, inertia and narrow responses to changing circumstances. There is consensus on only one point, the desirability of some schooling for employment in the modern sector. Apart from that, the relative importance of aspects like "adequate preparation," "identifying ability and potential," "screening for social compatibility" or even "political screening," is subject to dispute and wide variation.

Qualifications or educational credentials seem then to form simply a convenient starting point: they offer some fixedness or stability in situations of uncertainty. To use them to make a first distinction between people is accepted as non-arbitrary and fair. Whatever their drawbacks, everybody is subject to them. Such a convenience works well enough even for governments, when they are acting as employers, the largest in their countries.

But what implications might be drawn for governments, when they are acting as educators, also the largest in their countries? Perhaps they ought to recognize explicitly that the links between levels of schooling and particular jobs are largely arbitrary. They might then set about their educational reforms with less attention to manpower and much more attention to high-quality schooling from Grade 1 through to the point where they can afford to give everybody a place. Beyond that, let the selection and training for jobs be arranged by the job-givers, i.e., the employers. And let there be no underestimate of the ability of the employers to cope with such a situation. Earlier we noted that some school systems operate centralized examinations to qualify their young people. Other systems dispense with central examinations and permit individual schools to issue their own qualifications. In both cases, employers work with whatever the school system yields. Significantly, in self-graduating systems, where schools vary so widely that their certificates have no reliable standard meaning, employers have been wondrously creative in testing for competence, ability, aptitude, attitude and compatibility. Therefore let *them* work out what they want. Let the schools work at good education.

References

Brooke, N., Oxenham, J. and Little, A. (1978) *Qualifications and employment in Mexico*, Education Report No. 1. Sussex: Institute of Development Studies.

Deraniyagala, C., Dore, R. and Little, A. (1978) *Qualifications and employment in Sri Lanka*, Education Report No. 2. Sussex: Institute of Development Studies.

Hallak, J. and Caillods, F. (1980) *Education, work and employment*. Paris: UNESCO/ International Institute of Educational Planning.

JASPA (1981) *The paper qualification syndrome and unemployment of school leavers*. Vol.1, *Kenya, Somalia, Tanzania, Zambia* and Vol.2, *Gambia, Ghana, Liberia, Sierra Leone, Addis Ababa*. ILO/JASPA.

JASPA (1982) *Paper qualification syndrome and unemployment of school leavers, a Comparative Sub-Regional Study*. Addis Ababa: ILO/JASPA.

Kogan, M. (1984) An employer's perspective, Brunel University Expectation of Higher Education Project, Paper No. 3. Uxbridge: Brunel University.

Lewis, W. A. (1977) The university in developing countries: modernisation and tradition in higher education and social change. In K. W. Thompson, B. K. Fogel and H. E. Danner (Eds.), *Higher education and social change*, Vol.2 (pp. 516–529). New York: Praeger.

OECD (1970) *Occupational and educational structure of the labour force and levels of economic development*, Vol.1. Paris: OECD.

Oxenham, J. (Ed.) (1984) *Education versus qualifications?* London: Unwin Education Books.

Paul, J. J. (1985) Forecasting skilled-manpower needs in France, concepts and methods. In R. V. Youdi and K. Hinchliffe, (Eds.), *Forecasting skilled manpower needs: The experience of eleven countries*, pp. 35–56. Paris: UNESCO/IIEP.

Psacharopoulos, G. and Sanyal, B. (1981) *Higher education and employment, the IIEP experience in five less developed countries*. Paris: UNESCO/International Institute of Educational Planning.

CHAPTER 5

Captured by the American Dream: Vocational Education in the United States

WELLFORD W. WILMS

University of California at Los Angeles

SINCE it was created under Federal legislation in 1917, vocational education in US high schools has enjoyed a high level of public support. According to a recent report by the National Commission on Secondary Vocational Education, in 1984 nearly $9 billion was spent on high school vocational programs (National Commission on Vocational Education, 1984). Originally designed to help youngsters deemed unfit for higher education to get vocational skills and thus rise in sub-professional jobs, vocational education is a logical extension of the American Dream—getting ahead by one's own hard work. Recently, however, an increasing number of studies have called into question the degree to which vocational education in the US has an economic payoff for its students. Additionally, some critics maintain that vocational programs, rather than advancing social mobility, may in fact contribute to occupational and class stratification by substituting job training for education and tracking students into dead-end jobs.

Thus, it is puzzling how vocational education appears to flourish while evidence mounts as to its shortcomings. The answers appear to lie in vocational education's deep roots in the American belief in material success as well as in its distributive effects, by which it channels millions of Federal dollars each year into a long-established pipeline that feeds a powerful political constituency. In this way, the American belief system provides a social rationale for vested economic and political interests and insulates the vocational education system from external demands for change. This chapter also points out limits that may be inherent in attempts to transplant social programs from one culture to another.

The American Dream

Beliefs, like the American Dream, play a central role in all cultures. By accounting for experience, beliefs provide psychological and social order. Order and harmony replace chaos. As Murphey (1979) notes, humans, who have developed without the navigational aid of instinct, use beliefs as a basis for action.

Thus, the American Dream, whose central tenet is that material wealth is the chief measure of a man's success, provides the belief that guides the lives of millions of Americans. The outlines of those beliefs can best be seen in the nation's literature, which since the 19th century, has reflected those values that Americans hold dear. Horatio Alger, a 19th-century American author, is credited with popularizing the "rags to riches" dream by writing more than 100 books that sold more than 17 million copies. The titles themselves— *Ragged Dick, Mark the Matchboy, The Cash Boy, Risen from the Ranks, Andy Grant's Pluck* and *Bound to Rise*—reveal key elements of the formula for success. First was the conviction that all men are created equal. Material wealth stood for success, a necessary reinterpretation of the Protestant ethic to suit it to the American industrial revolution. The nation offered unlimited opportunity, but those who would succeed had to seize it. The belief held that men are responsible for their own positions in life, and the deserving ones would rise by their own effort. A law of mutual obligation was also a key element in the belief structure. Those who had already succeeded were obliged to help those who, because of circumstances beyond their control, were less fortunate.

Finally, certain behavior and characteristics set apart those who would ultimately rise from those who were destined to stay at the bottom. If nothing else was ingrained in American boys who wanted to succeed, it was the admonition: "be willing to start at the bottom and work hard." After all, hard work was morally right. Further, boys who would succeed had to learn habits of thrift and self-denial. Further, Alger's heroes were always faithful, passing up opportunities to profit at their employers' expense. Their hard work and habits of industry led them naturally to rise on the job. A crucial distinction between those who would rise and those who would not was that of individual initiative and self-reliance. Above all, young men who will succeed must have certain personality characteristics. Honesty, charitableness, cheerfulness and optimism set them apart from the others. Finally, courage and resolution, or pluck, were essentials. Alger's hero, Luke Larkin, was

> the son of a carpenter's widow, living on narrow means, and so compelled to exercize the strictest economy . . . [Luke] filled the position of janitor at the school which he attended, sweeping out twice a week and making the fires. He had a pleasant expression, and a bright, resolute look, a warm heart, and a clear intellect.

Thus, by clarifying and popularizing themes of the American dream, Alger helped to forge key axioms that undergirded the near-universal American belief in success that persists still in the late 20th century. This belief, like beliefs of other times, defined relationships between individuals and their environments and provided a basis for action.

The Development of Vocational Education

It was from this belief in success that vocational education grew. The notion that everyone was equal at birth and that success derived from one's own self-determination and hard work were at the belief's root. Further, those who were so determined and worked hard would naturally form those habits and characteristics that made them deserving. The advance of post-Civil-War industrialism, however, promised to alter some of the basic tenets of the American belief in success. Men were replaced with machines, and dreadful working conditions persisted in the factories. Late 19th-century public schooling, which sought to equalize Americans' opportunities came under heavy attack for being deadening and out of touch with changing labor market needs (Grubb and Lazerson, 1974). The restoration of these tenets of American life called for a powerful antidote, and reforming the schools became a priority. Ultimately, one of American public education's most progressive programs was developed—the Smith–Hughes Act, which ushered in vocational education.

The rationale that led to the development of vocational education grew out of the manual training movement of the 1880s and 1890s; that too was based on the American belief in success. Manual training was heavily influenced by a Swedish educational system known as "Sloyd," which literally means "skill" or "dexterity," emphasizing the use of carpenters' tools and mechanical drawing to develop the intellect and character through manual work. The Sloyd system found quick acceptance among American educators because, as the 13 December 1892 edition of the Santa Barbara *Morning Press* proclaimed:

> Sloyd develops the child physically, mentally and morally. It is intended to mean something more than mere mechanical skill—valuable as that is. Its object is the intelligent exercise of the whole body. It aims to develop character and to so train a child as to fit him in the future to become a useful and worthy citizen. (Ellenwood, 1960, p. 17)

Retrospectively, the nation's interest in manual training before the turn of the century seems inevitable. It was educationally sound, productive and wholly consistent with the American belief in success. But, unlike Alger, who credited the individual's habits and character for upward mobility, manual training put the burden on the school. Educators assumed that manual training would make school more interesting to children, who would then stay long enough to learn the basics and a few manual skills, and explore some likely occupations. The process, according to the common wisdom, would promote equality of opportunity.

Despite manual training's promise, it never took a firm enough hold on the American mind to endure. Because it was eagerly and visibly extended to juvenile delinquents and southern blacks, its image became one of "philanthropic education for social deviants" (Grubb and Lazerson, 1974). A national depression in the early 1890s also undercut manual training for the sake of economy (Ellenwood, 1960). In 1910 David Snedden, Commissioner of Education for Massachusetts and an important figure in the vocational education movement, faulted manual training for being liberal education in disguise, which rarely resulted in any recognizable form of "vocational efficiency" (Snedden, 1910).

Unfortunately, the ills of society that manual training sought to cure continued to worsen into the 20th century. Dreiser and other social critics of the early 1900s described how large cities such as Chicago were like huge magnets, attracting the "hopeful and the hopeless." Industrial expansion was well under way, and cheap, unskilled labor was in high demand. In a drive for efficiency and profit, factory jobs were broken down to their simplest components, so that they could be performed by interchangable, unskilled workers. As cities became crowded with the hopeful and the hopeless, the more fortunate took these blind-alley jobs, the less fortunate joined the growing unemployment lines and the specter of social unrest became apparent.

The nation intensified its consideration of solutions to remedy these national crises. In the years preceding World War I, many influential groups developed proposals to include vocational training in public schools to restore faith in the American belief of success and to boost productivity. In 1914, Congress, moved by the public tide, created the Commission on National Aid to Vocational Education to bring the proposals for vocational training together under a legislative proposal. The Commission's work resulted in the Smith–Hughes Act of 1917. Because the legislation was set deeply in the American belief system, remarkably dissonant groups, including the National Association of Manufacturers, the American Federation of Labor and the National Education Association, supported it.

An analysis of influential documents of the time, including the Commission's report and hearings that preceded the Smith–Hughes Act, reveals that the appeal for a national program of vocational education was based on the key tenets of the American belief in material success—equalizing opportunities, promoting individual effort or self-determination and emphasizing the morality of hard work and success. Supporters of vocational education further assumed that, according to the deeply-held American belief, students who worked hard would naturally develop those habits and personality traits that would make them deserving and thus help them rise.

Equality of Opportunity

Vocational education would help assure equality of opportunity by providing people with the broad technical skills necessary for employment in the new industrial order. Further, those who were fit and capable would be able to rise to their highest levels of ability.

Vocational education supporters acknowledge modern industry's powerful influence in creating a class-bound society. The stifling jobs that industry created in the name of efficiency brought into existence a lower industrial class from which the unskilled could not escape. By offering youngsters a wide range of vocational choices and insuring broad transferable training, the schools could break this cycle and become advocates for both working men and women and industry. Lapp and Mote gently put the blame at industry's feet:

> Perhaps industry is not to be held accountable for the cataclysmic peril of individualism run riot, but industrial education will free the workers from the enticements of "blind-alley" jobs, facilitate the realization of an economic democracy and in the end raze the bulwarks of class exploitation, an ideal from which industry certainly is not to emerge a loser. (Lapp and Mote, 1915)

Industry's quest to maximize profits through efficiency required a systematic approach to management. Pioneered by Frederick Taylor around 1885, scientific management was perhaps the first organized approach to work—analyzing work into its simplest clements, and directing systematic improvements in how the worker performed. The needs of efficiency militated against human development. According to Lapp and Mote, "manufacturers want men . . . who are content to stay at one machine process until they have become proficient in it." Vocational educators reacted against this dehumanizing attitude, and maintained that industrial skills were a way out of repetitive, stultifying work. Vocational education would promote equality of opportunity by providing all students with the chance for industrial training. Industrial training would also help working men to gain control over their own lives through economic self-sufficiency. Ultimately, some argued, the work-force would become so skilled that employers would become dependent on their employees, forcing them to include employees in vital decisions that affected their lives.

> As long as the worker is poorly trained, as long as he is an inefficient factor in production and his place is easily filled, he can be dominated through fear of losing a poor job. Let the worker become a skilled artisan or let him through a combination of cooperation gain control of the supply of the product that he has to sell, then he becomes a potent

factor in determining hours, wages and working conditions. More-over, as soon as he becomes a skilled worker, his power and impor-tance as a citizen are enhanced and he begins to tamper with the machinery at the source of his master's political strength. (Lapp and Mote, 1915)

These proposals to increase individuals' sense of potency in the face of rapid industrial growth were only peripheral, however, to their primary objective—to promote equal opportunity in the face of a rapidly advancing class system which was based on occupational status and education.

Reaffirmation of Individual Effort and Self-determinism

But, as a horse can be only led to water and must drink from his own determination, individuals had to be determined and self-reliant to rise in the American class structure. Thus, reaffirming the importance of individual effort was a focal point of the proposals to revolutionize American schools through vocational education. Secretary of Commerce, William Redfield, poignantly described the meaning of individual effort in his testimony supporting vocational education. He told of a boy "willing enough, but quite unable and quite untaught" who took the only employment he could find, which was driving a grocer's cart for $2.50 per week. The low wage was barely enough to live on, let alone support the boy's aging and unemployed parents. This low-level employment was, in Redfield's words, degrading to the boy's sense of manhood and fearfully injurious to his home. Low-level work was not inherently evil, but this boy, like Alger's heroes, was virtuous and always on the lookout for opportunity. The boy found training as an electrician through the help of a private organization. Two years later, through his own hard work and aided by the stewardship of this private training organization, he had increased his earnings tenfold. He was then able to discharge his responsibilities to his parents and take his rightful place in society.

Although it was proposed that vocational education be publicly subsi-dized, this was not at odds with an emerging early 20th-century American conception of individual freedom. It simply added a new dimension, which recognized and affirmed the responsibility of the more fortunate to help the less fortunate. In this more contemporary view of individualism, the public schools served as stewards, providing the avenue of skill training to work and material success.

Hard Work and Material Success

Vocational education also emphasized the importance of hard work to succeed. As an added benefit, students' diligent study and hard work would increase national productivity. Reaffirming this aspect of the American Dream found immediate support among legislators and their constituents who felt that the belief in an individual's hard work was losing its hold among the new class of factory workers, which in turn had a deleterious effect on national productivity. Accordingly, achieving greater economic productivity through vocational education rested with tapping children's life-career motives:

> Primarily it is the motive of personal advancement. Show a man how he can better his economic condition by acquiring further knowledge, and he will assiduously seek to acquire it if his ambition has not atrophied; show a youth how the knowledge that the school gives couples up with a life-work, and he seeks the knowledge eagerly. (Lapp and Mote, 1915)

The schools, vocational education advocates maintained, should point individuals toward a better economic condition. These advocates claimed that the schools of the day existed in a culture that valued the work of the mind over work of the hands, lacked usefulness for students and employers alike and failed to capitalize on students' life-career motives.

How Well Has It Done?

Between 1917 and the mid-1970s little research was done on how well vocational education actually fulfilled its social purpose. The lack of such information reflects, in part, a public acceptance that, like many religious beliefs, is based on faith. And, like the religious faithful, believers are less swayed by empirical evidence than by anecdote and example. Recognizing this fact, the American Vocational Association (vocational education's political arm) has for years orchestrated a highly successful public relations campaign through local newspapers about boys and girls who have pulled themselves up by their own bootstraps and succeeded through their vocational education programs, thus testifying to its value.

The lack of evaluative research can be explained also by the powerful grip in which the vocational education lobby held research funds. Until the early 1970s, vocational education was regarded by most policymakers and researchers as a moribund topic that held little interest for research. Further, the American Vocational Association, and the Federal bureau that dispensed research funds, had exclusive and undisputed control over the research agenda. Thus, until Congress created the National Institute of Education in 1973, which in its early years operated independently of special interests, evaluative research was limited to maintaining vocational education's political appeal through descriptive studies.

However, by the early 1970s, the issue of youth employment had attracted national interest. Also, the National Institute of Education had been set up and authorized to invest substantial amounts of money in research on pressing national educational issues. Since then, millions of dollars have been spent on vocational education and research, which have produced widely varying conclusions about its results. (See, for example, Michael Kirst, *Research Papers for Vocational Education: Compliance and Enforcement of Federal Laws, Planning Papers for the Vocational Education Study*, National Institute of Education, Washington, DC, 1979; National Planning Association, *Policy Issues and Analytical Problems in Evaluating Vocational Education*, US Department of Health, Education and Welfare, Washington, DC, 1972; M. Zymelman, *The Economic Evaluation of Vocational Training Programs*, Johns Hopkins University Press, Baltimore, 1976.) An important reason for the disparity between the studies' findings lies in the messiness of social science research and in the problem of adequately controlling for differences in students' backgrounds and abilities.

The evidence suggests that high school vocational programs may have superior holding power only for black women. Despite problems in adequately controlling for students' backgrounds, Bachman (1972) found that college preparatory students are the least likely to drop out. He also found very little difference in drop-out behavior among vocational, general and agriculture students. Grasso and Shea (1979) contrasted the holding power of occupational and general high school programs and concluded that black women in business and office programs persist better, but both black and white men in vocational programs drop out more frequently than do their general program counterparts. A study done by Mertens (1982) analyzed the propensity of a a large sample of students to drop out after the 9th, 10th and 11th grades. The study, which controlled statistically for students' backgrounds, found some increase in retention for vocational students, but the effect was small. In a study of drop-outs from California high schools, Stern *et al.* (1985) reported that drop-outs with vocational education backgrounds fared no better than other drop-outs.

Except for the experience of women graduates of high school office programs, little persuasive evidence exists that high school vocational programs, compared with other high school programs, pay off in placement and earnings. In two of the few studies that questioned the value of high school vocational education programs prior to the mid-1970s, Kaufman (1967) and Vincent (1969) found virtually no earnings advantage for vocational graduates over others. More recently, Grasso and Shea (1979) concluded that for males, enrolling in a vocational or general program makes no difference in their rates of pay. They report some evidence that vocational graduates experience slower rates of growth in wages over time than do general graduates. But they also conclude that women who enrolled in business and office programs and took conventional jobs earned 27 cents per hour more than women from other curricula. After reviewing the literature on high school vocational education, Berryman (1980) concluded that verbal and mathematical ability are more closely related to later earnings than are specific vocational skills.

More recent research by Rumberger and Daymont (1982), Meyer (1981) and a study by Mertens and Gardner (1983) fail to show any substantial gains in employment or earnings for graduates of high school vocational courses. To the extent that advantages are discernible, they are most likely to appear in cases where students take a concentrated vocational program and work in the area after graduation. As Stern *et al.* (1985) point out, any employment or earnings gains that are apparent, diminish over time.

Most findings at the secondary level can be extended to post-secondary vocational training as well. Wilms and Hansell (1982) found that dropping out of a post-secondary vocational program also had no effect on students' earnings. Students who dropped out early in their programs (who were also most often from less-advantaged backgrounds) earned as much as their classmates who graduated, after controlling for differences in backgrounds. In an earlier study, Wilms (1975) found that less than 20 percent of post-secondary students who trained for upper-level technical jobs got them. Most vocational graduates became clerks or took lower-level, unrelated jobs for which they could have been trained in weeks. On the other hand, 80 percent of the women who trained for lower-level clerical or service jobs got them, but with the exception of secretaries, they barely earned the Federal minimum wage. Though the study collected job histories for up to three-and-one-half years, it found no evidence of vocational graduates' upward occupational mobility.

In a federally-financed study of two divergent Los Angeles area locales, Wilms (1984) found that most employers do not favor hiring high school vocational education graduates or paying them more than others. To the extent that they voiced a preference for entry-level clerical, blue-collar and service jobs, employers tended to favor applicants with academic rather than vocational education backgrounds. Far from placing a premium on technical skills, most employers reported that good work habits and positive attitudes are essential to job success. The report noted that employers regarded educational credentials as valuable only insofar as they help to ensure that applicants have these attributes. Thus, they usually prefer to develop job skills informally through on-the-job training, and they expect the schools to inculcate proper work habits and attitudes.

Recently, the Committee for Economic Development, which comprises presidents of leading American businesses and universities, issued a report on education that commented flatly:

> However it is viewed, vocational education, with few exceptions, has failed to make measurable impact on the success of its graduates in the

VE—D

labor market . . . One exception to the poor track record . . . is secretarial training . . . Yet outside of this area and certain drafting, agricultural, auto mechanics, and crafts programs, there appear to be few vocational programs that justify the investment in them. (Committee for Economic Development, 1985)

Finally, in his epic study of American schooling, Goodlad (1984) inquired about the social value of vocational education. His line of questioning developed from observations contained in the Harvard University report, *General Education in a Free Society* (1945), which emphasized the social importance of a common high school curriculum. The report insisted that:

There are not and must not be two classes of citizens, separated by whether their diverse interests, gifts, and hopes depend on their heads or their hands. (*General Education in a Free Society*, 1945)

Nevertheless, 40 years later, Goodlad and his research team found a discernible split between the academic and vocational programs in high schools, a split that tended to substitute job training for general education. Within vocational programs, Goodlad noted another dimension of inequality. Frequently, white vocational education students were enrolled in programs with a general education content such as home economic or business while Mexican–American vocational students were disproportionately enrolled in programs aimed at preparation for lower-level jobs, such as cooking, sewing and auto repair. Goodlad commented:

I was forced to think about this issue as I walked through, and observed students in the vocational education classes of the high schools we studied. The antiquated equipment in most of them would not have bothered me if its apparent function had been to assure all students an alternative mode of learning which we hope they will acquire through general education. The fact that the equipment did not parallel that of modern industry would have been of no significance. But it suddenly became of significance when principals, counselors, and vocational teachers spoke eloquently about the preparation of the students using it for immediate successful entry into the job market. The incongruity often was startling. (Goodlad, 1984)

Constancy of the Belief

So, we now return to this chapter's original question: why vocational programs persist in the face of such evidence. Since 1917, funding for vocational education has increased from $10 million to nearly $9 billion today. Sixty-five percent of all high school students in the US are estimated to enroll in vocational programs of one form or another. However, the evidence indicates that, with the exception of typing and some business programs, little demand for it exists among employers and few vocational graduates achieve any notable success. Contrary to its founding vision, vocational education does not appear to staunch drop-out rates or live up to its potential as a superior pedagogical medium. Its failure no doubt stems from the lower-class stigma of manual work causing middle- and upper-class parents to avoid it. Vocational education's low status also derives from its being disproportionately targeted on low-income, minority students. The empirical evidence thus stands in sharp contrast to rhetoric of the original belief.

One reason for vocational education's persistence is revealed in a quip by Albert Quie, formerly the ranking Republican on the US House of Representatives Committee on Education and Labor. "It's just good politics", said Quie, meaning that vocational education gets the money back home to constituents who believe in the program's purpose and thus support its legislative advocates. Indeed, the resources commanded by the program are substantial. More than 350,000 teachers alone depend on the $9 billion that annually flows through the vocational education pipeline to 15,000 high schools.

Vocational education's popularity stems also in part from its practical social function. Empirical evidence notwithstanding, these programs continue to be substituted for general education for students who fail to achieve in the academics. Thus, frustrated educators and policymakers take comfort in the belief that these non-achieving students may nevertheless succeed.

Consequently, the American public, guided by the underlying belief in giving everyone an equal chance at success, continues to support vocational education. The program itself has changed remarkably little since 1917. Reflecting contemporary social values, girls are now included in more equal fashion with boys, as are the handicapped, displaced workers and other disadvantaged groups. Further, in response to public demands for greater economic productivity, vocational education has included economic development in its goals. And, as might be expected, the widespread belief in the American Dream still lies submerged beneath its surface. For example, at a 1984 legislative hearing, Jack Bailey, a member of one of Kentucky's vocational education advisory committee, testified:

> The higher level people you put out of these vocational schools, the more money they're going to make and the more taxes they'll pay, in my opinion. And if they go out there and ditch dig . . . , they're going to be paying very few taxes. If they are trained properly, they are going to go into higher tech, higher pay, higher paid jobs.

Not only is vocational education still regarded as a route to higher-paying jobs, it is still believed to be a medium through which positive work habits and attitudes can be inculcated. At a legislative hearing in 1983 a Virginia school official claimed:

> In the simplest way possible, let me explain what I see going on in vocational education. I see students who are busy. They are cutting hair, they are welding, they are laying bricks . . . I see them interested in learning skills, developing good work habits.

Despite the social turbulence of the 1960s, Americans still cling to the dream that all people are born with equal chances for success, and that, through individual effort and hard work, anyone can make it. The evidence is embedded in the culture. For example, "advance" obituaries written about famous living people and kept on file by newspapers for timely use at their deaths describe Ronald Reagan's career as, "From small-town Midwest boy to the most powerful man in the Free World". Richard Nixon's eventual death will mark, "the end of an American-dream career—from small-town boy to the nation's highest office" (Rawitch, 1986). Evidence of the American Dream is easily seen in the popular culture as well. "Success" books continue to be best-sellers. Mass advertising, whose themes must quickly establish themselves with prevailing beliefs, capitalize on success through individual effort. Daniel Yankelovich, a polster and observer of changing American lifestyles, notes that most Americans continue to believe that hard work and individual effort pay off (1981).

Implications for The Future

Thus, it appears that the constancy of the belief exerts a fundamental and powerful influence on vocational education. While the belief was originally instrumental in developing and popularizing vocational education, the evidence suggests that the belief may today impede the adaptation of vocational education to contemporary needs. Rigidity replaces innovation; programs become increasingly separate from the larger educational enterprise; narrow skill training is substituted for general education for students who can least afford the costs of being ill-prepared. The power of the belief, however, continues to protect vocational education from social demands for change. The abiding conviction that anyone who works hard can get ahead dulls the social need to rethink its educational strategies. The evidence doesn't really matter. Rhetoric and anecdote suffice.

Likewise, the implications of this analysis for developing nations seem important. As developing nations seek solutions to similar social problems through education, the cultural roots of promising programs in other cultures bear close scrutiny before attempts are made to adapt them.

Clearly, the applicability of the American approach that derives from a fundamental belief in individual effort, hard work and material success would be stranger in many other cultures.

References

Bachman, J. (1972) *Young men in high school and beyond: A summary of findings from the youth in transition project*, Final Report, Project #5–0916. Washington, DC: US Office of Education, Department of Health, Education and Welfare.

Berryman, S. E. (1980) *Vocational education and the work establishment of youth: Equity and effectiveness issues*. Santa Monica: prepared for Aspen Systems Corporation, The Rand Corporation.

Committee for Economic Development (1985) *Investing in our children: Business and the public schools*. Washington, DC: a statement by the Research and Policy Committee.

Ellenwood, D.S. (1960) A study of the Anna S.C. Blake Manual Training School from 1891 to 1909, unpublished dissertation. Los Angeles: University of California.

Goodlad, J.I. (1984) *A place called school*. New York: McGraw-Hill.

Grasso, J. and Shea, J. (1979) *Vocational education and training: Impact on youth*. Berkeley: Technical Report for the Carnegie Council on Policy Studies in Higher Education.

Grubb, N. and Lazerson, M. (1974) *American education and vocationalism: A Documentary History*. New York: Teachers College Press, Columbia University.

Kaufman, J. (1967) *The preparation of youth for effective occupational utilization, the role of the secondary school in the preparation of youth for employment*. Pennsylvania: Pennsylvania State University.

Lapp, J. and Mote, C. (1915) *Learning to Earn*. Indianapolis: Bobbs–Merrill.

Mertens, D. (1982) *Vocational education and the high school dropout*. Columbus: National Center for Research in Vocational Education, Ohio State University.

Mertens, D. and Gardner, J. (1983) The long-term effects of vocational education. *Journal of vocational education research*, **8**(2), 1–21.

Meyer, R. H. (1981) *An economic analysis of high school vocational education–IV. The labor market effects of vocational education*. Washington, DC: The Urban Institute.

Murphey, M. (1979) The place of belief in modern culture. In J. Higham and P. Conkin (Eds.), *New directions in American intellectual history*, Baltimore: The Johns Hopkins University Press.

National Commission on Vocational Education (1984) *The unfinished agenda*. Washington, DC: US Department of Education.

Report of the Harvard Committee (1945) *General education in a free society*. Cambridge, Mass.: Harvard University Press.

Rawitch, C (1986) The Persistence of American values. Los Angeles: Unpublished paper, University of California.

Rumberger, R and Daymont, T. (1982) The economic value of Academic and vocational training acquired in high school. New York: paper presented at the meeting of the American Educational Research Association.

Snedden, D. (1910) *Problems of vocational education*. New York: Houghton.

Stern, D. Hoachlander, E. G. Choy, S. and Benson, C. (1985) *One million hours a day: Vocational education in California public secondary schools*. Berkeley: Report to the California Policy Seminar, School of Education, University of California.

Vincent, H. (1969) An analysis of vocational education in our secondary schools. Washington, DC: unpublished manuscript, US Office of Education, US Department of Health, Education and Welfare.

Wilms, W. W. (1975) *Public and proprietary vocational training: A study of effectiveness*. Lexington: Lexington Books, D.C. Heath.

Wilms, W. W. and Hansell, S. E. (1982) The dubious promise of postsecondary vocational education: Its payoff to dropouts and graduates in the USA. *International journal of educational development*, **2**, 43–60.

Wilms, W. W. (1984) Vocational education and job success: the employer's view. *Phi delta kappan*, **65**, 347–350.

Yankelovich, D. (1981) *New rules*. New York: Random House.

PART 2
The Context of Policy Formation

Introductory Note

THIS section is concerned with the process of policy formulation and with conditions impinging upon that process.

Neave examines policy formation in the Commission of the European Communities. Within the Commission as a whole, vocationalization policies evolved from two divergent organizational origins with different legal bases. Initially, vocational training was perceived as an instrument for encouraging mobility of labor within the EEC. It was not viewed as part of "education" which was seen as part of "culture" and not covered by economic cooperation within the Community. Neave reveals that the evolution of EEC policy in this area has been fraught with tensions about the goals and locus of vocationalization activity, tensions which are traceable to different jurisdictional and institutional bases. Neave points to changing views of the nature of employment and unemployment in Europe which have mirrored shifts in the structure of industry, and the persistence of high unemployment. Change in the conceptualization of vocational education has thus been forced upon the Commission by external conditions, leading also to closer collaboration between the two service branches of the Commission.

Similar tensions often surround vocationalization policies within nation States, because different ministries or other agencies are often simultaneously involved. Thus, Wright asks with regard to Sierra Leone: who makes this policy? What are the main considerations influencing policy formulation? He notes that curriculum diversification (vocationalization) in developing countries has been replete with failures, but he asserts that negative project evaluations are not sufficient grounds for abandoning educational policy. Projects are mechanisms for translating policy into practice. If a project fails, this does not necessarily mean that policies are misconceived. But there is then a need to look for alternative mechanisms and to re-examine the rationales.

He argues that failure to distinguish and understand the links between policy, project and practice is one reason why diversification may be prematurely rejected. In Sierra Leone diversification is not so much a policy formulated by the Government as one thrust upon it by the World Bank. A major weakness in such policy formulation—with adverse effects on project implementation—is that it tends to be insufficiently rooted in the realities of the national context.

Formulation of vocationalization policies is often inadequately informed about resource requirements—let alone information as to whether economic benefits warrant the costs incurred. Cumming examines the cost of practical and vocational subjects, and discusses the concepts and methods involved in cost calculations. He concludes in a review of international literature that such subjects are considerably more expensive than other subjects. However, for subject costs in general, there is great variation

97

among schools in cost per pupil, due to differences in class size. He also notes that the data required for accurate estimates of subject costs are not readily available from school statistics and other routine sources. The difficulties in measuring the economic benefits of practical/vocational subjects are also dealt with.

THE EDITORS

CHAPTER 6

Policy and Response: Changing Perceptions and Priorities in the Vocational Training Policy of the EEC Commission

GUY NEAVE

University of London Institute of Education

THE perspectives involved in the study of vocationalization are many. From a sociological–historical context, it may be regarded as yet another step in the protracted process that has extended the period of childhood and, at the same time, reinforced institutional dependence. It may be seen from an economic context where vocationalization stands as one element or response to the twin imperatives, of on the one hand, "stocking up" skills which prolonged youth unemployment might cause to be lost or, on the other, as a way of dealing with that massive occupational change which, we are led to believe, a high-technology-based economy will bring about. Similarly, vocationalization may be interpreted from the standpoint of its curricular aspect, that is, from the operationalization of particular skills and their location in relevant points of the education or training systems. A further perspective from which this issue could be examined is that of educational planning and its various techniques, budgetary, human resource allocation and training, the levels and type of labor force to which they contribute. Last but not least, there is what, *faute de mieux*, could be called the perspective of political sociology. This latter might see vocationalization as an example of how governments seek to alter prevalent and established value systems in education towards what some might call "a new realism" and others, less charitably disposed, might see as a "new utilitarianism."

Thus, in discussing vocationalization, there is a plurality of interpretations that can be brought to bear. What most of these have in common, however, is their focus on policy at the stage of implementation—that is, within the school or within the training system, irrespective of whether these are located in the public sector, which is more likely to be the case, or in the private sector, which tends increasingly to be a major growth area as firms assume responsibility for the training of their work force.

Examining policy at the implementation stage is vital. It gives us a notion of how far set objectives have been met. It also gives us equally important

99

indications of how they have not. But there is another aspect to policy and to this vocationalization is no exception. This is the matter of policy formulation. It turns around the perceptions of priorities, how the *problèmatique* is conceived and negotiated by those who have either responsibility for developing such measures or, alternatively, who occupy a key role in scanning a range of options which set the outer bounds within which implementation is itself set. It is to the formulation aspect that this paper is addressed.

The Commission of the European Communities

There are several reasons that justify the choice of the Commission of the European Communities as a case study. The first is that policy formulation rests upon a "comparative dimension"; the second is that the Communities, unlike other international bodies, rest upon a juridical base which, in certain instances, provides for legislation that is binding upon Member States and enforceable by sanction. This, of course, is rarely used. But it is this feature that separates the Commission from say, OECD, the Council of Europe or UNESCO. From a constitutional point of view, the Commission occupies a rare and unique situation: it has powers both legislative and executive. Third, it provides a permanent and high level forum to debate, to consider proposals for action at Community level and, sometimes, to exercise a surveillance and monitoring function. Amongst these the Education Committee, composed of permanent delegates from the Member States and the Commission's representatives, and the Advisory Council for Vocational Training, made up of government, employers' and employees' delegates and the Commission officials, are the most salient. Fourth, considerable financial resources may back policy development. Without monetary backing, what passes for policy is little more than the hortatory statement of the impotent and the hamstrung! As an indication of the resources available, in 1984, some ECU 1,437,000,000 was disbursed by the European Social Fund in support of a range of measures to assist young people—in retraining, relocation and job creation ("Educational and Vocational training . . . ," 1985, p. 14).

Origins of Community Policy

If we take the process of vocationalization as being broadly aimed at introducing new skills into the curriculum as a means of creating a better match between the output of school and training systems on the one hand, with the perceived requirements of industry on the other, then it is evident that Community developments in this area have a dual origin. This dual origin is not merely organizational and administrative, it is also juridical. Organizationally, vocational training remained a responsibility separate from education. The former came under the purlieu of the Directorate General V in charge of Social Affairs. The latter was added to the general oversight of Directorate General XII whose remit covered research and science. To this, education was added in 1974 ("Education in the European Community," 1974).

Legally, vocational training is a matter of Community competence based on Articles 57, 118 and 128 of the Treaty of Rome. Education, however, is not formally mentioned and resides on a special formula designed to stress the *voluntary* nature of the meeting of Member State Ministers of Education ("Mise en oeuvre d'un programme . . . ," 1976).

There were, in effect, two clearly differentiated organizational contexts from which the issue of vocationalization emerged. The first of these involved vocational training *per se* and was defined in 1963. A number of general guidelines were set out as part of a general strategy to move towards a common policy in this area ("Council decision . . . ," 1963).

In essence, vocational training policy was seen as an instrument for encouraging mobility of labor across the then six Member States, an interpretation which corresponded to the prevalent view of the Community as primarily an *economic entity*. And the major element in such a policy was informational, that is, enhanced vocational guidance as a lever to this end. Though intentions were to move towards a policy common to all Member States, intention does not imply capability. Several reasons account for this. First, vocational guidance did not enjoy a high priority on the agenda of Member States; second, resources inside the Commission were relatively limited and third, because responsibility for this area tended to be dispersed across different Ministries—Education, Labor, Agriculture, etc.—within the Member States.

The second organizational context began to emerge in the course of the early 1970s urged on by a reinterpretation of the Community's long-term *raison d'être*. This interpretation took the view that the Community could not remain simply as an economic conglomerate, but had, if it were to engage the support of its citizens, to assume a *cultural* commonality as well. The establishment of an education service in 1974 and the creation of a Community Education Action Programme in 1976 was a response to an expanded view of the Communities' spheres of interest. However, in contrast to the basic goal of a vocational training policy which was to work towards harmonization, the education service, from the first, set its face against this imperative. "Harmonization of these systems and policies," it was stated, "cannot be considered as an end in itself" ("Resolution of 6 . . . June," 1974).

Issues involving vocationalization were split between two different services, with a different juridical base and different strategic assumptions permeating their respective remits. This organizational duality was heavily reflected in the basic areas from which each service sought to build its individual policy of vocationalization. Working from a traditional perspective, Directorate General V conceived policy formulation in terms of the effectiveness of various apprenticeship schemes in the Member States, to continue with exploring the potential for guidance for those moving from full-time schooling to full-time employment and to analyze current trends in Member State vocational guidance services ("Activities of Directorate General V . . . ," 1979a). The central assumption behind their activity was, first, to uphold the historic dichotomy between education on the one hand and training on the other, whilst seeking to extend the range of activities included in the former to wider target groups—for example, women and girls or those school-leavers with no opportunity for vocational training.

The stance taken by Directorate General XII ran parallel to this. The crucial difference lay in the fact that the education service was not prepared to accept the validity of the "binary model" of education versus training. From very early on after the drawing up of the Community Education Action Programme, the education service argued strongly in support of "integrating" vocational training into the education system ("Preparation of young people . . . ," 1976).

The policy to be pursued, it suggested, ought to be initiatory rather than responsive. It ought to be part of a long-term strategy, developed across broad areas of Commission responsibility and bear down on the linkage between education and work rather than industrial strategy and training. Beneath this disagreement about the focus and goals of the two series lay a more understandable, though covert, agenda—namely, was education to be ancillary to vocational training or, on the contrary, should vocational training be regarded as a service item in a policy whose running was made by education?

Different Policy Approaches

The concept of vocationalization therefore, had, like Janus, two faces. It also had two vastly different approaches in its development, depending on which particular section of the Commission's services had responsibility for it at a particular time. For those responsible for "vocational training" *stricto sensu* it was a matter of extending into compulsory education elements to strengthen the "vocational element." For those working within the framework of the education service, it involved strengthening within the vocational training system those elements of general education which might serve in a remedial function for "at risk groups." The former built from the training system back into school. The latter sought to build from school into the training system. Complementary though these strategies might be, wide differences existed in what might be termed "the formulative stage" of their development. It is probably correct to say that "policy formulation" as enacted by DGV tended to hew more closely to formal bureaucratic procedures and to involve negotiation within a legislative framework through the Advisory Committee on Vocational Training, the Economic and Social Affairs Committee and the "social partners," i.e., government, employers and trades unions. This was not the approach espoused by the education services. Here policy formulation was, at one and the same time, more extensive, more protracted and, equally important, based on the belief that educational research ought to be a prior stage to the formulation of policy. To be sure, the education section of Directorate General XII engaged in regular discussion and consultation with the Education Committee, the main forum representing the education ministries of the Member States. Nevertheless, the development of its policy relied on an extensive program of "action research," designed not merely to ascertain the most fruitful ways of tackling the transition from school to work, but also to involve the education world from the grass roots upward.

This program, perhaps one of the most sustained examples of collaborative research at international level to be undertaken, was launched in the autumn of 1977. Then, it involved some 28 projects, ranging from Denmark to Sicily, from Berlin to Ireland. Today, it is in its "second phase," the first having ended in 1981–82. Some degree of its scale can be gathered from its financial profile. In its first year of operation, total funding from all sources—Commission as well as Member State—was in the order of ECU 6,000,000 ("Implementation of the Resolution . . . ," 1980).

The focus of this "action research" lay in six areas. These were:

— education and training needs of school-leavers facing difficulty in obtaining employment;
— problems of poor motivation towards study and work and ways of stimulating greater participation by young people;
— compensatory action to provide better opportunities for specific groups, viz. girls, migrants' children, the handicapped;
— the association of vocational preparation before and after school-leaving age by strengthening cooperation between education and employment sectors;
— development of continuing guidance and counselling services;
— improvements in both initial and in-service teacher training the better to enable them to prepare young people for adult and working life ("Preparation of young people . . . ," 1976).

From the standpoint of policy development, the transition project had two main purposes: first, to provide a series of networks across Member States, in which examples in one might inspire initiatives in another; second, to cut across formal administrative boundaries which separated education from training and labor market bodies in an attempt to move towards a broadly coordinated policy. In short, the "transition program" stood as an operational expression of the conviction, aired earlier by the education service, which refused to recognize the established division between education and training.

Such a "bottom up" networking approach stood in marked contrast to the legislative "top down" perspective embarked upon by the vocational training services, an approach which emerged clearly in the Recommendation issued in July 1977, which called for the extension of vocational *preparation* to those categories of young people who were unemployed or faced the threat of unemployment in the future ("Activities of Directorate General V . . . ," 1979b).

Intervention of External Factors

Complementary though the two strategies for vocationalization might be, and despite the very marked differences in procedure, both services shared a common assumption at least up to 1978. This central assumption was the nature of youth unemployment itself. Prior to 1978, youth unemployment was held to be a cyclical phenomenon, a temporary fluctuation that would readjust itself once the economy began to pick up again. From this it followed that measures to extend vocational training were conceived in the same light as the problem they were designed to tackle—namely, as short-term responses of a sectoral nature. From the standpoint of the education service, the main task to be tackled involved a more thorough grounding in the basic skills the better to improve insertion to the labor market once the latter picked up. From the standpoint of the vocational training services, the goal of policy was, in essence, to extend provision by expanding the capacity of vocational training systems. This, effectively, was little more than a policy of holding youngsters off the labor market in a labor market context which itself, would remain broadly similar once recovery set in.

By 1978, few of these basic policy parameters held good. Unemployment in general and youth unemployment in particular appeared to have assumed a permanent dimension. Unemployment was then, not transitional, but structural. Second, unemployment itself hid more wide-ranging shifts in the structure of industry—a marked shrinkage in the secondary sector and an even more marked change in the nature of work and the skills required by the "new technologies."

These external factors had wide-ranging consequences for the "frame" in which policy was considered. First, they cast doubts on the validity of a policy based on short-term *ad hoc* responses. Second, and more specifically, they called into question the strategy of extending the intake capacity of traditional vocational training systems. They seemed to suggest that a prior requisite for policy development should be a reassessment of the role of traditional training systems and their ability to meet fundamental changes in the structure of the labor force. Finally, they re-opened a point that the education service had made virtually from the time that education had been included as part of Commission responsibilities—namely, the high degree of "administrative compartmentalization" in Member State systems between authorities with an educational remit and those with responsibility for vocational training. Though not recognized as such at the time, the upshot of these external factors was to give added weight to the strategy which the education service had been forced to adopt as a result of the absence of a firm legal base for education in the Communities' founding treaties.

Alternance: a New Approach to the Relationship between Education and Training

Thus shifts in the "contextual framework" brought about shifts in the "conceptual framework" in which discussion took place. The fact that youth unemployment was no longer confined to either "the disadvantaged" or to "marginal" groups caused the Commission's services to revise their approach. Such a revision took place over the four years from 1979 to 1983. Essentially, it turned around the development of what might be termed a coordinated, cross-sector strategy designed to bring together education, vocational training and employment authorities. It brought to an end what is best described as a "reactive" policy and replaced it by a medium-term, forward-looking perspective, in which vocational training was interpreted not as a vehicle for "stocking up" skills, so much as an active instrument for generating new skills and, no less important, new employment ("The development of Vocational training . . . ," 1982).

Naturally, such changes did not come overnight. The move towards a coordinated, cross-sector approach was, however, marked by two developments. The first of these involved recasting the "conceptual framework," the second, changes in the organizational context in which Commission policy was worked out. Central to the former was the emergence of the so called "alternance model" of vocational training. Essentially, the alternance model combines a "sandwich" course format with the principle of permanent education. It seeks to link practical knowledge derived from the work-place with a more theoretical grounding in training establishments. It takes the view that work experience is a central element in experiential learning. The significance of this concept is obvious, and may be seen as a key element in "vocationalizing" education. Seen from the school perspective, it seeks to supplement knowledge conveyed in the classroom with "real-life" experience. Seen from the perspective of vocational training, alternance departs from the view that such training is limited only to the under-25s or that it should take place on a "one-off" basis. The importance of the alternance model did not lie simply as a way to impart greater flexibility to established systems of training, nor yet as a means of re-skilling both the younger generation or those in mid career. It also had a particular significance in the conduct of policy inside the Commission. For just as the alternance model predicated a new type of linkage and relationship between work and training, so it also predicated a closer collaboration between the two services of education and training whose policies had, hitherto, operated like the classic definition of political parties in 18th-century England—two stagecoaches going down the same road, occasionally spattering one another with mud!

Changes in the organizational framework were equally significant. In January 1981, responsibility for both education and vocational training was brought together under a single Directorate. Directorate General V now assumed the remit for employment, social affairs and education. The bringing together of the two services set the stamp on the move towards a comprehensive strategy first, to use vocational training as an instrument to attack unemployment and second, to link in with policy developments in other areas of the Commission's activities ("The development of vocational training . . . ," 1982).

How far the two services were now agreed on the basic priorities may be seen from discussions in the Education Committee early in 1981. The Education Committee identified two areas as crucial to the Commission's policy development. These were:

— the preparation of young people for working life;
— the development of continuing education and training ("Outcomes of the proceedings . . . ," 1981).

Beneath these two priorities ran a particular vision of the school system which, itself, might eventually move towards the principle of "integration," at the upper secondary and the post-secondary levels. Included in this pattern would be general education, vocational training and certain elements of work experience.

Coordinate Planning: Towards Vocationalization?

The relocation of both education and vocational training inside a single Directorate accelerated the trend towards coordinate planning. By June 1981, the Ministers of Education endorsed the notion of interlinked planning for vocational training and education. Similarly, the previous month, their colleagues in charge of Social Affairs gave their blessing to this same principle. The following year, on 27 May 1982, the Social Affairs Council passed a Resolution on Community Action against Unemployment which marked a further step along this road. The new approach rested on five major points:

— strengthening the general level of education during compulsory schooling;
— the development of initial and complementary training grounded on a broad range of related occcupations (*famille de métiers*);
— the drawing up of new options for continuing education of a general character to be available throughout an individual's working life;
— the organization of such training, whether initial or in-service upon modular units in keeping with the alternance model;
— a corresponding reinforcement of guidance and vocational training services to underpin the development of vocational training.

A close examination of the documents circulated at this time amongst the Social Affairs Directorate reveals that coordinated planning had three levels. These were the political, technical and administrative levels. At the political level, the main objective was to bring together both the Ministers in charge of education in joint discussion at Community level with their counterparts in charge of employment policies, thereby securing agreement for the approach already under discussion inside the Commission. This objective was secured in June 1983, when for the first time in the history of the Communities, Ministers from both "sides" met, and agreed on a five-year program for vocational training policies up to 1988 ("Education and vocational training . . . ," 1985, pp. 11–13).

At thc technical level, the main objective was to redefine vocational training by setting up what was termed a "*stage de préparation*" on the one hand, and, on the other, to redefine its content to include the development of social skills, and finally, to place it firmly within the context of *éducation permanente*. At the administrative level, the main objective sought was to bring about coordination between the various services—education, vocational training, employment and social services generally—by local or regional authorities. Local or regional coordination was important for several reasons. First, because it formed the implementation of the principle agreed at Community level; second, following the experience of the transition from school to work program, local coordination was seen as key in developing successful transitional strategies ("Interim report . . . ," 1985). And third, because, seen from the standpoint of vocationalization, it showed most clearly, that the process was not limited simply to those authorities in charge of schools or training establishments. If it was to be part of an overall plan both to re-skill and to create employment, then it had, perforce, to involve local labor market agencies as well as both sides of industry.

The central item in Commission thinking was contained in the concept of "preparatory stage" which later emerged as the notion of a "Social Guarantee." From the standpoint of its location in education/training systems, it was to follow on immediately after the end of compulsory education. Its purpose was threefold: first to operationalize the notion of "alternance"; second, to develop a wider range of skills, including remediation, than the usual pattern of vocational training; third, to instill amongst its "clients" the notion that training itself was not a "one-off" activity, but rather part of life-long learning. Thus, what the Commission had in mind as an instrument of vocationalization was a parallel sector alongside full-time secondary schooling for all early leavers and those without formal qualifications. Originally, the notion of a Social Guarantee was to provide vocational training and work experience as a matter of right for all early leavers or youngsters without qualifications. Its salient features were one year's foundation training immediately after compulsory education with the additional possibility of a further year of a more advanced nature. This second year would be available at any period up to the age of 25.

If the nomenclature of the proposal was retained by the joint meeting of Education and Social Affairs Ministers in June 1983, the generous terms put forward were not. Instead the Council opted for a program consisting either of basic training and/or initial work experience for six months—and certainly no more than a year. The idea of a further year was not looked upon with delight! Even in this diluted form, the Social Guarantee represented one of the most comprehensive statements about vocational training policy the Commission had made since the original guidelines were drawn up in 1963. In addition to the usual categories of early school-leavers and the unqualified, access of women, particularly those in rural areas, was also given priority.

The Social Guarantee was not, however, the only example of cross-sectoral planning within the Commission, for equally radical proposals were also put forward for compulsory education. Some of these may be seen simply as extensions into the school system of those principles developed within the alternance model. Foremost amongst them was the notion of using the Community itself as a learning resource. School authorities were to be encouraged to develop close links with employment authorities as a first step in creating direct work experience for the 14–18 age range, either in firms or in the community. This theme was taken up and elaborated the following year in the joint meeting of Ministers of Education and Social Affairs. Vocational guidance, counselling and careers' education, the meeting recommended, should span the whole period from secondary school to training and, moreover, they should be closely interwoven into the school curriculum ("Education and vocational training . . . ," 1985).

These developments may, of course, be seen in terms of "lateral policy coordination," that is, the bringing together of administrative areas, both within the Commission and, hopefully, within the Member States as well, which cover a similar age range. But there is also an element of "vertical coordination." By "vertical coordination," I mean extending the planning perspective either to cover an older age range and thus other types of educational establishment relevant to it or introducing another issue transcending both areas of "lateral coordination" and thus linking them with a common theme. Two examples may serve to illustrate this process and, at the same time, show how vocationalization, first applied within the usual domain of post-compulsory links with training and the labor market, has been extended recently to embrace higher education.

The Emergence of a "Human Resources" Strategy

The emergence of "vertical coordination" as a policy mechanism can be traced back to 1978 and in particular to the Heads of State Conference at Bonn. One of the topics discussed was the potential of the so-called "new information technologies" and their possible impact on employment, culture and education. From the viewpoint of the education service, the new technologies merely emphasized, once again, the validity of its original thesis, namely closer coordination between education and training on the one hand, and better articulation with the alternance model on the other. Thus whilst the advent of the new technologies was seen as a catalyst to the overall task of redrawing the map of education and training, it did not change the overall policy perspective which the Social Affairs directorate had embarked upon. On the contrary, it appeared to add a new urgency to bringing education, training and labor market agencies into closer collaboration.

Even though the education service regarded the new information technologies as an element of reinforcement and thus, of continuity in their objective to redraw the links between education and training, they did introduce a new perspective into Commission thinking. This perspective involved wider consultation with other Commission services and at the same time brought education and training into a broader policy planning context. In effect, employment and social policy—the overall setting in which both the education and training services operated, was itself only part of a more complex issue. This issue was nothing less than the future industrial viability of the Communities, faced with the challenge in the field of high technology from the United States and Japan. As such, it touched upon such areas as industrial policy, the Communities' research and development strategy, the planning of regional affairs and finally, the question of innovation strategies and the development of what is known as "the internal market." The latter, scheduled to be complete by 1992, involves removing the final obstacles to the free movement of goods and services within the Communities. Within this "ecology" of different policy fields, the Ministry of Social Affairs occupied a very specific niche. Its main task lay in the development of a "human resources" strategy. This, in turn, meant that from the first, the measures designed to introduce the new information technologies into the education and training systems required extended consultation with

Directorate Generals III (Industry), XII (Research and Development), XIII (Innovation and the Internal Market) and XVI (Regional Affairs) ("Nouvelles initiatives . . . ," 1982).

The human resources strategy has come to dominate much of current Commission views on the development of both education and training, and was instrumental in changing, once again, the policy context in which vocationalization was placed. If, in the early 1980s, reform of vocational training was seen as a way of creating employment, now it became part of a broader plan to re-equip European industry by updating the knowledge base on which it rested. And, as Commission documents make clear, the central element in this knowledge base lay in raising the level of technical knowledge not only in the active labor force, but in those likely to join it in the future. From the particular confines of education and training, the advent of the new technologies imposed three specific priorities:

— training and in-service education of teachers and instructors through application of the new technologies;
— the appropriate adaptation of training programs for young people and, in particular, the young unemployed;
— recognition of the needs of specific client groups, including women and older workers.

By introducing the new information technologies into the policy equation as an element in re-skilling, the human resources perspective extended the scope in which vocationalization was set. If this served to reiterate the relevance of "alternance education," it also raised the issue of balancing opportunities and provision for re-skilling between young people and the older generation who, without it, were in a position no less precarious than that of their children. This latter consideration occupied a key place in redefining vocational training as a process of permanent up-dating, rather than a "once-for-a-lifetime" induction into industry.

Furthermore, just as the human resources strategy posed the need to cross-link policy options across a wide range of Commission activities, so it also posed the question of "highly qualified manpower," both in the field of research and in its supply and interlink with industry. The role of research in general and that carried out by higher education specifically in the development of "high technology" is a matter of record. A number of programs designed to accelerate knowledge transfer between universities and industry have been put in place by the Commission. ESPRIT (European Strategic Programme for Research into Information Technology), RACE (Research and Development in Communications Technology) and, more recently, COMETT (Community Action Programme for Education and Training in Technology) are amongst the more visible ("University–industry cooperation . . . ," 1985).

Strictly speaking, these programs—with the exception of COMETT—lie outside the purlieu of Social Affairs. They are important, however, in that they seek to develop closer ties between research, industry and universities and also because such links, originally laid down within the ambit of other directorates, are now becoming a central part of the human resources strategy being developed by Directorate General V. From this point of view, they are perhaps less an illustration of the vocationalization of higher education—though there are signs of this too, see below—than of the process of "vertical coordination" between different sectors of the education/training systems. To the extent that they involve higher education as a research base for industrial change on the one hand, and, on the other, as a source of supply of graduates qualified in the areas deemed relevant to the "high technology imperative," such programs are complementary to the objectives assigned to vocational training systems. They are, in short, a prolongation at a higher level of those objectives we have already seen applied both to schools and to training—realigning of skills in keeping with economic change, the expansion of "work experience programs" during undergraduate training whilst, at the same time, serving as a knowledge base to sustain the transition to a high technology economy.

Conclusion

In any organization with responsibility for defining policy and setting resources to achieve particular goals—and here the EEC Commission is no exception—the priorities chosen are in function to the perception of the particular issue and the organizational context in which perceptions are apprehended. The development of vocational training measures over the 10 years from 1975 to 1985 shows this clearly. From being an instrument for improving mobility of labor and confined within the usual bounds of training systems, vocational training has, over the years, assumed a central and crucial role not merely as a vehicle for modernization, but also in gaining some measure of acceptance of the consequences, social, occupational and cognitive, of that process. The role of vocational training, at least as it is reflected in documented discussion and proposals put forward by the EEC Commission, appears to have gone through three stages; the first when it was seen as responding to an established pattern of industry stocking up skills and acting as a palliative to what was held as to be short-term youth unemployment; the second, as part of a broader policy sweep designed to create better coordination between education authorities on the one hand and employment creation on the other; and the third when it assumed the status of a medium-term plan to accelerate the changeover to a new industrial base, and as such locked in firmly with compulsory schooling on the one hand and the university system on the other. These changes in role, as I have argued, reflect equally pronounced changes in the way the basic problem was understood, first in terms of youth unemployment, second as a vehicle for job creation and re-training and third, as a sectorial element in a more general mission, namely to ensure the industrial renewal of Europe.

Some may care to see these developments merely as the growth of the "vocational imperative" and the rise of a technocratic view in which education is subordinated to the overriding demands of industry. There may be some validity for such a view, though it should perhaps be pointed out that what is one generation's utilitarianism turns out often to be its success-ors' accepted orthodoxy until the next round of reforms hoves in to view, at which point it becomes—for those opposed to it—a new utilitarian ideology. What this view tends to forget is that whilst it may be the individual's right to refuse the opportunity to develop those competencies that may stand her or him in good stead at a time of social and economic change, this right can only be exercised once such provision is available.

There is, of course, another viewpoint on the issue of vocationalization and one which, if implicit throughout much of the Commission's thinking on the subject, remained largely unpursued. This is the question of control and authority. New elements in the school curriculum, new training policies for teachers or vocational educators, changes in the balance of student flows through higher education—all of which, in varying degrees, have been touched upon in the elaboration of the Commission's proposals—beg the question "control by whom to do what?" Even if aspects such as these have no part in Community level responsibility—which in essence, resides in drawing up an agreed framework within which national authorities operate *selon leur gré et selon leurs capacités*—the way the policy frame is drawn up implies some measure of shifts in the balance of power and responsibility.

The prevalent view of vocationalization tends to see the process in terms of an illegitimate intervention by authorities or agencies whose priorities do not accord with established practice and convention. The "industrialization" of the school curriculum can be seen as a particular instance of this. In point of fact, the process engaged in is a rather wider one. As it emerges in the reflections of the education of vocational training services of the EEC Commission, vocationalization contains another dimension which is often underplayed in the debates on this subject. This dimension involves the application of "power sharing" or co-responsibility which, first developed in the field of industrial relations, is now inserted into education or vocational training. The clearest expression of this principle, which can just as well be understood as a dispersal of power from a single monolithic administration or, for that matter, from a similar professional grouping, emerges in the various schemes for linking the school with its local community or in the various proposals for coordination between regional and local authorities as a way of developing more flexible vocational training initiatives. Not surprisingly, no specific details were mentioned as to the particular format to be used or to the exact balance of responsibility to be assigned to different interests. Nevertheless, the principle of "partnership" or co-responsibility is clearly stated. How it is to be effected remains a matter for the respective Member States to work out.

From this point of view, the evolution of vocational training policies in the EEC Commission casts a rather different light on the controversy surrounding the rise of vocationalization. For what can be seen as a negative development when viewed from the standpoint of corporative interests, may equally well be regarded as a positive one for those "social partners" hitherto excluded from the enterprise. At the present time, we tend to identify opportunities for acquiring new competencies and up-dating old skills in terms of "education" or "training" simply because that is the way they were defined in the past. But it is no less evident that, by redefining location in the education system, content, length and availability what is emerging is not merely a different type of relationship between the two areas education and training, but an entirely different "learning system"—despite the ghastly jargon of the phrase. It would be surprising if such a new concept did *not* require new partnership arrangements. That we happen to interpret this "new provision" in terms of the old—and, to be frank, in terms of ancient conflicts which accompanied the development of "education" versus "vocational training"—tells us nothing about the potential of the "new provision." What it does show is perhaps our inability at the present time to go beyond hide-bound concepts, or to maintain our debate within them.

In taking the EEC Commission as a case study in changing concepts and priorities, I am not suggesting that discussion of this issue has necessarily to follow the same path. But, by dint of being the focal point at which this issue has been debated at a supranational level, and proposals for dealing with it elaborated at a similar level, we can recognize more clearly some dimensions which are less evident within a national context.

If, as I have suggested, the process of vocationalization disguises the emergence of a "new learning system," whether such a system gives due recognition to established authorities or brings about changes in the hierarchy of status amongst subject areas, is magnificently irrelevant. What is relevant, surely, is whether such new provision will contribute significantly to "life, liberty and the pursuit of happiness" in a time of massive economic change.

References

Activities of Directorate General V in the field of vocational training July 1977 to May 1979. Document V/535/79, 28 May 1979(b).

Activities of Directorate General V in the field of vocational training. Document V/585/79, 29 May 1979 (a)(Mimeo.)

Council decision of 2 April 1963 laying down general principles for implementing a common vocational training policy. Document 63/226/EEC, Official Journal, 10 April 1963.

Education and vocational training within the European Community: activities of the Commission of the European Communities in 1983 and 1984. COCM (85) 134 Final, Brussels, 29 March 1985. (Mimeo.)

Education in the European Community. *Bulletin of the European Communities* (supplement) No.3, 1974.

Implementation of the Resolution of 13 December 1976: progress report on measures taken at Community level. Document 5471/80 (EDUC 30), 5 March 1980.

Interim report on the development of the Programme to the Education Committee concerning the implementation of the second series of pilot projects. Document CAB/XIV/170-EN, Brussels, Sept. 1985.

Mise en oeuvre d'un programme d'action au niveau communautaire. Document SEC (76) 216, 21 January 1976.

Nouvelles initiatives communautaires pour la période 1983 à 1987 concernant les nouvelles technologies de l'information et le changement social. Projet de Communication de la Commission au Conseil (version no.5), le 11 fevrier 1982 (typewritten).

Outcomes of the proceedings of the Education Committee, 23–24 April 1981. Document 6502/81 (EDUC 14), 29 April 1981.

Preparation of young people for working life and for transition from education to work. Document R/32290/e/76 (EDUC 52), 8 June 1974.

Resolution of 6 June 1974. Official Journal No. C,982, 20 August 1974.

The development of vocational training policies in the European Communities in the 1980s. Draft Communication to the Council, Bruxelles, 8 July 1982, pp. 1–2.

University–industry cooperation in promoting training policies to meet the challenges of social and technological change and industrial development in the European Community. Draft Communication to the Council, 13 June 1985.

CHAPTER 7

Curriculum Diversification Re-examined—A Case Study of Sierra Leone

CREAM A. H. WRIGHT

Milton Margai College of Education, Freetown

EDUCATION systems in Africa are continuously being subjected to major innovations and reforms, which invariably entail considerable external funding and expertise. Experience suggests that such external support is often orchestrated towards promoting those policies which are in vogue with aid agencies, rather than addressing the diversity of peculiar needs confronting each recipient country.[1] Given Africa's overwhelming dependence on external assistance, this may mean that aid agencies "inadvertently" determine which policies are pursued before they have to be abandoned in favor of a newer vogue. Decisions to continue or abandon support for a particular policy are often based on large-scale evaluation studies, focusing on generalized input–output models. Such studies provide indications of how far (and how efficiently) policy objectives are being achieved. However, they hardly give any systematic insight into the wide range of peculiarities and local complexities which impinge on the policies in a particular national context. It is precisely this type of insight that African countries need, increasingly, if they are to identify appropriate points of leverage through which policy implementation can be improved.

In their search for generalizable solutions which can be funded in many countries, aid agencies can afford to "write-off" major policies and projects, in spite of substantial investments already made, and then commit resources anew to "more promising" policies. In contrast, each African country needs to be fairly resolute about its own major educational policies, so that while a country should not stubbornly adhere to such policies in the face of overwhelming contrary evidence, it need not acquiesce to their abandonment on the grounds of negative evaluation studies.

A particularly striking case in point concerns the vocationalization of

[1] Since aid agencies operate in a large number of countries they tend to favor "generalizable" solutions which can be applied in all of these countries. Aid agency support therefore tends to concentrate on one or two of these generalizable solutions at a time.

115

education through such means as diversifying the curriculum in general schools or establishing fully vocational schools. Given the post-independence dearth of skilled manpower for industrialization, and the allegedly "academic" nature of prevailing educational programs, the idea of vocationalizing education was so pregnant with promise that it became at once irresistible and imperative to aid agencies and African countries alike. Most African countries, therefore, pursued some form of vocationalization with enthusiastic assistance from aid agencies such as the World Bank, which supported an impressive array of projects in a wide range of developing countries. After over two decades of implementation however, the promises of vocationalization appear to be largely unfulfilled. Indeed, it now seems that vocationalization might, after all, be simply an illusion which is too costly to pursue and unlikely to yield the expected outcomes.[1] Yet the lure of vocationalization still persists in most African countries.[2] If this resilience is not matched by continued support from aid agencies then African countries need to work out their own modalities and marshal their own resources if they wish to continue efforts at vocationalizing education. In such circumstances the need to re-examine this "elusive panacea" of vocationalization becomes urgent and significant. It is in this context that this chapter seeks to re-examine curriculum diversification as a major vocationalizing strategy, through a critical analysis of the Sierra Leone experience. The focus of the chapter is exclusively on the educational side of the education–employment link. This reflects my firm conviction that we need to develop key insights and a proper understanding of design and implementation problems pertaining to diversified education. We can then be in a position to understand how it can be made to work in practice. Without this it is rather premature and futile to engage in high-powered evaluation studies on the impact of diversified education in employment terms.

Within this context, my main contention is that there has always been a fundamental failure to distinguish between curriculum diversification as a policy, as a project and as a practice. Failure to appreciate these different senses of diversification, and a poor understanding of their inter-relatedness, often led to false judgment, undue pessimism and premature disillusionment with curriculum diversification. This case study of Sierra Leone attempts to reach much more pragmatic and progressive conclusions by examining curriculum diversification, first as a major policy actively pursued by Sierra Leone for over a decade before acquiring something of a

---

[1] This is the main impression one gets from the major World Bank study of diversification in Columbia and Tanzania (see Psachoropoulos and Loxley, 1985).
[2] In spite of many negative evaluation reports and implementation problems experienced over the years, Vocationalization of Education was chosen as the theme for the 10th Conference of Commonwealth Ministers of Education, held in Zimbabwe in 1987.

"latent policy" status;[1] second as a major project designed and implemented under the 1st and 2nd Sierra Leone Government/IDA Education Projects;[2] and third as an on-going practice which continues to exist in a multiplicity of non-spectacular forms throughout Sierra Leone. Finally the paper draws from these different senses of diversification in order to re-examine the whole issue of curriculum diversification as a crucial educational goal which is intimately linked to national development aspirations.

Diversification as Policy

When the Sierra Leone Government declared in its White Paper of 1970 that diversification of the secondary curriculum was a major policy (Sierra Leone Government, 1970), it was reasonable to assume that substantial resources and concerted action would be devoted to diversification, and that other aspects of educational development would receive relatively less priority in terms of resources and efforts. Policy, therefore, involves conflict, since it not only entails strong commitment to the pursuit of certain educational objectives, but also implies an accompanying willingness to sacrifice, or at least temporarily suspend, the intense pursuit of some other educational objectives. In functionalist terms the policy of diversification could be understood as an attempt by the Government to gear education towards providing manpower for development, and responsive aid agencies which see this as a sensible policy have provided the necessary support.[3] This is a dangerously misleading picture which often leads us to believe that we have given diversification our best collective efforts without much tangible benefits. A more realistic picture emerges only when fundamental questions pertaining to the politics of educational policy are raised. Who in fact makes policy? What are the main factors or considerations which influence policy formulation? How and why do such influences come into play?

The most important fact to emerge in response to this type of investigation is that diversification of the secondary curriculum was not so much a policy formulated by the Government as one thrust upon it by the World Bank in connection with the 1st Sierra Leone Government/IDA Education Project (Wright, 1984). This is not to imply any sinister motive on the part of the Bank, since it advocated diversification to African countries in line with what was then the most progressive thinking regarding development strategies (cf. Harbison, 1973). Moreover, the compulsive logic and rationale for diversification was readily accepted by Sierra Leone as it had presumably been by many other developing countries in which the Bank was already providing support for diversification. Importantly, however, because diver-

[1] A policy becomes latent when everyone insists it is still important but no one is willing to invest resources in its implementation any longer.
[2] IDA Education Project Implementation Unit, Sierra Leone/IDA Project Information Notes.
[3] This rather simplistic functionalist interpretation often absolves funding agencies and attributes failures to problematic characteristics of the recipient country's education system.

sification was perceived as a somewhat generalizable solution to the problems of developing countries, the Bank's advocacy of a diversification policy was not rooted in the peculiar realities of the Sierra Leone situation. More significantly, although the Sierra Leone Government was willing to go along with diversification as an important aspect of its educational development strategy, it was not quite prepared to sacrifice some of its more important educational goals in the name of diversification. The fact is that, at Independence, Sierra Leone found itself entangled in a complex web of rather ambitious educational aspirations such as expansion of the system at all levels, democratization of educational opportunities, universal primary education in the shortest possible time, qualitative improvements to the education system and improved linkage between education and national development. Unfortunately, however, Sierra Leone at the time lacked the necessary planning expertise to orchestrate these aspirations into some pragmatic order of priority and formulate educational policies accordingly. It, therefore, obtained external assistance first for a survey of education in relation to economic development (Sierra Leone Government, 1961) and, subsequently, for preparation of a detailed proposal for external funding of educational development in Sierra Leone (Sierra Leone Government, 1964). This proposal highlighted the need for substantial expansion of educational enrollment (Sierra Leone Government, 1964) and, with specific reference to secondary education, it recommended provision for

> Doubling the intake; diversifying the curriculum with increased provision for technical and vocational training; controlling the output to meet the needs of teacher training at all levels; providing sufficient entrants for Fourah Bay College, Njala University College and Teacher Training Colleges, and for employment. (Sierra Leone Government, 1964, Preface—statement by the Government)

This type of all-embracing approach to educational development reflected the complexity of Government's educational aspirations, and indicated that diversification was simply a single element within a package of priorities which formed the basis of Sierra Leone's initial proposal to the World Bank. The Bank's reaction was unfavorable as is evident from such a statement as:

> The proposed project comprised substantial expansion of general secondary, technical, vocational and teacher training capacity which the Bank's late 1965 appraisal mission judged premature in the absence of basic manpower and sector planning data. In particular, the Bank questioned planned expansion of secondary education in view of increasing unemployment among mainly academic secondary school leavers. (International Development Agency, n.d. p. 1)

In contrast to the all-embracing package submitted by Sierra Leone, the World Bank advocated and eventually approved a circumscribed package centered on quality improvements for a small number of existing institutions, and providing for

> modernization and diversification of facilities (mainly through construction of laboratories and workshops) at 11 secondary schools; modernization and expansion of facilities at one technical and three trade schools; reconstruction of the country's one in-service primary teacher training college; and selected technical assistance inputs. (International Development Agency, n.d., p. A6)

In these circumstances, project negotiations became a long-drawn-out affair lasting almost five years (1965–1969) and requiring an unprecedented number of full appraisals (International Development Agency, n.d., p. 1). The Bank attributed this to Sierra Leone's lack of planning expertise and general inexperience with IDA preparation requirements (International Development Agency, n.d., p. A6). From the Sierra Leone Government's viewpoint, however, there were much more crucial reasons to do with conflicts in policy priorities as well as the size and scope of the project, rather than with the technicalities of project preparation. Evidently, the Government's priority of expansion coupled with qualitative improvements and diversification contrasted with the Bank's perception of appropriate policies and strategies for educational development in Sierra Leone. Ultimately the package recommended by the Bank prevailed by virtue of what can be described as "funding power"—he who pays the piper calls the tune! It could be argued therefore that a high priority on diversification was not really a matter of Government preference but much more an offer that the Government was constrained to accept. Indeed, the fact that the Government's diversification policy (Sierra Leone Government, 1970) was outlined *after* the World Bank project had been "agreed" upon suggests that the policy itself was a *fait accompli* in line with World Bank terms for project funding. Undoubtedly, diversification was always an important educational concern in Sierra Leone. Equally so, diversification and other qualitative changes have always been regarded simply as necessary adjuncts to a major program of educational expansion.

As a policy then diversification was enveloped in considerable controversy and ambivalence, particularly in relation to its implications for curtailing expansion of educational enrollment. Sierra Leone officials felt that the Bank had imposed unacceptable constraints and accused IDA of implicitly attempting

> to influence Government policy in a highly sensitive area where social pressures cannot be ignored. (International Development Agency, n.d., p. A6)

The crucial point in all this is that such controversy and its resulting ambivalence has profound consequences for policy implementation. On the one hand, commitment to diversification as an exclusive priority and a willingness to curtail action on other goals implies an expectation that policy implementation will be finite, with a clear beginning and end. In these circumstances policy implementation could reasonably be expected to correspond with the life-span of one or more projects. On the other hand, if diversification is treated simply as one element in a package of priorities then the implied expectation is that policy implementation will be on-going, evolutionary and long-term. Against this background it could be argued that the World Bank approach implies that *policy* implementation is equatable to *project* implementation. Hence the Bank could feel justified in making profound judgments about diversification policy on the basis of its evaluation of diversification projects.[1] In contrast, the logical implication of the approach taken by the Sierra Leone Government is that implementation of a diversification policy will be a gradual long-term matter beyond the confines of one or two projects.[2] Indeed, the Sleight Report, which formed the basis of the Government's initial request to the World Bank, advocated a re-orientation of secondary education towards a more practical and vocational bias, but made it clear that this was essentially a gradual long-term process.

> This change will not immediately be reflected in national percentages, but it should establish a change of direction. (Sierra Leone Government, 1964)

In these circumstances a project is simply a finite episode in the life of a policy, and while feedback from project evaluation is important for reviewing policy it is most unwise to base major policy judgments on the outcomes of one or two projects. Quite clearly there has been a significant failure in many quarters to distinguish between diversification as policy and diversification as project. Consequently, project evaluation has been allowed to play an unduly decisive role in the decline of support for diversification *policy*. While most African countries still have an instinctive belief in the importance of diversification, there is now a curious reluctance to use local funding or request external assistance for this purpose. The adverse economic situation in these countries probably makes it inevitable that their policy options will list whithersoever the funding wind bloweth! The case of Sierra Leone has demonstrated that funding agencies and recipient countries sometimes operate at cross-purposes over policy, with bizarre consequences for implementation. Thus while the World Bank was

[1] As in the case of the study on Columbia and Tanzania.
[2] It is quite probable that at the time Sierra Leoneans did not interpret the policy in these terms, but their position logically implies such an interpretation.

apparently trying to ensure that the diversification policy would be reasonably well implemented within the life-span of one or two major projects, Sierra Leoneans were inadvertently detracting from this thrust by using every opportunity during project appraisal and implementation, to inject elements of educational expansion and improvement of academic content into the first project (Wright, 1984, p. 114). Indeed, by the time of the second project Sierra Leoneans were able to negotiate a project package within which diversification became simply one of several priorities (Second Sierra Leone/IDA Education Project, n.d.). This type of "distortion" during implementation makes diversification more of a long-term prospect than originally intended.

Diversification as Project

As a mechanism for policy implementation a project will have clearly defined objectives, and the business of project design is to ensure that the requisite expertise and supporting resources are effectively and efficiently harnessed towards the attainment of these objectives. Obviously, project objectives must have a strong bearing and logical link with the policy in question, but, more importantly, project design must be sufficiently realistic and pragmatic to ensure successful implementation. In Sierra Leone the objective of diversifying secondary education was stated as

> to prepare secondary school leavers better for employment through provision of facilities and curriculum revision specialists necessary to diversify and modernize programs. (International Development Agency, n.d., p. A2)

Project design should, therefore, be expected to ensure that diversified programs can be made to take root and become an integral part of the secondary education system. Amongst other things this requires substantial knowledge of the existing secondary school system and insight into possible strategies through which diversified programs can be made to take root.

Against this background, several features of project design and implementation have undoubtedly had a crucial influence on the outcome of the first and second diversification projects. First there tended to be far too much concentration on civil works and equipment, at the expense of program development and personnel training (Wright, 1984, p. 118). The Bank appeared to have an obsessive concern with equipment, civil works and the attendant formalities of tenders, contract packages, etc. Consequently, little attention was given to the *content* of a diversified curriculum beyond an implicit assumption that it would include what King (1980) has called the inevitable cluster of subjects, i.e., woodwork and metalwork. Sierra Leoneans also appeared to be strongly concerned with civil works and equipment rather than program development (International Development Agency, n.d., p. A10). This was undoubtedly due in part to lack of knowledge and experience relating to technical/vocational subjects and the general mechanics of developing diversified programs. Understandably also, Sierra Leoneans were anxious that concrete benefits should be derived from the World Bank loan used to fund these projects. Hence buildings and equipment held much greater attraction than program development.

Second, in the selection of project schools for both the first and the second project substantial pressure was apparently exerted on behalf of schools in politically favored regions and prestigious schools with sound academic track records. In terms of good design one would expect project schools to be selected so as to maximize the chances of successfully implementing a diversification project. Where this has not been done, it is doubtful whether serious value should be attached to evaluative studies which attempt to compare outcomes from project schools with those from so-called control schools.

Third, the training of technical and commercial teachers to implement diversified programs in the schools was surprisingly neglected during the first project. Although this was later remedied by the establishment of a Technical and Business Education Department at Milton Margai Teachers College, the neglect does reflect an underlying conviction that diversification is essentially about buildings and equipment rather than teacher training and curriculum development.

Fourth, when some attention was eventually given to the content of diversified programs this resulted in greater confusion than ever before. While most project schools still operated mediocre versions of traditional craft-based syllabuses in woodwork and metalwork, the teacher-education programs embarked on an innovative and integrated approach to technology known as "design technology." As will be argued later these conflicting approaches to technical subjects have profound implications for the way pupils perceive and relate to diversified programs in the schools.

The factors highlighted above indicate that project design engendered certain weaknesses which evidently militated against attainment of the diversification objectives. Similarly, project implementation involved anomalies, inconsistencies and inadequacies which reduced the chances of achieving the desired outcomes of diversification. For instance, technical and commercial equipment supplied to some schools remained in packing cases for one or two years because the skilled manpower for installing them was lacking in these schools. At the same time some schools which had the necessary manpower were either not allocated as much equipment as they required or failed to receive equipment promised to them (Wright, 1979). Again most of the equipment supplied to schools soon became non-functional because there was no provision for maintenance and repairs. Similarly, no provision was made for a regular and reliable supply of consumable materials (wood, metal, commercial stationery, etc.) to the schools, and the shortage of such materials soon resulted in excessive teaching of "theory" for subjects which were supposed to be pre-eminently practical. Most importantly perhaps, schools were left largely to their own devices in the matter of what was to be taught as part of a diversified curriculum. The number and combination of "diversified subjects" offered varied widely from school to school and no guidance or assistance was provided to help schools develop suitable content for each of these subject areas (Adams *et al.*, 1983). It is particularly significant to note that while this gross neglect of curriculum development in technical and commercial subjects was being manifested, substantial expertise and resources was being invested in curriculum development for mathematics, English, science and social studies, under the same project![1]

It is fair to indicate that many of these negative features pertaining to project design and implementation were recognized within the project and remedial measures proposed accordingly. Unfortunately most of these remedial measures failed to move beyond the proposal stage. Thus the idea of incorporating "installation and maintenance services" into equipment supply contracts remained just an idea; proposals for a "mobile maintenance unit" to service and repair equipment in project schools were not acted upon; and plans for establishing a centralized system for bulk purchase, storage and distribution of consumable materials to schools remained on the drawing board.[2]

The fact that so many negative aspects of project design and implementation have been highlighted does not imply that nothing good resulted from the diversification project. Undoubtedly there were some success stories and much was achieved by Sierra Leoneans, World Bank officials and external specialists working under adverse conditions to effect rather ambitious changes in a complex education system. In outlining these negative features, therefore, the concern of this chapter is not to minimize project achievements but rather to focus attention on the significant gap existing between policy ideals and the practicalities of project design and implementation. Given such a situation it would seem that the important question to be addressed by evaluative studies is not so much whether diversification has failed or succeeded, but the extent to which diversification has in fact been given a chance to become operative. Where such a fundamental issue relating to the diversification project has not been satisfactorily explored, it would be most premature to make pronouncements on the efficacy of the diversification policy! The extent to which diversification has been given a

[1] This was part of the compromise Sierra Leoneans were able to win from the Bank regarding their own priorities for improvement of "academic" curricula.
[2] Most of these proposals were repeatedly submitted to project officials without any serious response.

chance to work can only be assessed through an insightful study of the way diversification operates in the school system.

Diversification in Practice

As in most African countries, the idea of vocationalizing education has a long history in Sierra Leone, dating back to the colonial era. It is an ambivalent history characterized on the one hand by an enthusiastic advocacy, and on the other by considerable antipathy towards vocationalization.[1] At the heart of the matter is a fundamental contradiction between the aspirations of pupils (and their parents) who regard education as a means of upward mobility to "high status" occupations, and the popular perception of vocationalization as preparation for "low status" occupations. Thus while training for certain occupational levels is regarded by African governments (and colonial regimes before them) as crucial for national development, the use of the formal school system for this purpose conflicts with the perceptions and occupational aspirations of the school population. It is therefore somewhat naïve to assume that pupils in Sierra Leone would respond positively to subjects like woodwork, metalwork, typing, cookery, etc., because of the facilities and equipment provided or because of government exhortation about the importance of such subjects for national development. Such an assumption could only be justified if strategies have been worked out for influencing pupils' aspirations towards an acceptance of occupations related to these subjects, or if efforts have been made to develop diversified programs which will not be perceived by pupils as being merely a preparation for "low status" occupations. Both of these options are complex and difficult to pursue in practice since they require substantial understanding of the factors influencing pupils' aspirations, perceptions, etc., as well as insight into viable alternatives relating to the structure and organization of diversified curricula. It is only when these and related issues have been properly explored that we can begin to understand how diversification can be made to work in different school situations, and then proceed to make sensible pronouncements about the efficacy of a diversification policy for African countries such as Sierra Leone.

Institutional Factors

The up-take and operationalization of curriculum diversification in a school are strongly influenced by several institutional factors. In particular, up-take appears to be influenced by an amalgam of factors related to "institutional ethos." This concept embraces the philosophy and objectives

---

[1] Enthusiasm for vocationalization has been particularly noticeable in periods of economic depression when unemployment becomes a major problem. Otherwise it is seen mainly as a prescription for drop-outs and therefore resented by most pupils and parents.

underlying the establishment of the school, its present development goals, historical traditions, cherished values and ceremonial rituals. Thus a strong degree of up-take was evident in schools which were originally established for more pragmatic purposes than the mere pursuit of academic work,[1] even though these schools may have changed over the years to become highly academic in their orientation. Again schools which emphasize "work ethics" and the "dignity of labor" showed appreciable up-take of the diversification project.[2] Invariably these schools already had a tradition in which "vocational" subjects constituted an integral part of the curriculum.[3] In contrast, schools which were originally established as prestigious academic institutions geared towards preparation for higher education, showed poor up-take of diversification.[4] Indeed, the history and traditions of these schools indicate that vocational-type subjects have either been non-existent or have had an uneasy and precarious existence in the curriculum.[5]

Obviously, diversification stands a better chance of being successfully implemented in schools which have a high degree of up-take, but there is more to implementing diversification than the level of up-take shown by a school. Consideration has to be given to the way diversified subjects are organized and structured, as well as the staff strength and resources available to teach these subjects. These factors determine the extent to which a school can successfully operationalize a diversified curriculum. In some schools the structure and organization of programs requires every pupil to take at least one diversified subject during the first three years (lower secondary level) of schooling. Beyond this specialized streams are provided at the upper secondary level (Forms 4 and 5) for pupils who may wish to specialize in technical subjects or home economics or commercial studies, etc. At the other extreme the structure and organization of programs in some schools is such that a pupil could go through secondary education without having to take even a single diversified subject at any point (Wright, 1983). This latter situation trivializes diversified subjects and makes them rather peripheral to the main business of schooling. Essentially then the pattern of organization and structure of the school curriculum determines the opportunities available for pupils to participate in diversified subjects, and also reveals the importance that a school attaches to these subjects. On this basis it can be argued that some of the project schools in Sierra Leone

---

[1] For instance, the Albert Academy was established by a missionary society to prepare young people for mission work and community development.
[2] Albert Academy and Bumpe High School are major examples.
[3] There is a long tradition of vocational subjects being successfully implemented at both Albert Academy and Bumpe High School.
[4] The Prince of Wales School for instance was established as a government school to promote science and prepare those who would go on to become doctors and engineers (cf. Sumner, 1963).
[5] This is particularly true of the Prince of Wales School where efforts have continuously been made since 1935 to incorporate a viable technical studies program into the curriculum without success (see Sumner, 1963, p. 378).

attached surprisingly little importance to diversified subjects, in spite of their frequent pronouncements to the contrary, and also provided rather restrictive opportunities for pupils to participate in these subjects.

As regards staffing for diversification, schools in Sierra Leone have always suffered from an acute shortage of qualified and trained teachers in technical and commercial subjects. This has meant, for instance, that schools have had to use poorly qualified craftsmen to teach technical subjects. Apart from their lack of pedagogical and communication skills, such teachers are themselves examples of the "low status" occupations towards which pupils have shown considerable antipathy. This obviously affects the status of these teachers in the schools, and also influences the regard which pupils have for technical subjects. However since the establishment of training facilities for technical, secretarial and business studies teachers at Milton Margai Teachers College there are signs that the status of these teachers is on the ascendancy. This might well have a positive impact on the way in which pupils perceive and respond to diversified subjects.

An undoubtedly crucial aspect of curriculum diversification concerns the availability of facilities, equipment and materials for teaching diversified subjects. Because of the high costs involved in providing these elements it is often assumed that lack of such resources constitutes the major obstacle to successful diversification.[1] The reality in Sierra Leone schools, however, indicates that there is much more to diversification than the provision of workshops, equipment and materials, since these resources sometimes become little more than "white elephants" in project schools. To the extent that such resources are indispensable, however, many schools which have some capacity for utilizing them effectively have always been constrained by inadequacies of such resources and the recurrent-cost burden of maintaining equipment and providing consumable resources. In this regard the Government's allocation of funds to schools does not include special provision for these recurrent costs,[2] despite the professed importance attached to diversified subjects. This again raises the disturbing question of how far hard-pressed African economies can meet the inevitable recurrent costs emanating from the implementation of high-capital projects such as curriculum diversification. It is becoming increasingly evident that many such projects experience a downward spiral once large-scale external funding ends. This trend has significant implications for the role of large-scale externally-funded projects in the realization of educational policy objectives.

---

[1] This is probably the Bank's major rationale for emphasizing Buildings and Equipment at the expense of curriculum development and teacher training.
[2] Schools are funded mainly on a formula involving enrollment size but ignoring the range of programs offered and the recurrent-cost implications of vocational subjects.

Pupil-related Issues

All the resources and logistical provisions made in support of diversification would be in vain without the positive participation of pupils in the related subjects. A salient lesson from the history of vocationalization efforts in Sierra Leone is that it is futile to channel pupils into a situation where they become unwilling captives in diversified programs or vocational subjects. The end result can be counter-productive as was pointed out by one of Sierra Leone's leading professional engineers in the following observation:

> The late Mr Edmondson labored long and valiantly at the Diocesan Technical School to train young men in Carpentry, Drafting and Surveying. It is to the credit of the training he gave that some of his young men later became Barristers, Doctors and Physician Specialists in Government services, and Clergymen in the service of God. (Davies, 1968)

Planners often forget that education is as much a "buyer's market" as it is a "seller's market." Often, what is important is not so much what is on offer in the curriculum, but what pupils decide to take from the educational process. It, therefore, seems imperative for the success of diversification that proper insight should be developed into how pupils perceive and respond to diversified subjects. It is only through an understanding of the factors involved that we can hope to promote positive pupil participation in these subjects. In this regard it is commonly believed that most pupils hold vocational-type subjects in such low esteem that if they had a free choice they would refuse to take these subjects. A survey of pupils in sample project schools did not quite confirm the validity of this belief for the Sierra Leone situation. Pupils' subject preferences were elicited by asking them to list the first four subjects they would choose to study if they had a free choice, and the first four subjects they would reject or refuse to study under the same conditions. The responses indicated that pupils were strongly aware of the subject combinations needed for a good pass in the West African GCE "O" level examinations. Thus English language and mathematics which are compulsory for these exams were listed by all pupils amongst the first four subjects they would freely choose to study. Beyond this, other chosen subjects mainly reflected the pupils' bias towards science or arts streams. What was most significant was the high frequency with which business studies subjects were listed amongst the freely chosen subjects.[1] Also, although technical subjects did not feature appreciably in the list of freely chosen subjects, their occurrence in the list of rejected subjects was also

---

[1] There has been a phenomenal rise in the popularity of business studies subjects at both secondary and post-secondary levels. This is a phenomenon which needs to be more fully studied in relation to economic and employment trends.

negligible. The indications, therefore, are that pupils in the sample schools do not appear to have any obvious bias against studying diversified subjects as such.

Another common belief is that most pupils have a negative attitude to vocational-type subjects in the schools. An attitude survey however revealed that this was simply not true. For the 30-item questionnaire the maximum possible score was 150 (most positive attitude), while the minimum possible score was 30 (most negative attitude). Table 1, therefore, indicates that the mean attitude score (M) for all technical subjects is fairly high in the sample schools concerned. On average then there is a positive attitude towards all technical subjects amongst pupils in the sample schools. Interestingly, there is a consistent hierarchy in pupils' attitudes, with technical drawing having the highest mean score, followed by metalwork and then woodwork. Moreover, there was a much stronger correlation between scores for metalwork and woodwork ($r = +0.84$) than for metalwork and technical drawing ($r = 0.57$) or woodwork and technical drawing ($r = 0.46$). This seems to suggest that pupils have a more favorable attitude towards technical drawing which they perceive as being somehow different from and preferable to metalwork and woodwork.[1] What is most significant, however, is that the responses from sample project schools indicate clearly that pupils do not have a negative attitude to technical subjects.

TABLE 1 *Summary Statistics of Attitude Scores*

	Mean scores and (Standard Deviations)		
Sample school	TD	WW	MW
Albert Academy ($N = 35$)	113.69 (10.74)	108.70 (13.63)	110.37 (14.12)
Prince of Wales School ($N = 50$)	—	107.40 (7.35)	107.58 (11.53)
Bishop Johnson Memorial School ($N = 32$)	—	109.94 (13.00)	112.88 (10.39)
Magburaka Secondary School for Boys ($N = 50$)	—	110.60 (7.23)	118.57 (8.97)
Schlenker Secondary School ($N = 38$)	—	103.37 (13.80)	—
Bumpe High School ($N = 44$)	106.23 (12.50)	105.15 (12.84)	—

TD—technical drawing; WW—woodwork; MW—metalwork.

Yet interviews with teachers and school administrators revealed a persistent allegation that pupils "look down" on technical subjects or do not take these subjects seriously for some reason. Further investigations suggested

[1] A similar hierarchy in pupils attitude towards different technical subjects has been reported for Kenya by Lauglo (n.d.).

that pupils' antipathy for technical subjects becomes manifest in the context of career aspirations and expectations of schooling.

Clichés and stereotypes about the unrealistic career aspirations of secondary school pupils still persist in spite of the changing social and economic climate which is imposing a new sense of realism amongst pupils in Africa. Empathetic investigations in the Sierra Leone context revealed that pupils' career aspirations operate at two levels which could be termed idealistic and realistic. At the idealistic level when pupils are simply asked what job they would like "at the end of all their education," the occupations most frequently stated are prestigious ones such as medical doctor, lawyer, scientist, economist, etc. Two caveats to this general trend are worth mentioning. In some schools which are not particularly renowned for academic excellence pupils sometimes opted for less prestigious career aspirations (teacher, nurse, preacher) even at this idealistic level. Second, at one school which has a highly successful business studies program and a well-developed technical stream, the two most frequently occurring career aspirations were accountant and engineer. Almost all the pupils who wished to be accountants had also listed business studies subjects amongst the first four subjects they would choose to study if they were given a free choice. However, most of the pupils wishing to become engineers did not include technical subjects amongst the first four subjects they would freely choose to study. The significance of this will be discussed later. In consonance with their idealistic aspirations, pupils also had a highly inflated perception of the academic qualifications required for these prestigious occupations. Thus a doctorate degree was more frequently mentioned than professional qualifications or practical training.

Against this background certain constraints on pupils in relation to their career aspirations were extensively discussed. For instance, it was pointed out to pupils in some schools that the poor track record of the school in GCE examination results, and the negligible number of pupils who qualify for entry to university each year, made it very unlikely that most of them would acquire the high academic qualifications they felt necessary for their prestigious career aspirations. With these sorts of constraint in mind pupils were asked what would be their next choice of job if they failed to get the qualifications necessary for the first choice of occupation. It emerged from the responses that pupils' career aspirations operate at a realistic level which is often not revealed on initial questioning. In making a second choice of job most pupils were realistic enough to accept a downward shift in their original career aspirations (e.g. from accountant to office clerk).

What is perhaps most significant about pupils' career aspirations is its "long-term horizon," which implies a prolonged period of formal education before starting a career. In the Sierra Leone situation, most pupils' career aspirations (idealistic or realistic) are such that they entail some form of post-secondary education as a prerequisite for job entry. Since there tends to be an intimate link between pupils' career aspirations and their expectations of what can be got out of schooling, the predominant perception amongst pupils is that secondary schools serve to prepare them for post-secondary education (see Table 2). Beyond this, the expected outcomes of schooling which pupils regard as most important (Table 3) indicate that they

TABLE 2 *What Pupils Wish to do After Completing School (Form 5)*

Options	Percentage response according to school					
	AA[1]	POW	BJSM	MSSB	SSS	BHS
1. Get a job in a government department	20	2	12.5	6	18.4	20.5
2. Try to start own business	5.7	10	9.4	2	0	0
3. Go to college or university	57.1	86	37.5	60	68.4	50
4. Get a job with a private company or firm	2.9	2	0	0	2.6	0
5. Learn a trade at a trade centre	0	0	6.3	4	2.6	9.1
6. Go to a technical institute	14.3	0	34.4	28	7.9	20.5

[1] See Table 1 for names of schools.

TABLE 3 *Outcomes of School which Pupils Regard as Most Important*

Positive outcome	Percentage frequency of selection according to school					
	AA[1]	POW	BJMS	MSSB	SSS	BHS
1. Earning a high salary to repay your parents and family	88.6	74	78.1	80	76.3	81.8
2. Becoming someone your parents and relatives could be proud of	68.6	78	34.4	78	23.7	63.3
3. Being able to go to college or university	60	64	31.3	66	76.3	63.3
4. Becoming an important person or leader in the community	51.4	48	62.5	70	71.1	81.8
5. Being able to understand what is happening in the world	57.1	48	56.3	32	31.6	31.8
6. Getting a decent job with good pay	57.1	46	34.3	34	52.6	52.3

[1] See Table 1 for names of schools.

have a complex concern with high earnings and high status, strongly undergirded by a desire to please and reward parents or relatives. Pupils can, therefore, be expected to value highly those aspects of schooling which they perceive as contributing to the possibilities for high earnings or high status in the future. Conversely, pupils will pay little attention to aspects of schooling which they regard as detracting from such possibilities. Thus, if pupils regard subjects such as woodwork and metalwork as leading to low-status and low-earning occupations, it should hardly be surprising if they do not take such subjects seriously. Indeed, when pupils were asked to state which subjects they paid least attention to and to indicate why, the range of subjects included metalwork and woodwork. More importantly, however, by far the most frequent reason given for paying so little attention to these subjects is that they are not important for the pupils' future studies/career.

Curriculum Factors

In African countries such as Sierra Leone the school curriculum is under considerable pressure from different sources which sometimes make conflicting demands. Planners tend to give priority to national development needs and the role education is expected to play in meeting such needs. The diversification of the secondary curriculum is obviously a case in point. Beyond this, however, it is also important that in terms of its objectives, structure and content, the curriculum must reflect cognizance of the complex and changing forms of human knowledge. Finally, what is most important but often paid mere lip-service, is that the curriculum must be responsive to the aspirations of pupils and their parents.

Against this background it can be argued first that diversified programs in secondary schools reflect a major orientation towards the role of education in national development. To this end the important question to be raised is the extent to which diversified programs can turn out the caliber of trained or trainable manpower required for socio-economic development. While there was no systematic attempt to match diversified programs to needs indicated by a manpower survey for instance, it could be argued that diversification does not require such a close fit and that the spread of diversified programs (technical, business, secretarial, home economics, agriculture) was sufficiently wide to cover major areas of socio-economic manpower needs. Essentially then the diversified curriculum widens the scope of knowledge and skills offered, and improves the contribution that an otherwise general secondary education system could make to manpower development.

Second, in terms of the changing forms of human knowledge a major criticism of diversified programs is that they largely reflect an adherence to traditional and often archaic content and structure, which have little relevance to the Sierra Leone context.[1] This is particularly true of the technical subjects where the craftsmen engaged as teachers are left to their own devices and continue to teach woodwork and metalwork in the age-old tradition of manual crafts, oblivious of the major changes which have transformed studies in this area to a "design technology" approach (cf. Dodd, 1978). In these circumstances pupils are simply taught the rudiments of workshop practices and spend most of their time making minor artefacts or assisting the teacher to make and repair school furniture. Many school administrators understandably encourage such a state of affairs, and regard it as an indication of success if some pupils develop reasonable proficiency in making chairs, tables and beds, etc., for the school (and the staff)! It could well be asked, however, whether such proficiency is best acquired in the context of a general secondary education or more appropriately catered for in vocational/trade schools and through apprenticeships in suitable workshops. For one thing, diversification itself does not entail making pupils into skilled craftsmen, and it would be self-deluding anyway to assume that such an objective could be pursued in two periods a week over a few years. Yet it is difficult to see what other conceivable objective is being pursued under the traditional manual craft approach, beyond the bland contention of introducing pupils to manual skills and teaching them to appreciate the dignity of manual labor.

With the new breed of technical teachers there is some hope that the technical studies curriculum can be transformed to reflect a more relevant and effective approach involving a twin focus on design and technology. This approach is not only epistemologically viable in itself but also creates much more tangible links between technical studies and other school disciplines. Amongst other things it entails a scientific understanding of forces, materials and processes as a basis for problem formulation and problem-solving in the design process. It also involves the development of design communication skills using the "language of technology" (technical drawing). Beyond this of course there is strong emphasis on the development of practical skills involving the use of various materials (wood, metal, plastic, etc.) in the practical realization of a design solution. In their attempt to transform the technical studies curriculum the new teachers face formidable opposition from craftsmen who have become entrenched as teachers, as well as administrators who are far more appreciative of the material products of these craftsmen than any educational impact on pupils.

Finally, it needs to be asked how far the diversified curriculum meets the aspirations of pupils and their parents. It is in this regard that one can fully understand the relative neglect of technical subjects by pupils. In principle,

[1] These subjects are surprisingly much more dependent on foreign books and curricula than the so-called academic subjects. This might well be due to the shortage of competent curriculum specialists in these areas.

the traditional manual craft approach to these subjects is not only oriented towards preparation for low-status occupations, but effectively inhibits the possibilities for higher education and high-status jobs. In their present state, woodwork and metalwork are not even countenanced by the university as entry qualifications for engineering or any other courses. While most pupils are ready to accept that they may not succeed in entering university or achieving their preferred career aspirations, they are not necessarily willing to forfeit the opportunity to "have a go" at these objectives. Pupils who study biology and chemistry at school with the aim of becoming medical doctors may not gain entrance to university and may in fact end up being laboratory assistants, junior workers in the pharmaceutical industries, or even something unconnected with biology and chemistry. What is significant for such pupils however is that they did "have a go" at their career aspirations and had a chance to prove to themselves that their biology or chemistry, etc., was not good enough. In contrast, pupils who take woodwork and metalwork at school know that these subjects "lead nowhere" in spite of so much talk about their importance in professions like engineering, architecture and forestry, etc. Pupils are fully aware that it is subjects like physics, mathematics and chemistry which provide entry to university engineering courses, *not* woodwork or metalwork. Thus, pupils may well have a liking for woodwork or metalwork, and may well acquire an appreciation for the dignity of manual labor, but when it comes to their career aspirations they would invariably wish to keep their chances alive by concentrating on other subjects!

Diversification Re-examined

As a policy concerned with enhancing education's contributions to manpower development, the diversification of secondary education was well-founded and properly conceived. The two major factors which originally served to justify a diversification policy are still very much in force in contemporary Sierra Leone, and have probably become more intensified. First, Sierra Leone still suffers from an acute shortage of manpower for industrialization and modernization. This can readily be appreciated from the mediocrity prevalent in manufacturing and other modern sector services, as well as in the agricultural sector, government administration and most parastatals. The fact that economic growth has not been sufficient to generate employment opportunities is quite another matter, and it is extremely foolish to infer from a shortage of employment opportunities that a policy of diversification is inopportune in any way. Second, the secondary school curriculum in Sierra Leone is still overwhelmingly "academic" in its orientation and, therefore, continues to offer a rather narrow range of knowledge and skills in relation to further studies and career possibilities.

Significantly, this is still the case at a time when the usual safe havens for employment (government departments and parastatals) have become over-saturated. Against this background it is difficult to understand how the policy of curriculum diversification could conceivably be regarded by any-one as being inappropriate or inopportune for a country like Sierra Leone. The main issue to be resolved is whether the diversification policy is to be pursued on an on-going, long-term and evolutionary basis, or whether it should be abandoned simply because the finite experience of two World Bank projects did not yield expected results.

As a project seeking to establish "diversified subjects" in the secondary school curriculum, diversification was poorly designed and badly implemen-ted. This is nothing unusual since as far as major educational projects in Africa are concerned success stories are few and far between. Poor design and bad implementation do not necessarily add up to failure, but they do indicate that strategies could have been improved and that resources could have been more efficiently deployed and more effectively utilized. Gen-erally, there can be little doubt that the diversification project has made a significant impact on Sierra Leone's education system. For almost a decade it concentrated the thoughts, skills and resources of Sierra Leoneans on trying to make diversification work. Throughout this period, it also provided substantial input of external expertise and resources, and afforded a healthy dialogue on educational priorities and strategies in Sierra Leone, as well as sponsoring an impressive range of essential overseas training for Sierra Leoneans. Most importantly, although the diversification project might not have yielded the ambitious outcomes expected, it has offered new insights and important lessons as well as providing a major catalyst for the on-going process of diversification which in a sense has been in existence since the colonial period.

As a practice dating back to the colonial period diversification has experienced a considerable boost since the formal policy was enunciated in 1970. An unprecedented input of buildings, equipment and materials has substantially improved the practice in some schools while enabling others to take on the challenge of diversification in a manner they could not have afforded under normal conditions. The practice has also been greatly enhanced by the establishment of teacher education facilities and programs in diversified subject areas. However, much remains to be done by way of developing responsive diversified programs which can be properly struc-tured and organized within the school curriculum. In this regard there are important lessons to be learnt form the diversification project and subse-quent developments in project schools.

There can be no doubt that business studies subjects are now very popular, eagerly chosen and enthusiastically pursued by an increasing number of secondary pupils. This is a phenomenal change from the situation 10 or 15 years ago when pupils with "low academic ability" were being channeled to commercial streams where they studied business and secretarial subjects. Yet, there is nothing dramatically new or radically different in the business studies curriculum or the way in which business studies subjects are taught. What has happened in fact is that in a period of economic decline the business sector has increasingly become the main area of major employment, and is certainly the only sector which can still afford to pay lucrative salaries. Educational institutions with well-developed business studies programs have been able to capitalize on this phenomenon. Thus for instance pupils from the Albert Academy who take a certificate in business studies in place of the usual GCE "A" level subjects are very much in demand and now command higher salaries than most university graduates. Moreover, it is now becoming clear that such qualifications as the Certificate in Business Studies provide significant advantages in further professional courses in accountancy, banking, etc. Consequently, not only do we have a situation in which business studies subjects are highly popular amongst the brightest pupils in a school like Albert Academy, but there are increasing incidents of bright pupils from some of the other leading secondary schools *transferring* to a school such as the Albert Academy, in order to study business studies subjects. There could hardly be a more fitting testimony to the success of diversification when the pieces finally fall into place. In this case the success is largely externally induced in the sense that changes in the economy, employment opportunities and earnings pattern have resulted in a phenomenal change in pupils' perceptions of business studies subjects.

In the case of technical subjects, we do not have to wait for such an external eventuality, although it will be most welcome when it does occur. The solution meanwhile appears to be largely in promoting enthusiastic pupil participation, coupled with improving the logistics of operationalizing curriculum diversification. A sober start is being made in this direction now that the euphoria of a major project has faded. Curriculum planners, teacher educators and some of the experienced new-breed of technical teachers have already done substantial work on developing an integrated technical studies curriculum for Form 1 to Form 3, involving the "design technology" approach.[1] Also, there are plans to develop a curriculum for specialist studies in design technology up to Form 5, which would be acceptable for entry to university. Such a program of technical studies leading to university courses would hopefully transform pupils' perceptions of technical subjects in a healthy way. Those who enter university courses in engineering, architecture, etc., would be much better prepared than the current catchment of students who have only studied mathematics, physics and chemistry. Pupils who do not succeed in entering university would still do well in technical institutes and trade centers or simply as technologically

---

[1] The hesitation to invest in diversification efforts is such that funds to pay a token honorarium for these curriculum development activities have not been readily available from the Government.

literate employees. There are also hopes that the ideas of a mobile maintenance unit and a central purchasing/storage system will become operational
sometime in the future. It is quite ironic that all of this now has to be
attempted without the benefit of external funding which seemed to be so
readily available for all sorts of abstruse uses during the project years. But
then diversification is such an important educational goal with such profound implications for national development that we must do the best we can
with our limited resources. Most importantly we cannot afford to be
discouraged or side-tracked into pursuing new panaceas by those who can
afford to play a game of fashion with issues so crucial to our future. As with
most African countries, the story of curriculum diversification in Sierra
Leone is as much about unexplored potentials and under-utilized opportunities, as it is about unfulfilled promises and unrealized expectations.

References

Adams, S., Sengova, T. and Wright, C. (1983) Diversification in existing secondary schools—
interim completion report No. 3 (Draft) (p. 4). Evaluation of Second Sierra Leone/IDA
Education Project (Credit 573–SL). Freetown: prepared for the IDA Education Project
Unit. (Restricted circulation.)

Davies, E. J. (1968) Problems of educating and training the Sierra Leonean engineer of today.
In Thomas, K. (Ed.) *Co-ordination of engineering activity for progress in a developing
country* (pp. 18–29; see p. 19). Freetown: Fourah Bay College Bookshop.

Dodd, T. (1978) *Design and technology in the school curriculum.* London: Hodder and
Stoughton.

Harbison, F. H. (1973) *Human resources as the wealth of nations.* New York: Oxford University
Press.

International Development Agency (World Bank) (n.d.) Project Performance Audit
Memorandum; Sierra Leone First Education Project (CR 170–SL). (Restricted
circulation.)

King, K. (1980) Education and self-employment. In *Education, work and employment—II*
(pp. 219–283). Paris: UNESCO IIEP.

Lauglo, J. (n.d.) *Practical subjects in Kenyan academic secondary schools (general report).*
Stockholm: Swedish International Development Agency (SIDA) Education Division
Document No. 20.

Psachoropoulos, G. and Loxley, W. (1985) *Diversified secondary education and development:
Evidence from Columbia and Tanzania.* Baltimore: Johns Hopkins University Press.

Second Sierra Leone/IDA Education Project (Sierra Leone II) Draft Working Papers (W.P.)

Sierra Leone Government (1961) *Educational and economic development in Sierra Leone: An
interim report of the Education Planning Group.* Freetown: Government of Sierra Leone.

Sierra Leone Government (1964) *The development programme in education for Sierra Leone
(1964–1970) "The Sleight Report".* Freetown: Government of Sierra Leone.

Sierra Leone Government (1970) *White paper on educational policy— 1970.* Freetown:
Government of Sierra Leone.

Sumner, D. L. (1963) *Education in Sierra Leone.* Freetown: Government of Sierra Leone.

Wright, C. A. H. (1979) *Situational analysis of technical and commercial education in Sierra
Leone* (p. 16). (Report on a series of surveys undertaken by staff of the Technical and
Business Education Department between September 1977 and April 1979.) Freetown:
Milton Margai Teachers College.

Wright, C. A. H. *et al.* (1983) The politics of streaming and subject choice. Interim Research
Paper Series. Freetown: CREST Research Centre, Milton Margai Teachers College.

Wright, C. A. H. (1984) Curriculum diversification in Sierra Leone as a basis for a theory of
educational innovation. Unpublished Ph.D. Thesis, University of London.

CHAPTER 8

Curriculum Costs: Vocational Subjects*

C. E. CUMMING

Moray House College of Education, Edinburgh

It is so self-evident that it hardly needs an entire chapter devoted to demonstrating that practical subjects are, by their very nature, more expensive than "normal" or chalk and talk subjects. Or so a sceptic might argue. However, the meaning of costs and their behavior in education invite close scrutiny by academics and policymakers alike. What is it about practical subjects that makes it seemingly imperative for the "factors of production"—the mix of resources used to produce the intended outcomes—to exceed those deemed fit to achieve outcomes in other non-practical subjects? Could it be that ostensibly higher costs of practical subjects are justified in terms of benefits that accrue both while studying and, perhaps more importantly, while participating in the labor force? How far does it matter if practical subjects are more expensive as long as the mechanisms by which the costs are financed take account of the distribution of "benefits"?

The coverage of the paper is, in the main, restricted to second-level schools with one or more practical subjects where those subjects have links to jobs, either as "pre-vocational" or as more directly "vocational" components of general secondary schooling. Some of the evidence cited, on the other hand, concerns technical/vocational schools with diversified options or streams.

It is necessary to establish a definition of costs, a "concept map" to which inevitable questions of inclusion and exclusion can be addressed. However, much more than with other curricular subjects the issue of whether it is at all possible to discuss *costs* without reference to putative *benefits* demands consideration. A profile of benefits is therefore described. The question of who should bear the costs of specifically "vocational" education rounds off the first part of the chapter. The first part of the chapter consists then of a framework for appraising the costs of practical/vocational subjects. The second part aims to obtain guidance from the published literature on the costs (and benefits) of practical/vocational subjects relative to other curricula.

* The author is grateful to John Mace for a critique of an earlier version of this chapter.

137

Part I. Conceptual Framework

A Concept Map of Costs in Education

All real resources used in education could in principle be allocated to other uses. Hence, the costs of education—as of other economic activities—amount to what is sacrificed with respect to the best alternative use of those resources used in education. Measurement of costs implies that all the alternative uses of the real resources can be both imagined and valued (a price tag attached to them). If this ideal of the economist is accepted, it is immediately clear that all of the true costs of education do not appear in, for instance, budget statements. An example of such an omission occurs when in courses, offered by technical colleges and some universities and purporting to be directly related to raising productivity in industry and commerce, the convention is to price the time of the students as zero. A statement of the accounts of such institutions will include *direct* costs of labor, buildings, plant, equipment. Further rummaging in the byeways of official statistics would unearth other costs such as transfer payments (allowances paid to students) and extra living costs associated with being in the student role. Students' time is, however, "free." Yet, time and again in studies of educational costs, the opportunity cost of students' time, calculated as the income forgone by students during study, has been reported as high as or higher than the direct costs of education (Schultz, 1961; Selby Smith, 1970, pp. 70–71; Judy, 1971, pp. 46–53).

Two further distinctions are necessary before sketching a usable map of costs. First, current or recurrent expenditure is made on goods and services that are used up and/or have to be bought regularly. Capital expenditure is made on goods that last more than one year, and possibly as long as 60 years; renewal is therefore sporadic. Second, budget and account statements are meant usually to render a form of public accountability and, therefore, the costs identified in such statements are some part of *social* costs. Social costs are those that are borne as a result of the social decision to have some education activity and such costs fall upon society. *Private* costs are borne by students or their families as a result of and in return for education.

Figure 1 attempts to map the broad field of costs of education.

Putting price tags on costs

It is one thing to set out what is meant by costs: yet another to actually measure costs especially, as it will become evident, to measure costs at levels below that of an institution. Not only is there the difficulty of accessing reliable data on actual expenditures but for some of the cost components there is controversy over the meaning of the data.

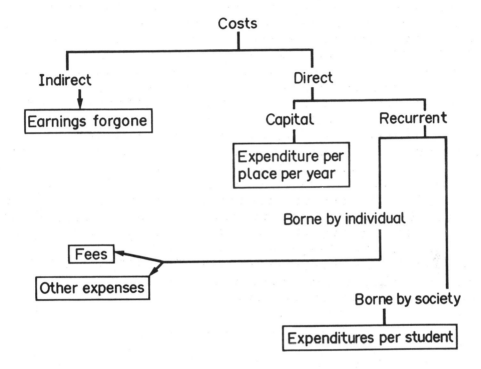

FIG. 1 Concept Map of Costs

Indirect costs: If remarks are limited to students on practical/vocational courses the convention is to assume that such students forgo a certain proportion of the income earned by their peers in work adjusted for unemployment (Schultz, 1961). There are problems with the validity of such estimates: for instance, what happens to wage rates when one-time students are released to the labor market? Which unemployment rate to use?

Direct costs: The most straightforward element in costing in principle, if not in practice, is to measure recurrent expenditure. Out-turns of expenditure are normally available for levels of aggregation above that of the individual institution. Where institutional records are available, allocation of expenditure to functions, e.g., teaching and administration and organizational units such as departments remains to be done by the cost analyst.

Hence curriculum costs are seldom given. In a paper prepared for a recent conference entitled "Economics and Educational Management," it was reported that "we need ultimately to examine the combined impact of separate resource allocation decisions on the costs of the curriculum that schools provide . . . Curriculum costing studies of these kinds are relatively rare" (Simkins, 1986).

Those recurrent costs borne by individuals, such as school transport, special clothing, books, extra food costs, are not routinely available. Household survey data and research studies do, from time to time, produce such data. The alternative route to their measurement is to impute them on the basis of their size relative to income forgone or direct social recurrent expenditure. Fees present a more manageable component since scale charges are normally available for both private and public sectors of education.

Direct costs, capital components: Even if a capital sum is "spent" in one year it would clearly be inappropriate to include the sum spent in that year, thereby implying the real resources "free" use in future years. An annualized capital expenditure is necessary. To do this, account must be taken of the expected lifetime of the real resource—50 or 60 years for a school building in the UK but only 20 years in, for example, a harsh African climate—and an estimate made of the interest "lost" by having purchased the real capital resource instead of, say, investing the money in the best (and safest) bond market. The annualized expenditure can be regarded as the annual rental value; what one would pay if one had to lease the building or equipment rather than buy it outright. Costing of capital is obviously sensitive to interest rates chosen for the best alternative investment.[1]

Figure 1 attempts to state what the present writer means by the social costs and the private costs of education. Such "definitions" of costs work well enough as guidelines to measuring costs at aggregate curriculum levels. Cost of separate subjects—mathematics, geography, home economics—are in principle derived using the same definitions. Measurement of resources actually used by different subjects is the more complex the nearer one gets to the actual site of delivery of the curriculum.

Conceptual Framework

In a chapter on the costs of education it would be perfectly legitimate to proceed to the specific case, namely the costs of practical/vocation subjects. Various reasons can be given for costing in education.

[1] In UK school buildings and those of local authority colleges are not bought outright, since the capital sum is normally borrowed on the local authority bond market. Thus the annual charges on loans can be used as a proxy for annualized capital expenditure.

Reasons for costing in education

(1) to describe fully the provision and allocation of resources in an education system;
(2) to note differences in unit costs and highlight decisions that lead to those differences;
(3) to alert decision-makers to cost consequences of their decisions;
(4) to carry out cost-benefit and cost-effectiveness studies for alternative programs.

It may seem naïve, but the strongest reason, to me, is the first reason, namely, simply to describe fully the resources allocated. (No one would seriously quibble with a manager in industry who set about costing his marketing operation.) But, and it is a big *but*, costs have costs. Curriculum costing may require, at least at present, some additional justification.

As Levin (1981) argues, "any educational program that purports to improve the labor market success of its students represents a prime candidate for cost–benefit analysis because the benefits of such programs can be readily assessed in monetary terms in order to make them comparable with costs."

Profile of benefits to vocational education

The dominant element in the profile of benefits to vocational education is that of increased lifetime earnings of the successful participants in vocational education programs. The reasoning is that the benefits of the program consist of the increased output directly attributable to the investment in the vocational program. One of the sacred canons of human capital theory holds that the output gains can be measured tolerably well by summing the lifetime earnings differentials (suitably discounted) of students who have and have not received the program under investigation. There is a vast library of doctoral theses and other researchers applying this approach to education, mainly at the level of stages of education, e.g., primary against secondary. Psacharopoulos (1973, 1981) is the doyen of this approach and fairly stable patterns of findings do emerge.

While the patterns of findings are stable—for instance, private returns outstrip social returns, returns to primary education exceed those to secondary education—they do not lack critics from supporters of other explanations of why people with more education generally earn more. All the competing explanations (the screening hypothesis, the dual labor market hypothesis and the radical neo-Marxist explanation) refute the key assumption of the human capital explanation, namely that observed wages' differentials reflect marginal productivity differences. The current state of the debate demands caution in performing and interpreting rate of return studies. The present writer stands by the managerial necessity of costing in education and by the logic of evaluating the likely and actual benefits from a decision to spend. What weight in a decision is ultimately given to a calculation of a rate of return will depend on the context for that decision.

Other claimants to being a benefit generated by specifically vocational education programs are (a) reduction of aggregate unemployment below the rates that would otherwise have existed; (b) redistribution of income to low-income groups; (c) external benefits such as lower incidences of social deviation; (d) it is often claimed that practical subjects will improve the prospects for self-employment if regular wage-earning employment fails to materialize. In the literature on cost–benefit approaches in education it is not usual to find price tags put on these last four aspects of benefits.

Conceptual Framework—Financing Issues

For practical subjects offered at secondary level education, *prima facie* there is no case for arrangements for financing to differ from those that pertain in a country for the study of other curricula. The problem of financing only becomes insistent when there is an explicit and intended link between the curriculum and subsequent employment. Candidates for financing specifically vocational education are the State (at national or more local level), employer(s) or industry and the student/employee. There is no need to open up here the labyrinth of the training/education conundrum. It is enough to posit a broad dimension of education–training where vocational education is located along that dimension adjacent to and overlapping with training. The nearer one is to the training end of the dimension the easier it is to justify the costs of that training being borne by firms or the industry as a whole. Governments may intervene and support such training because of the need to stimulate a higher volume (and perhaps quality) of training than would occur otherwise. Individuals may, and noticeably do in developing countries, pay for their own training. At the other end of the dimension, the costs of general education, whether at primary, secondary or tertiary level, are seldom shared with industry though they are with individuals. The benefits to industry are just too tenuous for cost-sharing to be justifiable. However, a case for cost-sharing can be made for vocational education at secondary and higher levels of education. Partly because of the same principles of equity and efficiency that drive the engine of State support to lower and general education and partly because of attempts to manage the economy through long-term manpower planning, governments are the major partners in funding vocational education. But, with the high costs of such vocational education (most of which is also "practical" and skill based) governments look to industry to *share* some of the costs. There is, for instance, in the 1985 Green Paper on higher education in the UK a proposal that industry be asked to bear the costs of those components of degree courses that are specifically vocational. If employers do share the costs of vocational education it is reckoned they may be more concerned with the curriculum of those courses. Such a concern may result in a better match between the curriculum and the attitudes, knowledge and skills demanded at work.

To sum up, three points need to be highlighted. First, the concept of cost and its meaning to the various interested parties when costs are discussed in education is not commonsensical. The concept map shows the main features of a still largely unsurveyed land. Second, while the process of costing in education can be justified in its own right, when attention is focused on vocational education, for which many would claim there are or ought to be measurable returns, an additional pretext for costing is to hand. Third, the question of who should bear the costs of practical subjects, where these are the main components of vocational education, can be answered only after a thorough scrutiny of who benefits from the subjects—the State, industry or individuals—and whether the practical subjects are offered as vocational education or vocational training. We turn now to what can be gleaned from the literature on curriculum costs to examine it within the theoretical framework of Part I.

Part II. Obtaining Guidance on the Costs of Vocational Subjects

One must bemoan the paucity of published and easily accessible studies of both curriculum costs and of their sub-set, practical/vocational subjects. There is a faint possibility that somewhere administrators in education beaver away doing just such studies as a routine part of their work. The near ubiquity of computer-based accounting in the education systems of the developed world certainly makes costing of subjects an administrative possibility whereas, before computers, such a task was for the persistent researcher! An ERIC search brought forth a crop of possibilities which were, in the main, irrelevant on follow-up. The UNESCO organization, the International Institute for Educational Planning, did more school cost studies than any other organization during the tenure of the last director, an economist. Only one such study, as yet not available in English, has been done on the costs of curriculum including vocational subjects (Tibi, 1986).

Some Guidelines for Curriculum Costing

In a study of school subjects the present writer focused on the direct recurrent expenditures incurred by society (Cumming, 1971). A distinction that proved worthwhile was that between *staffing* costs of subjects— covering expenditures on teaching staff only—and *teaching* costs—covering staffing costs plus all other expenditure unambiguously allocable to the teaching of a particular subject. Three separate unit costs were calculated and the resulting comparison of subjects was significantly affected by the choice of unit (cost per pupil, cost per pupil-period and cost per teaching group or class). The cost per pupil-period, which is the product of pupils and the time for which a subject is studied, was concluded to be the most robust unit for comparison. Using the pupil-period as the divisor, the unit costs of teaching English in 12 secondary schools varied by the order of 500 percent (Cumming, 1971, p. 106). Classics turned out, on average, to be the most expensive subject at more than 200 percent greater than English. The unit teaching costs of technical subjects were less than half those of classics but 50 percent above those of English. No attempt was made in those studies to scale the peaks of indirect costs and capital costs. A later attempt (Cumming *et al.*, 1972) to apply the same curricular costing methodology to courses in further education colleges revealed that the unit costs of departments (the loci of courses) varied as much across colleges as they did between different courses. In both schools and colleges unit costs are particularly sensitive to even small changes in class size.

In general, the staffing costs of a subject are determined by the age/experience of the teachers, the initial qualifications of the teacher, the size of class and the number of periods allotted in the timetable. The teaching costs are subject to the same determinants plus the instructional supplies and equipment, auxiliary services (such as workshop assistants) and subject-specific administrative overheads.

A second study of British further education (Selby Smith, 1970) did go beyond the above Scottish studies by including (a) direct capital charges (based on allocating loan charges to departments) and (b) imputing the costs of students' time. Selby Smith goes beyond the costing of courses in calculating partial (benefit–cost) ratios using discounted median values of future earnings (Selby Smith, 1970, p. 130).

Taussig (1968) did a cost–benefit analysis of vocational education in New York City high schools. He found that vocational education did not increase "the market productivity of the graduates of the vocational high schools." He goes on to conclude that the unremarkable market productivity was achieved despite "the large incremental costs shown to be devoted to vocational training relative to the alternative high school programs." He found that unit recurrent "teaching" costs in vocational high schools and academic high schools were in the ratio of 1.66:1 while overall institutional unit recurrent costs were in the ratio of 1.43:1. (He adopts a short-cut method for capital costs, assuming those would be 22 percent of recurrent costs!) Notice, Taussig does not cost vocational subjects, merely the institutions with a "bias" towards vocational education. His study is similar in design—at least in the costing element—to those of Hinchliffe (1983) and Tibi (1986), see below. He does not *show* that "vocational training" has high incremental costs relative to other curricula. Logically the possibility exists that at least some of the incremental costs in the vocational high schools were due to the other curricular elements in these schools.

In another and more elaborate study, Hu *et al.* (1971) compared the costs of vocational and comprehensive secondary education and the labor market successes of the two types of high school in three American cities. In contrast to Taussig, they concluded that not only were the monetary returns of the vocational graduates higher than those of comprehensive graduates but also for one city, using three measures of comparison, the returns greatly exceeded the costs. Unfortunately the treatment of costs in the study is relegated to two pages compared with 18 pages of the benefits. What is clear is that Hu and his colleagues did not undertake the costing of the schools themselves, but relied instead on data from the school districts. The average unit recurrent expenditures of the two types of high school were in the ratio 1.44:1 (vocational : comprehensive). Elsewhere Levin (1981) quotes Hu and Stromsdorfer (1979) as reporting that vocational curricula show unit costs of from two to five times as much as other curricula.

A third American investigation concentrated on the differential costs of curricula in junior colleges (Warren *et al.*, 1976). In an effort to untangle the costs of the component courses of curricula, Warren *et al.* compared costs of all baccalaureate and occupational curricula relative to an invention of their own—the Baccalaureate Curricular Cost Base (BCCB) for each institution studied. The BCCB is the weighted average of the annual costs of educating a student in three broad baccalaureate areas, viz., business, education and liberal arts. They found that a majority of courses in highly specialized fields in both the occupational and baccalaureate categories were more expensive than courses represented in the BCCB. For instance, "health occupations curricula cost on the average approximately 1.8 times as much per student as curricula comprising the BCCB, both technical occupations and trade and industrial occupations curricula cost approximately 1.5 times as much."

A novel feature of the study is the notion of *equipment centeredness*, curricula that require major investments in instructional equipment. High *equipment centeredness*—calculated as the depreciation of instructional equipment divided by salary expenditures for each field of instruction— explained some of the high relative costs for certain fields of instruction.

In the small literature on curriculum costs one of the most detailed studies, as far as various courses are concerned, is reported by Cage (1968). He reports the ratio of 16 different vocational–technical program unit costs (recurrent only) to the unit cost of arts and science curricula during 1967–1968 in Iowa. For instance, ratio of unit costs of auto-mechanics courses to those in arts and science fall in the range 1.21–3.23 with a mean of 2.27 over 10 community colleges. The wide variation of unit program costs was a feature of another American study by Semple and West (1982). Their investigation concentrated on a single institution, Nash Technical College. Unit costs per student-hour ranged among 19 different programs from $0.81 to $3.58 with a mean of $1.91.

Tibi (1986) has been studying the costs of vocational education in Thailand. He writes "it has been difficult to get costs by specific field of study because of the diversity of fields and levels of education or training within the same school."[1] What he can report is the unit costs (recurrent, direct and social only) according to types (biases) of each institution. Recurrent costs per student are highest in agricultural colleges, followed by those in technical colleges and then by those in so-called professional colleges, where arts and crafts are taught. (The ratios were 1.96:1.54:1.) More interesting are Tibi's observations of the relative labor intensiveness of the colleges. In the agricultural colleges expenditures on personnel account for 39 percent of total recurrent expenditure; in technical colleges they are 55 percent and in professional colleges they are 58 percent.

It is a cliché of curriculum costing that "practical" subjects are more expensive because of the kinds of resource employed. The problem is that seldom is there quantification of the resource gap. Moreover, it is necessary to state that other things must be equal for the obvious to hold. (Recall the finding that classics was the most expensive subject in a Scottish authority's schools.)

To conclude this review of the literature in a search for guidance on the costs of vocational subjects we turn to two recent studies. Hinchliffe's (1983) work, part of the DiSCus project, concerns cost structures of secondary schooling in Tanzania and Colombia. Like the studies of Tibi, Taussig and Hu *et al.*, Hinchliffe costs schools with biases rather than costs separate subjects. Hinchliffe's approach is to cost directly four categories of school in Tanzania and six in Colombia. All the cost components in the cost concept map are included. Earnings forgone are established in a novel way. This indirect cost is identical for all the four biases in Tanzania, while in Colombia indirect costs do not vary by more than 17 percent between the highest (the academic bias) and the lowest (the commercial bias). The intriguing aspect of Hinchliffe's results is the apparent proximity of costs whatever the bias. In Tanzania, academic biased schools are cheapest. Total annual unit *recurrent* costs are 19 percent higher in agricultural-biased schools, 13 percent higher in technical-biased schools and 9 percent higher in commerce-biased schools compared with the academic schools. However, in terms of total unit *social* costs the differentials almost disappear. Thus, the total unit social costs are 2, 3 and 4 percent higher in the commerce-, technical- and agricultural-biased schools respectively than in the academic schools. (The only study from the developed world which supports the *relatively narrow* cost differential between vocational and other studies is reported by Meeth (1974). He established that the *mean* cost per student hour (direct costs only) of vocational subjects in 75 two-year colleges was 29 percent higher than that of a humanities curriculum.) The data for Colombia are complicated by a

[1] Personal communication to the author, 24 March 1986.

comparison of World Bank project schools—INEMs[1]— and other schools. The INEMs combine academic and pre-vocational curricula and include several pre-vocational tracks. Within INEMs variation in unit costs between tracks are very small. Hinchliffe remarks on the finding: "[perhaps] . . . the nature of the problem is such that the methodology is not picking up". In other words, he was surprised by the results.

A possible explanation of the observed low unit cost variations between schools offering apparently different curricula—apart from the obvious one that there really *are* no great cost differentials— is that real variations in subject costs are damped by (a) costs of subjects that loom larger in the curriculum than the biases, e.g., maths and language; (b) common or shared costs of services such as administration, boarding; (c) random variations caused by staffing ratios and class sizes. Turning that explanation round, the costs of curricula depend on a complex mix of factors.

Finally, attention turns to the SIDA study of practical subjects. For reasons connected with the overall design of the study and the small period of fieldwork (less than three weeks actually gathering data) the full rigors of costing, implied in Fig. 1, were not applied. No data on indirect costs were gathered. Nor was any estimate made of direct costs borne by students. Direct costing, using primary sources, was made of capital expenditures and of recurrent expenditures. The former expenditures refer to the four industrial education (IE) subjects, while the latter refer to the secondary schools as a whole. The resulting recurrent costs suffer from the same deficiencies as those cost studies of Hinchliffe, amongst others.

In an effort to get at curriculum costs, a method based on a model or an "identikit" timetable for the IE subjects was employed (Cumming *et al.*, 1985, pp. 90–93). The staffing costs of IE, on this method, were approximately twice those of "talk and chalk" subjects.

The greatest portion of fieldwork was devoted to using payment vouchers to establish capital costs of the SIDA-supported schools. In annualizing these costs the imputed interested rate on the capital was set at zero, on the assumption that SIDA, in giving a grant, surrendered the choice of investing in bonds. The effect is to understate the true social costs. (Hinchliffe adopts the same procedure.) The cost per place per year is, for a facility costing Ksh 750,000 to erect, some Ksh 940 with zero interest charges, Ksh 3600 at 7.5 percent interest and Ksh 4400 at 10 percent interest. Unfortunately, data was not available in Kenya for the actual costs of building/equipping schools other than for the IE facilities. Comparisons were, therefore, made between *estimated* capital costs for a range of facilities—classrooms, science labs, etc., and the *actual* costs of IE subjects. IE is estimated to be more expensive than (a) classroom subjects—by a factor of 5; (b) other practical subjects— by a factor of 2/2.5. Compared to science, one of the IE subjects is nine times more expensive in terms of initial equipping.

[1] INEM—Institutos Nacionales de Éducacion Diversificada Media.

TABLE 1. *Summary of Findings on Relative Costs of Practical/Vocational Subjects Compared to Academic or Other Classroom Subjects*

Author	Year	Country	Cost approach	Findings
Cage	1968	USA	Whole program costed in individual colleges	Wide variation of unit program costs across colleges
Taussig	1968	USA (New York)	Costing of institutions (high schools) with vocational bias	Unit teaching costs 66 percent greater, unit recurrent costs 43 percent greater in vocational high schools than academic high schools
Hu et al.	1971	USA	Costing of high schools with vocational bias	Unit recurrent costs 44 percent greater in vocational high schools than in academic high schools
Warren et al.	1976	USA	Comparison of costs of occupational courses with a liberal arts base course	Technical and trade and industry, curricula cost 50 percent more than the basic baccalaureate course
Meeth	1974	USA	Costing of vocational subjects in two-year colleges	Mean cost per student-hour 29 percent higher in vocational subjects than in humanities
Hinchliffe	1983	Tanzania	Costing of high schools with various biases	In Tanzania, unit recurrent costs 19 percent in agriculture-biased schools, 13 percent in technical biased schools, 9 percent in commerce-biased schools
Cumming et al.	1985	Kenya	Costing of industrial education subjects	Staffing costs of IE subjects twice those of classroom subjects: capital costs five times as expensive as classroom subjects
Tibi	1986	Thailand	Recurrent costs of three kinds of college compared	Unit costs in agricultural colleges were 98 percent higher and in technical colleges 54 percent higher than in professional colleges

The thin literature on curriculum costs is notable for its lack of consideration of financing issues. That there is some cost-sharing at secondary level is evident by the report that students of industrial education subjects in Kenya pay a fee that is, in principle, earmarked for purchase of materials in IE (Lauglo, 1985, p. 136). A subsidiary motive for the Cage study seems to have been to produce data which could be used to charge fees to students in proportion to the costs of their courses. Cost sharing with industry is nowhere evident, as yet, in the academic research literature.

Conclusions

First, while a fairly rigorous scheme for costing in education can be designed, its full application in the field of curricular costs is seldom achieved. Second, the unit for comparison of costs of one subject or curriculum with another demands attention. These two conclusions would apply equally to any subject of the curriculum. A third conclusion is that a full discussion of the costs of vocational subjects is seldom complete without consideration of the benefits of those subjects. (High costs may be justified by high benefits.) Table 1 attempts to summarize the various findings from the literature. Fourth, the complexity of costing individual component subjects of vocational curricula has led investigators to cost "biases" in curricula. The resulting differential costs of various biases may distort the true cost differences of component subjects. In calculating the costs of biases the weighting of the component subjects in the curricula must be reflected in the cost analysis (Warren *et al.*, 1976, pp. 60–62). Fifth, where costs of vocational/practical subjects can be compared to other subjects in the curriculum they are likely, other things being equal, to be more expensive in terms of costs per student-hour because of (1) the higher capital intensity/ lower labor intensiveness of practical subjects, (2) lower average "norm" class size for pedagogical and safety reasons and (3) lower *actual* class size because of the "experimental" nature of subjects, leading to a lack of optimal uptake. Sixth, recent international trends towards cost-sharing amongst the various benefitees of vocational education are not as yet reflected in reports of the costs of practical/vocational subjects.

References

Cage, B. (1968) Cost analysis of selected educational programs in area schools of Iowa. Iowa: State University. (Mimeo.)

Cumming, C. E. (1971) *Studies in educational costs*. Edinburgh: Scottish Academic Press.

Cumming, C. E., Davies, M., Lillis, K. and Nyagah, B. (1985) *Practical subjects in Kenyan academic secondary schools*. Stockholm: SIDA Education Division Document No. 22.

Cumming, C. E., Keenan, K. and Wilson, T. R. (1972) *College costs: The first part of the report of the Further Education Resources Project*. Glasgow: Glasgow University.

Hinchliffe, K. (1983) *Cost structures of secondary schooling in Tanzania and Colombia* (a DiSCus working party). Washington, DC: Education Department, World Bank.

Hu, T., Lee, M. L. and Stromsdorfer, E. W. (1971) Economic returns to vocational and comprehensive high school graduates. *Journal of human resources*, **6**, 25–50.

Hu, T. and Stromsdorfer, E. W. (1979). Cost–benefit analysis of vocational education. In T. Abramson *et al.* (Eds.), *Handbook of vocational education evaluation*. Beverly Hills, CA: Sage.

Judy, R. W. (1971) *Cost and benefit study of post-secondary education in Ontario, school year 1968–69*; Toronto: The Queen's Printer.

Lauglo, J. (1985) *Practical subjects on Kenyan academic secondary schools: General report*. Stockholm: SIDA Education Division Document No. 20.

Levin, H. M. (1981) Cost analysis. In N. L. Smith (Ed.), *New techniques for evaluation: New perspectives in evaluation*, Vol. 2. Beverly Hills: Sage.

Meeth, L. R. (1974) *A curricular and financial cost analysis of the independent two-year college of America*. Washington, DC: National Council of Independent Junior Colleges.

Psacharopoulos, G. (1973) *Returns to education: An international comparison*. Amsterdam and New York: Elsevier.

Psacharopoulos, G. (1981) Returns to education: an updated international comparison. *Comparative education*, **17** (3).

Selby Smith, C. (1970) *The costs of further education: A British analysis*. Oxford: Pergamon Press.

Semple, R. and West, D. (1982) *Cost analysis of curriculum programs: A technical report*. Raleigh: North Carolina State Department of Community Colleges.

Simkins, T. (1986) Economics and the management of schools. Birmingham: paper presented at the conference of the British Educational Management and Administration Society, University of Birmingham, 24/25 April 1986.

Schultz, T. W. (1961) Investment in human capital. *American economic review*, **51**, 1–17.

Schultz, T. W. (1960) Capital formation by education. *Journal of political economy*, **68**, 571–583.

Taussig, M. K. (1968) An economic analysis of vocational education in the New York City high schools. *Journal of human resources*, **3** (supplement), 59–87.

Tibi, C. (1986) Report on costs of technical and vocational education in Thailand (as yet untitled). Paris: IEEP. (Draft mimeo, in French.)

Warren, J. T., Anderson, E. F. and Hardin, T. L. (1976) Differential costs of curricula in Illinois public junior colleges: some implications for the future. *Research in higher education*, **4**, 59–67.

PART 3
Policy Implementation

Introductory Note

THE chapters in this section address select issues in policy implementation or describe more broadly how vocationalization policies have been implemented throughout the education system of a particular country.

Saunders studies the Technical and Vocational Education Initiative (TVEI) operating in British schools since 1983 to identify unintended effects of the implementation strategy on the institutions in which TVEI projects are embedded and reviews the literature on the impact of pilot projects when they are expanded into a system of education. His notion of "pilot enclaves" is similar to Gallart's observation that in Latin America, innovations related to technical–vocational subjects tend to form "islands" within the institution, isolated from the mainstream curriculum. One characteristic of such enclave culture is a vigorous supportive rhetoric. Equally important, TVEI tends to form an enclave in terms of administration, curriculum, resource base and pedagogy. A condition which gives rise to the enclave phenomenon is external pressure to adopt a heavily resourced innovation, leading to resistance from school staff who themselves are not involved in implementing the innovation and who do not benefit from the extra resources entailed.

Marklund's paper on Sweden is more concerned with the macro level of national policy. He describes measures within school, and measures involving cooperation between schools and the world of work aimed at preparing individuals for their future livelihood regardless of the social status of the job concerned. He is concerned not only with the goals of these measures, but equally with the means adopted to realize these goals, and with the likely results. He argues quite pointedly that the nature of the programs depends upon the level at which they operate in the education system. At the same time, the notion of levels has itself become less distinct as the Swedish system is currently changed by the forces of democratization and comprehensivization in order to facilitate recurrent education. Marklund argues that if left to the "market forces" of private demand, recurrent education could become a new mechanism of social segregation in contrast to the egalitarian principles which have guided Swedish education over the last 40 years.

O'Dell provides a broad review of the evolution of vocationalization in the Soviet Union. Hand in glove with the objective of training people in practical skills exist ideological goals relating to political and moral education. She pays special attention to the present educational reform which is based on resolutions at the 1986 Party Congress, within the context of Gorbachev's emphasis on the need to improve economic productivity. The present reform has its implementation problems, and O'Dell analyses these in some detail.

VE—F

Gallart contrasts the case of vocationalization of Brazilian mainstream secondary schools—which met with opposition from their clientele, with that of "secondarization" of technical training in Argentina, which has been a success. One reason, she argues, is that the former sought to provide terminal education of a pre-vocational kind, discouraging ambitions of further academic study. But the latter was more of a "strong polytechnical branch of secondary education which would give the student a basic training to perform as a middle level technician or to continue studying for a technical career." Gallart addresses a range of other issues associated with these two innovations, but a major conclusion is that vocationalizing reforms "should not appear as diminishing the chances of students for mobility in the labor market or as formally cutting access to higher education," in order to be attractive to their clientele.

Gustafsson's chapter outlines the ideology of the "education with production" program in newly independent Zimbabwe. Tracing its origins to the Brigades of Botswana as well as to socialist and populist views of education, he places the movement within theoretical and contextual frameworks to examine the implementation constraints and potentialities of this movement.

THE EDITORS

CHAPTER 9

The "Technical and Vocational Education Initiative": Enclaves in British Schools

MURRAY SAUNDERS

Lancaster University

IN June 1986 the Secretary of State for Education in Britain announced, without any lead-up or warning, that the Technical and Vocational Education Initiative (TVEI) sponsored by them, was to be "extended" and opened to every Local Education Authority in Britain. The estimated average annual expenditure over the 10 years will be about £90 million (HMSO, 1986). The program originally included 14 local education authorities in its first year (1983/84), in subsequent years, these 14 have been joined by 48 (1984/85) and then another 12 (1985/86) with a further 29 in September 1986. The extension was the latest phase in an unprecedented strategy, in the recent history of British educational policy implementation, of government interventionism in the curriculum of British schools.

While the main thrust of this chapter is a general account of the unintended effects of the strategy for implementing TVEI adopted by the Government, it is important to locate the significance of the shift in policy in a more general context.

There have been several useful accounts of the overall context of educational policy development of which TVEI is a part, focusing in the main on a notion of "new vocationalism." Its newness is predicated on the gradual drift of education practice into the center of political and economic discussions of the "decline" of Britain's industrial infrastructure and the rise of unemployment since the early to mid-1970s. This drift has turned on the examination of the explicit connection between what goes on in schools and what goes on in "employment."

Clark and Willis (1984) argue that the analysis which underscores such governmental action in the educational arena assumes a *deficiency* in both young people and the schools which are charged with their education. Young people are deficient because they "lack both the necessary skills and the appropriate work experience and the habits of mind that go with it" (Clark and Willis, 1984, p. 2) to survive in a highly competitive labor market. Schools are deficient because they were "failing to equip their pupils with the necessary basic skills and attitudes to enter work" (Clark and Willis, 1984, p. 3). Thus, to use Watts' (1983) basically functionalist terminology, the "traditional bonds" between education and employment were becoming increasingly loosely tied. In terms of socialization, orientation and preparation (Watts' terms), schools were failing miserably and the relationship between schools and employment was becoming more and more "dysfunctional." Perhaps the only "bond" outlined by Watts still working relatively effectively was that of selection. Other, more informal or subtle processes of socialization and differentiation may also still have been in evidence (see Willis, 1977) although the rationalistic governmental explanations would tend not to encompass these. Other writers (Dale, 1985, p. 49; Pring *et al.*, 1985) have suggested that the industrial infrastructure and youth employment are connected through the pace and nature of technological change. The decline of apprenticeships and the subsequent "need" for flexible and "generically" skilled young workers are also responses to shifts away from the manufacturing to the service employment base. Pring *et al.* argue that there is "little chance" of the unskilled worker finding secure employment even after the age of 18 (Pring *et al.*, 1985, p. 6). The paradoxical analysis began to emerge that students were ill equipped both in terms of their world view and in specific skills for the "new" or emerging industrial needs. These needs were, at the same time, specifically for highly (in areas of technology) yet generally (and flexibly) skilled young workers. However confused or muddled the apparent deficiency of schools was articulated, the argument has rapidly gained momentum and credibility. Another paradox which has become increasingly a feature of the discussion of responses to the Government's analysis, is the way in which their "deficiency model" cohered with a quite different "deficiency model" which emanated from the educational progressives in the schools which characterized "normal" schooling as sterile, irrelevant, academic, didactic and abstract.

These background features provide the context in which shifts in government policy can be more readily explained. As the functionalist and educational progressive critique began to swell, how did the Government respond? Hudson (1980) in a paper given to the 1980 British Educational Research Association (BERA) conference applied the economic categories of exchange and use value in the analysis of teachers' professional ideologies. A similar re-interpretation of these categories to analyse shifts in the policy rhetoric of schools and government may be appropriate here. As youth unemployment deepened, apparent technological changes in the production process accelerated and industrial productivity became a central issue, national government in Britain since the mid-1970s has developed a two-stage policy shift with respect to their stance on education. The first stage was to publicly signal that courses of study in schools and the educational systems as a whole were too concerned with exchange value of qualifications in abstract knowledge areas (if a course of study is characterized predominantly by its exchange value, then its use to students lies primarily in what it can be exchanged for i.e. *access* to jobs, higher education, etc., irrespective of the skills and capacities the courses were intended to develop). The connection between the curriculum and employment areas, in this conventional model, was too loose, too indirect and was unsynchronized. The antidote was to tighten the coupling between the curriculum and employment by fostering the "use value" of courses, in which the skills and capacities that courses were meant to develop in students should *actually* be intended for use at work. Although these categories are not mutually exclusive, a shift in emphasis from one to the other is significant. Thus in October 1976 (see Callaghan, 1976, p. 332) James Callaghan, the British Prime Minister, made a key intervention by signalling, in a speech made at Ruskin College, Oxford, the embryonic functionalist critique outlining schools' deficiencies in terms of progressive teachers' ideologies, the "inappropriate" states of mind that this produced in students and the lack of an appreciation, understanding and commitment on the part of students to industry's needs and work (see Dale, 1985, p. 47). He inaugurated a "Great Debate" on these issues which was taken up with considerable vigor by the popular as well as the educational press. The whole issue of educational effectiveness was presented as important enough in the public and political "mind" for government to readjust its traditional view on the relative autonomy of schooling and consider more "direct" forms of influence. Gorbutt (1984, p. 50) outlines the growing pace of this influence through successive speeches and government circulars until we reach the second stage of the policy shift in 1982, which was the move from public articulation of the "diagnosis" and the attempt to influence through government circulars the curriculum awareness of schools (in particular Circular 14/77) to a more direct form of intervention. However, the strategy used to force home the shift from influence to intervention was quite unprecedented and did not cohere with preceding trends. Intervention required a quite different vehicle from that used for "influence." Gorbutt (1984, p. 53) points to the disjunction between themes and solutions emerging during the period of "influence" and those that appeared as we enter the period of "intervention." Dale (1985, p. 43) argues that TVEI as an interventionist strategy does not follow any of the main routes previously used to bring about educational change in Britain. It is suggested that direct intervention was impossible under existing frameworks and conventions, in particular via the Department of Education and Science (DES). This, added to the increasing government concerns with youth employment, pointed to a quite different agency to puncture the shield of autonomy that schools had hitherto enjoyed. The

Manpower Services Commission (MSC), unfettered by the constraints of custom and the procedural straitjacket of a government ministry, its recent history of intervention in youth training and its close ties with the National Economic Development Council (NEDC) was an obvious choice. So, on 12 November 1982, the Prime Minister, Mrs Thatcher, announced the launch of the TVEI as a vehicle for the direct intervention of the Government into the curriculum of British schools.

While Fig. 1 outlines the formal features of the initiative, other operational, less obvious yet highly significant features are worth a brief mention. Although there were many expressed fears (see Saunders, 1986a) concerning the new strategy, it took a comparatively short time (three years) for most Local Education Authorities (LEAs) to become complicit in the new vocationalism. Many believed (see Saunders, 1986b) that they could retain their independence. What has emerged is complicity with broad policy guidelines (National Priority Areas), with local authorities retaining local operational control and design. The new funding arrangements for these developments (called by some "categorical funding") has involved LEAs in a quite new form of operation (see Harland, 1985; Dale, 1986; Fulton, 1987) in which the contract, accountability, monitoring and evaluation were key characteristics.

SPONSORS: H.M Government

AGENCY: Manpower Services Commission

MANAGERS/DESIGNERS: LEA

USERS: Teachers/students

PURPOSES: To explore and test methods
                             of organizing ⎤
                                 delivering ⎜ replicable programs
                                 managing   ⎟ of TV education
                                 resourcing ⎦

STATED AIMS

To widen and enrich the curriculum
     prepare students for the world of work
     help students lead a fuller life
     enable students to contribute to the life of the community
     enable students to adapt to a changing occupational environment
     help students to "learn how to learn"

Fig. 1 TVEI Policy Description

AGENCY OPERATIONAL PRINCIPLES

LEAs should be direct line managers, designers and responsible parties of schemes.

There are centrally devised general criteria with specific design features developed locally

Funding will be met by the agency of all *extra* costs incurred in educating the cohort within a scheme under strict financial accounting procedures

Participants should be consulted during the development of project proposals.

The agency will accept a variety of approaches in order to meet "purposes" and "aims" above

FEATURES OF THE "DESIGNATED" PROGRAM: AGENCY GUIDELINES

Target group

A scheme should include 1000 students during its life

Two cohorts of students should complete the course in the 14–18 age range

Participation by students in the scheme should be voluntary

Students should be attracted from the full ability range

Both sexes should be equally represented

Mixed sex classes should be the norm

Some provision should be made for students with special educational needs

Curricular features

Curricular designs should be for four years between the 14 and 18 age range

Designs should link to subsequent training or vocational opportunities

Designs should include a "work experience" component

Designs should be responsive to local and national shifts in "employment opportunities"

Designs should consist of both general and technical/vocational (the provision of courses which lead to students' acquisition of generic or specific skills with a view to employment) education

Assessment

Courses should lead to nationally recognized qualifications

Assessment of performance should be continually and terminally negotiated, with records of achievement or "profiles" which should express student achievements *not* readily deducible from formal qualifications

Management and staffing

Each LEA scheme should appoint a coordinator

Each participating institution should appoint a coordinator

Local management by a "support arrangement"

FIG. 1 TVEI Policy Description (continued)

This chapter is an account of some important features of the implementation of TVEI as a *pilot* project to change the shape of curriculum practice in the 14–19 age range in the British education system.

Figure 1 is a synthesis of the various guidelines issued to LEAs for the submission of proposals for funding TVEI projects. It will be noticed that the projects should last five years with two cohorts of students completing the course in the 14–18 intended age range. In general practice, this has resulted in a group of secondary schools (14–16/18 years) and colleges of further education (16–18/19 years) varying from two to 14, being involved in each LEA project. Cohorts of students in the 14/15 age range, in the first year of operation in the participating secondary schools would include a subgroup, ranging from approximately 10 to over 100, of students who would constitute the TVEI cohort, i.e., that group to which the initiative specifically referred in terms of its effects. It should also be noted, and this is important, that the purpose of the TVEI is to *explore and test* methods of organizing, delivery, managing and resourcing replicable programs of technical and vocational education. In other words, TVEI is intended as a "pilot," on a massive scale, of particular approaches, with a systematic need to identify TVEI effects on students, staff, resources and curricula, etc. This chapter builds on some existing general observations on the problems of "piloting" as a strategy to promote change in curricular relevance and identifies some internal tensions inherent in TVEI as a specific strategy.

Problems with "pilots".

By highlighting some recently made observations by Crossley (1984) I intend to introduce some general problems associated with "pilot innovations" as a strategy for change in educational institutions. He puts "relevance" education in a socio-economic context by referring schematically to the tendency of its introduction to create dualist systems of education, i.e., academic schooling existing alongside vocational schooling. At the same time, these two systems tend to be experienced by different "classes" of students leading them into hierarchically arranged positions in the division of labor. The systemic constraints on developing more "relevant" curricula which emanate from this tendency, in particular resistance from teachers, students and parents of students participating in such programs, have led to a more "sensitive" approach to the issue of implementation, if only to discover the limits of incremental changes when carefully thought out. The SSCEP project (see Saunders and Vulliamy, 1983) in Papua New Guinea is a practical case in point and in the literature, the "step-wise" approach to innovation advocated by Sinclair and Lillis (1980) is another.

Crossley argues that, as a reaction against the clumsy and sociologically naïve nationwide attempts at relevance innovation, step wise, local or pilot strategies have become enthusiastically endorsed. However, he identifies four characteristics of "piloting" which have intended and potentially adverse effects on the capacity of pilots to generate wider applications and replicability. These characterizations are summarized below.

(1) Pilots are often associated with or dependent on key individuals who provide particularly gifted or "charismatic" leadership almost impossible to replicate.

(2) Pilots which embody alternative or culturally oppositional forms of curricula, teaching and learning styles or organization are accommodated while they remain pilots or limited in scope. The full weight of resistance will not therefore be experienced until replication is attempted.

(3) Pilots of vocational or "relevant" education, when sensitively developed, have to run alongside academic curricula, particularly in the long transitional phase associated with step wise or pilot approaches to innovation. Thus, the transformation of vocational schooling into the "practical side" of a conventional curricula map, with all that implies, is difficult to prevent during long periods of development.

(4) Pilot projects cannot be equated with experimental trials because of the unique circumstances, commitment and resourcing associated with their often flexible and shifting evolution. This sort of intensive support and the specific conditions associated with them can seldom be replicated on a wider scale.

To these cogent observations, we can add the summary point made by Leithwood *et al.* (1974) concerning the way pilots may be intended to create "shock waves emanating in concentric rings" (reminiscent of the ubiquitous "ripple effects" of TVEI) from the small, massively resourced initial group of innovators. What tends to happen at the same time, however, is that there is less investment in unique services the further one proceeds from the source. The logical inconsistency in this approach lies in the fact that the initial adopters are likely to be in what Leithwood calls the "high innovator" portion of the target population, subsequent adopters tend to be low innovators, less intrinsically motivated, receiving less extrinsic motivation to change (in-service, resources, time, etc.). He concludes by suggesting that

strategies for change that apply diminishing forces to increasing resistance are unlikely to be successful. (Leithwood *et al.*, 1974).

To extend these observations I will draw on the experience of evaluating 12 TVEI projects in England. The Lancaster TVEI Evaluation Programme began in 1984 and complies with the characteristics of the "new strategy" outlined above which emphasizes and expands the role of "evaluation" (it may be, however, that the Government's view on evaluation is less than serious in the light of the national extension of TVEI in 1986 after only two years of operation for most of the projects). Notwithstanding this point, the Lancaster program has been tracking all TVEI students in one cohort in 12 authorities, along with a comparison group of non-TVEI students, for three years. Alongside this exercise, the program has been "debriefing" key participants at all levels of the "implementation staircase." The following analysis is drawn from regular debriefing interviews with project coordinators, school coordinators, participating teachers and non-participating teachers in some 30 schools in all 12 authorities (for a full account of the Lancaster strategy see Saunders, 1986c). While Crossley (1984) and Leithwood *et al.* (1974) focus on some general problems associated with the attempt to extrapolate from the experience of a "pilot" to the wider case, our evaluation has highlighted the effects of the pilot itself on the wider institution in which it has been embedded which will further condition replication.

The Pilot Enclave

As our analysis proceeded, it seemed increasingly that a key feature of TVEI implementation was its capacity to create an "innovation enclave." To the extent that "pilots" are sets of practices or materials, usually expressed in a policy text, which may be clearly and self-consciously distinguished from established or ascendant sets of practices, they may be said to form "pilot enclaves" which are inserted or which intervene in the established institutional context.

A characteristic of a pilot enclave derived from our work in the Evaluation Programme based at Lancaster University, and related to points (1) and (2) made by Crossley above, is that it produces "vigorous rhetoric" (used literally to refer to a set of "rallying" or "mobilizing" concepts and ideas) which draws participants together and, by mutual identification with an "enclave" culture, distinguishes adherents from non-adherents. This rhetorical practice should, however, be distinguished from "policy realization." Indeed, it may be that the stronger the rhetoric, the greater is the gap between rhetoric and actual practice.

While it is plausible to identify the creation of enclaves as a general outcome of a piloting strategy, the conditions under which TVEI has been implemented, as well as the specific character of its implementation, has compounded the likelihood of enclave creation. The general conditions in the British system include real funding contractions, falling rolls, the "popular" critique of its "effectiveness" outlined above and a bitter and unresolved struggle between government and teachers over salaries, policy priorities and terms and conditions of service. In this situation, the special and particular attention to a group of students, teachers and curricular areas, intrinsic to "piloting," would inevitably exaggerate the enclaves thus created.

The MSC took the "exploration and testing" element of the brief outlined above seriously, in that pilot "discreteness" was, at least in the initial stages of implementation, an intense preoccupation of its monitoring of TVEI. Elaborate mechanisms for the separate identification of TVEI cohorts were insisted upon, as was the use of TVEI-funded resources, plant use, INSET, etc. The outcome of these preoccupations was to put considerable pressure on schools to separately account for what was happening to those involved with TVEI.

As I have identified TVEI implementation as having the general characteristics of a pilot enclave, and some specific conditions which have amplified the tendency, how are they manifested?

TVEI has developed a strong administrative and management identity with its line management of central teams, regional advisers, LEA project coordinators and school coordinators/liaison officers. This set of management roles may cut through the existing arrangements of LEA adviser, officers, headteachers and heads of department. Although guidelines were relatively open, TVEI in practice has a strong and broadly identifiable curricular orientation. Most proposals contain technology courses, including information technology, computing, food and catering, business and office skills courses and electronics. Proposals also contained personal and social, residential and work experience education.

TVEI proposals contained a set of teaching and learning practices as "characteristic" of TVEI orthodoxy which include student centeredness, inquiry, problem-solving, group and co-operative work, less teacher direction, less literary or text-based activity, experiential rather than symbolic, unspecified links between "theory" and "practice," new, more "egalitarian" relations between students and teachers, although from a long tradition in educational thinking, this orthodoxy often countered conceptions of "conventional practice" in schools and colleges.

Finally, and most importantly, in terms of enclave effects, it is separately and lavishly funded and staffed in comparison with current real and perceived spending. Projects starting in the second round of submissions (1984), for example, had budgets of approximately £2 million each.

In summary, TVEI has a strong tendency toward the development of enclaves in terms of its administrative, curricular, teaching/learning and resource characteristics. It should be noted, however, that enclave development is usually unintended and, indeed, expressly opposed by many participants in TVEI. What is of interest are the effects that enclave creation has on schools in TVEI and the differing strategic responses of key participants.

Depending on the responses of staff and the management style and ethos of each particular school, the enclave characteristics of TVEI have been variously managed. If, for example, the implications of participating in TVEI were not anticipated by a school, the various disruptions, curriculum changes and activities generated by TVEI have "competed" with school interests, resulting in the perception of TVEI as "divisive." This may have been exacerbated by more general fears about increasing government intervention and control of the secondary school curriculum. In such cases senior staff, accustomed to control over school organization, resource allocation and curriculum, found themselves officiating over a series of decisions on which they did not have direct control but which were implied by TVEI participation. Some general issues and tensions, arising from TVEI's pilot enclave characteristics, follow from the enclave "sites" identified above.

The differential allocation of extra resources to some curriculum areas and not to others in a period of general contraction has inevitably generated resentment amongst some non-TVEI staff. The offer of extra resources for whatever reason was a prime incentive for school participation in TVEI. In some cases the control over use of TVEI resources conflicted with internal school decisions on whole school use. The limits on the extension of TVEI-funded resource use have not been clearly demarcated by the MSC and there has been great variation between schools on "extended" use.

Some TVEI teachers expressed the concern raised above by Leithwood *et al.* and Crossley, that TVEI was, fundamentally, a "resource-led" curriculum innovation. This perception implied several long-term problems for the "ripple effects" TVEI was intended to create. Unless resource provision at present rates is extended, how can the gains of TVEI be generalized? It may be that this interpretation of TVEI tends to understate the changes in teaching and learning strategies that have characterized at least the "rhetoric" of TVEI in some schools.

The distribution of resources, increased in-service education and the allocation of extra scale points to subject areas associated with TVEI (more by custom than any implied association in the policy guidelines) has inevitably created buoyancy and dynamism in such areas. These inputs are conspicuous by their absence in other areas in the curriculum, creating a "natural" feeling of exclusion on the part of non-included teachers. As one teacher put it, in a marvellous mixed metaphor, "It was like being left out in the cold when the cookies were handed out."

Less obvious, and certainly more difficult to articulate, is the sense that the conventional shape of the curriculum is irreversibly changing, threatening the departmental credibility of erstwhile "safe" areas. Arguments have been presented which focused on the feelings of rejection and irrelevance that TVEI had prompted in some subject teachers. The perceptions which resulted in these responses characterized TVEI as narrow practical/vocational education, which they found difficult to identify with. At the same time, the fear was expressed that more traditional "literary"-based skills would be seen as redundant. In an interesting analogy, a teacher described the TVEI enclave as the *"nouveau riche"* of the curricular village, offending and threatening the old status hierarchy by its brashness and tradesmanlike culture.

In real terms, the expansion of the option choices at the end of the third year, as long as conventional forms of curriculum organization are retained, inevitably reduced the potential number of clients for each subject, particularly if option blocks contain popular, or fashionable, subjects with which more conventional areas are competing. Related to this problem was the way, in small departments, the requirement to provide for small numbers in TVEI classes had actually reduced the normal curriculum provision across the whole of the fourth year.

In some cases the demands of TVEI in-service, coordination and administration meetings have created management problems relating to staff cover for involved TVEI teachers. Some head teachers observed that the organizational effects and demands of TVEI have far outstripped the expected demands associated with the numbers of students engaged within it. In this sense the needs of the whole school and the needs of the TVEI pilot enclave are not congruent. Added to this senior management problem has been the demands of TVEI participation (courses, meetings etc.) or TVEI staff which has considerably cramped already well-loaded general time tables, e.g., exam preparation, marking, etc.

In general, the speed with which schools were asked to submit proposals and the late stage at which final budget clearance was given by the MSC has had several effects. The choice of particular items of equipment may have been different if more time for the examination of alternatives had been available. Because proposals were often in skeleton form, decisions about appropriate resources were made without a full understanding of the implications of proposed course provision. In some cases, courses were designed in the expectation of levels of resource funding which in the event did not materialize. A final effect of the speed of adoption has been the overload on school co-ordinators and school management as they have struggled to develop, as well as administer, TVEI provision. This has resulted in the initiation of courses which have not been fully written, which have not been adequately equipped, and in a large amount of administrative data-gathering, particularly in the early stages, for MSC monitoring purposes. Importantly, in many cases courses have been initiated without final accreditation. This has been the case particularly for those schools which have developed a "stronger" interpretation of TVEI (I will return to this later), involving the breakdown of traditional two-year courses into smaller modules, which in some cases include cross-curricular combinations.

Models of School Responses

In the light of these contradictory pressures, the senior management of schools have in effect to balance the gains of TVEI in the form of increased resources, and, for some, the provision of a platform on which to innovate the curriculum against some difficult management decisions and implied changes in curriculum control.

For a minority of schools, TVEI has provided an opportunity to begin to revamp the whole curricular map of the 14–18 age range, involving changes in organization, content, assessment and teaching approaches. This option we have characterized as an *adaptive extension*, or strong interpretation of TVEI.

For the majority, TVEI has been one of a number of competing concerns, and thus its implementation is characterized by *accommodation*, in which TVEI curricula are adapted to fit the general shape of already existing curricular arrangements. For these projects the potential benefits of TVEI tend to be assessed and activated slowly, with innovatory elements being introduced continuously over time.

For another proportion of schools, TVEI has afforded an injection of funds but the general implications in curriculum change, organization, timetabling and teaching approaches have been muted, with extensions of the option choices being the principal manifestation of TVEI presence in the curriculum. Such response may be characterized by *containment*, or a weak version of TVEI, in which its effects have been confined and absorbed by existing school practices. In actuality, a school may have traces of all three of these "model" responses. In effect, the placement of a school, in general, in one or other or these crude categories may depend on a combination of factors:

(1) the already existing shape of the curriculum, which may include TVEI-type developments;
(2) the previous experience of school staff in curriculum review and discussion;
(3) the strong or weak interpretation of TVEI adopted by senior school managers;
(4) the extent to which both school (or their equivalent) and project coordinators are perceived as "change agents" in curriculum development and, in turn, their capacity to generate within schools and across projects a "TVEI ethos" which includes the desired characteristics.

The capacity of school and project coordinators to influence curriculum development may well depend on factors 1, 2 and 3, above and the communication channels that each level has been able to develop. The teachers' action during TVEI implementation has had the effect of severely limiting curriculum and organization meetings. Important developments in these areas have been held back in many cases.

The effects of TVEI management enclaves

Enclave tendencies in TVEI implementation have their expression in the shifting and ambiguous position of coordinators at both LEA project and school points in the implementation staircase. (See Saunders, 1987 for a discussion of the Implementation Staircase.)

In the case of LEA project coordination, coordinators have been charged with a role of both "administrator" and "change agent." These two sets of "practices," while not mutually exclusive, do not cohabit easily. The coordinators' relative power to execute changes in schools and their more general role as administrators (coordinating information flow, equipment procurement, establishing continuity of the TVEI proposal expressed in schools across the LEA) has by no means been explicit. It has, in true TVEI fashion, been "negotiated" with the key participants, in this case the heads of schools, the advisory service and LEA officers. Particularly difficult for project coordination has been the establishment of the boundaries of their legitimate influence in project schools. These boundaries exist between the authority of the senior managers and their "whole school" concerns on the one hand, and the interests of the TVEI pilot enclave on the other (with all its rights and obligations). The boundary is essentially concerned with the appropriate degree of influence, cooperation and control over such matters as curriculum organization, teaching strategy and assessment which has been established between the parties with varying degrees of success. Where the project coordinators and senior managers have broadly congruent perceptions of TVEI and its implications, possibly coinciding with "strong" school interpretations of TVEI, then the relationship may be characterized as collaborative. The "irksome" management tasks associated with TVEI participation—covering for meetings, data-gathering, visits to the school, etc.,—arc sccn as necessary evils. On the other hand, if there is a lack of congruence between project coordinators and senior school management perception of TVEI, possibly associated with a "weak" school interpretation, then the relationship is more "abrasive." Issues relating to the boundaries of legitimate influence on the internal affairs of the schools are more prevalent in these cases, and the incidence of minor skirmishes over the management tasks identified above is higher.

A complicating factor in the development of these "negotiations" is the ambiguous position of the project coordinator with respect to the LEA and the MSC. By the nature of the position, project coordinators are faced with continually shifting advocacy depending on the issue. On the one hand, they may be outlining the interests and the preoccupations of the LEA to both schools and the MSC (staffing ration, for example), and on the other, the preoccupations of the school to the MSC and the LEA (equipment shortages, time-tabling, the need for administration time, etc.); and finally, they are faced with processing and interpreting MSC guidelines and requirements to the schools and LEAs (identification of TVEI cohorts, questions of funding, etc.). The factors influencing the project coordinator in successfully picking his way through these conflicting pressures are complex. A clear and agreed job specification (amongst all participating interests) in which the coordinating role and the proposals' orientation were stated may have been a desirable yet unusual prerequisite. The previous experience and status of the project coordinator may well have established preconceived limits and possibilities to the role which were difficult to transcend once in post. Variations in previous status do coincide with variations in the degrees of overt influence from project coordinators which schools appear to tolerate.

The briefs given to school coordinators or liaison officers have varied from school to school. These variations are conditions by the previous status of the coordinator and the weight given to school project coordination in terms of administration time for TVEI management (varying from below half a day to a whole week). In some cases, aspects of TVEI, e.g., profiling, residential education, etc., have been given to members of staff, for which "points" may or may not have been allocated.

In many cases the workload concerned with both administration and curriculum and with teaching and learning innovation has been underestimated. Some form of "slack" in both these capacities is seen as desirable by coordinators to accommodate shifts in emphasis in planning and INSET.

In general, the role of the school coordinator has reflected the ambiguities mentioned above between the demands of the established administrative hierarchies in school and those derived from TVEI participation. In a majority of cases the function of the school coordinator has been confined to the organization of administrative directives, essentially communicating requests for information of policy action. This reduced platform (in terms of status and legitimacy) on which to initiate changes in teaching/learning strategies or curriculum development has resulted in more active control by the senior management of the school. In schools in which TVEI is "contained" with little impact on the whole curriculum (timetable, options, teaching/learning, etc.), school coordinators are without the necessary influence, or, perhaps, skills or brief, to act as "change agents" with the functional emphasis on administration. Schools which are either adopting or "accommodating" TVEI are more likely to enhance the status of school coordination, either by giving the role to a senior post-holder or by providing the "climate" in which the efforts of the coordinator are supported and given the necessary credence.

In most cases the "change agent" aspect of the school coordinator's role has been difficult to achieve, if indeed the brief included such a mandate. The many evaluation studies on curriculum change suggest that changing conventional practice in schools is a difficult and protracted business. The lack of a high commitment to change on the part of some senior staff, the related issue concerning the insufficient influence of some coordinators and the considerable burden of TVEI administration, combine to limit school coordinator initiatives in internal change.

However, where the school climate is supportive (approved by senior management), coordinators have developed strategies to subvert the resistance to or suspicion of TVEI amongst whole school staffs. These strategies tend to increase the workload on coordinators because a "ground rule" appears to be to minimize any disruption or burden on other members of staff derived from TVEI, creating what has been termed elsewhere the "grafting syndrome," centering on the "servicing" of colleagues' organizational needs. In such circumstances the "inclusion" tendencies of TVEI orthodoxy are more apparent and, correspondingly, the "exclusion" and thus resistance of teachers outside, or at least perceiving themselves as outside, the enclave, becomes more pronounced. In this Catch 22, in which "success" hatches increased resistance, school coordinators have developed the following strategic responses.

In order to minimize the establishment of a TVEI enclave (i.e., the danger inherent in the more positive or oppositional TVEI style) solely associated with particular departments or individuals, and to enhance the perception of TVEI as a "whole school" endeavor, a maximum flow of information about TVEI appears to be a prerequisite. School coordinators who have been able to establish a regular communication channel within and across schools and informally consolidate this via chance discussions, etc., have been able to undercut exclusion and coopt their colleagues and drawn them into the planning exercise.

Those schools which have chosen to spread the use of resources have greatly enhanced the development of a "whole school" approach to TVEI. This has been achieved informally by the use of the equipment for in-house training for staff, teaching materials preparation or simply "having a go," and by students in clubs or supporting their work in other areas of the curriculum. More formally, teachers and students have used the resources during classes, and have developed teaching and learning materials themselves or in conjunction with members of staff directly involved in TVEI teaching.

I have mentioned above the conception by some members of staff of TVEI as inappropriate, irrelevant or threatening to their curricular specialisms. Where school coordinators and senior staff have been able to broaden the base of TVEI ideas in the curriculum and encourage departments to participate in curriculum review and design to include teachers outside the narrow definitions of "technology" or "vocation," the effect has been to "activate" the whole school. Where these strategies have not been left to chance but have been initiated, either in part or together as an implementation strategy, the effects are marked. The principal constraint, in implementation terms, appears to be located with the relative influence of both project and school coordinators on internal school policy.

Some Conclusions

In adopting the strategy it did, the Government faced both schools and itself with a double bind in which projects needed both to adhere to pilot discreteness while, at the same time, undermine the severest effects of enclave creation outlined above. In order to minimize the demoralizing effects of enclaves, the most effective strategy was to try and spread or diffuse the TVEI input throughout the institution. This might be called *pre-emptive replication*. While this serves the interests of the whole school management and dismantles the enclave created by TVEI, it also begins to dismantle the structure of the "pilot," intrinsic to the initial TVEI conception of "testing methods of organization, delivering, managing and resourcing replicable programs of TV education." Thus, in order for TVEI to be managed effectively, it is necessary for the "pilot discreteness," once such a preoccupation of MSC monitoring, to be minimized. If pilot discreteness is *actually* retained, however, then the headteacher has to contend with the severe internal school dislocations created by the TVEI enclave. One of the great ironies in TVEI may be that the most daring and genuinely innovative school exponents of TVEI orthodoxy are precisely those which have contradicted the terms under which their initial involvement with the MSC was negotiated. In other words, by using strategies such as those outlined above, they have dismantled the enclave and have made TVEI, as a pilot, all but disappear. This collection of factors may be diagrammatically represented as in Fig. 2. The question is, if the notion of pilot breaks down in the "best" school exponents of TVEI, does this matter? Although only a speculation, the difficulties of sustaining this strategy may in small part, along with political expediency, help to explain why the MSC has allowed its vocabulary to drift. In guidelines on the extension of TVEI, phrases like "piloting and testing" have been replaced by "preparation."

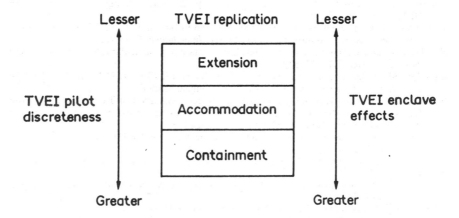

Fɪɢ. 2. Model Management Responses in TVEI

However, it is important not to let the specification of the TVEI case distract from more general lessons to be drawn from its three-year development. While the use of a pilot is a useful antidote to the brutish way in which national governments have engaged in educational engineering, to introduce enclaves into education institutions in order to test its effects, appears to be fundamentally misconceived and offends a "practical logic," particularly where the system is characterized by the relative autonomy of single institutions. Whether extended, accommodated or contained, the innovation is transformed and cannot deliver the objectives the initiator may have hoped of it.

References

Brockington, D., White. R and Pring, R. (1985) *The 14–19 curriculum: integrating CPVE, YTS, TVEI?*. The Youth Education Service Ltd., Bristol.

Callaghan, J. (1976) in *Education*, 22 October 1976.

Clarke, J. and Willis, P. (1984) In Bates *et al.* (Eds.),*Introduction to schooling for the dole*. Basingstoke: Macmillan.

Crossley, M. (1984) Relevance education, strategies for curriculum change and pilot projects: a cautionary note.*International journal of educational development*, **4**, 245–250.

Dale, R. (1985) In R. Dale (Ed.), *The background and inception of the technical and vocational education initiative in education, training and employment*. Oxford: Pergamon Press.

Dale, R. (1986) Examining the gift-horse's teeth: a tentative analysis of TVEI. In S. Walker and L. Barton (Eds.), *Youth unemployment and schooling*. Milton Keynes: Open University Press.

Fulton, O. (1987) The TVEI: An assessment. In *Education and training, UK 1987*. A. Harrison and J. Gretton. (Eds.) *Policy Journals*.

Gorbutt, D. (1984) The new vocationalism: a critical note. *Perspectives* **14**. University of Exeter.

Harland, G. (1985) TVEI: A model for curriculum change. Paper given in the BERA TVEI Symposium 1985.

HMSO (1986) Working together—education and training, Cmnd. 9823. London.

Hudson (1980) Use and exchange value in teachers' professional ideology. Paper given in the BERA conference 1980.

Leithwood, K. A., Russell, H. H., Clipsman, J. S. and Robinson, F. G. (1974) School change: stages, constructs, and research methodology. *Interchange*, **5**, 33–48.

Saunders, M. and Vulliamy, G. (1983) The implementation of curricular reform. *Comparative education review*, **27**, 351–373.

Saunders, M. (1986a) *Managing the enclave—Teachers outside TVEI*. In C. McCabe (Ed.), *The organisation of the early years of TVEI*. Multilingual Matters.

Saunders, M. (1986b) Developing a large scale "local" evaluation of TVEI: Aspects of the Lancaster experience. In D. Hopkins (Ed.) *Evaluating TVEI: Some methodological issues*. Cambridge: Cambridge Institute of Education.

Saunders, M. (1987) Perceptions on TRIST: implications for INSET: *Research Papers in Education* **2**, 28–47.

Sinclair, M. E. and Lillis, K. M. (1980) *School and community in the Third World*. London: Croom Helm.

Watts, A. G. (1983) *Education unemployment and the future of work:* Milton Keynes: Open University Press.

Willis, P. (1977) *Learning to labour*. Farnborough: Saxon House.

CHAPTER 10

Integration of School and the World of Work in Sweden

SIXTEN MARKLUND
University of Stockholm

VOCATIONAL education is an ancient phenomenon, but as a form of schooling it is relatively new, only a century or so old. And coordination between general and vocational education became a general issue of school policy only during the post-war years.

The concept of vocationalization is unclear, and so too are its practical manifestations in new school structure and curricula. This is partly because education and vocational training have often been considered incompatible. Education was an escape route away from physical work, i.e., the very thing which vocation or trade stood for. The Greek and Latin words for school meant this very thing—freedom from physical labor, the cultivation of intellectual pursuits. The British teacher or doctor calls his occupation a "profession" but hardly a "vocation." In France the word "*profession*" generally refers to an occupation or livelihood, regardless of its academic social status; the street-cleaner in the Rue des Écoles has a "profession" just as much as the research scientist in the Sorbonne University nearby. In Germany, the word "*Beruf*" denotes both vocation and profession, and the same is true of "*yrke*" in Scandinavia. To obviate the discussion otherwise prompted by the usual distinction between vocation and profession in English usage, I propose using the term "vocationalizing of education" to denote all the measures *within* school and also measures involving co-operation *between* schools and the world of work, aimed at preparing the individual for a future occupation and livelihood, whatever the social status of the job concerned.

Levels of Vocationalization in Education

Vocationalization can also be classified by other criteria than social status. One such criterion may refer to differences concerning the goal of this vocationalization. Another concerns the means and methods employed in

173

its realization. When discussing questions of objectives nowadays we can hardly avoid such questions as the democratization of education, equality of opportunities and comprehensivization of education. Similarly, as regards means and methods, we immediately come up against questions concerning the differentiation of pupils and curricula in different schools, different tracks, streams, settings, etc. A classification of vocationalization at different *levels* can refer both to its means and to its ends, as follows:

(1) During his education, the individual should be made aware of his future role as a member of the world of work.

(2) In addition, and preferably as part of his compulsory schooling, the individual should be informed about the world of work, about general characteristics of economic activity and specific characteristics of different occupational fields.

(3) In addition, the individual should be trained to perform special tasks, i.e., tasks belonging to a field of occupations or a particular occupation.

(4) The next level of vocationalization takes the form of specialized and supplementary job training, now usually as part of the job itself.

(5) A further level involves updating with references to new and changing occupations, as well as further training for positions higher up in the same occupation.

All these levels of vocationalization imply some form of integration of school and world of work. Moreover, at the highest levels school and work can be integrated to form a single entity. The above-mentioned classical distinction between "work" and the "freedom from work" associated with school then fades out of existence.

One practical problem concerns the school levels or educational levels with which these different levels of vocationalization are to be integrated. Traditionally speaking, schooling has been divided into primary, secondary and tertiary. As a result of the democratization and "comprehensivization" of schooling, these organizational levels have tended more and more to include not only academic (traditionally professional) but also vocational education. This tripartite division is becoming more and more of an anachronism and is being superseded by a division into compulsory and post-compulsory education, with the latter tending to imply an integration of school and world of work within an overriding system of recurrent education or what has been termed, with slightly different emphasis, life-long education.

Vocationalization as a Matter of School Curriculum and School Structure

The school curriculum has always been regarded as the territory of the professional educationalist. As a rule, teachers and headteachers have taken the role and tasks of their own school for granted, as well as the selection of pupils and the qualitative criteria of acceptable results. Teachers and headteachers have tended less often to view the role of their own schools in a wider social and educational context. They have regarded them as something defined *a priori* by nature and culture or else as a problem for politicians and rulers. Questions of this latter kind, which have become more and more pressing in our own time, include this very question of how one can and should try to coordinate school and the world of work. The transition from school to employment concerns everybody. It can assume various forms, with various apportionments of responsibility and with various degrees of vocational specialization. The essential requirement for each individual proceeding from school to employment is that these two things should be coordinated, that there should be no friction between them and that they should not be mutually contradictory.

"Vocationalization" as a curricular and organizational question thus becomes, when viewed in the context of educational organization, very much a question of educational differentiation and integration. These two terms—differentiation and integration—refer to the study program and the pupils. Study programs can be differentiated (for which read: vocationalized) with respect to content and methods. And pupils, similarly, can be divided into groups both within and between different study programs, e.g., according to individual interest and ability or with reference to labor demand in the community.

If this latter aspect, the needs of the community, is taken to include the official and, mostly, universally accepted goals of recent years concerning equality through education, the vocationalization of education is also bound to concern the differentiation and integration of teaching. Whichever level between general introduction to the world of work and specific vocational training and development we are referring to, it cannot be viewed as an isolated addition to general education. Instead it is more likely to be an essential dimension of general education.

Vocationalization of Compulsory Education

During the 1950s and 1960s Sweden introduced a compulsory nine-year comprehensive school, otherwise known as basic school, for all children and youngsters between the ages of seven and 16. This school is now attended by 98 percent of all pupils of compulsory school age. The remaining 2 percent comprise pupils with physical and mental disabilities who attend special institutions and pupils attending a number of independent schools, e.g., schools run by religious denominations and schools employing alternative methods of education. Most of the private schools formerly existing came to be integrated within the basic school system.

Until 1962, the new school existed on an experimental basis. Several forms of vocationalization were tested. Between 1962 and 1969 the new basic school was gradually introduced throughout the country, with essentially uniform time schedules and syllabi. At the same time the pre-existing forms of primary and lower secondary schools at this age level were abolished.

A new subject, civics, was made compulsory for all pupils from Grade 4 onwards. This subject always included what was termed *theoretical vocational orientation*, referring to the world of work at first locally and later on in larger areas. Field trips had to be organized to a number of work-places. These visits were to be prepared in class and then reported in writing. Starting in Grade 7, where in addition to the compulsory subjects pupils were able to choose elective subjects for a few periods per week, theoretical vocational orientation also included questions concerning education for different occupations. *Practical vocational orientation* was introduced as a new subject in Grade 8. This subject was allotted three weeks, or longer in individual cases. During this time the pupils were to acquire hands-on experience at two or three different workplaces out of school. Placement arrangements were made by special educational and vocational orientation (SYO) teachers, who were usually also in charge of theoretical vocational orientation in school. In addition, most of them were employed part-time in local youth employment offices. The goals of these activities were stated as follows in the central curricular instructions:

> Practical vocational orientation is designed to supplement vocational theoretical orientation and other civics instruction by means of work experience at a number of workplaces, in this way giving the pupil, firstly, an opportunity of acquiring personal experience of a limited number of jobs or vocational fields and, accordingly, a concrete view of the implications and demands of duties and working conditions in these occupations or occupational fields; secondly a practical opportunity of investigating whether he has the aptitudes, interests and other qualities required for the jobs in question; and thirdly a closer knowledge of the world of work, e.g., concerning the division of labor and specialization, employer–employee relations, relations between superiors and subordinates and between individual employees, educational opportunities, occupational safety and health and occupational hygiene.

In the terminal grade of compulsory school, until 1962, pupils had to choose between different study routes—known as lines—which were organizationally segregated but still kept within the framework of the compulsory school system. These lines were essentially of three kinds, viz., academic, general and pre-vocational. Until 1962, pupils taking the latter two lines had to complete their practical education by working in local industry and enterprise. The results of gearing pre-vocational education to local enterprise were not always encouraging. This was a difficult matter to organize, especially in communities with one-sided economic structures. And 15 was considered too early an age for pupils to be stationed away from school. From 1962 onwards, accordingly, this pre-vocational training was transferred entirely to schools. The number of vocational lines was reduced and the main upshot was technical education divided into the following principal fields.

Line	*Dominant subjects*
General practical	Engineering trades Domestic work Office and retail skills
Technical–practical	Materials, tools and machinery Technical drawing and arithmetic Engineering trades
Commerce	Practical Swedish Commercial arithmetic and accounting General product science Typing Office and retail skills
Household line	Housing and interior design Economics and work organization Diet and cooking Textiles and sewing Child care and family studies

These vocational subjects, which as can be seen were of a fairly general and preparatory nature, were allotted 22 periods per week altogether in each line. In addition, all pupils also had to take Swedish, civics, geography, biology, physical education and either music or art.

Lines were freely chosen. Pupils—and their parents—decided whether they were to take an academic, general or pre-vocational line. From the very outset there was a heavy bias in favor of the academic lines. Between 1955 and 1968, the proportion of pupils opting for pre-vocational tracks fell from 55 to 20 percent of each year. There were some schools where pre-vocational lines frequently attracted so few pupils that only one or two of the four study programs mentioned above could actually be organized.

In 1968, at the instance of the National Board of Education, the Riksdag (i.e., the Swedish Parliament) passed legislation thoroughly revising the system of differentiation in compulsory schooling. As a result, basic school acquired a new curriculum which was gradually introduced from 1969 onwards. The lines of the terminal grade were now completely abolished. Grades 7–9 acquired time schedules and syllabi, 85 percent of which were common to all pupils. These included English as the first foreign language, which was now made compulsory for all pupils in Grades 3–9. For the remaining 15 percent of their time, pupils could choose one of the following elective subjects: one foreign language (German, French or—for immigrants—home language/mother tongue); economics; art; technology. Theoretical educational and vocational orientation as part of the teaching of civics continued on much the same lines and with much the same scope as before. Practical vocational orientation was reduced from three to two weeks and transferred from Grade 8 (where it had previously been included in preparation for the choice of line in Grade 9) to the terminal grade. Educational and vocational orientation (SYO), both theoretical and practical, included all pupils in the terminal grade (age 15–16), regardless of whether they had chosen a foreign language, economics, art or technology. The distribution of pupils between these four options remained virtually constant until 1980. Most of them, about 60 percent, opted for a second foreign language. Technology was taken by 20–25 percent (almost exclusively boys), economics by about 15 percent (mostly girls) and art by only a small percentage.

The compulsory school curriculum was revised once more in 1980. This involved little change as regards our question of the vocationalization of education. The division into lines remained abolished as in the 1969 curriculum. Elective subjects in Grades 7–9 retained the same proportions as before, i.e., roughly 15 percent of the time. A change was made here, however, in that apart from a second foreign language, which schools always have to offer, the elective subject can now be taken from any school subject field whatsoever. It is interesting to note that a new subject, technology, was made compulsory, with two periods per week in Grades 7–9 for both boys and girls. The curriculum says that this subject is intended to contribute towards the pupils' "everyday knowledge and skills." In addition, the term "practical working life orientation" or "work experience programs" (PRAO). At the same time its duration was increased from two or three weeks to a total of 10, which can now be spread out through all nine grades of compulsory school with no reference to the individual pupil's educational or vocational choices. These activities, then, have become more of a wide-ranging introduction, at the same time as their element of vocational preparation has grown less specific and more generalized. The curriculum has the following to say on the subject:

> Through work experience programs and the educational and vocational orientation provided by schools, pupils are to acquire a knowledge of different fields of activity, working environments, jobs and occupations, as well as the importance of work to human beings and society. They are to gain an insight into employer–employee relations at work, into the different attitudes and interests represented by the parties, a knowledge of laws and collective agreements, of the rights and obligations of employers and employees, of connections between these factors and of the preconditions of enterprise. They are to acquire a knowledge of the tasks of employment offices and the services which they provide for job-seekers and employees. At school, in their studies of various subjects, pupils are to be given opportunities of analyzing their experiences, so as to help them to arrive at mature educational and vocational decisions.
>
> Work experience, like other school activities, must counteract restrictions of educational and vocational choice imposed by traditional sexual stereotypes or status thinking or by social and cultural background. It must be aimed at promoting equality between the sexes in the family, at work and elsewhere in the community.
>
> Like other educational and vocational orientation in the broad sense, work experience concerns everybody at school. It must, in various forms, be included in school activities from the first to the final grade and in the transition from school to employment. A knowledge of working life and the labor market can be acquired both as a result of practical activity in school and outside it and through the teaching of the various school subjects. All job experience, including the pupils' own experience from their leisure and holidays, should be utilized in schools. Thus attention should also be paid to the working life of the school itself and to the duties and situation of the various personnel categories.
>
> In grade 9, educational and vocational orientation has to be intensified, partly by bringing the pupils into direct contact with various educational opportunities. In connection with upper secondary school admissions and outgoing educational and vocational orientation, schools must provide the special guidance needed by certain pupils in preparation for educational choice and contacts with the world of work.
>
> Direct contact with working life has to take the form of field trips and longer periods during which the pupils are actively occupied at workplaces. The local education authority has to decide the total duration of employment contacts (between 6 and 10 weeks) and their

distribution between school levels and individual grades. These decisions have to be prepared within the local committee for co-operation between schools and the employment sector.

Under work experience schemes, pupils at the senior level of compulsory school (ages 14–16) have to acquire at least one week's experience of each of the following three sectors of employment:

- Technology and manufacturing.
- Trade, communications, services, agriculture and forestry.
- Office work and administration, caring and teaching professions.

Schools must endeavor to ensure that pupils combine their choices in these three sectors in such a way that boys will acquire an insight into occupations where women predominate and girls into occupations where men predominate.

Rounding off our consideration of the ways in which Sweden has tried to achieve vocationalization within a school system which, on the whole, is one and the same for *all* pupils, we can draw the following conclusions:

(1) Ever since about 1950, vocationalization in basic schooling up to the age of 16 has had two main components, viz., an introduction to educational opportunities, occupations and the world of work, and pre-vocational education.

(2) The introduction of orientation in turn has been of two kinds, viz., theoretical orientation in the teaching of science and social subjects, and practical orientation at workplaces.

(3) Until 1969, pre-vocational education was organized within special vocational lines of the terminal grade (for 15- and 16-year-olds). Otherwise there were academic lines and lines of general studies.

(4) The lines pupils followed depended on the educational choices made by themselves and their parents. The proportion opting for vocational lines declined rapidly until 1969, when the system of lines in compulsory schools were abolished entirely.

(5) The vocational orientation and work experience aspects of school vocationalization have been expanded and deepened and have acquired a more generalized content, at the same time as pre-vocational studies focusing on individual occupations and groups of occupations have diminished or disappeared entirely.

(6) To begin with, the target group for vocationalization in schools comprised non-academic students. Over the years, however, it has expanded to include all compulsory school pupils, i.e., even those planning to pursue higher theoretical studies.

(7) The general consensus among teachers, parents and pupils, as well as politicians and administrators in education and the employment sector, now seems to be that the best form of vocationalization in compulsory school is a good general education and, within this framework, good work experience programs.

Vocationalization of Post-compulsory Education

The evolution of compulsory schooling as described above entailed the postponement and, subsequently, the complete abolition of the organizational differentiation of curricula and pupils. On completing the now fully integrated course of compulsory schooling, all pupils can go on to upper secondary school, where they are eligible for both academic and vocational study programs. Due to competition at this level, however, not all pupils gain admission to their study route of first preference.

Experience of the vocationalization of compulsory schooling during the experimental period of the 1950s and during the general implementation of the compulsory school system in the 1960s "trickled upwards" to a great extent into post-compulsory schooling. Vocational education, which in the course of the reform came to be located exclusively at post-compulsory level, was thoroughly transformed. Whereas previously it had comprised more than 800 different occupations and positions, specified with reference to earlier craft traditions, it was now divided into about a dozen wide-ranging and less specialized occupational groups geared to the demands of industrial society.

Before 1971 Sweden had had a large number of schools for the post-compulsory ages 16–19 years. These schools were grouped into three types:

- upper secondary schools (the domestic "gymnasium" for students aged 16–19);
- continuation school (two-year courses in social, economic and technical studies for students aged 16–18);
- vocational schools, schools of agriculture, schools of forestry, rural schools of home economics (from age 16 and onwards).

Legislation passed in 1968 by the Riksdag abolished these schools as three distinct types of school with separate organizations and objectives. They were replaced by the single integrated upper secondary school.

This new school became a natural continuation of the compulsory comprehensive school, which the students completed at the age of 16. The integrated upper secondary school offered 25 lines of study, to be pursued for either two or three years. In technical studies there was also a four-year line. In addition to these lines there were a number of special vocational courses of varying duration.

The range of lines and special courses now varies from district to district. The directives issued for planning work on the upper secondary school system laid down that efforts should be made to include the majority of study alternatives in every upper secondary school area, but it would not be possible to provide the full range everywhere.

Politics Behind the Integration of General and Vocational Education

The partition of general and vocational education before 1971 was both a reflection and a cause of certain social attitudes. The distinction was, and had always been, an artificial one. Many people have credited academic subjects with a superior status to the practical ones. It was hoped that the introduction of a single school would eliminate or at least reduce the social connections attached to different subjects and make them equally attractive. Only then, it was said, would it be possible for the individual student to choose a line of studies on the basis of his or her wishes, interests and aptitudes.

The different sectors of upper secondary education had been separately housed. The physical segregation of the academic and the practical studies had produced one-sided groups of students bearing little or no resemblance to the social realities of subsequent working life. This physical segregation has since 1971 been gradually eliminated or diminished.

These *social reasons* for integrating vocational and academic education at upper secondary level coincided with other considerations. The integrated upper secondary school was also aimed at making it easier to deploy resources of staff and equipment more effectively. Coordination would facilitate a better range of teaching posts, so that more qualified teachers would be available for more subjects and students could be taught by the teacher best qualified for the work in hand. This meant that there were also *educational reasons* for integration. And education would make it easier for studies to be conducted on the best premises for each subject.

To the social and educational reasons there were also added *financial* ones. Integration should give economic advantages, above all at municipal levels. Not only would it reduce administrative costs to a certain extent, it would also make for a more competitive utilization of resources such as expensive special facilities and technical equipment.

The change in 1971 also aimed at a substantial widening of the very *concept of upper secondary education*. This education, the Riksdag said, should no longer be restricted to general studies or academic studies serving to prepare students for further education at universities and colleges. It should also include technical and vocational education. The boundary between theoretical and practical education was no longer accepted. The educational decisions of the individual student, it was said, should be less binding and final than they had hitherto been.

These reasons for an integration of school and world of work, social as well as educational and financial, were all presented in a series of reports by governmental *ad hoc* committees during the 1960s (SOU 1962:30, 1963:42, 1963:50 and 1966:3, see References). They were all followed up by governmental proposals and decisions by the Riksdag (proposals 1962:54 1964:171, 1968:129 and 1968:140, see References). It should be noted that all these proposals and decisions were part of a larger program for the introduction of an over-arching social welfare system, in which education, general as well as vocational, was an integrated part (Marklund and Bergendal, 1979: Marklund, 1980: Boucher, 1982). (Most documents about this, including the national curricular guidelines for vocational education, integration of general and vocational education and also integration of school and world of work, so far exist only in Swedish).

Upper secondary studies can from 1971 be grouped into three main sectors: a first sector for arts and social studies, a second for economic studies and a third for technical and scientific studies. The 25 lines of the upper secondary school are divided as follows between the various sectors:

- *Arts and social study routes* comprise the following: two-year domestic line, two-year nursing line, two-year social service line, two-year music line, two-year social line, three-year arts line and three-year social science line.
- *Economic study routes* comprise the following: two-year distribution and clerical line, two-year economics line and three-year economics line.
- *Technical and scientific study routes* comprise the following: two-year lines for clothing manufacturing, food manufacturing, workshop techniques, motor engineering, woodwork, building and construction, electro-telecommunications, process engineering, forestry, agriculture, gardening, a two-year maintenance and repair line, a two-year technical line, a three-year science line and a four-year technology line.

It should be noted that within these three sectors there are both academic and general–vocational lines. Seventeen of the 25 lines are mainly vocational or pre-vocational, while the remaining eight have a general or academic outline.

It has to be admitted that this structure of simplified vocational education in a restricted number of study lines and this grouping of vocational as well as academic studies in upper secondary school were bought at the price of a large number of specialized vocational courses within the framework of upper secondary school. The *specialized courses* became more than 400. They do not form part of any line. The duration of these courses varies from 10 weeks to three years.

Most specialized courses follow on directly from comprehensive school. Others, known as higher specialized courses, must be preceded by at least two years of upper secondary schooling or comparable studies.

The students in integrated upper secondary school attending these special courses and higher specialized courses have decreased in number since this type of school was introduced in 1971. They now make up about 5 percent of the student population at this level.

The New Deal in Vocational Education—Recent Developments

With the introduction of the integrated upper secondary school, vocational education was given a new content and organization. The salient points of the new organization for vocational education were as follows:

- All lines replacing vocational schools became of two years' duration. A number of special courses were also provided.
- Students following the vocational lines were given a broader general education than previously. Specialization proceeded successively.
- More scope was given to the so-called general subjects.

Specialization was effected gradually by means of sub-alternatives. This meant that more definite decisions by the students about their course studies could be taken at a later stage. It also meant that they could be given a more all-round education making it easier for them to adjust to changes in the labor market.

The new vocational education was based on the so-called *block principle*, whereby similar occupations are merged into larger vocational sectors. The basic block, i.e., the initial course of studies, contained items common to the entire sector. Studies were then gradually specialized in keeping with the character of the various occupations.

One important innovation was the great increase in the study of so-called *general subjects* included in vocational education. Swedish, labor market orientation and physical education were compulsory for all lines. Students also had to choose at least one of several optional extra subjects of a general character. These were English, German, French, civics, religious knowlege, psychology, mathematics, domestic science, music or art. A student could also dispense with one vocational subject in order to study subjects belonging to another line within the upper secondary school. This form of substitution, which might not comprise more than 12 periods per week, was generally confined to the second year.

Labor market orientation was a new subject included in all vocational lines. This subject was designed to provide students with a general background to their subsequent careers, e.g., through information on the labor market and working life. Students were also introduced to social economic affairs, trade unions and other labor market organizations, industrial safety, industrial democracy, personnel welfare and other matters concerning joint determination and cooperation.

At present the integrated upper secondary school can take all students finishing their compulsory education at 16. And the number of students attending upper secondary school now corresponds to about 90 percent of the year group.

This means that the frequency of upper secondary studies has increased enormously during recent years. It more than doubled between 1971 and 1980. The vocational lines have become more attractive than before. One reason for this change is that the entrance requirements to universities and other kinds of higher studies were changed in 1977. It is no longer necessary to have a traditional three-year academic upper secondary line to go to university. A two-year upper secondary course is sufficient, provided that this course includes Swedish and English. This confers *general* eligibility for higher studies, which is enough for the majority of university courses. In certain kinds of higher studies, i.e., to become a teacher or a doctor, it is necessary to have also a set of *special* admission qualifications usually full academic courses from upper secondary school.

According to follow-up studies during 1979–1983 (so far only reported in Swedish) more than 90 percent of the students fulfilling an upper-secondary vocational course had a job four years after ending their secondary vocational courses. And three quarters of them had got jobs in a working area related to their training. Unemployment for 20-year-old men and women with no or interrupted post-compulsory studies was twice as high.

The fear, very often expressed when the integrated upper secondary school started, that the quality of vocational education might deteriorate, is hardly heard nowadays. It has been found, however, that the integrated upper secondary school is a fairly expensive kind of school. One reason for this is the investment in school buildings of a specialized kind, investments in machines, learning materials and equipment. Another reason is the cost of teaching staff. The student/teacher ratio is 12 for the Swedish upper secondary school as a whole. As a rule, vocational lines have smaller classes than academic lines. In most upper secondary vocational courses the student maximum is 16. With 17 or more students there are organized two classes, with 33 three classes, etc. The reasons for these low figures are that the training in these lines of study are seen as in need of a more individualized teacher guidance than general and academic training on the same age level.

It is interesting to see how the distribution of pupils between different lines has developed since 1971. The two-year vocational lines have risen steeply in popularity and scope. During the 10-year period ending in 1981, this vocational education increased its share of the school population from 19 to 37 percent. Specialized short-cycle courses moved in the opposite direction, from 39 to 27 percent. (Since they are mostly shorter than the vocational lines, these courses only account for about 5 percent of the upper secondary school population altogether.) The traditional university and college entrance academic lines did not change appreciably during the same period. The number of applicants for the two-year vocational lines showed the heaviest increase. The vocational lines for food manufacturing, clothing manufacturing, woodwork, electro-telecommunications engineering, caring professions, and agriculture and forestry have attracted more applicants per place than the theoretical university entrance lines. This is a point which is frequently overlooked in the debate on the equalizing effects of the new school: two-year vocational education within the integrated upper secondary school has risen in status.

The amalgamation, from 1971 onwards, of vocational education with general academic education at upper secondary level to form a single school was a direct consequence of the underlying reform of basic schooling. Experience of the integrated upper secondary school has on the whole been encouraging, but changes have been found necessary in a number of respects. Widespread experimental schemes of work experience are now being conducted in the general and academic lines, during the two or three years of their duration. Work experience can total up to eight weeks per student, divided into fortnightly periods. Another experimental scheme involves the coordination of studies in these lines with corresponding courses of municipal adult education.

It is also very interesting to note the recommendation made by a Government Commission for the prolongation of two-year vocational lines of study to three years. Only a minor portion of the third year would be spent at school, the greater part being devoted to work experience outside.

Another Government Commission has recommended that university entrance qualifications for applicants from non-academic lines be tightened up so as to stipulate a certain minimum level of achievement in academic subjects as a condition of formal eligibility.

Recurrent Education and Life-long Learning

The changes which took place in Swedish education during the 1960s principally entailed a prolongation of continuous youth education, an augmentation of its general components and a postponement of specialization and vocationalization. In the meantime, adult education, in its various forms, developed into a necessary supplement to youth education. Discussions of educational policy during the 1970s were mostly concerned with the achievement, with due regard to the needs of both individual and community, of a good balance between educational inputs at different stages of the life-cycle. A deliberate policy has evolved of alternating between periods of education and periods of employment or other activity. In 1975 the Riksdag declared that educational planning as a whole should be based on the principle of recurrent education, thereby renouncing the idea that education ought preferably to be concentrated within a continuous period during childhood and adolescence, followed by uninterrupted economic activity right up to retirement.

There are several indications of an emergent pattern of recurrent education. Of the 90 percent students per year going on to upper secondary school from compulsory school, many have an intermission of one or more years in between. This now applies to about 15 of the 90 percent. An equal number suspend their studies for a year or so for practical employment. In other words, they alternate in this way between education and employment of their own volition. There is now reason to support this kind of development through various measures of educational and employment policy.

National and municipal adult education has provided additional opportunities of alternating between or otherwise combining education and employment. This adult education now has a larger student population than upper secondary schools, although with a shorter duration of studies per individual. The study circle activities organized by the adult education associations attract almost two million people annually, which is a very large number of an entire national population of just over eight million. Circle studies, admittedly, are confined to a few dozen hours and are to some extent concerned with arts and hobby subjects, but they still give many people an opportunity of combining gainful employment with education.

Similar tendencies are to be observed in the popular educational activities of folk high schools. The number of full-time students at these schools has not increased during the past ten years, but the number taking short-cycle courses has risen since 1970 from about 16,000 to almost 200,000 per annum. Similar activities occur in the form of small package courses arranged by companies and organizations at training and conference centers. These activities too have expanded appreciably. Arrangements of these kinds can be described as building bricks in a growing system of recurrent education.

Developments at the universities since 1970 have resulted in about half the students enrolling every year being 25 or older, which means that in one way or another they have alternated between education and gainful employment. The number of part-time students at the universities, i.e., students who as a rule probably combine or alternate between education and employment, has increased from a mere 12 percent in 1970 to more than 30 percent in 1987. It has also become common for students to express a preference for individual courses and subjects, instead of reading for a full degree. The proportion studying on this basis has risen since 1970 from about 10 percent to 40 percent of annual enrolments.

The new university entrance regulations introduced in 1977 make adults with job experience eligible for higher education. Gainful employment has a credential value in competition for popular studies. Generally speaking, this has led to appreciable changes in the age, previous knowledge and experience of students enrolling for higher studies. In time, the pattern of recurrent education which is now evolving may transform not only recruitment for higher studies but also the content of the studies themselves and perhaps also patterns of recruitment in the employment sector.

One of the purposes of recurrent education is to bring about a more vigorous interchange between the employment sector and education. It should be possible for upper secondary schooling and higher education to build increasingly on the students' own practical experience. Theoretical studies can be made to focus more on the analysis of such experience. It is clear that with developments moving in this direction, experience from adult education will have an essential bearing on teaching in both upper secondary school and higher education. The boundaries between adult education and regular post-compulsory education are becoming less and less rigid, at the same time as the need for a wide variety of educational inputs remains and, if anything, is growing.

Thus the development of the employment sector will do a great deal to determine the future structure and content of education. Technical progress may lead to a polarization of the labor market, with a widening gulf between skilled and unskilled jobs. The implications this holds for the organization of work and the vocational preparation provided by schools are a fundamental question. Efforts to improve the occupational environment and to augment co-determination at work will also involve special demands on education.

Schools are being reformed and changed all the time, not least in response to the changes undergone by working life. But changes in schools are still being made in disturbing isolation. Schools are being adjusted as far as possible to a world of work which "is just there." The same goes for working life and the labor market. Some adjustments, it is true, are being made in relation to schools, but on the whole working life and the labor market are planned as if schools "were just there," standing immobile to one side. The simple fact—a truism but an increasingly obtrusive one—is that schools and employment cannot be kept in watertight compartments. Any change in one of them is bound to affect the other. Schools and education are investigated and reformed essentially in a vacuum, and the same goes for work and employment. They are less often treated conjointly. Schools need to be planned more with scope for work. Similarly, the world of work will have to be organized more consistently and broadly than at present with scope for students from the age of 16 and upwards.

One of the main questions here is whether a new system of recurrent education is to be allowed to develop freely or whether it must be made subject to some form of political influence. Free development governed by the market mechanisms can, if the worst comes to the worst, result in recurrent education, based on alternation between employment and education, becoming a new mechanism of social segregation and rejection, i.e., contrary to the egalitarian education and social policies which have been characterized developments in Sweden over the past 40 years. The choice of development in this form of vocationalization of education rests with everybody, viz., individual and society, national and local authorities, public authorities and organizations, politicians, administrators and researchers. It is, moreover, to be hoped that analyses and investigations will indicate how persons of different ages can share what appears to be an insufficient pool of employment and how older persons can tutor younger ones.

In this way the vocationalization of education will acquire a slightly different meaning from what is generally termed vocational training. There is a danger involved in training large social groups of young persons at an early stage for limited positions in industry. In modern industrial society, less than 10 percent of the work force is directly productive. The large categories of skilled workers today are employed in public and private services of a general kind, in hospitals, child care, care of the elderly, teaching, distributive trades, communications, information, administration and suchlike fields. To these are added research, performing and other arts, leisure activities, entertainment and a great many other things which today we regard as both good and necessary. Preparations for employment in all these things also constitute vocationalization, but they must be given to the persons concerned through both generalized and vocationalized education, and this can best be provided through an integration of school learning and everyday work.

References

Boucher, L. (1982) *Tradition and change in Swedish education*. Oxford: Pergamon Press.

Marklund, S. (1980) The role of central government in educational development in Sweden. In E. Hoyle, and J. Megarry (Eds.), *World yearbook of education 1980: Professional development of teachers*. London: Kogan Page.

Marklund, S. and Bergendal, G. (1979) *Trends in Swedish educational policy*. Stockholm: The Swedish Institute.

Swedish *Ad Hoc* Governmental Committee Reports: SOU 1961:30 ("Compulsory Education"); SOU 1963:42 ("A New Gymnasium"); SOU 1963:50 ("Continuation Schools"); SOU 1966:3 ("Vocational Education").

Swedish Governmental Proposals to the Riksdag: Prop. 1962:54 ("Basic School"); Prop. 1964:171 ("The New Gymnasium"); Prop. 1968:129 ("Revised Basic School"); Prop. 1968:140 ("Integrated Upper Secondary School").

Swedish National Curricular Guidelines: Grundskolan ("Basic School") 1962, 1969 and 1980; Gymnasieskolan ("Integrated Gymnasium") 1971.

Swedish School Law (1962) Stockholm: SFS 1962:319.

Swedish School Statutes. Stockholm: SFS 1962:439 and 1971:235.

CHAPTER 11

Recent Soviet Vocationalization Policies

FELICITY O'DELL

Cambridge Eurocentre

VOCATIONALIZATION has been an important element of Soviet education from the very beginning. The very first Soviet schools were faced with the problem of how to educate people with the necessary skills to rebuild the economy after the ravages of both World War I and the Civil War. To this end, people had not only to be trained in practical skills but Soviet schools had also to engage in considerable social and moral education so that school-leavers had the discipline and the motivation to work hard for the Soviet cause.

An emphasis on the practical rather than the theoretical has thus, from the start, been at the center of Soviet educational programs. There has never been any question of practical work being only for the less academic children.

Throughout the Soviet period, there have been a number of educational reforms, yet the problem of training for work has remained central. Each reform—including the most recent one in 1984—has tried simply to improve on the ways in which people are prepared for work in Soviet society.

One question often raised by educational reformers since 1917 has been that of *where* training for work should take place. Should schoolchildren learn their practical skills on an actual farm or in a real factory? Should school-leavers get their training for their chosen specialism in a vocational school or on the job? Some argue that the youngster can only really learn how to work from experiencing work on the shopfloor, holding real tools and producing real goods. Others say that this hinders the work of factories and does not give young people the theoretical foundation they need for their training. At different times during the Soviet period the question of where to train has been answered differently.

The whole of Soviet ideology, however, is based on equality of opportunity for all regardless of sex, race or social background. Children must, therefore, not seem to be separated for vocational training at too early an age nor must their choice of one type of training appear to deprive them of the chance to transfer to another type later on.

Another significant factor to bear in mind when considering vocationalization in the USSR is the fact that there is a continuing demand for workers of most types. Some might explain this as being caused by the inefficient organization of work, but the fact remains that there is no shortage of jobs. As a result, the problems faced by Soviet society and Soviet schools are fundamentally very different from those being faced by Western societies and schools at the moment.

In this chapter I shall examine the ways in which the Soviet system attempts to deal with the sometimes conflicting problems of efficient vocationalization and provision of equal opportunity. The particular problems which the 1984 reform has addressed itself to will be considered. Finally, I shall look at remaining problems relating to the question of vocational education in the USSR.

Basic Structure of Soviet Vocational Training

The structure of Soviet vocational training, as described below, existed before the 1984 reform and none of the basic points made below has been changed by the reform.

Vocational training begins for the Soviet child from the very first day s/he enters a kindergarten or school. From the first class of the general school, the Soviet child has a couple of lessons a week which are called *"trud"* (labor). These continue right through his or her school career and, like all subjects in the Soviet curriculum, are compulsory for all children. Unlike other subjects in the Soviet curriculum, the labor-training syllabus is not identical throughout the USSR for all children. Much of the work done is related to the particular economic needs of the area where the school is situated.

There are three main components of the labor lessons: (a) practical skills; (b) socialization for work and (c) vocational guidance. The practical skills a child is taught enable him or her to do work with the hands, to hold and use tools, to operate machinery. Obviously, what is taught increases in complexity with the children's age. Exactly what kinds of tools and machinery the child learns to work with varies, particularly as the child gets older. While all children—boys and girls—should learn the basics of woodwork and metalwork, older children may specialize according to their own interests or the facilities available in their area. There is also a tendency for boys to specialize later in woodwork and metalwork and girls in sewing and other traditionally female skills.

As the children get older, they frequently go outside the school for their labor lessons. They may go to a study workshop set up at a local factory or they may go to an "inter-school production combine," a large building used by all the schools in the area and incorporating workshops of a range of different types. An important part of the practical skills training received by schoolchildren is a month's practical work which all children have to do in the ninth year of the secondary school. In this month children engage in full-time work on production or on the farm. This gives all children some taste of what working life is like and it is felt to have considerable moral as well as practical benefits.

The socialization component of labor lessons is considered to be of no less importance than the practical side. There are two main strands to this part of the program. Firstly, and more abstractly, pupils are trained in what are felt to be the correct Soviet attitudes towards work. They are, for example, encouraged to see their own personal fulfilment as being through work; they are trained to respect their own work and that of other people; they are told to see all jobs as being equal while at the same time being encouraged to study hard so as to be able to contribute more to the working life of the Motherland. Secondly, and more practically, pupils are trained in the habits and attitudes which will help them to be efficient Soviet workers in the future. They are encouraged, for example, to be disciplined and to work as part of a team.

The third component of the labor lesson relates to vocational guidance. This is different in nature from vocational guidance in the West. As here, it is concerned with pupils choosing jobs. In the West, the aim, however, is to analyze the interests and abilities of the child in question and then to select a job which seems to fit that individual. In the Soviet Union, on the other hand, the starting-point is an analysis of the jobs where workers are required. The role of vocational guidance is then to guide schoolchildren into those jobs where they are most needed. This is often a matter of encouraging children to join industries local to their area or to go into fields where the demand for workers exceeds supply. Much of the vocational guidance program in the school centers around talks and visits organized by local parents and workers. Vocational guidance is probably the area of labor training which comes in for most criticism.

The three elements of the labor lesson that we have considered above are reinforced in other lessons given in the Soviet school. Science lessons, for example, purport to stress the practical applications of any theoretical points taught. History lessons deal with working conditions and emphasize the importance of workers' movements. Geography lessons devote far more time to economic geography than to physical geography. The reading syllabus includes, for instance, more poems extolling the joys of work than odes to the beauties of nature.

Similarly, the extra-curricular activities provided for the Soviet child include many that have a direct relevance to work. In clubs like the Young Technicians' Club and in activities organized by the youth movements, youngsters can develop practical skills further and they also have the same work ethic reinforced.

The education of all Soviet children is, with minor exceptions, identical until the end of the eighth class. School is compulsory until the end of the tenth class. After the eighth class, there are two possibilities.

(1) The pupil may stay on at the general secondary school. After this, he or she may (a) do a course in a PTU (a vocational trade school); (b) go on to higher education or (c) go straight to work, receiving training for this on the job.

(2) The pupil may leave school and go to an SPTU (a secondary vocational trade school). In this school pupils not only complete their secondary schooling, following the same syllabus as that used in the general secondary school but also get a qualification in a particular trade.

Throughout the 1970s the trend was to discourage pupils from going straight to work without any kind of institutionalized job training. More and more PTUs of different kinds were constructed and larger numbers of young workers are now receiving their initial job training in them. Institutionalized job training is favored for a number of reasons, the main one being the nature of the scientific–technical revolution. It is felt that it is not enough for people today just to learn the specific skills necessary for one particular job. Job requirements are changing so fast that workers need to be very flexible. Most people will, it is felt, have several different specialisms in the course of their working lives. The vocational trade schools can make this easier both for industry and for future workers by giving basic theoretical technical courses which will help workers to adapt to changing conditions in the future.

Among vocational schools, SPTUs have an especial significance. One reason for the importance of SPTUs is the fact that specialist job training is begun at the age of 15, a relatively early age. However, general schooling is carried on at the same time so that paths to higher education are not, theoretically, blocked off for children who opt to get a practical qualification at the earliest opportunity.

The provision of alternative routes to higher education is an important factor in Soviet education. Universities and other higher educational institutions have evening and correspondence departments which have almost as many students as the day departments and these are of particular benefit to people who started working straight after school or vocational school. For those who have been away from study for a long time, preparatory departments have been set up at a number of higher educational institutions. These retrain people in study habits for a year before they start a full higher education course. Workplaces are encouraged to support their workers who wish to follow a belated course of higher education. In a number of ways, then, the Soviet educational system provides for people who decide to return to higher study after having worked. These provisions are the major way whereby equality of opportunity is seen to be encouraged by the Soviet educational system.

Having looked above at the basic structure of vocational training in the Soviet Union, let us now turn our attention to certain problems within that system which have been highlighted by the Soviet press. As was pointed out above, vocational training can be seen as the pivot of the 1984 Soviet education reform. What are the problems which Soviet vocational education must urgently address itself to? Most of the measures proposed by the reform are aimed primarily at producing more efficient workers for the future, though some focus on socialization aspects of training for work and some deal with the more practical skills felt to be required by the socialist society of the future.

Problems in Vocational Education

What are felt to be the particular problems for Soviet society in the future? In a recent speech Gorbachev said that the Soviet Union is going through a critical period in its current need to intensify production. Intensification, he said, is as revolutionary and as all-consuming a process for the present day as industrialization was in the past. Of prime importance in the move for intensification is the preparation of workers, a preparation which begins in the schools and is carried further by PTUs and higher educational institutions.[1] A recent article in *Izvestiya* neatly sums up the significance attributed to schools when it states that what is done in the kindergarten sandpit today will have its effect on the factory shopfloor in the future.[2] It is significant that the Minister of Education who took office in 1985 is an engineer by training.

In the last few years the Soviet press has highlighted a number of problems relating to the training of citizens for work. These criticisms fall into five main categories. First, the training given frequently does not produce the kind of workers desired in that they do not have the creativity or knowledge of modern technology necessary for maximizing production in a modern society.

Second, the moral aspect of labor training is also not always satisfactory as many workers do not have the committed attitudes to their work that the authorities would like. It has been felt for some time that the best way to train workers who are not only creative and knowledgeable but also committed is through institutional training rather than totally at the factory or on the farm.

Training vocational skills in PTUs has also given rise to a third set of problems, however. Since the early 1970s an increasing number of PTUs and SPTUs has been set up, but the prestige of these is still not as high as is wished. Part of the problem here results from the large number of ministries which have been involved in vocational education and from the differing standards of the courses which they provide. It is felt, moreover, that the

[1] Zhivoe tvorchestvo naroda. *Izvestiya*, 11 Dec. 1984.
[2] Zastavit "vospityvat"? *Izvestiya*, 24 Dec. 1984.

level of academic education given by many PTUs is lower than that given by general secondary schools. The extent to which courses actually give students practical experience under realistic conditions also varies and is not always adequate.

Fourth, the prestige of particular types of work, most notably agricultural labor, is not high. This is increasingly viewed with concern by the Soviet press as the performance of Soviet agriculture is becoming disturbingly unsatisfactory.

A final area which has regularly undergone criticism in the Soviet press is vocational guidance work. This has been frequently criticized for being both qualitatively and quantitatively unsatisfactory.

The problems outlined above are those which one would have expected the reform to try to solve.[1] To what extent and in what ways has it done so? How far can it expect to be successful in achieving its aims? In the next section we will attempt to answer these questions.

The Reform

Some of the changes in the reform are concerned primarily with structure and some concentrate on the content of vocational training.

Structural Changes

A fundamental principle of the reform is that young people should receive their basic labor training from professional instructors in schools or colleges rather than from older workers directly on the job. The trend of the 1970s is thus continued.

There is to be some re-organization of the structure of schools and colleges providing labor training. The trend is towards simplification. PTUs are eventually to be all of one type—they are all to become SPTUs or colleges which give both the last two years of a general secondary education and a vocational training. These SPTUs will in addition have courses for those who have already completed their secondary schooling as well as for those who have not. They will also have courses for the re-training of older workers. Day, evening and correspondence students may all be catered for by the SPTU.

The number of pupils who leave the general secondary school after the eighth class to attend a SPTU is to be increased. It is felt that the current intake should eventually be doubled.

SPTUs are to be established at any enterprise where there are more than 2000 workers. To train workers for enterprises with fewer personnel,

[1] For a more detailed discussion of these problems see the chapter on vocational education in the USSR by F. O'Dell in J. J. Tomiak (Ed.), *Soviet education in the 1980s*, London: Croom Helm, 1983.

colleges will coordinate the needs of enterprises in the same branch of industry. In rural areas they are to be in each administrative region.

Ministerial control is also to be simplified. At present PTUs are under the aegis of a range of ministries. Over the period 1984 to 1988 all ministries involved are expected to pass over control of their vocational colleges to the State Committee on Vocational and Technical Education. The aim is more efficient coordination of the needs of society for particular types of worker with the vocational courses provided and with the student intakes allowed. It is hoped to systematize the content and attestation of courses.

In 1985–1986 the State Committee on Vocational and Technical Education together with the education ministries was to prepare a list of the jobs for which SPTUs should provide courses. In cooperation with the industrial ministries involved, the State Committee will then work until 1987 on drawing up suitable curricula and syllabi for vocational courses.

Particular importance is to be given to the development of agricultural SPTUs. As one measure to improve the standards and prestige of such colleges, teachers are to be given material incentives to take up jobs in rural colleges. Graduates from these colleges may be given an allowance to help them set up a home if they decide to work on the land in their specialism. If they leave within a short time they will have to return the money.

Changes in Content of Vocational Training

It is re-emphasized in the reform that labor training is not mere instruction in practical skills; it is perhaps even more importantly a matter of inculcating the desired attitudes towards both work and society. Official articles on the reform deal with this before they go on to describe more practical aspects of the proposals. Thus it is stated that each young worker of the future must be a patriot, an internationalist, a collectivist and s/he must uphold high standards both at work and in everyday life.

The need to provide young people with up-to-date labor knowledge and skills is emphasized. Creativity in work and the ability to make use of the new technology are now seen as vital characteristics of the future worker. The central press has recently pointed out that it is not enough today to know the three Rs, it is also necessary to be familiar with electronics.[1]

General secondary education is recognized as having an important role to play in the overall process of labor training. To this end teaching of science subjects is to be improved and their practical relevance is to be emphasized. Optional and extra-curricular activities with a practical application are to be encouraged. Vocational guidance work with pupils is to be improved.

One way in which it is hoped that some of these problems may be resolved is by attaching secondary schools to a base enterprise. This means that each school has very close links with either a factory or farm in its local area.

[1] Gorizonty elektroniki. *Izvestiya*, 1 Dec. 1984.

These enterprises share with the school the responsibility for labor training.

Where exactly do the responsibilities of the base enterprise lie? The reform re-emphasizes that labor training tasks for the first to the seventh classes are concerned with general labor skills of a polytechnical character. From the eighth class on they concentrate on preparation for the mass work specialisms. Training may be carried out in school, on production or at inter-school production combines. It is now, however, the responsibility of the base enterprise, no matter where training takes place, to keep equipment used for training up-to-date and in good repair, to provide specialist clothing and, most importantly, to enlist experienced workers as tutors. The enterprise also pays for work done and assesses children's skills.

Although most practical training is to be based in schools or colleges, the need for pupils to learn production skills in a real environment is acknowledged and so base enterprises are to give pupils real tasks to complete under the guidance of experienced workers and tutors. Special training workshops are to be set up at base enterprises so that youngsters can do some of their work practice there. Enterprise administrators must take responsibility for the level of production training that goes on within their place of work.

Pupils gaining work experience at an enterprise do not count as workers as far as the firm is concerned but they must be paid at least half of what their work earns them. Base enterprises must also help to finance buildings and equipment required by their SPTU.

What are the responsibilities of the school towards its base enterprise? The school has not only to organize the pedagogical side of vocational training but also to further the comfort and attractiveness of the base enterprise; it organizes concerts, provides pot plants, paints rest areas and helps with pre-school facilities, for example. The involvement of the pupils in many of these tasks is felt not only to be of benefit to the base enterprise but also to have an important socializing role for the children themselves.[1]

The need to improve the caliber of teachers is not ignored. Increases in pay for teachers and all workers involved in education are being introduced to encourage people to go into this profession.[2] Incentives and training are to be given in particular to experienced workers who decide to become instructors in schools or colleges.

All organizations which have any connection with vocational training are called on to play their part in improving the system. The Academy of Pedagogical Sciences is to do research into problems of vocational instruction. Trade unions are to help with proposals. The Komsomol is to be involved in work carried out in the schools and base enterprises. The Party is to pay attention to raising the prestige of vocational training as well as to general party work within the SPTUs. The State Committee on Vocational

[1] Bazovoe predpriyatie i shkola. *Izvestiya*, 12 Oct. 1984.
[2] Osnovnye napravleniya ekonomicheskogo i sotsial'nogo razvitiya SSSR na 1986–1990 gody i do perioda do dvukhtysachego goda. *Izvestiya*, 9 Mar. 1986.

and Technical Education is to work out a system of control over the work carried out by the colleges and the base enterprises. Facilities, training and administration are to be regularly checked and improved.

The aims of the 1984 education reform have been re-emphasized by the 27th Party Congress held in February 1986.[1] As all the measures proposed by the reform show, the proposals relating to vocational education are extremely thorough. They aim both to extend the network of institutional vocational education and also to improve its standards and prestige by simplification of the structure and by coordination and improvement of its aims and curricula.

Problems of the Future?

Certain of the areas of the reform mentioned above seem bound to give rise to difficulties and can already be seen to be doing so. The rhetoric is grand but unfortunately the practice does not, perhaps cannot, always live up to it. The first problem is the question of automation. Automation is being encouraged at the factory; it is said that it can already double or treble productivity. It is also felt that automation can encourage creativity among the work-force. In the last five year plan more than a hundred models of robot were produced and thousands of these are already in use in factories.[2]

In a recent speech, Gorbachev has again stressed the importance of a transformation of the economy, emphasizing the need for automation, computerization and robotization. He said that by the year 2000 the amount of manual work being done would decrease by 15-20 percent. In connection with this he noted the need to have a constant system of education, enabling pupils and workers at all ages and levels to train and retrain to fit the ever-changing needs of modern society. The contemporary education reform is just one step towards this end but it cannot do everything that will be necessary.[3]

Familiarization with electronics is being verbally encouraged for young people. Schools are urged to start introducing children to computers—through games—at the earliest possible age. Even home computers are essential in today's world, writes *Literaturnaya gazeta*. Both the schoolchild and the minister must have access to one in the future. They are invaluable for the future engineer, draughtsman and journalist. From an early school level microcomputers can both amuse and instruct. Simulation games can give the child an impression of what it's like to drive a car or a plane, for example. Working with a computer, it is claimed, can help the child to understand how his or her own mind works and can train pupils to do their own work in a more systematic, and therefore, creative way.[4]

Soviet educationalists have frequently made the point that working with

[1] See note 6.   [2] See note 4.   [3] Doklad M. S. Gorbacheva. *Izvestiya*, 26 Feb. 1986.
[4] Chelovek, EVM i obshchestvo. *Literaturnaya gazeta*, 30 Jan. 1985.

computers will help develop pupils' creativity. It is arguable whether flourishing creativity is in fact a by-product of using computers. Many Western teachers with experience of working with computers in education feel that they encourage a particular type of thinking rather than an originality of approach.

Recent exhibitions in the Soviet Union of Western computer technology bear witness to a general interest in computers, as does the purchase in 1984 of a small number of BBC "B" microcomputers, yet the central press criticizes the Ministry of Education for not paying enough attention to the practical aspects of training to work with computers; the computer, *"Shkol'nitsa"* ("schoolgirl"), which is planned to be usable with schoolchildren of all ages, is still only in an experimental form. Software, as usual, lags even further behind hardware in its development.

Not only general secondary schools but also PTUs are in no way prepared for tomorrow's automation, more specifically for the predicted boom in industrial robots. At the level of higher education too, specialists are said to be trained using out-of-date equipment. As a result, specialists at all levels are felt to have a fear of tomorrow's machines; their earlier training is felt to be a hindrance rather than a help in coming to terms with the new technology. When it happens, re-training is so slow that many are afraid that the new equipment which is coming into the factories will never in the end be properly used.[1]

The problem of automation is one that is unlikely to be solved quickly in the Soviet Union. The reasons for problems in this area are not hard to find in that there seems to be a certain conflict of interests here between what is economically and what is politically desirable. *Literaturnaya gazeta* is right to say that computers are invaluable for journalists but the ease of writing enabled by word processors has implications that are more likely to excite the producers of *samizdat* than the political authorities. Similarly, the true—and fictional—stories which have circulated in the West of schoolchildren finding their way into police and military files will certainly have encouraged the political authorities to view home computers with a certain apprehension.

Another basic problem which the reform seems unlikely to solve fully is the bureaucratic one. Large organizations—and the USSR *par excellence*—seem to tend towards an excess of paperwork and ill-thought-out controls. The advantages of the simplification of the system of vocational training are clear but the resulting centralization of control is not likely to rid the system of bureaucratic problems.

There are already press reports of young and talented teachers who leave their jobs because all the paperwork they have to do does not allow them the freedom to teach in the way that they would like.[2] Izvestiya similarly reports how a parent was invited to contribute a session about his job for a school

[1] See note 4.   [2] Opyat' dvoika. *Izvestiya*, 17 Oct. 1984.

evening activity. He wanted to accept but requested that he do it the following week because he felt he needed more time to prepare adequately. The school told him that that would be no good because it was just that one particular week that the theme was vocational guidance and that next week they would have a different topic![1]

Other examples concern formal inspections of educational institutions; specialist lecturers complain that their work is constantly being inspected by people who know nothing of their field.[2] The factory, Chaika, in Moscow is famous in that it is organized and staffed almost completely by schoolchildren. It makes a profit of millions of roubles but the director of the factory is said to spend almost all of his time undergoing either pedagogical or economic inspections.[3]

Nervousness about taking responsibility for unusual decisions is also a feature of large bureaucracies and this has resulted in, for example, the director of an experimental school in Novosibirsk losing his job three times for being innovative in the spirit of the reform but in an original way.[4] He has similarly been repeatedly reinstated but at undoubted cost.

Centralized regulations lead to abuse in all sorts of areas. Optional courses are set up at schools because the Ministry says they are necessary but the courses are not always based on the interests of the children or the needs of the local economy so much as on what the teachers can already do without any extra preparation. Thus teachers use the optional program to get some overtime payment for themselves rather than to find specialist workers from outside the school who could give the pupils a worthwhile course.[5]

The agricultural problem is unlikely to be solved quickly. In recent articles in the central press, the problem of finding enough people to work on farms is often blamed on the fact that, when the fashion in the USSR was for having everything of a large size, then it was not considered practical to keep a full secondary school in every village. Older children were sent away to boarding schools in local towns. Having once left the village, those children are unlikely to return. It is now stated that it is necessary to build full secondary schools for children to attend without leaving home—even if these schools have relatively few pupils. An eloquent statement of this problem can be found in an article called "Who will milk the cows tomorrow?"[6] It indeed seems likely that a large-scale school-building program for rural areas may be necessary for the solution of the difficult problem of finding adequate agricultural workers. This is as yet beyond the scope of the reform.

The question of raising the prestige of vocational schools is also a difficult one. An increased prestige has happened to some degree in the past through

[1] Trebuyetsya prizvanie. *Izvestiya*, 23 Jan. 1985.
[2] Vysshaya shkola, rabota i lipa. *Izvestiya*, 7 Dec. 1984.
[3] See note 13.　　[4] See note 13.　　[5] Snova o fakul'tative. *Izvestiya*, 12 Nov. 1984.
[6] Kto doit korov zavtra? *Izvestiya*, 6 Feb. 1986.

the improvement and extension of PTU facilities and opportunities. There has not, however, been much success in making vocational schools attractive to the children of the intelligentsia rather than to those of a working class or agricultural background. If the Soviet Union finds itself able to provide vocational training in SPTUs together with an academic education that is not inferior to that given in the general secondary school, then it will be able to serve well the interests of both the State and the individual. Under such circumstances perhaps the children of the intelligentsia may not then feel that going to an SPTU is an unsatisfactory move as compared with staying on at the general secondary school. For this to happen, however, some fairly dramatic changes of attitude are required.

A final problem, but perhaps the most significant, is that of finance. Considerable cost is involved in carrying out all the measures which have been proposed. It is already clear that money problems—in the USSR as elsewhere—limit the extent to which a grandiose rhetoric can be put into practice.

The organization of vocational training always seems to bring problems. If youngsters are trained in schools or colleges, they may learn a lot of theory but do not know how to hold a tool properly when they eventually come to work. If schoolchildren do their training on the job they may at first hinder the work of the enterprise. Once they have picked up the necessary skills, they may be used by the work-place administration as a means of cheap labor. The difficulties here are certainly not confined to the Soviet Union but they have not been fully solved by earlier Soviet educational reforms.

The close links which the reform seeks to establish between the SPTU and the base enterprise together with their shared responsibility for vocational training would suggest that they may be able to work out a theory/practice balance that is in the interests of both industry and education. The other problems outlined in this section seem less open to solution. It will be interesting to see what the following years will bring.

CHAPTER 12

The Secondarization of Technical Education in Argentina and the Vocationalization of Secondary Education in Brazil

MARIA ANTONIA GALLART

Centro de Estudios de Poblacion, Buenos Aires

THIS paper presents a particular point of view on the problem of vocationalizing secondary education. It draws on the considerable experience of Argentina in secondary technical education, from its early creation at the end of the 19th century up to its present status as a branch of secondary education which includes more than a fifth of total secondary school enrollment, and more than a third of male enrollment.

There occurred a paradox in the history of Argentine education. The attempt at vocationalizing academic education failed, but the technical branch grew, integrating general education into its original curriculum of predominantly technological subjects and stressing a double purpose of both preparing its graduates to enter the university and teaching them skills for the world of work.

Examining these failed reforms,[1] one can see that two goals underlie the attempts at vocationalizing post-primary education. The first is to teach skills which would permit the secondary school graduate to compete advantageously in the labor market. The second is to diminish the pressure on higher educational institutions by making vocational education terminal. There are several problems with this approach. One is the presence of very strong demand for access to the upper levels of the educational system in Latin America. A second is the difficulty in integrating general preparatory and vocational education in one and the same curriculum when a dual-purpose secondary school is chosen. The third is the projection of the skill profile that will prevail in the labor market in the future. And last but not least, that the supply of educational variants coincides with the actual social

---

[1] Since the creation of a national educational system in Argentina a century ago, with a French style predominantly academic secondary level, several reforms have been introduced. Two large reforms (in 1916 and 1969) were put into effect but soon had to be aborted because of political opposition. In both cases the reforms implied vocationalization and the specialization of post-primary education. See Gallart (1983, Chapter II).

demand, in order to avoid the "vocational school fallacy of educational planning."[1]

The evolution of technical education in Argentina, along with its present curriculum and outcomes, illustrates some of these problems. Even though they are a school-based branch of secondary education, Argentine technical schools are the product of a process of convergence between terminal trade schools, vocational schools and industrial technological schools which nowadays take the form of a technological branch of secondary education. Most of its graduates continue to both study and work. The evolution of technical education in Argentina was not so much a process of vocationalization of academic education as a process of secondarization of vocational education. Nevertheless, the forces at work are the same as those that act when vocationalization of academic secondary education is introduced, i.e., strong social demand for secondary education linked to mobility aspirations; competition among social sectors for access to the upper levels of the educational ladder with the consequent segmentation between tracks, schools, and/or optional courses; the influence of the characteristics of the labor market on the social demand for the different tracks; and in the positions open to school-leavers, given the labor market's segmentation, the devaluation of credentials, and changes in salary differentials. These elements enter into the process and weigh on the success or failure of vocationalization. The point is that the analysis of the evolution of Argentine technical education in comparison to the vocationalization of secondary education in Brazil may give us some clues leading to a more realistic implementation of vocationalization policies.

The Evolution of Argentine Technical Education

The original development of elementary education in Argentina, which made elementary education available to half of the 6–13 age group as early as 1914, also sustained the development of secondary education (in 1915 the level included approximately 3 percent of the 13–18 age group and was predominantly academic). At that time, industrial education, i.e., the secondary technical branch of it, begun in 1899 as technological post-primary schools whose goal was the training of middle-level technicians, accounted for only 5.4 percent of secondary enrollment, while commercial schools had 10.9 percent. Terminal vocational trade schools were created in 1909 to feed the newborn industrial sector. By the mid-1940s they accounted for approximately 5000 students, almost a fifth the size of the enrollment in the non-terminal industrial schools. Trade schools lost their clientele during the first Peronist government (1946–1951) when the Ministry of Labor

[1] See Foster (1977, pp. 356–365), the classic paper on the relationship between students' preference for academic studies and the advantages in the labor market of these academic diplomas for white-collar and upper level occupations.

created the CNAOP[1] system which were vocational schools that permitted the student to pursue higher studies in a particular technical institution, then called the Worker's University. At the time these schools contained just as many students as the industrial schools run from the Ministry of Education. In the early 1960s all of these various vocational branches of post-primary education were unified under an autonomous office of the Ministry of Education. Thus the present technical system was born. These schools are non-terminal, providing degrees to middle-level technicians in a number (25) of fields. But their enrollment is concentrated in only a few fields: electricity, construction, mechanics and chemistry. In 1985 the total secondary enrollment rate was around 60 percent, with a majority of students in the commercial and technical areas of the vocational non-terminal branches.

Characteristics of Technical Schools

While they stress mathematics and sciences over the humanities, these schools have a mixed curriculum which begins with three years of academic subjects common to all fields of specialization, in addition to shopwork. These three years are equivalent to the basic course cycle in the other branches of secondary education, and consequently students can change tracks. The final three years are distinct for each field of specialization. They include a strong mathematics curriculum (including calculus), scientific and technological subjects, technical drawing, laboratory and shopwork. This curriculum extends technical education a year longer than the other tracks of secondary education, and furthermore is full-time (commercial and baccalaureate schools are only half-day schools). Even given these extra requirements one out of three boys enrolled in secondary education was in a technical school in 1985.

Does this curriculum meet the expectations resulting from the dual purposes of preparing the student for both technical work and a university career? In a recent in-depth study of technical schools,[2] the articulation among the humanities, scientific and technological subjects, and the integration of shopwork with classroom subjects was analyzed, taking into account the double purpose of technical education. This study examined technologically very different fields of specialization: electronics, construction and mechanics. As regards the integration of the curriculum, in all schools analyzed a gap developed between the technical subjects and the general education subjects, and also between classroom and shop. Different teachers, and even different spaces (classroom, laboratory, shops), signalled "islands" which supported divergent poles of technical education. General

---

[1] Comisión Nacional de Aprendizaje y Orientación Profesional, i.e., the National Commission for Apprenticeship and Professional Guidance.

[2] This was a "thick description" study of 15 schools. The researchers spent a month in each, interviewing principals, teachers and students, and observing classrooms and shops. See Gallart (1985).

TABLE 1. *Latin America: Secondary Education Crude Enrollment Rates by Country, 1950–1975*

Percentage	1950[1]	1960	1970	1975[2]
Less than 15	Honduras (1.9) El Salvador (3.3) Guatemala (3.5) Mexico (4.0) Dominican Rep. (4.7) Colombia (4.8) Nicaragua (5.0) Costa Rica (5.0) Paraguay (6.1) Ecuador (6.1) Bolivia (6.2) Cuba (6.4) Brazil (6.5) Peru (7.1) Venezuela (7.5) Chile (13.2) Uruguay (13.3)	Brazil (4.3) Guatemala (4.8) Nicaragua (5.3) Honduras (5.4) Dominican Republic (5.6) Mexico (7.9) Paraguay (8.4) El Salvador (9.5) Bolivia (10.7) Colombia (10.8) Ecuador (10.9) Cuba (12.4) Peru (13.8)	Dominican Rep. (8.9) Guatemala (9.1) Honduras (10.2) Brazil (11.3) Bolivia (14.3) Paraguay (14.9)	Dominican Rep. (9.0) El Salvador (10.0) Honduras (11.1) Guatemala (11.5)
15–35	Argentina (15.2) Panama (16.3)	Venezuela (17.7) Costa Rica (20.3) Chile (20.9) Argentina (23.3) Panama (25.0) Uruguay (30.1)	Nicaragua (15.9) El Salvador (16.3) Mexico (20.2) Colombia (21.8) Costa Rica (21.8) Cuba (22.1) Chile (22.4) Ecuador (23.8) Peru (26.9) Venezuela (27.7) Argentina (32.3)	Brazil (16.9) Boliva (17.7) Nicaragua (19.0) Paraguay (23.0) Venezuela (30.1) Chile (31.1)
35–50			Panama (36.2)	Costa Rica (35.2) Ecuador (35.8) Mexico (37.4) Colombia (39.4) Peru (40.3) Argentina (41.1)
More than 50			Uruguay (51.5)	Panama (52.9) Uruguay (53.7) Cuba (58.3)

Source: UNESCO/CEPAL/PNUD, DEALC, *Informe final 4*, Vol. 2, Cuadro IV.28

[1] There is no information for Uruguay and Costa Rica.
[2] 1974: Brazil, Nicaragua, Venezuela.
  1975: Ecuador, Honduras, Dominican Republic, Uruguay.
  1976: Bolivia, Cuba.
  1977: Argentina, Colombia, Costa Rica, El Salvador, Guatemala, Mexico, Panama, Paraguay, Peru.
  1978: Chile.

education did not prepare the student to think critically about scientific–technical culture but was rather only a bad copy of the humanities as taught in the encyclopedic academic schools. Technological and scientific subjects were both too many and too broad, and their material was impossible to cover as scheduled. As a consequence the teachers' strategy was to choose what they considered key topics necessary either for work or higher education, and within each subject they stressed the things that were required in order to understand the focal concepts. This policy broke the horizontal coordination of the curriculum, and at times it became more a presentation of technical recipes than a real knowledge of science and technology. Shop and laboratory suffered from a double challenge. The first derived from the uniformity of design forced upon different fields of specialization. The curricular links between scientific subjects, technological subjects and shopwork (including questions of timetable and location) were borrowed from a metalworking model (where it is easy to interlink, e.g., physics, thermodynamics, study of machinery, materials analysis, shopwork with machine tools, etc.). Such an educational model for instance is greatly different from the model that would have to be applied in, e.g., training in electronics, where the relationship between the laboratory and the theory is much more profound and dynamic. The understanding of symbology is much more developed (and required) in the manipulation of electronic circuitry. As a consequence the articulation of the subject matter with the laboratory and shopwork is much more complex and simply cannot function in separately compartmentalized educational programs.

The second challenge dealt with the difference between teaching science and technology for future engineering students and the apprenticeship of a technician in a situation similar to the world of work. Some shops made an effort to work like a production unit. Several even produced goods. But the reproduction of this "world like work" is very difficult in the context of a scholastic organization. The values and rationale behind learning to climb the educational ladder are very different from the effort to earn and preserve a place in an enterprise. In school the demands of production and commercial competition are absent. Productive work degenerates into "make believe," defended by the belief that the student only needs to "learn to do so that he can command," as some students and teachers put it.[1] Given this pedagogic point of view, the student is not required to become a good lathe operator.

Are these problems insurmountable? Is it possible to provide general education and at the same time train a middle-level technician in an integrated way? A recent essay by Moura Castro (1984) on vocational education puts forward some interesting ideas in this regard. The author examines different occupations and locates them within a two-dimensional typology. The first is the continuum between tasks which follow strictly

---

[1] Some of these dangers of technical school curricula are presented in a broader context in King (1985).

simple rules as, for example, in semi-skilled jobs and those that follow complex rules as in technical occupations. The second dimension deals with occupations that manage simple decision-making tasks as, for example, in lower administrative positions, or else are required to deal with many exceptional situations, and thus accept responsibilities and take risks, as in managerial jobs. In the continuum between the extremes of the typology, technical training which stresses the mechanical learning of rules and their applications is useful for the first type of occupations, but as one advances toward the other end some kind of training which prepares the student to respond to the challenges of uncertainty is necessary. The author calls this latter general education. General education, then, is not academic encyclopedism, but rather what was the original purpose for teaching and learning the humanities, that is, a strong paradigm which enables the individual to think and to solve problems. In other words general education is not an all-embracing education, but rather an education which teaches a way to think. The author posits a scientific technological education which runs from the analysis of the machine to physics, from applied electronics to Boolean algebra. General education is not a matter of width but of depth. Moura Castro asks whether specific education is not the best general education. To apply this criterion to Argentine technical education could be one way to respond to the challenges presented here, by training the technician who can both manage a broad spectrum of occupations and master a method of thinking and studying.

A second aspect of technical education worth examining is its outcome in terms of the performance of graduates. This issue can be broached using the results of a follow-up study of 400 technical school-leavers who finished school in 1973–74 and were interviewed in 1985.[1] Some preliminary results may be presented here. Although there is a considerable social mix, the surveyed alumni come mostly from lower middle class families. Most of them have reached a higher educational level than their parents (72 percent of the respondents' fathers had elementary education or less). And among the technicians surveyed 80 percent had entered the university, while 20 percent are higher education graduates (most of them in engineering and architecture). The historical period since their finishing school was a very critical time for the Argentine economy. Inflation continued and increased. Industrial employment decreased. And since 1981 open unemployment— very low before—grew. Nevertheless, the follow-up study showed a high level of employment (97.7 percent), more than the Metropolitan average for that date.

Technical school leavers occupied a variety of occupations.[2] Around 40

---

[1] This study is part of the project "Education and Work: The Role of Technical Education in Argentina," in CENEP, Buenos Aires.
[2] A detailed description of the tasks performed by the respondent was compiled, and occupations were categorized along different continuums: knowledge and skills applied, occupational category and hierarchical status.

percent were technicians or professionals. But there were also entre-preneurs (approximately 10 percent), self-employed in small enterprises (20 percent), executives (6 percent) and skilled workers (3 percent). Only a third worked in the manufacturing sector, but 42 percent worked in tasks related to their fields of educational specialization. And an additional 24 percent applied general technical knowledge to tasks not directly related to their particular field of study. But only 26 percent were in occupations that had nothing to do with the training they had received. Regarding mobility, 55 percent had attained an occupational level higher than that of their parents (with only 20 percent lower than the parents).

It is interesting to note in this regard that this high level of mobility was compounded by a high degree of social reproduction. In the case of technical schools' graduates there was a strong correlation between their parents' and their own occupational status. This occurred because the whole population had been upgraded. Of the parents, 65 percent were in the three lower occupational levels, though only 27 percent of the graduates were in these kinds of occupation. But the children of parents in the upper strata tended to enter the best jobs, and most of the ones from the lower strata stepped up one or two occupational levels. At the same time, that permitted a high degree of mobility and a reproduction process which took the form of a "queuing order model," where the children tended to maintain the same relative position as their parents, while improving their absolute situation (Schiefelbein and Farrell, 1982, Chapter 12). This was possible because there had been a process of growth of middle-level occupations in society. This phenomenon is observed also in other Latin American countries (Ciavatta Franco and Moura Castro, 1981) and questions the common assumption of the contradiction between social mobility and social reproduction.

The Process of Secondarization of Technical Education

The forces at work in changing secondary education presented above can be seen now in the light of the evolution of technical education. The demand for non-terminal vocational education was always greater than the demand for terminal streams. Even when trade schools were demanded by workers' children as a first step into post-primary education, these trade schools never accounted for more than 20 percent of industrial school enrollment. With the appearance of CNAOP schools, enrollment in trade schools declined rapidly. In the 1960s attempts to make the technical branch terminal found strong opposition. Present technical education with its dual purpose and non-integrated curriculum is the result. How to better integrate general, preparatory and vocational education continues to be a problem, as we have seen above. But the performance of the technical school graduates in the world of work reveals a profile which is much wider than the one defined by the authorities of technical education (which is that of providing strictly middle-level technicians who have specialized in a particular field), but a profile which has a good chance of competing in the labor market. The amount of recorded intergenerational mobility reveals some of the reasons for the demand for that type of education by low middle class and workers' children.

Concerning the forces at work, resistance to the vocationalization of academic curricula and to the specialization of preparatory courses over a long period points to the desire to keep all the tracks oriented towards possible entrance into the university and to maintenance of the general education character of the academic branch. If these trends are related to enrollment patterns, it appears that actually the main function of secondary schools—to foster mobility toward higher education—had tacked on to it the vocational function of teaching skills (within commercial and technical schools at least), so that students of lesser economic means could more advantageously enter the labor force. This dual purpose was aided by the fact that Argentine universities allow students to work, accommodating schedules to that end. The vocational objective is therefore not incompatible with the preparatory goal in terms of a student's plans (Gallart, 1983, p. 136).

Regarding the competition among social sectors for access to the upper levels of the educational system, the few studies which take into account the social background of Argentine secondary students show a high participation rate for students from the lower middle class (and obviously from the upper strata), while the children of blue-collar workers have low levels of participation in the last years of secondary education. There exists a great deal of educational mobility, particularly among the children of parents who have completed elementary school, while at the university level the children of highly educated parents are over-represented (Echart de Bianchi, 1976; Klubitschko, 1980).

Most students expect to enter higher education, even admitting in many cases the need to combine study with work. The hierarchizing among the choice of studying only, working and studying, or working only is closely correlated with socio-economic status and chosen branch of secondary education (which two variables are interrelated, technical and commercial schools having a larger probability of receiving lower class students).

Thus it seems that seeking educational mobility (and ultimately occupational mobility) appears for many lower class students to be a possible objective, while for upper class students higher education and exclusive private schools are a way to maintain the status attained by their parents (Gallart, 1983, p. 213).

The Brazilian Case

Brazil traditionally has had a selective academic secondary education, accompanied by a less prestigious vocational branch,[1] the latter covering half of secondary enrollment in 1971. This vocational stream included different schools for agricultural, commercial and industrial tracks (Piletti, 1984, Chapter 1). The vocational tracks were aimed at the lower classes,[2] though since 1953 their graduates have had access to university, although they had to take special equivalence examinations, until in 1961 they were given the same rights as students in other tracks to continue higher studies.

The Reform

In 1971 the government decided to vocationalize the entire second cycle of secondary education across the whole country. The first cycle was integrated with primary education in a basic elementary cycle of eight years with a general education focus. The second cycle (second grade) was to be taught in all schools and was to be mainly vocational. The debate on the reform revealed the importance attributed to vocational education during the second cycle in order to prepare the student for work, by granting professional qualifications. Nevertheless, an amendment was introduced, allowing, as an exception, special preparatory studies for bright students. The idea behind the law was to train middle-level human resources for the labor force and dissuade the student from the pursuit of university studies.[3]

The Process

The reform was difficult to implement even in the richest state, São Paulo. Some schools retained their old curricula by cheating. Under the cover of new names they kept the old subjects. Others chose "easy" vocational fields without taking into account labor market requirements in order to allow the students to concentrate on their study for university entrance examinations. Many vocational courses were aimed at the tertiary economic (70 percent), and only 20 percent at the secondary economic sector. Some schools did not have the means to even implement vocational courses, and these were second rate (Piletti, 1984, p. 111). The certifications discriminated between two kinds of qualification in order to avoid the pitfall of granting professional degrees to incompetent graduates: a basic qualification which was only a professional initiation to be complemented by learning on the job, and a full certificate (Piletti, 1984, p. 115). Courses leading to this latter accounted for approximately a third of second cycle enrollment in São Paulo in 1977 (Ribeiro Leite and Cassia Barros Savi, 1980, p. 11).

[1] In 1909 trade schools were founded in state capitals for apprenticeship courses for poor children. Only in 1942 was secondary technical education institutionalized with the "Lei Orgánica do Ensino Industrial." Franco (1983, p. 21) and Ribeiro Leite and Cassia Barros Savi (1980, p. 3).
[2] Constitution of 1937, Art. 129.   [3] Law 5692/71.

The contradiction between the intended purposes of the reform and the resultant disorganization of the second cycle, the funding problems (costs were 60 percent higher than those for academic courses) (Ribeiro Leite and Cassia Barros Sari, 1980, p. 5), affected the decision to change the law in 1982. The new law (Law 7044) replaced the old "qualification for work" with a new "preparation for work" as part of the "integral education of the student." Moreover, compulsory vocationalization aimed at producing qualified professionals was made optional for schools (Warde, 1983).

Enrollment in second cycle schools grew during these years. In 1976 there were 345,842 students in the state schools of São Paulo. By 1980 there were 416,216 (Piletti, 1984, p. 116). In 1982, 35 percent of the 15–18 age group of the city of São Paulo was in second cycle schools, allowing for wide differences among districts. In one blue-collar district there was only an 11.25 percent enrollment rate. In a study of second cycle students in São Paulo only 45 percent of them thought to take higher education entrance examinations. Others preferred to work for a while to save money for higher education. Most thought that their schooling was not preparing them sufficiently to compete in those examinations. A majority also think that they are not qualified to work as technicians, and as a consequence expect to follow some specialized training in SENAI (Franco and Durigan, 1984).

Some differences between Argentine and Brazilian education must be stressed. There is a small coverage of formal education in Brazil—34 percent of school-age children had never been in school when the law of vocationalization of the second cycle was introduced (Piletti, 1984, p. 35). The enrollment growth in both cycles is a recent phenomenon compared with Argentina (Tables 2 and 3). However, non-formal education, vocational and technical training for the industrial and service sectors had been developed early and with a significant coverage in SENAI and SENAC (Edfelt, 1975). In Argentina non-formal technical training was never important. In any given year there are more graduates of six-year technical schools than short-course trainees. The development of the industrial sector was also different. Instead of an early development, followed by stop-and-go cycles and stagnation as in the Argentine case, Brazil's development is more recent and has been stronger and more sustained, at least until the present crisis.

Conclusions

We can now turn to the problem of implementating the vocationalization of secondary education as presented at the beginning of this chapter, drawing some conclusions from the experience of both countries. The demand for non-terminal secondary education in Latin America will continue to be very strong as long as the private rate of return of subsidized higher education is high. And the political costs of diminishing enrollment in

TABLE 2. *Argentina: Secondary Education Enrollment by Tracks, 1915–1985*
(in thousands)

	Baccalaureate	Normal	Commercial	Industrial	Others (trade schools, agricultural)	Total
1915	11.1	10.6	3.6	1.8	6.0	33.7
	(33.5)	(32.0)	(10.9)	(5.4)	(18.1)	(100)
1925	22.3	17.5	6.5	3.8	10.9	61.0
	(36.6)	(28.7)	(10.7)	(6.2)	(17.8)	(100)
1935	41.0	24.4	11.0	9.2	19.3	104.9
	(39.1)	(23.3)	(10.5)	(8.8)	(18.4)	(100)
1945	62.3	50.3	27.9	26.7	34.0	201.2
	(31.0)	(25.0)	(13.9)	(13.3)	(16.9)	(100)
1955	110.7	97.3	83.3	86.4	94.2	471.9
	(23.5)	(20.6)	(17.7)	(18.3)	(20.0)	(100)
1965	178.6	184.9	178.7	113.5	133.4	789.1
	(22.6)	(23.4)	(22.6)	(14.4)	(16.9)	(100)
1975	454.2	—[1]	411.9	335.1[2]	41.9	1243.1
	(36.6)	—	(33.1)	(27.0)	(3.3)	(100)
1985	715.5	—	564.8	367.0	36.2	1683.5
	(42.5)	—	(33.5)	(21.7)	(2.2)	(100)

Source: Ministry of Education, Department of Statistics.

[1] Teacher training was transferred to higher education and normal schools became baccalaureate schools.
[2] Women's professional schools were transformed into industrial schools.

TABLE 3. *Brazil: Educational Enrollment in First and Second Cycles, 1963–1983*
(in millions)

	First cycle[1]	Second cycle[2]
1963	10.62	0.37
1965	11.57	0.51
1967	13.38	0.69
1969	15.01	0.91
1971	17.07	1.12
1973	18.57	1.30
1975	19.55	1.94
1977	20.37	2.44
1979	22.02	2.66
1981	22.41	2.82
1983	24.55	2.94

Source: Anuario Estatistico do Brasil, Secretaria de Planejamiento da Presidencia da Republica. 1981, 1983 data from the Ministry of Education.

[1] Years 1–8 of formal schooling.
[2] Years 9–11/12 of formal schooling.

non-terminal secondary education or higher education seem too great for democratic governments, and even for many authoritarian ones. As far as formal education is concerned, terminal courses meet very little demand. The problem then seems to be focused on how to attain a mix of general education, preparatory studies and vocational education in secondary education in a way that would permit a significant proportion of graduates to continue on to higher education, but at the same time would furnish most of them with the skills necessary to compete in the labor market. One must take into account that either because of attrition at the higher levels (as in the case of Argentina) or because they cannot pass entrance examinations, for a majority of students their secondary education will be their last completed educational cycle.

There are several possible responses to this problem. One is to provide a strong polytechnical branch of secondary education which would give the student a basic training to perform as a middle-level technician or to continue studying for a technical career. Another possibility is a comprehensive school with the option of training courses for specific occupations. The Argentine way seems to be closer to the first option, while the Brazilian case is nearer the second. But the latter seems to be difficult to implement in a country with a very strong non-formal professional training (as the history of SENAI and SENAC shows) and with a tradition of predominantly academic formal secondary education, which at the same time reaches only a minority of the target age group even in urban settings. Indeed, perhaps the articulation between in-school general education and post-school non-formal technical training is a better answer for Brazil.

The definition of general education is important in this case in order to avoid the danger of a contradiction between a 19th-century baccalaureate curriculum and short courses for middle or low level occupations. The idea is to strengthen the scientific–technological content of formal educational curricula in a problem-solving perspective, followed by a choice of short vocational courses for specific occupations. These short courses should be structured in modules that could be adapted over time according to labor market demands. They should not be stable structured courses that tend to outlive their usefulness.

A second issue concerns the way to introduce reforms that would vocationalize secondary education. The examples from the past history of Argentina and the recent experience of Brazil show that it is very difficult to change an entire level of the educational system by decree. There are a number of factors that must be taken into account. A few are listed below.

First, there is a group of factors related to the role of education within society and its relationship to the labor market. Given that in Latin America there is a strong tradition of social mobility through education, the vocationalizing reforms should not appear as diminishing the chances of students for mobility in the labor market or as formally cutting access to further education. It is necessary, therefore, that the reforms channel the demands of parents and students. In other words, individual choice (processed through the social demand for the different options) should be taken into account.

TABLE 4. *Net Enrollment Rate of the 15–19 Age Group by Educational Level in Brazil and Argentina, 1980*

	Brazil	Argentina
Basic education[1]	26.5	5.6
Secondary education[2]	14.4	32.6
Higher education	1.4	3.5
Net enrollment rate	42.3	41.7
Total population 15–19 years	100	100
	(13,277.662)	(2,335.407)

Sources: Brazil: Anuario Estatístico do Brazil, Secretaria de Planejamiento da Presidencia da República, 1981 (Census Data). Argentina: Censo Nacional de Población y Vivienda 1980, Serie B, Características Generales, INDEC, 1982.

[1] Brazil: Years 1–8 of formal schooling.
  Argentina: Years 1–7 of formal schooling.
[2] Brazil: Years 9–11/12 of formal schooling.
  Argentina: Years 8–12/13 of formal schooling.

TABLE 5. *Distribution of Time Among Subjects in Second Cycle Brazilian Professional Schools (Electronics) and Argentine Technical Schools*

	Brazil[1] (3 years) (hours) (hours)	Argentina	
		Basic cycle (3 years) (hours)	Superior cycle (3 years)
Language, national and English	17.5	14.2	3.7
Social sciences	12.4	14.2	4.4
Mathematics and sciences	18.6	26.8⎱	85.2
Technology and shopwork	42.3	37.8⎰	
Physical education	9.2	7.0	6.7
	100	100	100
Total	(2910)	(4445)	(4725)

Sources: Brazil: Piletti (1984, p. 80). Argentina: Weinberg (1967).

[1] Minimal Program for Electronics Technicians. Dictamen No. 45/72. This is the special field with full professional qualifications with most time alloted to scientific and technological subjects.

The processes seen above (the vocationalization of academic education and the secondarization of technical education) cannot be understood without taking into account the aspirations of new strata reaching secondary education, the possibility of their continuing on to higher education, the prospects of vocational education for them as compared with the other options available in secondary education, and the changing opportunities within the labor market for graduates from the different levels and tracks of the educational system. As long as the educational system in developing countries does not cover the entire age group, the mechanisms of segmentation by tracks will have a different meaning from those in developed countries. Wastage in elementary, secondary and tertiary levels is the hidden mechanism of differentiation for the lower social sectors of society.

The former stresses the point that educational expansion is related to changes in the labor market but has a different rationale and a different timing, depending on the kind of society one is dealing with (e.g., Argentina versus Brazil). The fact of an early growth of the formal educational system with almost universal coverage of elementary education and an extended secondary level, joined to a labor market with a shrinking manufacturing sector (as in Argentina's case), is very different from a recently expanded formal educational system, a very strong non-formal vocational education and a growing export-oriented industry (as in the Brazilian case). Both the social mobility processes and the relationship of education with the labor market should turn out to be very different. All of these make the fitting of education to the productive system an elusive goal.

A second group of factors deals with the organizational pattern of educational systems and non-formal training institutions. The characteristics of the educational system as a nationwide bureaucratic organization, divided into thousands of semi-autonomous units (i.e., the schools), make the process of change slow and difficult, not only in the case of reforms, but also in adaptation to changes in the labor market. In addition, the strength of the training institutions and the defense of their autonomy hinder the possibility of integrating their programs with formal education, and sometimes even increases the danger of duplicating efforts between formal educational systems and training institutions (e.g., long technical courses that last several years). Finally, the problem of costs must be taken into account, as vocational education is more costly than traditional academic education. Laboratories and shops, if they are really to be useful, are more expensive than blackboards and chalk. One of the Brazilian authors' constant criticisms concerning the failed reform is that the funds to finance vocational education in all schools were not available.

One final important comment concerns the difference between learning a cultural heritage in successive steps, acquiring a capacity for problem-solving, or even acquiring practical skills at an early age in a formal educational system, and the experience of learning to work in a competitive context with controls on one's efficiency, a particular division of labor, conflict and accumulation, and all this throughout life. This contrasting experience, as seen in the life histories of technicians, implies a different rationality for schools and enterprises, and is one of the reasons for the contradictory relationship between school and work. But it is also one of the reasons that makes this link so difficult to elucidate, yet so crucial for individuals and society.

References

Ciavatta Franco, M. A. and Moura Castro, C. (1983) La Contribución de la educación tecnica a la movilidad social: Un estudio comparativo en América Latina. *Revista Latinoamericana de estudios educativos (México)*, **1**, 9–42.

Echart de Bianchi, M. (1976) *Los determinantes de la Educación en Argentina.* Buenos Aires: FIEL.

Edfelt, R. (1975) Occupational education and training: The role of large private industry in Brazil. In T. LaBelle (Ed.), *Educational alternatives in Latin America* (pp. 384–413).

Foster, P. J. (1977) The vocational school fallacy in educational planning. In J. Karabel and A. H. Halsey (Eds.) *Power and ideology in education.* New York: Oxford University Press.

Franco, M. L. P. B. (1983) O ensino de 2º grau: Democratizaçao? Professionalizaçao? Ou nem una cosa nem outra? *Cadernos de pesquisa*, **47**, 18–31.

Franco, M. L. P. B. and Durigan, M. I. S. (1984) O aluno de curso professionalizante a nivel de 2º grau: Un retrato sem retoques. *Cadernos de pesquisa*, **48**, 47–56.

Gallart, M. A. (1983) *The evolution of secondary education in Argentina.* Ph. D. Dissertation, University of Chicago.

Gallart, M. A. (1985) *La racionalidad educativa y la racionalidad productiva: Las escuelas técnicas y el mundo del trabajo.* Buenos Aires: CENEP.

King, K. (1985) *The planning of technical and vocational education and training.* Paris: UNESCO/IIEP.

Klubitscho, D. (1980) *El origen social de los Estudiantes de la Universidad de Buenos Aires.* Buenos Aires: UN/ECLA.

Moura Castro, C. de (1984) *Educación vocacional y productividad: Alguna luz en la caja negra?* Brasilia: Instituto de Planejamiento Economico e Social–Centro Nacional de Recursos Humanos.

Piletti, N. (1984) *La profesionalización obligatoria de la enseñanza de Segundo grado en Brasil.* Montevideo: OIT/Cinterfor.

Ribeiro Leite, M. and Cassia Barros Savi, R. de (1980) Ensino de 2º grau professionalizante. *Cadernos de pesquisa*, **36**, 3–25.

Schiefelbein, E. and Farrell, J. P. (1982) *Eight years of their lives: Through schooling to the labour market in Chile.* Ottawa: IDRC.

Warde, M. J. (1983) Algunas reflexoes en torno de Ley 7044. *Cadernos de pesquisa*, **47**, 14–17.

Weinberg, D. (1967) *La enseñanza técnica industrial en la Argentina 1936–1965.* Buenos Aires: Instituto Di Tella.

CHAPTER 13

Work as Education—Perspectives on the Role of Work in Current Educational Reform in Zimbabwe

INGEMAR GUSTAFSSON

University of Stockholm

"EDUCATION with production" (EWP) is the main theme of current educational reform work in Zimbabwe. This article is an attempt to explain what it means in the context of Zimbabwe and to analyze the role that work is expected to play as an integral part of the curriculum of ordinary primary and secondary schools. The term "work" is used to mean the production of goods or services which are useful to the school or to the surrounding community. Hence, it refers to "real" work situations being part of the education process as distinct from practical activities that prepare for work or which are meant as applications of theoretical concepts. The assumption has been that education reform efforts can be explained, at least partly, by the theory of education and development which prevails in a particular society and therefore that it is important to analyze the role of work in a broad perspective of education and development.[1]

The principles of EWP in Zimbabwe have been concretized in an experimental program, set up after independence in 1980, under a semi-autonomous body called the Zimbabwe Foundation for Education for Production (ZIMFEP). It comprises eight secondary and four adjacent primary schools established mainly for students who returned from the camps in Botswana, Mozambique and Zambia after independence. They had developed schemes for education with production, which grew out of necessity in the camps. When there were no classrooms, students had to build them; when there were no materials, the teachers had to create them. It was also a model that was marked by a high degree of political mobilization closely linked with the struggle for independence. This group of students and teachers, grouped together in the ZIMFEP schools, were selected to spearhead the transformation of the formal system of education to respond to the socialist policy of the Government.

[1] See Fägerlind and Saha (1983) for a discussion about theories on development and educational reform.

219

Zimbabwean Reform in the African Context

There has, during the last 10 years or so, been a widely expressed view among politicians in Africa, that work should be made part of the curriculum of ordinary primary and secondary schools. This has been seen as a solution to a number of economic, social and pedagogical problems facing their countries, notably increasing youth unemployment and the increasing costs of formal education.

Nyerere (1967) was amongst the first fundamentally to question the relevance to development of the essentially liberal type of education that a country had inherited.

In 1976, the African Ministers of Education resolved that "African States should provide a new form of education so as to establish close ties between the school and work: such an education based on work and with work in mind should break down the barriers of prejudice which exist between manual and intellectual labor, between theory and practice and between town and countryside . . [and therefore] productive, practical work should generally be introduced in schools, offering technical and vocational courses whether at primary, secondary or higher level."[1] Many programs have been initiated to reflect this concern. One of the first and perhaps the most well known, is the program of brigades in Botswana,[2] started on private initiative by van Rensburg long before the statement referred to above. The Brigade originated from Swaneng Hill secondary school without any Government subsidy, and operated under severe cost constraints. It was seen as a necessity for the students to assist in the construction and building and to contribute to the up-keep of the school through work. In 1965 a group of unemployed Standard 7 leavers, who could not gain access to the school or any other secondary school, were organized into a so-called "builders brigade" which worked for the school and for the surrounding community and learnt a trade on the job at the same time as their work generated income to cover the costs of their training. The secondary school students and the brigade trainees combined, although in different proportions, intellectual and manual work, theory and practice. Work was used as a means to generate income, to prepare for a future occupation and last but not least, as a means to "combat elitism." In the early 1970s, the secondary school and the brigades were separated and the brigades evolved into a separate and unique system. Ten years after the first builders' brigade there were 20 brigade centers in Botswana with nearly 1100 trainees in 12 different trades. After 1978, numbers declined to 650–700, but are now increasing again. During these 20 years, the brigades have suffered many constraints but they offer a rich source of experience for the study of how

---

[1] Resolution adopted at the Conference of African Ministers of Education, held in Lagos 1976 and quoted in NEIDA.

[2] For a description of the origin and development of the Botswana brigades see, for example, van Rensburg P. (1967, 1974, 1984), Parsons (1983) and Gustafsson (1985a).

education can be combined with work. Such a phenomenon was not entirely new to Africa, of course. Many mission stations had had work as an important ingredient in their education program, both as means to "civilize" the African and to finance their schools and stations. The objectives then and the particular circumstances in which these programs were established is, however, outside the scope of this chapter. The program in Zimbabwe will be discussed within two partly contrasting, perspectives on education and development, both of which have originated as a reaction against capitalist development.

Mainstream Development and its Counterpoint

Hettne (1982) has used the terms "mainstream" and "counterpoint" to characterize two, partly contrasting, theoretical perspectives on development. The first tends to equate development with growth, structural differentiation and increasing complexity. Within this category he places liberal, State capitalist as well as Marxist perspectives on development. The second, the counterpoint, stresses the inherent superiority of small-scale, decentralized, ecologically sound, human and stable models of societal development.[1] The analysis of what causes/prevents development varies between Adam Smith, Ricardo and Marx, but it is also true that Marx was inspired by evolutionist thought which considered technological development and increasing specialization of tasks as characteristics of and necessary conditions for development. The focus was on production and the most important factor, according to Marx, was the mobilization of the productive forces.

The counterpoint puts emphasis on distribution, meeting the basic needs, as the overriding concern. The strategy usually gives small-scale agriculture a key role. Self-reliance is the alternative to capitalist domination and there is reluctance towards urban development. Culturally it seeks support from the traditions of rural life, the village and the family rather than in ideals of modernization. Nyerere's form of "African socialism" can be seen to represent the counterpoint as do Gandhi's ideals of development and social change. As Kitching (1985, pp. 64–70) has shown, these ideals show striking similarities to agricultural populism in 19th-century Russia. The arguments are also familiar to Swedish agricultural development strategies, which, at the beginning of this century, led to the "back to the land movement" (*"egnahemsrörelsen"*), a scheme to provide land for those who wanted to return to the rural areas. It had strong support in the agrarian party but also in various socialist groupings (see, for example, Seyler, 1983, pp. 290–295). Culturally it implied revival of rural cultures, the "wholeness of life" as opposed to the devastating effects of industrialism and urban life (Sundin,

[1] See also Fägerlind and Shaha (1983, pp. 26–27) for a distinction between linear and cyclical theories.

1984). It was argued that small-scale agriculture was the most efficient form of agricultural production.

The term "populism," has been used to describe widely different social movements and intellectual traditions.[1] It will be used here to describe the strategy of development which sees the alternative to capitalist domination to be to increase the degree of self-reliance mainly through small-scale rural development and for which urban industrial development is only reluctantly accepted or given less priority. It could be noted that Marx saw the peasantry as a class that would disappear as a result of polarization between capitalists and the proletariat. Technological advancement and increasing division of labor were necessary stages on the road to socialism. The difference on this point between the two traditions can be illustrated by Mikhailovskij's law of progress, which represents the counterpoint: "Progress is the gradual approach to the integral individual, to the fullest possible and the most diversified division of labor among man's organs and the least possible division of labor among men. Everything that diminishes the heterogeneity of society and thereby increases the heterogeneity of its members is moral, just, reasonable, and beneficial." (Quoted in Hettne, 1982, p. 96.) The question is how education should respond. In the Marxist tradition the answer has been polytechnical education, which according to Marx would, "in the case of every child over a given age combine productive labour with instruction and gymnastics, not only as one of the methods of adding to the efficiency of production but as the only method of producing fully developed human beings."[2] Nyerere reaches the same conclusions, although, as illustrated above, from a partly different strategy of development. His most important concern is that schools and pupils must recreate the contacts with rural life which they have lost through the colonial system, which has educated an urban elite. Or, in the words of Nyerere, "there must be the same kind of relationship between pupils within the school community as there is between children and parents in the village. And the former community must realize, just as the latter do, that their life and well-being depend upon the production of wealth by farming and other activities [therefore] every school should also be a farm the school community should consist of people who are both teachers and pupils and farmers" (Nyerere, 1967). In both cases it is an education with strong moral objectives in relation to work and participation in the process of development. It seeks the wholeness of the individual, in the case of Marx, to counteract the negative consequences of an increasing but necessary division of labor in the case of Nyerere as a reflection of small-scale and less specialized forms of production.

[1] See Conovan (1981). Conovan illustrates the difficulties in finding a common denominator of the term. Historically it has been used for such diverse social and intellectual movements as Russian rural populism in the 19th century to political populism in Peronist Argentine. Here it refers to rural populism as an alternative to capitalist development.

[2] As phrased by Marx in *Das Capital*, Vol. 1, Section 9: Machinery and modern industry.

Education and Development in Zimbabwe

Independent Zimbabwe inherited many of the features associated with a dual economy—large, highly mechanized farms, mines and industries in white hands and the majority of the black population employed as farm workers or living in the so-called Tribal Trust Lands, which gave only a small surplus. At the time of independence only 10 percent of the surplus value of agricultural production came from the small African units. This proportion has later increased. The industrial expansion that had taken place from 1945 had, by and large, widened the differences between the two sectors rather than narrowed them. The modern sector essentially served the white population and "African consumption or the lack of it was of little concern to the white ruling class" (Simson, 1979, pp. 65–66).

The strategy adopted after independence was to restore and increase the capacity of production and at the same redistribute the benefits more evenly without drastic measures to nationalize industries or to expropriate the so-called European farms. This policy was labeled "growth with equity." In the agricultural field change would come about through integration between commercial and self-subsistence sectors. This would include support to communal private/family as well as to State farms. In particular, assistance would be given "to those communities which are democratically organized and run farms in which local initiative is highest." Also the development of small- and medium-scale manufacturing and commercial enterprises around small centers would be encouraged. In the industrial sector it was emphasized that efficiency ought to be improved so that Zimbabwe could compete internationally. At the same time it was important to direct production towards internal demand (Government of Zimbabwe 1981).

One of the benefits to be distributed more evenly, particularly between blacks and whites, was education. Primary education was made free and the examination for Africans after Standard 7 was no longer used as a selection instrument for access to secondary education. Everybody was allowed to continue up to "O" level (Form 4). As a result, the formal education system has grown very rapidly, at the primary level from 820,000 in 1979 to 2,500,000 pupils in 1984. At the secondary level (Forms 1–4), expansion has been even faster with numbers growing from 66,000 in 1979 to 416,000 in 1984.

Not surprisingly, the "O" level results in 1984 were below expectations. Described as, appallingly low by the Prime Minister,[1] they gave new impetus to the reform work, of which the ZIMFEP schools are an important part. Discussions are now going on about the future direction and content of secondary education.

The theoretical basis for the reform of education is in the Marxist tradition of polytechnic education, with frequent references to Marx, Lenin and Kim

[1] As quoted in an article in the *Sunday Mail*, 31 Mar. 1985.

Il Sung (Chung and Ngara, 1985). But what does it mean in practice, given the existing social and economic structure? Can a formula be found which breaks with the traditional liberal education of formal education without being associated with the adaption concept of the past, which meant a practically-oriented education for the African students? If we should judge from the speeches made by the Minister of Education and others, in connection with the ZIMFEP program, this is how the problem has been seen. The overall objective has been, as expressed by the Minister, to "link learning with job creation, the school with industrial and cooperative development."[1] In other speeches he has talked about the new idiom as "the highest academic, practical and managerial skills to be combined."[2] At the same time, the Minister has taken great pains to explain that the ZIMFEP schools are not the "resuscitation of F2 schools under another guise." He has done this, he says because "many people confuse it [the ZIMFEP program] with having a school garden or doing some manual labor and others tend to equate it with the F2 schools of the past."[3]

More specifically, the objectives can be summarized as in Table 1.

What has been achieved?

The ZIMFEP schools, which in 1985 had about 5400 students in the eight secondary schools and about 2000 in the four primary schools, are all located on former European farms, varying in size between 800 and 6500 hectares. The schools offer the common core of subjects and the students sit for the same Cambridge Examination as students in other schools in the country. For this they are fully funded by the Ministry of Education. For their productive activities (defined as work in this chapter) they have depended on their income, or funds from various donor agencies, through ZIMFEP. The productive activities have therefore tended to come as additions to, rather than as an integral part of, a new and different curriculum. However they involve themselves in a number of activities which make their profile different from other secondary schools.

First, they have an impressive record of student participation in construction of the schools. Few negative reactions have been reported against student participation in such work. Students are also involved in gardening, poultry-keeping and handicrafts and some schools have started workshops

[1] Speech by the Minister of Education at ZIMFEP Textile Exhibition, 5 Dec. 1983.
[2] Speech by the Minister of Education at Workshop on Education with Production, 8 May 1984.
[3] Speech by the Minister of Education at the ZIMFEP Textile Exhibition, 5 Dec. 1983. The F2 schools were introduced by the Smith Government in 1970 as an alternative to secondary education for African students. They had a heavy bias towards practical subjects. Politically they came to represent the very essence of discrimination of the African population in a racially segregated system of education. They were abolished in 1978 due to opposition from students and parents.

TABLE 1. *Summary of Objectives of the ZIMFEP Schools*

Level/dimension	Ideological	Economic	Pedagogical
Students	Positive attitude towards manual work; understanding of one's role and the role of work in a context of socialist transformation; respect for peasants and workers	Students to become self-reliant through knowledge and skills applicable to work	Learning through practical experience; application of book-learning in real-life situations
School	Schools to become mini-community, which combines manual and mental labor; management practices to become more democratic	Schools to become partly self-supporting; schools to develop and seek linkages with the local community	Integration between theory and practice within and between subjects
National	Bridge the gap between manual and mental labor in society; promote participation in decision-making	Education to promote economic growth; employment creation through formation of cooperatives	Promote national education reform

Source: Gustafsson (1985b).

for production of school uniforms and school furniture. Up to 1985, students were also involved in large-scale commercial farming. The schools had by then started to cultivate only a small proportion of their arable land, varying between 25 and 140 ha; some schools had cattle. In view of a planned expansion of commercial farming it was then decided that large-scale farming should be separated from the daily activities of the school and be run by professional farm managers. Students would work on smaller demonstration plots. The schools have also had the ambition to create links with the community, through community theatre and literacy work. However, with the exception of one school (J.Z. Moyo Secondary), which launched a food-for-work program for the inhabitants in surrounding drought-stricken villages, this whole field of community participation has been largely unexplored. ZIMFEP has helped to place former students in jobs and has supported students who have established cooperatives after completion of their studies. A democratic form of government is an important feature of EWP. As expressed by one headmaster (Rusununguko Secondary School) "it is the revolutionary participatory democracy that we thirst after." This school has made deliberate attempts to build up a democratic committee system with representatives of students and staff at various levels, rotating chairmanship, prefects being elected by their fellow-students, etc. Although some other schools report on committees being set up for various tasks, there is no reference made in relation to democratic forms of government. Schools in Zimbabwe are hierarchical by tradition and this has probably been reinforced rather than lessened by the fact that the ex-refugees were used to military organization and discipline during the war.

The main problem, however, has been to define the role of the schools in a national context. They are innovative and experimental at the same time as they conform to existing rules and regulations. This has also created confusion among education officers in the field who, at least initially, saw them as a new and disturbing element in the existing system. Or, in the words of the Minister: "It is because I knew that the task would be controversial and that it would meet with opposition that I proposed that an independent welfare organization—ZIMFEP—be set up to lay the groundwork for substantive change. I believed that such an organization would have more freedom to experiment and would not be a prisoner of the bureaucratic structure inherited from the past."[1] Unlike the brigades in Botswana, the ZIMFEP program is closely related to the reform going on within the Ministry of Education. It was set up by the Minister and there are close linkages at the personal level, the Chairman of the ZIMFEP board being Head of Curriculum Development within the Ministry of Education. Their future is therefore closely linked to and a reflection of the discussion taking place at the national level. So, what are the options? This will be discussed below in light of the previous distinction made between mainstream and counterpoint perspectives on development. It should be noted then, that in the real world the dichotomies used, urban–rural, small-scale versus large-scale, are relative rather than absolute categories. However, within this framework there are many questions raised in Zimbabwe, for example to what extent it is of value that schools are partly self-financing? Should schools prepare students for small-scale rural production or should this type of production be seen as something of the past, or very temporary until this sector has been completely transformed and modernized? What should be the balance between ideological and economic objectives?

The Zimbabwean Discussion[2]

Following the socialist policy of the Government, the ideological objectives are important in Zimbabwe. Typical passages to express this are the following: "our socialist struggle will succeed or fail depending on our ability

[1] Speech by the Minister of Education at the ZIMFEP Workshop on Finance and Administration, 6 May 1983. Quoted in Gustafsson (1985b).
[2] Dr Uschevekunze addressing students and staff at Morgenster Teachers College 11 Nov. 1982.

to integrate manual and intellectual work in all spheres of life."[1] Therefore it should be important also for people in offices to know "how to do manual labor" (Gustafsson, 1985b, p. 12). In this context, work is something for all, irrespective of future occupation. A new syllabus for political education worked out within ZIMFEP, democratic forms of government within schools and work, could be seen as the cornerstones of this ideological objective.

In the economic perspective, ZIMFEP has worked out a curriculum for technical education which, if accepted, would drastically alter the balance between the arts subjects and the technical/practical subjects. It has even been suggested that students should sit for the "O" level examination and take a trade test (Gustafsson (1985b, p. 15).[2] The ZIMFEP schools themselves have tended to emphasize this point when asked to define EWP. The teachers of the practical subjects have often been asked to respond to questions about EWP and they usually talk about skill training or production of useful articles as the essence of EWP. This can be seen as a reflection of the broad discussion about the diversification of the secondary school curriculum, but this does not necessarily mean that work should form part of the curriculum. Preparation for employment may or may not imply training in real work situations; and it may or may not mean that the training should generate income to finance the education. Therefore, it has been argued by some that work as a means to finance education was only necessary during the initial stages, in the camps as a means for survival. In independent Zimbabwe it is the role of the State to finance education and besides, it is very difficult, as experience seems to suggest, to combine education with commercial farming. The Minister has touched on this problem indirectly when he said that it will not be possible for all schoolchildren to get access to factory floor experience, because there are not enough places.[3] Given the present economic structure, EWP is, therefore, in the economic perspective, small-scale agriculture and related productive activities. This is where schools can practice EWP, create employment and seek linkages with the local community. This is the reasoning of Nyerere and has always been important for the brigades in Botswana.

The third dimension, according to our classification of objectives above, is pedagogical, work as a means to link theory and practice. This seems to be a common denominator of EWP in Zimbabwe, whatever views are expressed

---

[1] Mrs Mudenge, who was the Director of ZIMFEP in 1984, argued strongly at a workshop on EWP, 8–11 May 1984, for a stronger bias towards vocational training. For a recording of the full texts of the speeches at this workshop see: *Education with Production*, the Report on the First National Workshop on Education with Production, 8–11 May 1984, Harare 1984, ZIMFEP Secretariate.

[2] This section is also based on interviews with staff at ZIMFEP and officials in the Ministry of Education in Zimbabwe.

[3] The Minister of Education, as quoted in an article in the *Herald*, 18 April 1985, "Phenomenal strides in education."

otherwise on the need to create socialism or to make schools partly self-financing. Also, this point relates to frequent criticism against teaching in African schools for being concerned with rote-learning, being "too bookish," etc. It does not necessarily follow, however, that work should be part of the curriculum. The ZIMFEP schools offer many interesting examples of how work can be used to link theory and practice, but those who want to object may find support in alternative methods to reach the same objective. In view of the above one may ask what the likely position and role of work is going to be?

Conclusions

The role given to work in education in Zimbabwe can probably best be understood in the ideological perspective. Derived as it is from the idiom of polytechnical education, the policy of the Government has become to integrate work with education at all levels of the system. The overall objective is moral/social rather than economic. Work is important for all, irrespective of future occupation, perhaps even more so for those who are not going to work with their hands. The curriculum development work undertaken by ZIMFEP should also be seen in this perspective. Rather than making secondary education more specialized and directed towards specific occupations, it has sought to alter the balance of subjects in favor of the technical/practical side. These efforts should not be seen as "diversification," in the sense of making secondary education more relevant to future manual occupations. It is an effort to counteract the negative effects of increasing specialization and division of labor, rather than adjusting to it.

If this is accepted, the question is how the ZIMFEP model can be replicated in all primary and secondary schools in the country. These schools are, for the most part, small day schools and they are located in the rural, communal areas (formerly Tribal Trust Lands). In addition to this, as the Minister has pointed out, the mere scarcity of places in the industries and mines, prevents integration between schools and industry on a large scale. The experience from student involvement in commercial farming on the ZIMFEP farms, seems to suggest that the best opportunities for EWP will be in small-scale, cooperative units of production in the rural areas or at growth points. It seems, therefore, reasonable to conclude that the replication of the ZIMFEP model will depend, at least in part, on the strength of the ideological argument on the one hand, and on the other, the priority given to small-scale cooperative forms of production in the rural areas, i.e., features of development typical of the counterpoint.[1]

[1] This article covers developments up to the beginning of 1986. Important policy decisions have been taken since by the Government. For further details and analysis of recent developments see: Gustafsson I. (1987), pp. 130–156.

References

Chung, F. and Ngara, E. (1985) *Socialism, education and development—a challenge to Zimbabwe*. Harare: Zimbabwe Publishing House.

Fägerlind, I. and Saha, L. (1983) *Education and national development* (pp. 139–143). Oxford: Pergamon Press.

Government of the Republic of Zimbabwe (1981) *Growth with equity—an economic policy statement*. Harare: Government Printers.

Gustafsson, I. (1985a) *Integration between education and work at primary and post-primary level—the case of Botswana*. Stockholm: University of Stockholm, Institute of International Education, Working Paper No. 95.

Gustafsson, I. (1985b) *Foundation for education for production—a follow-up study*. Stockholm: SIDA, Education Division Documents No. 29.

Gustafsson, I. (1987) "Schools and the transformation of work. A comparative study of four productive work programmes in Southern Africa." Stockholm: Institute of International Education, University of Stockholm.

Hettne, B. (1982) *Development theory and the third world*. Stockholm: SAREC Report R2, Swedish Agency for Research Cooperation with Developing Countries.

Kitching, G. (1985) *Populism, nationalism and industrialisation*. New York: Methuen.

NEIDA (1982) *Education and productive work in Africa* (p. 9). Dakar: UNESCO Regional Office for Education in Africa.

Nyerere, J. (1967) *Education for self-reliance*. Dar es Salaam: Government Printer.

Parsons, Q. N. (1983) *Report on the Botswana brigades*. Gaborone: National Institute of Development Research and Documentation, University of Botswana.

Rensburg, P. van (1967) *Education and development in an emerging country*. Uppsala: Scandinavian Institute for African Studies/Almqvist and Wixell.

Rensburg, P. van (1974) *Report from Swaneng Hill*. Uppsala: The Dag Hammarsköld Foundation.

Rensburg, P. van (1984) *Looking forward from Serowe*. Gaborone: Foundation for Education with Production.

Seyler, H. (1983) *Hur bonden bler lönearbetare, industrisamhället och den svenska bondeklassers omvandling* (How the independent farmer became a wage labourer). Lund: Studentlitteratur (Summary in English).

Simson, H. (1979) *Zimbabwe—a country study*. Research Report No. 53. Uppsala: Scandinavian Institute of African Studies.

Sundin, B. (1984) Ljus och jord. In T. Frängsmyr (Ed.), *Paradiset och vildmarken—studier kring synen pa naturen och naturresurserna*. Stockholm: Liber Tryck.

PART 4
Empirical Evaluation Studies

Introductory Note

LAUGLO and Närman present a study of industrial education (IE) subjects (woodwork, metalwork, power, electricity) which exist within the mainly academic curriculum of Kenyan junior secondary schools. They conclude that it has been possible to establish such practical subjects as "viable pedagogic systems" in terms of attraction to students, teacher morale and competence. But they have very high unit costs, have benefited greatly from foreign aid and exist in a small number of schools. They also find that the IE subjects do increase aspirations towards practical/technical occupations, but this occurs in a context where there is an acute shortage of opportunity—not of interest in such work. Crucially, however, IE subjects give no labor market advantage. Indeed, "good" school credentials in general do not seem to confer any advantage, suggesting that conventional assumptions about the importance of school certificates for access to jobs need to be re-examined. They suggest that policymakers, students and parents alike interpret the labor market opportunities associated with IE subjects "through a glass darkly": hopes are generated which do not match reality, but which make such subjects seem attractive to students as a way of "hedging one's bets" on further academic study.

Also within the context of the wider international debate, Psacharopoulos reports the results of a large-scale empirical evaluation of diversified secondary school systems in Colombia and Tanzania. He finds that, relative to schools offering conventional curricula, the schools with diversified curricula (pre-vocational subjects) recruit more students from poor origins, and that diversification does produce cognitive learning gains in the intended direction. But graduates from these schools do not find jobs more easily, nor do they earn more than graduates from control schools. Since "diversified curricula" are more costly than conventional ones, they are therefore, in terms of economic cost–benefit analysis, a poor investment.

King presents a critique of the interpretations and data base in the Tanzanian part of Psacharopoulos' study. He notes, *inter alia*, the importance of ideals relating to pedagogy and political socialization, not only economic relevance and "equity" aspects.

Chin-Aleong examines recent thrusts towards diversification of the secondary curriculum in Trinidad, pinpointing goals and modalities for different vocationalization models which have operated there. He argues that these innovations are based upon intuitive responses to economic and labor market conditions and not grounded in empirical evaluation. He argues the case for cost-effectiveness analysis, especially when allied with other evaluation techniques. Like Lauglo and Närman, and Psacharopoulos he provides evidence on the labor market performance of

233

graduates, and concludes that insignificant labor market advantages do not justify the costs of pre-vocational subjects (though training in greater depth and in a growing economy could be a different matter).

These studies are remarkably similar in finding that it is a costly policy to introduce pre-vocational subjects into the curriculum of general secondary schools, and that policy effectiveness is dubious if the goal is to help school-leavers find a source of livelihood under difficult labor market conditions. Wilm's conclusion in the review of empirical research in the United States (cf. Chapter 5) was a similar one. However, training in greater depth and under less depressed labor market conditions, might show greater effectiveness.

THE EDITORS

CHAPTER 14

Diversified Secondary Education in Kenya:
The Status of Practical Subjects and their Uses
after School*

JON LAUGLO

University of London

ANDERS NÄRMAN

University of Gothenburg

IN many countries, present policy for mainstream secondary schools favors curriculum change in a practical or vocational direction. A number of recent literature reviews and studies have examined some of the reasons and rationales for such policies, the problems of implementing them as viable pedagogic systems in the schools, and aspects of their external effectiveness in some countries (Grubb, 1985; Lillis and Hogan, 1983; Lillis, 1985; Psacharopoulos and Loxley, 1985). It is a truly international trend in that it transcends the divide between rich and poor countries, and it is manifest both in socialist countries and liberal democracies.

There are long-established concepts of general education which support the inclusion of practical subjects within general education. Thus both North American prevailing concepts of general education, with the pragmatist philosophical underpinnings, as well as the socialist ideal of polytechnical education, provide rationale for such subjects as part of general secondary education, regardless of the immediate labor market context (Lauglo, 1983). But in the main, the reason for the present trend lies outside educational ideology. It has become politically important because of the internationally depressed labor markets for secondary-school-leavers. Thus, the goals of "curriculum diversification" in a practical direction often include that of transmitting skills and attitudes which will be useful in gaining jobs and within employment. The common feature is a quest for more directly vocational relevance than "academic" curricula are said to have. In developing countries, particular emphasis is sometimes also given to

* The sponsorship by the Swedish International Development Authority of the reported research project is greatly appreciated, as is the personal interest taken in the project by Kenth Wickmann of SIDA. This paper has appeared as a journal article in another Pergamon publication: *The International Journal of Education Development*, Vol. 7, No. 2, 1987.

generating favorable attitudes to living and working in rural areas and to the goal of preparing for self-employment.

The patterns of such "vocationalization" vary. Establishing or expanding school-based vocational education that is institutionally separate from the prevalent "academic" secondary schools is one example. But often policies aim to establish compulsory or optional vocationalized components within otherwise academic curricula in mainstream secondary schools. In the latter case, the goal tends to be "pre-vocational": developing skills and attitudes conducive to acquiring more specific work skills after leaving school—either in further schooling or on the job. In either case, the aim is to prepare pupils for entry into occupations which are manifestly related to the practical subjects they study at school. In practice, there is no clear distinction between vocational and pre-vocational education, especially since school-based vocational education often is also regarded as incomplete and requiring further on-the-job training.

There is a long-standing controversy about how far such curriculum diversification in fact increases the economic usefulness of education (Foster, 1965; Weeks, 1978; Blaug, 1973). Even about higher education, Psacharopoulos (1980) has presented evidence that questions the superiority of purportedly more "applied" and technology-orientated subjects in terms of better economic cost–benefit ratios. But follow-up studies of students into the labor market have been few and far between. In the main, recent large-scale (but short-term) tracer studies support the pessimists (cf. Wilms and Hansell, 1982 (in the United States) and Psacharopoulos and Loxley, 1985 (in Colombia and Tanzania)). But long-term tracer studies are needed for more reliable data about the degree to which practical subjects give a labor market advantage, especially so in developing countries, where school-leavers often face a period of job search that may take several years during which they undertake a variety of short-term economic activities (Hoppers, 1985 p. 22).

Quite apart from their external effectiveness for labor market advantage, practical subjects are fraught with a number of difficulties which need to be overcome before they can be established as viable pedagogic systems. They are invariably more expensive than those academic subjects which at a minimum can be taught on a purely chalk-and-talk basis, partly because of the cost connected with equipment, workshops and materials requirements, and partly because they usually need to be taught in smaller classes. Their facilities, equipment and materials also pose greater demands in terms of managing logistics requirements and the initial establishment of these subjects. Competent teachers are difficult to recruit and train—and to keep, if their competence is better paid in other jobs. A pervasive problem in many countries has been the lack of attraction of practical subjects to parents and pupils. Such subjects are commonly said to suffer from demoralization among teachers and pupils alike. It is often claimed that both groups are reluctant participants in this area of education, and would veer towards better rewarded activities if they were given the opportunity.

The status of such subjects is likely to reflect the perceived post-school opportunities to which they lead—even when the subjects officially are defined as part of "general education." The labor market advantage—or lack of such—that these subjects are thought to give will be one important factor in this regard. Another important factor will be whether the study of these subjects implies that opportunities for further education of an "academic" kind will be curtailed. Thus, the status of practical subjects in the schools and the post-school opportunities to which they are perceived to lead, are closely interrelated issues.

In the present study, which is more fully reported in a series of documents from the Education Division of The Swedish International Development Authority (Lauglo, 1985a; Närman, 1985; Cumming *et al.*, 1985), we shall examine the status of "industrial education" subjects in 35 Kenyan academic secondary schools, the aspirations of students and their destination after leaving the lower stage of the secondary system.

The "Industrial Education" Subjects in Kenyan Schools

The "industrial education" subjects (hereafter referred to as IE) consist of wood technology and metal technology, which are taught as a combination at 24 schools, and of power mechanics and electrical technology, which are taught as a combination in 10 schools. Moreover, there is one school which offers wood technology. Each school is typically provided with two IE workshops, one for each IE subject offered. In these 35 government-maintained secondary schools, IE is usually compulsory in the two first forms (grades). But in Forms 3 and 4, IE is offered as an optional subject that is usually available to about one-third of the students. The students continuing with IE prepare for the lower secondary Kenya Certificate of Education (KCE) examination ("O" level) in one of the two IE variants available at each school. The IE subjects are partly assessed by a practical project or exam, and partly by an examination in related theory.

Students taking IE also prepare for at least five KCE examinations in academic subjects. In each form, students usually devote about six weekly class periods to IE—only a small proportion of their total weekly timetable of some 40+ class periods. Thus, IE functions as a "practical" supplement to an otherwise entirely "academic" course. By taking IE as a KCE subject, students may still hope to qualify for academic upper secondary school; and their range of subjects for that purpose will be only slightly restricted. IE subjects do not continue in the upper secondary stage which prepares for higher education. Nor does IE confer any officially recognized qualification or priority for selection to jobs or training schemes. The sole exception is teacher training in IE itself, but access to such training also requires upper secondary credentials.

With few exceptions, the IE schools are boys' schools. The schools constitute a small part of the government-maintained Kenyan secondary school sector of 413 schools. There is also a much larger number of Harambee (local self–help) schools. The government-maintained sector is very superior to Harambee schools in terms of examination results. Within the government-maintained sector, IE has been introduced disproportionately in "advantaged" schools. Thus, IE is found in a small number of schools of relatively high status (larger, longer-established schools with "good" exam results). The great majority of them (27 schools) were in the old Kenyan grading system classified as "A" schools—the very best grade. One might expect that this has eased the management of introducing the IE subjects (cf. Lillis, 1985). But one could also argue that the appeal to students would be greater in schools where the prospect of continued academic education would seem more remote than in these "elite" institutions from which more than 40 per cent of the students continue to the upper academic stage (Form 5), as shown in Table 4.

During 1969–1981 IE received substantial support from Swedish Aid. SIDA provided volunteer teachers to establish and teach IE until Kenyan IE teachers could be trained; it established and initially staffed teacher education in IE; it built/renovated and equipped/upgraded IE workshops. SIDA also established a unit to assist nationally in the maintenance of these workshops. Thus, the IE subjects benefited from substantial and comprehensive external assistance until 1981.

All four types of IE workshop were provided with relatively sophisticated equipment including a number of power-driven machines. One may query the appropriateness of the equipment in terms of expense and students' opportunity to use their skills later in life. But it is likely that the equipment's connotation of "advanced technology" helped to raise the status of the IE subjects in the eyes of students. The level of equipment may also have conveyed an exaggerated impression of the vocational opportunity associated with IE. Officially, the IE subjects aimed to be part of general education. But the IE subject syllabuses have a distinctly pre-vocational character. Further, IE tends to be perceived, both by teachers and students, as preparatory for work or further training in the different IE specialties.

The Scope of the Research Activities

The research extended from 1983 to 1985 and was carried out by an international team. In addition to the authors, it included: C.E. Cumming (Moray House College of Education), Martin Davies (SIDA Nairobi), Kevin Lillis (University of London), B.G. Nyagah (Inspectorate, Nairobi) and Daniel Sifuna (Kenyatta University).

The sources of data were: documentation, examination results, interviews with Kenyan and SIDA officials, observation of workshops during visits to most IE schools and a number of surveys which used a mixture of group and individual interviews and questionnaires. These groups were surveyed: headmasters of IE schools, Swedish former volunteer teachers of IE, Kenyan IE teachers and teachers of other subjects, parents of IE students, groups of students with varying degrees of experience of IE (four years of IE, two years of IE, no IE), and a small exploratory survey of employers. The student surveys included several small-scale tracer studies and one large-scale follow-up of students one year after the lower secondary KCE examination.

The evaluation sought to answer a wide range of questions: What are the aims and objectives of IE? What has the international experience been with similar subjects? What influences have shaped the development of IE in Kenya? How do the schools offering IE compare with other secondary schools? What do students, parents, teachers and headmasters expect from IE? What is the status of IE in the schools? Do the various IE subjects differ in their attractiveness to students? What kind of student takes IE as an examination subject? Is IE a "soft option" that attracts students because it is thought to be easy to pass or do well in? How do IE teachers compare with academic teachers in terms of rated competence and professional morale? How are the practical skills taught and how does the style of teaching accord with the declared aims of IE? What do IE teachers perceive to be the main problems related to IE and to their own job? What role did the Swedish volunteer teachers play in developing IE in the schools? How well are the provided facilities utilized? Is the level of equipment too advanced? What happens to IE students after lower secondary school? What uses do they make of IE? In particular, does IE help them in earning a living? How does IE compare with other subjects in terms of recurrent costs and development costs? What has SIDA spent on aid to IE and what have these expenditures been devoted to?

The main report (Lauglo, 1985a) from the project addresses the full range of these questions. In the present chapter we shall focus more narrowly on the status of IE in the schools and on the destination of students.

The Status of IE in the Schools

Ratings by School Staff

Three groups of staff answered questionnaires: headteachers of IE schools, teachers of IE and at each school certain designated "other teachers." These "other teachers" were the heads of department in mathematics, science, English, geography and the teacher with special responsibility for careers guidance. A very high rate of response was obtained from all these categories. Only from five out of the 35 government-maintained schools did we end up with no response from one or more category of staff. Nearly complete returns were obtained from the schools that were reached.

TABLE 1. *Teachers' Ratings of the Popularity of IE Subjects*

Response option	IE teachers (%)	Headteachers (%)	Other teachers (%)
Much more popular	28.6	12.1	9.6
More popular	35.7	36.4	18.4
About the same	18.8	39.4	44.9
Less popular	16.1	9.1	25.7
Much less popular	0.9	3.0	1.5
Total	100.0	100.0	100.0
No. of cases	(112)	(33)	(136)

They were asked: "How popular is IE among students compared to other school subjects?" Table 1 shows that even amongst "other teachers"— these take the least generous view—the vast majority rate IE to be "about the same" or "more" popular than other subjects. "Popularity" is not necessarily an indicator of "high status." It could be that students are attracted to a subject because it is widely perceived to be a "soft option", i.e., that it is relatively easy to pass and do well in. But few teachers perceive IE to be a "soft option." They were asked: "In your school, is it easier for a student to get a good grade in IE than in other KCE subjects?" In each category of staff, only 30–33 percent answered "yes" or "yes, very much" to these questions, whilst 47–58 percent across the three categories said "no" or "no, not at all"—the others answered "don't know."

Further, most school staff do not think that IE is more suited for academically weak students than for those who do well. They were asked: "For what group of students do you think IE is better suited? 'the academically above average' or 'those below average'?" Again one sees (Table 2) that it is the "other teachers" who have the least generous view of IE. But even among this group, the vast majority do not see IE as a subject that would be especially appropriate for "academic rejects."

Analysis of Examination Results

One might suspect that these ratings are subject to bias in favor of what teachers and headteachers think the Ministry of Education and SIDA would like to see. If so, IE could still be a "soft option" which as an examination subject would tend to recruit students who do poorly in academic subjects. Is this the case?

TABLE 2. *For What Type of Student do School Staff think IE is Especially Suited?*

Response option	IE teachers (%)	Headteachers (%)	Other teachers (%)
Those above average	59.8	42.4	11.9
Equally suited for both groups	40.2	45.5	66.4
Those below average	—	12.1	21.6
Total	100.0	100.0	100.0
No. of cases	(112)	(33)	(134)

Examination results at IE schools were consulted in order to answer these questions. It was found that at most schools, the IE results were on the average poorer than the results in English and Mathematics. IE could still be a "soft option" in the exam if those who take it are academically weak and do worse than others in Maths and English. To shed light on this question, we examined the examination results of only those students who did IE. Do these students perform better in IE or in maths and English? Data were available for 22 schools in the 1983 KCE examination. It was found that in all but four of these schools, the same students did on the average marginally or substantially *better* in the compulsory academic subjects of English and maths than they did in IE. Thus, if IE is popular, it is not because it is an easy subject to excel in.

In these circumstances, who takes IE as an examination subject "high flyers" or those who perform below average in key academic subjects? The former would indicate that IE has high status in the schools; the latter would suggest the opposite. By comparing students taking IE as an exam subject with the greater number who do not (but who also took it as a compulsory subject in Forms 1 and 2), in terms of their *academic* achievement, an answer is provided. Figure 1 gives such a comparison for mathematics, Fig. 2 for English. In these charts, a numerically low grade indicates a good result on a marking scale from 1 to 9 (9 is a failure). The diagonal line in the charts runs through the points where these two groups of students would have the same average grade. At all schools falling below the diagonal, the IE students did on the average better than students not continuing with IE beyond Form 2. Figure 1 shows a very clear tendency: at most schools the IE students do better in mathematics than the non-IE students. This is also true for the "top elite" schools of Alliance, Mangu and Lenana. Further, one notes that the schools teaching the more "advanced-technology" versions of IE— power mechanics and electrical technology—stand out more clearly in this respect than those teaching wood technology and metal technology. A similar affinity between practical/technical subjects and maths performance is also found in the technical secondary schools in Kenya (Lauglo, 1985b).

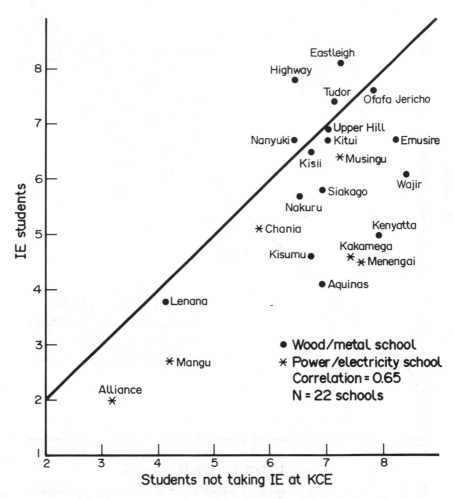

FIG 1. 1983 KCE. School average grade in mathematics: Comparison of IE students
and non-IE students at same school.

As to English achievement (Fig. 2) a different picture emerges: Here the
schools are quite evenly distributed below and above the "equal average
grades" diagonal. But also in this case there is clearly no general tendency
for IE students to be academically inferior to non-IE students.

For both of these core academic subjects, especially for mathematics,
there are considerable differences among the schools. What lies behind
these differences? One possibility is the streaming practices. At most
schools there are restrictions on what optional subjects students may
combine in Forms 3 and 4, within the range of offerings. The IE teachers
were asked (group interviews supplemented by questionnaires): "Are there

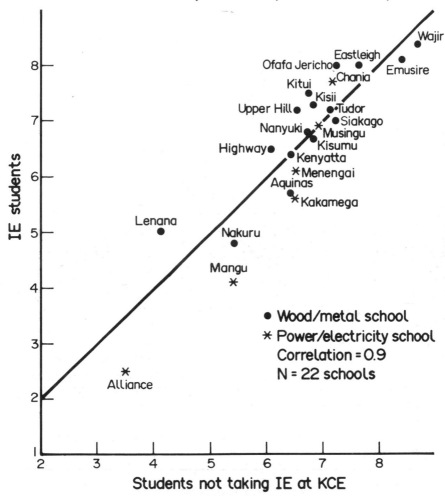

FIG 2. 1983 KCE. School average grade in English: Comparison of IE students and non-IE students at same school.

any KCE subjects which may be taken by students in other streams, but not in the streams that take IE at your school?" The subjects most frequently mentioned among the 35 schools for which data were obtained, were: business subjects, religious education, history, pure science (rather than the "integrated" physical science which tends to have lower status) and agriculture. They were also asked: "Does this streaming discourage brighter students from taking IE at Form 3 level?" How far does the perceived disadvantage or advantage due to streaming arrangements explain the relative academic caliber of IE students, as compared with non-IE students, in the different schools? Figure 3 presents some pertinent findings, using mathematics as the indicator of "academic caliber".

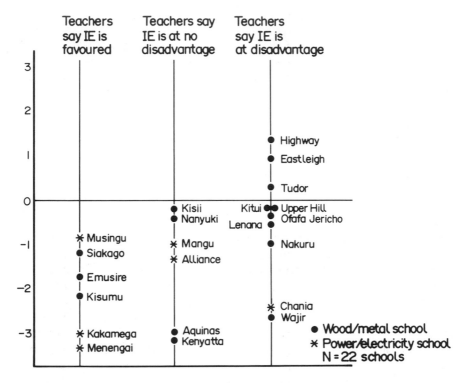

FIG 3. 1983 KCE. The difference between average maths grade of IE students and other students at same school, by IE teachers' impression about the effect of IE of streaming/setting arrangements at the school.

Information was available for only 22 schools. These are grouped according to the IE teachers' assessment. The scale shows: (maths average grade for IE students) minus (maths average grade for non-IE students). Since a "good" grade is a numerically low one, a negative difference means that IE students did better than non-IE students. The chart shows a pattern in the expected direction. IE students tend to stand out more favorably in maths, compared to non-IE students, when IE teachers think their subject is favored by the streaming arrangements. But the attraction of IE to students of good academic ability is shown by the fact that even when IE teachers feel their subject is discriminated against, IE is in most cases able to "hold its own" in attracting students who do well in mathematics.

It could be argued that IE has been favored with so much special assistance that the findings above are unlikely to apply to other pre-vocational or practical subjects which have not similarly benefited from comprehensive external support. To examine this possibility, other practical or pre-vocational subjects which also happened to be taught in IE schools were studied—again in terms of the mathematics achievement among students taking these subjects as compared with students not taking such subjects for examination purposes. Ten schools offered courses in "principles of accounts". In six of these schools, students taking accounts did better than other students in mathematics. Twelve schools offered courses in commerce. At five of these schools, the commerce students did better than other students in mathematics. Finally, five schools offered courses in Agriculture. At four of these schools, students taking agriculture did, on average, better in mathematics than other students. Clearly, on the whole, the limited data available do not suggest that other practical/pre-vocational subjects suffer the fate of being inferior options that mainly attract academically "inferior" students.

Teacher Morale

Headteachers were asked to rate their IE teachers in terms of relative competence: "In general, how good are your IE teachers compared with your other teachers, in teaching their subject?" Forty-eight percent of 34 headmasters answered either "Better" or "Slightly better," and 59 percent gave "About the same" as their answer. Only one headteacher gave the rating "Slightly worse." None rated the IE teachers as clearly "Worse." Most of these ratings were obtained during face-to-face interviews with the impression of frank answers. A very great response bias would indeed be required to invalidate the conclusion that headteachers do not regard the IE teachers as professionally inferior to teachers in academic subjects. But the headteacher did tend to think that the IE teachers were not as competent as their Swedish volunteer predecessors (before 1981) in establishing workshops and maintaining/repairing equipment. Those IE teachers who had worked alongside a volunteer tended also to have this view themselves.

IE teachers have the same official weekly allocation of teaching periods as academic teachers. During group interviews, the IE teachers invariably argued that IE teaching requires more time than academic teaching—for preparing materials, sharpening tools, maintaining equipment and keeping inventories. Headteachers and the sample of "other teachers" were asked: "Actual teaching time is only a part of the teacher's work. How much extra time do you thing is needed in IE as compared with academic subjects in order to prepare, maintain equipment, etc.?" Seventy-six percent of the 34 headteachers and 75 percent of 132 "other teachers" who answered, said either "Much more time" or "More time." The remainder answered "About the same" with the exception of only three "other teachers" who checked "Less time." Clearly, the IE teachers are supported in their claim of having more work.

With few exceptions, the IE teachers have been formally qualified to also teach either mathematics or physics—either for the full four-year course leading to the KCE exam, or for the first two years. Research currently underway by Närman shows that most of those who trained as IE teachers at Kenya Science Teachers College, teach maths or physics in the secondary school system. Only some 20–25 percent actually teach IE. What about our present sample, which only includes those who are teaching at schools offering IE? Given the extra work required in IE teaching, one might expect that they would prefer to do more teaching in their academic subject—especially since maths and physics are subjects of high status. In fact, in these schools, IE teachers are almost exclusively deployed to teach IE. About 70 percent teach no other subject. Nearly all teach more periods in IE than in their academic subject. Yet we found that IE teachers with few exceptions prefer IE teaching to the teaching of mathematics or physics. They were asked: "In your case, are you happy about the balance in your present teaching load between IE and your academic subject?" Only 8 percent of them checked the answer "I would like to teach more in my academic subject." The others answered either "It is OK as it is" or "I would like to teach more IE." This is an indication of good morale, even if allowance is made for considerable response bias favoring an answer perceived to be the "desired" one.

Other indicators point in the same direction. The IE teachers were asked: "How satisfied are you with being an IE teacher?" The "other teachers"—who as a group had experienced greater career advancement because they are mainly a sample of heads of departments, whilst only 30 percent of IE teachers were head of department—were asked a similar question: "How satisfied are you with being a teacher?" Table 3 shows the answers from these two groups.

TABLE 3. *Satisfaction with Being an IE Teacher/with Being a Teacher*

Response option	IE teachers (%)	Other teachers (%)
Very satisfied	39.3	33.3
Satisfied	46.4	48.6
Not sure	5.4	0.7
Dissatisfied	8.0	13.8
Very dissatisfied	0.9	3.6
Total	100.0	100.0
No. of cases	(112)	(136)
No answer	(1)	(3)

The findings show that IE teachers are, if anything, slightly more satisfied than their academic colleagues. Again, a dramatic response bias would be needed to invalidate the conclusion that most of these teachers are, on the whole, satisfied with their profession. Of course, they might still have wished to enter a more lucrative career if they had the opportunity. Nor should it be taken to mean that there are not aspects of their work which they find difficult to cope with (cf. Lauglo, 1985a). The IE teachers also often lament the lack of opportunities for further education and promotion within IE. But it is still safe to conclude that professional morale among IE teachers is at least as high as among teachers of academic subjects. Thus, the status of IE seems quite high, both in terms of attraction to students and teacher morale. The findings in the survey of parents/guardians of Form 2 IE students at 13 schools also showed near universal parental support for IE, as a desirable exam subject for their child (Lauglo, 1985a, Chapter 7). Interestingly, there was no tendency for more educated parents to be any less keen on IE, than were those with only primary school or less, possibly because the former are more aware about the declining labor-market value of a purely academic secondary education. This greater awareness may offset the tendency which one would otherwise expect: that more educated parents would be less interested in subjects which have connotations of being part of a "terminal" secondary schooling.

Student Aspirations and Destinations after school

Surveys were conducted of students while they were in the final year of their lower secondary course (Närman *et al.*, 1984a) and of students followed up about *one year* after their lower secondary KCE examination (Närman, 1985). In both surveys, it was generally found that students who had experienced IE had a positive view of these subjects, and there was great interest both in continuing their education *and* in entering occupations of a technical/practical kind.

In the follow-up study three categories of student were traced: students who had taken IE for the full four-year lower secondary course in preparation for the KCE exams (Category I); those who had experience of IE in the first two forms but who had not opted for/been selected for IE in Forms 3 and 4 (Category II), and students from five schools which did not offer IE but which were deemed suitable as a control group in terms of location and reputation of overall quality (Category III). An attempt was made to reach the 1514 students who sat for the KCE exam in 1983, by means of a postal questionnaire. Direct information was obtained from 1080 (71 percent). These are the students for whom data on occupational aspirations and expectations are to be analysed, see below. (Some of these were also contacted for personal interviews.) In respect of the educational/occupational activity of ex-students, secondhand information was obtained for an additional 16 percent—giving a total sample of 87 percent (1320 ex-students) for whom at least some information was obtained. The validity of the findings presented in this section gains support from this very high rate of success in tracing ex-students.

Aspirations and Expectations

In the follow-up study, the students were asked: "What kind of job would you wish to have if you could choose freely?" as an open-ended question. The answers were not specific enough to allow a classification as to educational prerequisites or level of pay. Hence, the category "Technical/practical jobs" includes jobs at various levels ranging from clearly manual work to technician jobs. Similarly, "Office jobs" range from clerical job to those of very high status; "Agriculture," ranges from "plucking tea" and "food production on own farm" to "veterinary"; "Medical jobs" include, e.g., doctor, nurse, and local health worker. The categories should mainly be understood as a sectoral classification. Figure 4 gives the categories and the percentage share of all "mentions" falling into each category. A few respondents gave more than one answer. Further, the ex-students were asked: "What kind of job do you actually expect to get?" Using the same occupational groupings, the percentage distribution of answers for the three ex-student categories, is shown in Fig. 5.

The figures show that technical practical jobs are highly rated both in terms of "job if freely chosen" and the actual expectation. This is more true for "job if freely chosen." Thus, technical/practical jobs are not jobs that ex-students would end up in reluctantly. The opposite is true: the aspirations for such work exceed the expectation of being able to obtain it. In terms of "job if chosen freely," technical/practical work is even preferred by one-third of those who had no exposure to IE at all during their years in the lower secondary school (Category III). Clearly, such work is typically not a second choice, but quite popular.

Another striking finding in Figs 4 and 5 is that with greater exposure to IE, both aspirations and expectations for practical work rise very strongly. This suggests that exposure to IE has had a striking effect on students' aspirations for practical/technical work, and that it has also given those with an IE background greater confidence in eventually being able to find such work. Yet, as will be shown below, relatively few ex-students are able to realize such aspirations and expectations in the short term (one year after "O" levels). In the main, small-scale tracer studies over several years (Närman *et al.*, 1985b; Davies, in Cumming *et al.*, 1985) suggested that the same has been true for their career experience over a longer period, though there may be interesting differences among schools and localities.

It might be argued that the strong association of aspirations/expectations with degree of exposure to IE might result from a stronger response bias among former IE students in favor of favorable impression about a subject which they had chosen in school—and to please a foreign aid donor. Such a

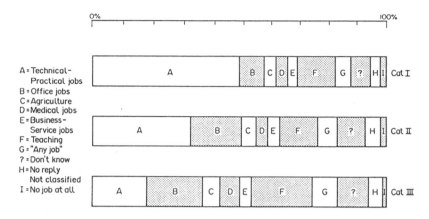

FIG 4. Jobs "chosen freely". Distribution of choices by type of job and category of ex-student.

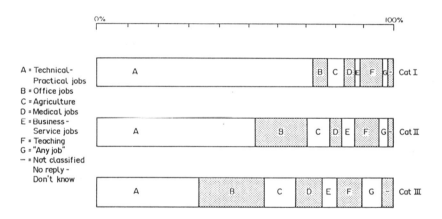

FIG 5. Jobs "actually expected". Distribution of answers by type of job and category of ex-student.

bias might be stronger for Category I students who chose to take IE as an examination subject than Category II students who did not choose IE or who were not selected for it. The difference between Category I and II could also reflect differences in initial interest, prior to their different experience after Form 2. But such explanations would not fit the observed difference between Category II and III. Indeed, if self-selection of students with kindred occupational attitudes were a strong factor, one would expect Category II to be intermediate between I and III in their attitudes, which is clearly not the case. In view of these considerations, and of the quite strong observed differences, it seems reasonable to infer that IE has indeed had the effect of interesting students in technical or practical work as a future career, so that contrary to what some critics have argued (Foster, 1965), curriculum can change students' occupational aspirations. But it should be noted that to interest these students in practical or technical work is hardly the problem. The interest is quite strong even among those with no exposure to practical subjects. The problem that students face is being able to realize their ambitions.

It is striking that teaching—the modern sector job that all students are regularly exposed to over many years—is not popular. Only in some 8–9 percent of the answers is it the job aspired to. But it is more often the job an ex-student expects. For many ex-students who start teaching, it is not a choice at all but simply an available opportunity which they settle for when they are unable to realize their hopes. Conversely, both technical/practical jobs and jobs in agriculture stand out as quite popular occupational areas to which access is perceived to be difficult. The fact that these answers were given by former lower secondary students one year after their "O" level examination indicates that these perceptions are based on some experience about how difficult it is to gain access to various types of work or further schooling after "O" levels.

The Destination of Ex-students and the Uses of IE

Table 4 shows the main activity about one year after "O" level examination, of ex-students with varying degrees of exposure to IE. One notes that the percentage differences among the three categories are negligible. In the short term, students with greater exposure to IE cannot be said to possess any advantage over others in finding employment.

TABLE 4. *Main Activity of Ex-students one Year after Form 4*

Main activity	Category I: Students who had 4 years of IE (%)	Category II: Students who had IE in Forms 1 and 2 (%)	Category III: Students at non-IE schools (%)	Total (%)
Form 5	40	39	43	40
Repeating Form 4	4	5	6	5
Work	6	7	5	6
Training	5	5	6	6
Looking for work or education	45	43	40	43
Total	100	99	100	100
No. of cases	(320)	(551)	(205)	(1,080)

Table 4 includes only those ex-students for whom direct information was obtained. If one also includes the additional 240 ex-students for whom some secondary information was obtained (usually from students who had some knowledge about what others were doing), we would get 44, 46 and 48 percent in Form 5 for Categories I, II and III respectively; and the rates of unemployment (looking for work or education) would be reduced to 40, 38 and 34 percent respectively. However, since one could most easily obtain second-hand information about those ex-students who had continued in school, these adjusted figures would understate the true percentage "looking for work" and exaggerate the percentage continuing to Form 5.

Clearly, not even the negligible differences that do exist indicate that IE confers any labor market advantage. One should also note that the Category I students in this sample were in no way academically inferior to the others. In fact their maths results were slightly better.

The survey showed that not less than 90 percent of the students aspired to enter Form 5. Many fail to realize this ambition. But the table nonetheless shows that a strikingly high percentage of students from all three categories succeed in entering Form 5. This is a reflection of the high academic caliber of the IE schools as a group. A further striking finding is the high proportion in all three categories who after one year are still looking for work. In comparison, the percentage who have either found employment or succeeded in gaining access to an employment-based training program is quite low. Thus, also for these relatively elite schools, school-leavers face very great difficulty in finding employment. The hope which many parents and students have had, that IE can make a difference in this respect, is not borne out by the post-school reality, at least not in the short run. It should however be emphasized that a one-year follow-up is too short a period for a definitive answer to the question of labor market advantage. We therefore hope to extend the follow-up to a three-year period.

Data presented by Närman (1985) did show a slight tendency for ex-students with an IE background to leave home in search for work less often than did others, possibly because they thought their IE skills gave them a better chance of making a living at home.

In view of the negative findings in Table 4, the question arises: What gives school-leavers an advantage in the quest for jobs after Form 4? Is it general academic achievement? Predictably, it was found that those with good exam results stand a much better chance than others of gaining admission to Form 5. More than 90 percent of those who obtained Division I (the best results), and 70 percent of those with Division II were able to continue to Form 5, as compared with 22 percent of those with Division III and even 3 percent of those who barely passed (Division IV). Our concern is, however, with those who did not continue to Form 5 or who repeated Form 4, but who entered the labor market in search of jobs or employment-based training opportunity. Table 5 shows how these 564 ex-students fared in the labor market during their first year out of school.

TABLE 5. *Do KCE Examination Results Give Those who Leave School, Rather than Going on to Form 5, any Advantage in the Labor Market During their First Year after School?*

	Examination Results				
Do they find work?	Divisions I and II (%)	Division III (%)	Division IV %	Fail (%)	Total (%)
Work or "training"	16	13	30	36	21
Looking for work or education	84	87	70	64	79
Total	100	100	100	100	100
No. of cases	(91)	(252)	(176)	(45)	(564)

Chi-square = 26.32; P(Chi-square) <0.001.

The pattern in Table 5 is quite startling. It is in fact the ex-students with the poorest examination results—Division IV or Failure, who most often have become employed or gained access to a job-related training program. Indeed, the trend is highly statistically significant. Superficially at least, this finding flies in the face of much writing, often based on impressions rather than empirical reseach, about the credentialist mentality of employers in developing countries.

It is likely that those with better exam results set their sights higher and that they therefore are willing to hold out longer for "suitable" employment. Further analysis is planned to examine the strength of a possible tendency of this kind. But the strength of the zero-order negative association between exam results and being employed or under training, in Table 5, is considerable. It seems at the moment unlikely that the above-noted possible tendency would be so strong that it would mask a true *positive* association of any importance between examination results and labor market advantage for this sample. It is therefore reasonable to question the conventional wisdom that credentials and exam results are of great importance in access to jobs in the highly competitive labor market facing lower secondary school leavers in Kenya.

What does give advantage, then? We can reasonably speculate that personal contacts must be of considerable importance. Connections through kinship networks or networks related to home location are likely to matter greatly. Employment may be obtained through sponsorship by persons known to the employer, sponsors who vouch for the applicant's integrity, willingness to learn and to work hard. If school credentials in general play a very small part in selection to jobs, it is not surprising that specialist subjects also fail to give any advantage—and especially so in the case of IE which is only offered in a small number of schools and unlikely to be known by many employers. Indeed, nearly all IE teachers complained that their subject suffers from lack of awareness among employers (noted during group interviews). Also, the exploratory survey (Sifuna, 1984) of employers who were known to have hired former IE students, showed that they often had low awareness of IE and doubted the value of school-based training as preparation for practical work. Such scepticism among Kenyan employers has been noted by others (e.g., King, 1977.)

The questions raised above point to the need for research on the process of search for opportunity which school-leavers embark upon. With the notable exception of Hoppers' (1985) study in Lusaka, the research literature on the search for opportunity which school-leavers embark upon, is very sparse. Our research also indicates the need for long-term tracer studies of ex-students with different types and quality of credentials from school. It may be that skills acquired in IE and other pre-vocational subjects are of economic value for those who succeed in gaining access to the type of employment which enables the ex-students to put these skills to use. Our findings too suggested that, when ex-students had succeeded in finding a job, those with some exposure to IE did seem to be employed in technical/practical work more often than students with no experience of IE at all—in spite of the fact that IE seemed to give no overall advantage in securing some kind of employment. But the sub-samples are in this case so small that firm inferences are not warranted. Very few ex-students (only six out of the 1080) were self-employed. But some others may occasionally engage in activities which are kindred to "self-employment." During interviews with ex-students, it appeared that there are a number of persons who do not see themselves as "self-employed" but who nevertheless are engaged in various short-term activities from which they derive some contribution to their livelihood. But the long-term tracer studies of small samples of IE students from four schools (Närman *et al.*, 1984b; Davies, in Cumming *et al.*, 1985) showed very few cases of self-employment of any durable kind. When self-employment did occur, it seemed to be of an episodic character: a short-term activity engaged in between periods of education or employment.

In general, our findings from surveys of students after school support the view that the economic usefulness of pre-vocational subjects needs to be assessed in light of the realistically available opportunities that students have after school, for work or further training. If such opportunities are strictly limited—and allocated largely according to other criteria than school credentials—it is fallacious to expect that training will lead to much utilization of skills even when students are keen to pursue careers that would enable them to use these skills.

In the case of IE, the skills seem to find little use after school as a means of earning a livelihood or for further training. But that is not to say that students do not value the usefulness of IE. The former IE students (Category I and II) in the one-year follow-up study were asked: "Have you had any use of IE so far?" Fully 75 percent of them answered "Yes." But the kind of usage they most often reported was of a private character: repairing or making articles in their homes or helping relatives. Only a small minority reported any usage in working life or in their further schooling. Thus, the pattern of usage accorded with a definition of IE as general education rather than with the view that IE has a pre-vocational function. For such general education purposes, it is skill in the use of quite simple handtools which is most readily utilized, not skill in the use of power tools and machines.

Concluding Remarks

The findings have implications for international debate about pre-vocational subjects and the merits of "diversified secondary education." In accord with critical commentary, we also conclude (cf. Lauglo, 1985a) that such subjects are considerably more expensive than academic subjects and that they demand more managerial expertise and initiative for their establishment and maintenance. But the case of IE in Kenya does show that such subjects can be established as entirely viable pedagogic systems. There is no international "iron law" by which such subjects are relegated to inferior status in the schools in terms of teacher morale and attraction to parents and students. On the other hand, what can be achieved in a limited number of schools over a decade or so, by comprehensive resource inputs that included teacher training, expatriate volunteer teachers, external assistance to workshop establishment and equipment, and the provision of an external support system for maintenance and supplies—is not necessarily indicative of what can be achieved on a large scale in an entire national system.

It is likely that the increasingly difficult labor market for secondary-school-leavers is interpreted by students and parents alike—as it is by policy-makers—to mean that practical subjects will give a labor market advantage. These subjects gain status from that perception, especially when taking them does not imply that students forfeit opportunities for further study of an academic kind. In such conditions of relatively high status for practical subjects, exposure to them seems in the Kenyan case to influence the occupational aspirations of students in spite of the counter claim that "curriculum does not shape occupational aspirations, the structure of opportunity does" (Foster, 1965; Blaug, 1973). But, under present labor market conditions, lack of student interest in practical or technical work is not a problem in need of remedy. There is no shortage of such interest among Kenyan secondary school students today.

Our research supports the view that the status of pre-vocational subjects will reflect, *inter alia*, the perceptions that students and parents have of the labor market and training opportunities towards which such subjects point. But these perceptions are "through a glass darkly": the hopes appear to be an optimistic distortion of labor market reality.

Present policy in Kenya and many other countries favors the expansion of pre-vocational subjects in secondary schools, and also in the upper classes of primary school. Our research supports the view that because such subjects are expensive and have demanding logistics requirements, they should not be launched as large-scale programs for quick implementation throughout a national system of education. Equally important, the most realistic justification for such subjects are their merits on general education grounds, rather than relevance for employment or self-employment. The curriculum and the tools and equipment required should reflect such justifications. Policymakers should face the question: do the general education benefits of these subjects merit the expense and development effort which they require?

References

Blaug, M. (1973) *Education and the employment problem in developing countries*. Geneva: International Labour Organisation.

Cumming, C., Davies, M., Lillis, K. and Nyagah, B. (1985) *Practical subjects in Kenyan academic secondary schools. Background papers*. Stockholm: Swedish International Development Authority, Education Division Documents No. 22.

Cumming, C. E. and Lauglo, J. Reflections on an evaluation in Third World education. (forthcoming journal article).

Foster, P. J. (1965) The vocational school fallacy in development planning. In C. A. Anderson and M. J. Bowman (Eds.), *Education and economic development*. Chicago: Aldine.

Grubb, W. N. (1985) The convergence of educational systems and the role of vocationalism. *Comparative education review*, **29** (4).

Hoppers, W. (1985) *From school to work: Youth, non-formal training and employment in Lusaka*. The Hague: Centre for the Study of Education in Developing Countries (CESO).

King, K. (1977) *The African artisan*. New York: Teachers College Press/Heinemann Educational.

Lauglo, J. (1983) Concepts of "general education" and "vocational education" curricula for post-compulsory schooling in Western industrialised countries: When shall the twain meet? *Comparative education*, **19** (3).

Lauglo, J. (1985a) *Practical subjects in Kenyan academic secondary schools. General report*. Stockholm: Swedish International Development Authority, Education Division Documents, No. 20.

Lauglo, J. (1985b) *Technical secondary schools in Kenya. An assessment*. Stockholm: Swedish International Development Authority, Education Division Documents, No. 26.

Lillis, K. (1985) Processes of secondary curriculum innovation in Kenya. *Comparative education Review*, **29** (1).

Lillis, K. M. and Hogan, D. F. (1983) Dilemmas of diversification: Problems associated with vocational education in developing countries. *Comparative education*, **19** (1).

Närman, A., Hegmar, E., Oksanen, P. and Wallenheim, A. (1984a) *Industrial education students in Kenya. Who are they? How do they perceive industrial education?* Gothenburg: Department of Human and Economic Geography, University of Gothenburg, Occasional Papers, No. 5.

Närman, A., Hegmar, E., Oksanen, P. and Wallenheim, A. (1984b) *A tracer study of ex-industrial education students from three schools in Kenya*. Gothenburg: Department of Human and Economic Geography, University of Gothenburg, Occasional Papers, No. 4.

Närman, A. (1985) *Practical subjects in Kenyan academic secondary schools. Tracer study*. Stockholm: Swedish International Development Authority, Education Division Documents, No. 21.

Psacharopoulos, G. (1980) *Higher education in developing countries: A cost–benefit analysis*. Washington: World Bank Staff Working Paper No. 440.

Psacharopoulos, G. (1985) Curriculum diversification in Colombia and Tanzania: An evaluation. *Comparative education review*, **29** (4).

Psacharopoulos, G. and Loxley, W. (1985) *Diversified secondary education and development: Evidence from Colombia and Tanzania*. Baltimore: Johns Hopkins University Press.

Sifuna, D. (1984) Report on employers' views of industrial education. (Manuscript, report for industrial education evaluation, Oct. 1984.)

Weeks, S. (1978) *The Foster fallacy in education planning*. Port Moresby: University of Papua New Guinea, Education Research Unit Research Report No. 32.

Wilms, W. W. and Hansell, S. (1982) The dubious promise of post-secondary vocational education: its payoff to dropouts and graduates in the USA. *International journal of education development* **2** (1).

CHAPTER 15

Curriculum Diversification, Cognitive Achievement and Economic Performance: Evidence from Tanzania and Colombia

GEORGE PSACHAROPOULOS

The World Bank

DIVERSIFYING the secondary school curriculum to include pre-vocational subjects has been an educational policy that has flourished over the last decade in many Third World countries. The often cited objective of diversification is to provide a wider set of future career options than could otherwise be had if the more uniform curriculum were followed. Many governments have invested heavily in diversified schools as a means to make the rapid expansion of secondary education consistent with a better match between the skills learned in school with those needed in the labor market.

In spite of numerous arguments put forth in support or opposition to diversified education in the Third World, little empirical evidence exists to confirm or reject hypotheses in favor of this type of school.[1] The purpose of this study is to begin to compare any advantages that might have accrued to diversified school students and graduates relative to more conventional types of formal training. Potential advantages stemming from diversification could be measured in several ways: first, wider access to secondary schooling by less privileged socio-economic groups of the population (equity); second, higher cognitive attainment measured by test scores in both pre-vocational and academic subjects (internal efficiency); and third, better labor market

This paper is based on a more comprehensive World Bank research project on Diversified Secondary Curricula (DiSCuS, RPO 672–45), in collaboration with the Colombia Ministry of Education, the Instituto SER de Investigacion, the Tanzania Ministry of Education and the Institute of Education, University of Dar es Salaam. For a more extensive treatment of the subject see Psacharopoulos and Loxley (1985) and Psacharopoulos and Zabalza (1984). The views expressed here are those of the researchers and should not be attributed to the World Bank.

[1] For variants of the basic rationale see Ahmed and Coombs (1975), Dore (1975) on Sri Lanka, van Rensburg (1974) on Botswana, Court (1972) on Kenya, Orata (1972) on the Philippines, Lourie (1978) on Panama, Benoit (1974) on Colombia, Nyerere (1967) on Tanzania, King (1978) on Kenya, Ruddell (1979) on Ghana, Weeks (1978) on Papua New Guinea, Schiefelbein (1979) on Colombia and Chile and Unger (1980) on China.

outcomes, e.g., better employment opportunities or higher returns to investments in acquiring a combination of academic and pre-vocational skills as opposed to merely one or the other (external efficiency).[1]

Countries selected for the empirical investigation of diversification should meet at least two criteria that would allow a proper evaluation: first, programs should have been in place long enough and be well implemented, and permit appropriate sampling. Secondary school diversification has proceeded farthest in Latin America and East Africa. Colombia has been chosen as a case country in Latin America because it extensively implemented public diversified education alongside purely vocational and academic secondary schools. Tanzania has been selected as a case country in East Africa because diversification there is a well-established policy based on self-reliance and has been well spread throughout the educational system.

Historical Background

Adaptation of a pre-vocational element to the traditional secondary academic curriculum in the Third World has developed over the past two decades in response to economic, social and political pressures. Such pressures continue to profoundly shape schooling policies today, often leading to educational reform of the type that is evaluated in this study.[2] There have been at least two major lines of reasoning which argue for and against the introduction of a vocational bias in the traditional academic secondary curriculum—one economic and one political.

The economic argument in favor of diversification centers around the perceived need to orient the formal education system to the needs of the world of work.[3] It is based on the assumption that economic growth and development are technology-led, and that traditional education, apprenticeship and on-the-job training are not adequate means to train sufficient numbers of workers to meet current and future demand for skilled labor required by the growing sectors of the economy. This is further bolstered by the allegation that a system of academically-oriented education instills attitudes in most students towards white-collar occupations in the urban–modern wage economy and not towards manual occupations and skills that are in short supply.

A second major stated reason for diversifying secondary education is based on a socio-political strategy which pursues equity considerations. It is believed that an academically-oriented system will produce gross inequalities between a small elite of educated (those who succeed in the system) and their uneducated counterparts.

[1] See Klingelhofer (1967), Oxtoby (1977), Evans and Schimmel (1970), Silvey (1972) and Ruddell (1979).
[2] For a review of implementing educational innovations, see Lillis and Hogan (1983).
[3] Cliffe (1973), Diyasena (1976), Figueroa et al. (1974), Lema (1978), Price (1973), Sato (1974), Tchen (1977) and Vulliamy (1980).

Those expressing opposition to diversification have emphasized its inability to attract competent teachers and suitable equipment, the possible diminution of the overall quality of education causing the graduate to be neither proficient in academic knowledge nor in specialized vocational skills, thereby retarding the possibility of skill formation on the job.[1] At best, students will acquire only a vague general orientation to vocational skills, it is contended. Opponents of secondary diversified education programs also complain that since vocational secondary schooling is often more costly than academic secondary programs, such a curriculum hardly qualifies as a cost-effective method to eliminate enrollment discrepancies between rich and poor, urban and rural students.

If vocational knowledge can less easily adapt to work-place conditions and needs than general academic knowledge, it may restrict future employment and earnings opportunities (Blaug, 1979; Conroy, 1979; Dore, 1975; Evans and Schimmel, 1970; Godfrey, 1977). If so, this deficiency might imply that school systems should leave highly differentiated training to firms in the private sector and/or specialized vocational organizations, such as SENA in Colombia, and instead gear instruction toward teaching the use of established knowledge and analytical methods for problem solving.

The implementation of diversified education differs according to country-specific conditions. Put simply, however, either vocational subjects are taught in schools physically separated from academic schools, or they are placed parallel (side-by-side) in a "comprehensive school style". In the diversified setting, vocational and academic curricula are taught to respective students with some crossing-over permitted. For our purposes, diversified education refers to secondary schools which provide a wide range of curricula encompassing courses of study which are typically found only in all-academic or in all-vocational schools.

The Case Study Models

Colombia and Tanzania have both extensively experimented with diversified secondary education over the past decade. As each nation was faced with reconciling its developmental needs with the capacity of secondary education systems to meet these objectives, diversification was expected to play an increasing role in matching educational enrollments with employment prospects.

Colombia: A Multi-Track Diversified System

The diversified secondary schools, called INEM (*Institutos Nacionales de Educacion Media*) combine academic with pre-vocational subject tracks under one roof in a six-year program. During the first two years, students are

[1] See Foster (1965), Blaug (1979) and Grubb (1979).

exposed to pre-vocational subjects in order to acquaint them with knowledge and career options in the various trades. The second two years are devoted to a vocational orientation, such as agriculture or commerce, along with some additional academic study, but the emphasis is clearly placed on the vocational course work. During the last two-year cycle, further specialization takes place. A student enrolled in the general industrial training program in the preceding cycle might now focus on metal work, construction or perhaps electrical mechanics, or he may concentrate in an academic option. There also exist the CASD (*Centros Auxiliares De Servicios Docentes*), which pull students out of their formal school setting two or three days a week to give them special hands-on training in vocational skills deemed important in the local labor market.

In addition to the diversified education system operating in Colombia, there remains the traditional academic course of study in private and public secondary schools. It was hoped, however, that diversified education would ultimately attract many students away from poorer quality private academic secondary schools and give them a chance to pursue vocational subjects of their choice, in addition to continuing a lighter load of academic coursework.

Tanzania: A Uni-Track Diversified System

The Tanzanian educational system is better understood when placed in the context of the country's economic system which stresses public ownership and control of most major enterprises. The public sector predominates and it is the educational system which is geared to providing the trained manpower needs if this sector is to run efficiently. Because education and employment growth is monitored by the Government, Tanzania, unlike Colombia, has not introduced diversification only as a means to match the supply of middle-level skills to manpower requirements. Rather, the main impetus for diversification in Tanzania stems from a strong sense of commitment to the ideals of work education similar to that found in the Chinese, Cuban and Soviet vocational educational systems.

Because of Tanzania's philosophy of self-reliance and self-sufficiency in producing skilled manpower, students are required to gain experience in practical subjects in addition to academic by "majoring" in a vocational subject of their choice while in secondary school.

Methodology

The central research question is whether the outcomes of diversified education vary substantially from those of conventional academic and purely vocational secondary schooling. Two clusters of outcome have been identified as the main "dependent variables" in this study: (1) what is learned in school and (2) what is later accomplished in post-school, economic activities.

Given the time span between the socio-educational inputs and outputs, a longitudinal tracer study was chosen (Psacharopoulos and Hinchcliffe, 1983). We have defined three testing points in time for assessing the possible effects of diversified curricula: (a) effects observable while the student is *still in school*; (b) effects observable about *one year after graduation*, when the graduate might be in his first employment or further education; and (c) a fuller assessment of the graduate *after he has been out of school for some years*.

The starting point in the two country cases was the schools in a given district where diversified curricula have existed for a number of years, along with other non-diversified schools. Random sampling was used to obtain representative national coverage of high school students in proportion to their numbers enrolled in particular curricular programs. A survey administered to high school seniors just prior to graduation was used to collect base-line information. A follow-up survey was administered to the same cohort one year after graduation in order to assess the initial post-school outcomes.

Of course, in order to assess the performance of diversified schools (target group) on a set of agreed criteria, information was raised on a number of students who did *not* attend such schools (control group). Thus, the testing of hypotheses reduces to the statistical significance of differences between target and control group mean performance on a set of indicators, standardized for a set of non-school-related factors.

In Colombia, the baseline sample consisted of 8051 students in INEM schools and the remaining 4800 students, the control group, in traditional vocational schools pursuing specialties which correspond to INEM specialties or in standard academic secondary schools. The Tanzania sample consisted of 4181 students with 1025 (the control group) in traditional academic secondary school settings.

Three sets of instruments have been used in each country study designed to raise the necessary information for hypothesis testing:

(a) an individual student questionnaire, administered to those still in the last year of target and control secondary schools;

(b) a school questionnaire, filled in by the headmaster of the schools included in the survey;

(c) a graduate follow-up questionnaire, administered to those who left school one year earlier (and also three years earlier, in the case of Colombia).

The questionnaires raised information on:

- *background indicators*, such as parental education, occupation and income level;
- *personal characteristics*, such as age, sex, verbal and mathematical ability;
- *future plans and aspirations*, such as the students' educational and occupational expectations;
- *exposure time to curriculum subjects*, such as the number of class periods attended per week;
- *school quality variables*, such as the condition of buildings, expenditure per pupil, and teachers' qualifications;
- *cognitive achievement on subject-matter* by means of special tests administered to each individual student in the various core curriculum subjects (e.g., commerce, agriculture, technical as well as academic subject matter);
- *general ability tests*, resulting to verbal and mathematical scores that are supposed to be unrelated to education;
- *non-cognitive outcomes*, measured by psychological modernity tests;
- *further training and employment indicators*, such as for those who were in training or further education the type of institution and field of post-secondary study; for those in employment, the sector of economic activity, occupation, earnings and hours of work.

TABLE 1. *Family Characteristics by School Type and Curriculum Subject, Colombia 1981 Cohort*

Subject	Family characteristics	INEM	Control
Academic			
	Family income (monthly pesos)	24,602	37,564
	Father's education (years)	6.9	7.8
Commercial			
	Family income	22,859	31,080
	Father's education	5.6	6.6
Industrial			
	Family income	21,367	25,517
	Father's education	5.6	6.3
Agricultural			
	Family income	17,230	19,342
	Father's education	5.4	4.7
Social services			
	Family income	19,595	29,556
	Father's education	5.5	7.4
Overall			
	Family income	22,220	30,282
	Father's education	5.9	6.8

Who attends Diversified Schools?

Table 1 shows that in Colombia INEM and non-INEM academic tracks recruit more from the higher income families, and that INEM tracks are less differentiated than control schools in terms of the parental education. Namely, compared to control schools, INEM schools draw more students from lower socio-economic backgrounds. (INEMs were built in the poorest areas of the cities.) Thus, as intended, the diversification strategy has successfully drawn more secondary school students from lower socio-economic backgrounds. Presumably, some of these students might not have attended high school if INEMs had never been introduced. But, of course, such students might have enrolled to *any type* of secondary school built in their area.

Regarding Tanzania, Table 2 shows that students from the high income families tend to pursue programs which specialize in commerce, while those coming from low income families attend agricultural programs. Although it is probably at the entrance to secondary schools where the largest social class differences sort themselves out, technical and agricultural programs were attracting students from socio-economic origins.

TABLE 2. *Father Characteristics of Secondary School Students by Curriculum Bias, Tanzania 1981 Cohort*

Curriculum bias	Income (in shillings)	Education (in years)
Agricultural	6,656	5.7
Technical	7,088	5.2
Commercial	7,834	6.6
Academic	7,181	5.9

Cognitive Achievement

Colombia

The achievement rankings by school type and program revealed that INEM schools frequently outperform control schools, especially on academic tests. But because these mean differences do not take into account out-of-school influences such as sex, age, ability and social origins which might differentially affect achievement independent of school placement, regression analysis was employed to control for those out-of-school influences which might account for higher scores before students were assigned to various schools or curriculum programs.

Results show that when background and school factors are held constant, mean vocational score depends strongly upon placement in the corresponding specialty track. There is also a strong relationship between academic ability measures and school characteristics on the one hand, and mean vocational achievement on the other.

TABLE 3. *Achievement Score Gain Associated with the INEM Programs, Colombia 1981 Cohort*

Curriculum sub-sample	INEM test score gain	
	Own curriculum specialization	Academic
Academic	3.28	3.28
Commercial	5.10	0.43
Industrial	15.71	8.01
Agricultural	—[1]	—
Social services	4.47	—

Notes: Background, ability and school factors controlled for. All marginal coefficients are statistically significant at the 5 percent level or better.

[1] Non-significant gain.

In Table 3 the sample is divided into five groups on the basis of curriculum bias. After statistically controlling for background and ability factors as well as for mean teacher salary (a school quality proxy) in a multiple regression, it is possible to determine the effect of curriculum bias on achievement. For example, in the academic subsample, INEM program students earned 3.28 points more on average than control students on the academic achievement test, after adjusting for differences in background, ability and school quality. Industrial program students placed in INEM schools performed substantially better than control students on the industrial achievement test (15.71 points higher) and on the academic achievement test (8.01 points higher). This implies that industrial learning was not acquired at the sacrifice of academic learning. This is true of commercial and social science students as well, though the advantage of the INEM program is less marked. There were no significant differences between the adjusted cognitive score means of INEM and non-INEM agricultural students.

Thus, the INEM vocational program is clearly superior to non-INEM programs in imparting vocational knowledge.

Tanzania

As with Colombia, regression analysis was employed to compare the scores of specialty track students relative to the academic control group, after statistically controlling for background and school characteristics. For each vocational test, the group trained in the subject of that test scored highest.

In Table 4 the advantage of the vocational curriculum is evidenced by the higher mean scores obtained by the vocational students on measures of vocational learning. In all cases, the gains in vocational learning are obtained at the expense of some English language achievement.

TABLE 4. *Achievement Score Gain Associated with Vocational Curricula Bias Compared to Academic Control Curriculum Bias, Tanzania 1981 Cohort*

Curriculum bias	Diversified school test score gain	
	Own specialization	English
Technical	5.26	−4.05
Commercial	5.43	−2.27
Agricultural	1.61	−2.24

Notes: All achievement score differences are statistically significant at the 5 percent level or better. Background, ability and school factors are controlled for.

Comparing Costs to Outcomes

The cost of schooling can be looked at from three viewpoints—society, government and the individual (or household). The specific cost components which may be relevant to these factors are (a) forgone output or earnings, (b) capital cost of buildings, furniture and equipment and (c) direct recurrent costs.

Colombia

Table 5 provides three pieces of relevant information: annual unit costs (capital and recurrent) of keeping a student in secondary school, group test score means in academic achievement, and the test score mean in each vocational specialization for the students taking that specialization. (Scores are adjusted for ability and out-of-school characteristics.)

TABLE 5. *Annual Direct Cost per Student and Achievement by School Type and Subject, Colombia 1981 Cohort*

School type/subject	Unit cost[1] (pesos)	Adjusted academic achievement	Adjusted vocational achievement			
			Agr.	Comm.	SS	Ind.
Academic INEM	25,700	53	—	—	—	—
Academic control	22,200	50	—	—	—	—
Agriculture INEM	26,200	49	62	—	—	—
Agriculture control	33,700	48	58	—	—	—
Commercial INEM	25,200	49	—	61	—	—
Commercial control	23,200	49	—	56	—	—
Social services INEM	25,000	48	—	—	57	—
Social services control	27,800	48	—	—	53	—
Industrial INEM	25,300	55	—	—	—	62
Industrial control	31,900	47	—	—	—	46

[1] Cost refers to public schools only and includes school-related expenses by students, government-financed recurrent cost and annualized capital cost. It excludes forgone earnings. Achievement scores are adjusted for out-of-school characteristics.

Looking at the recurrent costs it is noted that:

(a) Variations between tracks in INEMs are small;
(b) INEM academic and commercial tracks are around 20 and 14 percent more expensive, respectively, than the control counterparts;
(c) INEM agriculture and industry tracks are significantly less expensive than the control counterparts (28 and 25 percent), and the same is true for the social services specialty but to a lesser extent (11 percent).

There are two relevant sets of cost and achievement comparisons—the first comparing students following the same subject but within different types of school, and the second the academic control group of students with students who have taken pre-vocational subjects.

Based on comparisons of costs with achievement, INEM schools are certainly no worse than non-INEM schools in imparting desired cognitive and non-cognitive outcomes to secondary school students. The fact that they seem to teach vocational skills more effectively than academic skills is certainly consistent with their supposed function and mandate. Also, the fact that the INEM academic track produces an above-average crop of graduates suggests that such schools are not allowing vocational standards to rise at the expense of academic outcomes.

TABLE 6. *Recurrent Costs and Achievement Scores in Public Schools, Tan-zania 1981 Cohort*

Bias	Annual unit cost (shillings)	Adjusted mean achievement score				
		Vocational			Academic	
		Agric.	Tech.	Commerce	Math	English
Agricultural	3449	<u>52</u>			52	50
Technical	3263		<u>53</u>		55	48
Commercial	3160			<u>55</u>	49	49
Academic	2888	51	49	50	<u>51</u>	<u>53</u>

Note: Means are for public school students only and adjustents have been made to remove the effects of ability and out-of-school characteristics on achievement.

Tanzania

Table 6 presents average annual recurrent costs by curriculum program along with achievement scores in both academic and vocational subjects so as to allow a contrast between cost differences and achievement outcomes by program track. Test score means have been adjusted to remove the influences of ability, sex, age and other factors influencing school achievement.

Thus, it appears that technical schools, though costing more than control schools, yield a substantial increase in both academic and vocational knowledge over the academic control group. Likewise, both agricultural and commercial students gain in levels of vocational knowledge for increased per student costs. However, they do so at the expense of academic knowledge relative to the control group.

Graduate Destinations

Colombia

The results reported below are based on a 62 percent response rate, slightly above the 60 percent minimum required by the sample design to yield school-type curriculum cells with sufficient observations for testing statistical significance. Table 7 gives the main activity destinations by school type and curriculum program. Thus, one year later, roughly one-third of the graduates were in school, one-third were working full-time, and aside from 11 percent studying and working part time simultaneously, about one quarter of the sample was neither studying nor working.

TABLE 7. *1982 Destination by School Type and Subject, Colombia 1981 Cohort (percent)*

School type/subject in 1981	Post-school activity, 1982			
	Study	Work	Study/Work	Other
INEM	37	29	10	24
Control	37	30	11	22
Overall	37	30	11	22

Contrary to the expectation that INEM graduates would differ from traditional graduates in terms of employment status, no major post-school activity differences can be documented between the distributions of INEM and non-INEM respondents, meaning that the type of school attended does not alter the initial destination of graduates.

Table 8 gives the probability of being in employment one year after graduation. Those coming from control vocational schools have more chances to be working one year after graduation, relative to all other groups.

TABLE 8. *Propensity of Working Full-time in 1982 by School Type and Subject, Colombia 1981 Cohort (percent)*

Subject	INEM	Control
Academic	29.6 (39.1)	28.7 (42.2)
Vocational	28.1 (39.3)	33.7 (43.9)

Note: Figures in parentheses include those who both work and study.

Table 9 gives the mean earnings of INEM and control graduates working full-time. Earnings differences are very modest. But academic graduates earn more relative to the rest. With the exception of INEM academic graduates, actual earnings are clearly less than what graduates were hoping to earn before entering the labor market.

TABLE 9. *Monthly Earnings by School Type, Colombia 1981 Cohort*

School type	Mean earnings (in pesos)
INEM	9854
Control	9980
Sample	9887

Do those coming from vocational curricula experience less unemployment before getting a job? The data for Colombia do not substantiate this hypothesis. If anything, they show the reverse, as is indicated in Table 10, i.e., those who have followed vocational courses in either INEM or control schools have significantly longer periods of unemployment.

TABLE 10. *Period of Unemployment Before First Job by School Type and Track, Colombia 1981 Cohort (in weeks)*

Subject	School type	
	INEM	Control
Academic	21.2	21.6
Vocational	25.6	26.4

Note: Between-*subject* differences are significant at the 0.01 level.

Thirty-one percent of all graduates reported in the 1982 follow-up that they were currently looking for work. Are INEM students less likely to be seeking work? Clearly, those in full- or part-time study or employment cannot be classified as unemployed. Twenty-six percent of those already employed full-time are looking for other employment and 58 percent of those neither studying nor working are actively seeking work, the rest representing non-labor-force participants. When we examine responses by INEM/non-INEM membership, we note that in 1982, 30 percent of control versus 34 percent of INEM students are currently looking for work. The percentage difference in this case is statistically significant ($P = 0.001$) and suggests that INEM students are more likely to be job hunting.

Of those seeking jobs, 85 percent claim to be still financially dependent on their parents or relatives, with no difference between INEM and non-INEM affiliation. On average, job seekers have been looking unsuccessfully for work during the past 22 weeks and would be willing to work for 12,000 pesos per month, a reservation wage which is much higher compared to going wage rates of those already employed. Proportionally more control group graduates search for clerical work than INEM students, and these job seekers come just as often from agricultural and industrial tracks as from commercial tracks.

In summary, while proportions of INEM and control graduates looking for work are much the same, and while both groups expect to earn much the same once a job is found, a few differences can be discerned regarding the kind of employment sought by individuals from the two groups.

The Class of 1978 Three Years Later

Given the long inherent gestation period associated with longitudinal studies, it was felt that the study could yield some early indications on the labor market destination and performance of secondary school graduates by introducing a pseudo-panel component to it. After the selection of the sample of schools and students for the 1981 cohort, addresses were obtained from the same school of the graduates of the 1978 class. A target sample of 2000 such graduates were randomly selected from the school records and attempts were made to locate the graduates for the administration of a special questionnaire. This questionnaire raised retrospective information on the student's further education and occupational record between 1978 and the Fall of 1981 when the interviews took place. The questionnaires were completed by personal interview at the house of each selected graduate. This data set was used to test the same hypotheses related to diversification as with the 1981 cohort, except of course those related to achievement as it was not feasible to administer cognitive tests to the 1978 cohort.

It was found that INEMs draw students from the lower socio-economic groups. This is a similar finding to the one obtained using data from the 1981 cohort. INEM school graduation and an academic subject are strongly associated with the propensity to study after secondary school. Also, those who study agriculture in INEMs have a much higher chance of continuing further studies than entering the labor market immediately after secondary school. Those coming from INEM schools are less likely to participate in the labor force or hold a job three years after graduation. Standardization for other factors influencing the employment probability by means of a logit regression accentuates the INEM disadvantage in producing employable graduates.

Eighteen percent of the entire cohort reported they were looking for a job in 1981, with a very small overall difference between INEM and control schools. However, most of those looking for a job either already hold a job or are studying. Excluding such cases, the overall unemployment rate among the cohort in 1981 is 6 percent with a negligible overall difference between INEM and control schools. But the unemployment rate is especially pronounced among control agricultural graduates (17.3 percent). According to logit-adjusted probabilities of searching, control industrial graduates are the least as likely to be searching for a job in 1981.

The 1978 graduates spent on average 14 weeks looking for their first job. Those coming from INEM schools had an advantage of one week over the control group in getting a job. However, school type and subject are statistically insignificant in explaining job search duration. By contrast, inspection of the minimum acceptable salary among those looking for a job reveals that job seekers have a reservation wage much higher than their classmates who are already employed. Clearly, most of the job search activity among the respondents is for improving their present economic situation.

Our overall conclusion is that INEMs have not increased the propensity of high school graduates to enter the labor force. In fact, in those cases in which a significant difference can be identified, we find that the influence of INEMs has tended to go in the opposite direction. INEMs have not influenced earnings either. But a final conclusion on this must await the availability of data from university graduates, since one of the differential effects of INEMs has been to increase the chances of attending university to a greater extent than traditional schools.

Tanzania

The major post-Form-4 avenues available to graduates are: entry into Form 5; placement in teacher training or other public sector training; private sector salaried employment or self-employment; looking for a job or further training or voluntarily inactive.

The allocation of Form 4 students by graduate activities (Table 11) shows no major differences in the way employment, further education and training are distributed based on the student's Form 4 curriculum bias. But technical students are more likely to be employed and less likely to be seeking schooling, work or training. If one aggregates the Form 5 and training categories, one is still struck by the similarities among biases in terms of post-secondary-school activities. Consequently, it is possible to infer that with the possible exception of technical students, all other ex-Form 4 students stand nearly the same chances of going into employment.

TABLE 11. *The 1982*
Activity of Form IV
Graduates, Tanzania
1981 Cohort (percent)

Form V	29.5
Training	41.6
Working	14.4
Looking	14.5
Total	100.0

In the-follow up survey, those who were currently attending Form 5 were asked to list the courses they were presently taking. Such courses were clustered into the major fields of "technical" "commercial" and "agriculture." Seventy-eight percent of all those in Form 5 take academic subjects exclusively (e.g., maths, history, languages, social and physical sciences) and they are evenly distributed by Form 4 bias. When the remaining 22 percent of respondents are considered, technical students pursuing technical courses in Form 5 are drawn mostly from the Form 4 academic track and those majoring in agricultural science subjects were recruited heavily from commercial graduates. In short, there is little continuity between Form 4 and Form 5 subject specialization.

The group of nearly 1000 Form 4 graduates placed in training programs (including teacher training) comprised 42 percent of the 1982 follow-up respondents. When we subdivide this group by Form 4 curriculum bias and examine the current training program graduates are enrolled in, we observe that nearly one-half of the group are engaged in teacher training, most of them coming from the Form 4 agricultural and commercial biases. The proportion of academic bias graduates who enter teacher training does not appear to be out of line with the rest of the graduates. The most interesting result is the small proportion of commerce bias graduates who take clerical training courses and the high proportion of technical bias students who take these courses. This would seem to imply, on the one hand, that post-Form 4 clerical courses are not seen as adding anything to similar studies in schools and that on the other hand a substantial proportion of technical students who opt for training see openings in the clerical field. Finally, the proportion of agriculture bias students taking agriculture training courses is slightly lower than for the other biases.

Nine percent of the respondents had found salaried employment one year after graduation and another 5 percent were self-employed. Salaried persons were primarily public sector workers in the 1982 follow-up. Forty-eight percent were in government, 12 percent in private, and the rest in parastatal employment. By economic sector, 29 percent were in commerce, 9 percent in agricultural jobs and 17 percent in manufacturing, with the remaining 45 percent in all other sectors. Roughly 47 percent of those employed were in secretarial–clerical jobs. Most job holders found their job after waiting six months. They worked, on average 44 hours per week and earned 726 shillings per month before taxes.

When we examine workers by bias graduated from in 1981, we find 20 percent of agriculture students went into private sector employment, 57 percent of technical graduates went into government work exclusively, as did 55 percent of commercial graduates. Thus agricultural students are not as readily hired into the public sector as others. Their private sector activities do not necessarily include farming since one-third of these agricultural graduates work in commercial–secretarial occupations. Among those with salaried employment one half are employed in public sector clerical jobs, with no differences by Form 4 curriculum bias, or public–private school graduate status. However, girls are twice as likely to end up in non-public-sector employment. No significant differences emerge in earnings and weeks worked by curriculum bias.

About 7 percent of the respondents were looking for full-time schooling or further training and another 6 percent were looking for work. Similar ratios of males to females, and public to private school group is disproportionately looking for training. Regarding those looking for work only, 65 percent are looking exclusively for government employment, 29 percent for employment in parastatals and only 6 percent seek private sector work. This tendency for government employment varies little across Form 4 curriculum bias, sex or public–private graduate affiliation and further suggests that those holding out are actually still looking for placement in government activities. The notable exception is technical school graduates who will seek private employment in greater proportion to the rest.

About one-half are looking for secretarial–accounting positions regardless of curriculum placement in 1981. All but 15 percent started looking for jobs sometime in 1982, although private school graduates (24 percent) started looking as early as 1981.

Among those looking for work 70 per cent are supported by families, and 30 percent by doing odd jobs. Of the 70 percent who are supported by the family, slightly more come from the Form 4 agricultural bias, and more are boys or private school graduates. On average, they expect to wait 11 more weeks before finding a job which 50 percent describe as secretarial–clerical in nature. In brief, among students looking for work, no major differences arise across sex, public–private school attended or Form 4 curriculum bias.

It is interesting to note that those still looking for work put the level of "minimum acceptable earnings" at a much higher level of Sh 957, ranging from Sh 859 for academic students to Sh 1051 for commercial students.

According to one of the main purposes of diversification, it would be expected that graduates of agricultural, technical and commercial biases would experience a shorter period of unemployment than those from academic schools. The data, however, do not support this, as Table 12 shows.

TABLE 12. *Unemployment*
Rates in 1982 Tanzania
1981 Cohort (percent)

Subject	Unemployment rate
Agricultural	16
Technical	8
Commercial	16
Academic	13

One year after graduation, 13 percent of academic students were still looking for either work or training while the percentages for technical, commercial and agricultural students were 8, 16 and 16 respectively. Similarly, these academic graduates did not believe that they had any longer period of time to wait for some activity than other students. Those graduates either in Form 5 or in training courses again showed no differences by bias in the period they expected to have to wait to acquire employment once they entered the labor force.

The Returns To Investment in Diversified Curricula

Earnings function adjusted 1981 mean differentials were used to estimate rates of return to investment in various curricula. The fact that in the case of Colombia we are dealing with a three-year-old cohort allows us to approximate a more valid "flat equivalent" earnings differential at age 22 and hence use the "short-cut" rate of return method. (See Psacharopoulos, 1981).

Abstracting from the particular vocational specialization, INEM schools appear to have slightly higher returns (Table 13). But the academic subject taken in control schools appears to be associated with a higher rate of return. Given the nature of the earnings and cost data and the simplifying assumptions of the short-cut formula, the differences in the rates of return between INEM and control schools cannot be regarded as significant. While some tracks appear to have higher profitability than others, the differences are not sufficiently wide to conclude that the introduction of pre-vocational tracks results in secondary schooling being less economically efficient. Conversely, there is no evidence to suggest their introduction increases economic efficiency.

TABLE 13. *Approximate Social Rates of
Return to Investment in Secondary
Education by Subject and School Type,
Colombia 1978 Cohort (percent)*

Subject	INEM		Control	
Academic	7.7		9.3	
Agricultural	9.1		7.2	
Commercial	8.4	8.8	9.3	8.3
Social services	7.2		7.2	
Industrial	9.2		9.9	

Note: Based on earnings adjusted for ability and socio-economic factors.

The data set for Tanzania is not appropriate for a social rate of return to investment in secondary education calculation. To mention three reasons: (a) only a very small fraction of the 1981 cohort was in employment in 1982,

(b) most of those employed work in the non-competitive sector of the economy, hence their earnings do not necessarily reflect the marginal product of labor, and (c) the relative earnings refer too early in the career of the graduate to approximate the flat lifetime equivalent earnings differential assumed by the short-cut method.

Subject to the above qualifications, the set of adjusted earnings reported above has been used to calculate indicative social rates of return to investment in the four curriculum biases, if nothing else in order to summarize the cost and benefit differentials associated with them. Table 14 presents the estimated "rates of return" which in fact highlight the interplay of costs and benefits differences between the four curricula. Thus the academic (control) bias exhibits the highest rate of return (6.3 percent) and the technical bias the least (1.7 percent). Of course the usefulness of this calculation lies more in the relative comparison between biases rather than the absolute level of the returns.

TABLE 14. *Indicative Social Rates of Return to Investment in Secondary Education, Tanzania 1981 Cohort (percent)*

Form 4 bias	Rate of return
Agricultural	5.4
Technical	1.7
Commercial	3.2
Academic (control)	6.3
Overall	3.7

Note: Returns based on mean earnings adjusted for ability and other socio-economic factors.

Conclusions

Education authorities in a number of developing countries have committed themselves to the diversification of curriculum in secondary schools. Such diversification, in which practical and occupational subjects are substituted into an otherwise completely academic program, was adopted in order to provide a more balanced education, has been supported by international agencies. But beyond the argument of a more balanced education, the main objective of secondary school curriculum diversification has been economic, i.e., to improve the fit between the school and the world of work, or to develop skills and aspirations in secondary school students that more closely match the expected job opportunities of the developing nation's economy.

This study has been concerned with whether the introduction of diversified curricula into secondary schools has resulted in any differences between those groups of students who enrolled in pre-vocational courses and those who concentrated solely on academic programs on a number of "outcomes" such as equity, higher cognitive achievement or better labor market performance.

The results of the study indicate that the above objectives of diversification were not met, and that the expense of the diversified schools was considerably more than that of the conventional academic schools. In particular, evidence from the study implies that diversified school students who continue their education are more likely to be found studying in a completely different subject area than the skill area in which they received their pre-vocational training, that graduates from diversified secondary schools do not find employment more quickly than graduates from conventional schools, and that graduates from diversified schools do not demonstrate higher initial earnings than those from traditional academic schools. These findings, along with the substantially higher costs of diversified schools, require the educational policy-maker to be far more cautious in the future about adopting such educational reform.

Although limited in the number of countries and years of follow-up, this study has provided a new set of empirical evidence—evidence that should be considered when making decisions about secondary school systems. In particular, when contemplating a new diversified secondary school system, the policy-maker should think how the planned schools would differ from the schools in this study, and why the effects of the planned schools are expected to be more positive than the findings reported above.

Specifically, the following issues should be addressed before a new diversified school project is entertained:

(1) Results indicate that traditional academic school graduates are just as likely to find jobs as diversified school graduates. How, then, will the proposed diversified school increase the employment prospects for their graduating students?

(2) The findings demonstrate that students in specialized curricular programs tend to change their fields when pursuing further training. How can the proposed diversified school ensure that continuing students will choose to stay in their fields and not enter programs that have little to do with earlier training?

(3) Experience shows that diversified school graduates fail to earn more than academic control graduates. How could proposed diversified schools ensure higher earnings to their graduates?

(4) The analysis of school costs shows that the less specialized the curriculum, the less costly the program. The teaching of more general

skills also may offer a greater degree of employment flexibility to students entering an uncertain job market several years ahead. What pedagogical or labor market benefits would results from the proposed diversified school to outweigh the higher costs?

Experience has shown that diversified secondary school systems are substantially more expensive than traditional schooling. These types of school are not just difficult to implement but they are particularly expensive to sustain in a low growth economy. Instructional equipment, laboratories, tools and other relevant curricular material must be obtained, maintained, modified and replaced to suit changing technical needs. Institutional and instructional designs must be adapted. There is a continuing need for specially trained instructors. Overall, the diversified school requires a range of expenditures foreign to the traditional academic school. Yet, despite the higher unit costs of diversified schooling, this study was unable to identify any demonstrable major benefits.

We must remind ourselves that it is the developing country's economy which will have to maintain the school. Thus, the question is: Can diversification continue to be supported with its comparatively high recurrent costs without any evidence that such schools will be more effective than traditional ones? Or are there cheaper and more effective alternatives to providing a well-rounded education as well as creating the labor skills to be used by the economy?

References

Ahmed, M. and Coombs P. (1975) *Education for rural development: Case-studies for planners*, prepared by the International Council for Educational Development under sponsorship of the World Bank and the United Nation's Children's Fund. New York: Praeger.

Benoit, A. (1974) *Changing the Educational system: A Colombian case-study*. Munich: Weltforum Verlag.

Blaug, M. (1979) The quality of population in developing countries, with particular reference to education and training. In P. Hauser (Ed.), *World population and development: Challenges and prospects*. New York: Syracuse University Press.

Cliffe, L. (1973) The policy of Ujamaa Vijijini and the class struggle in Tanzania. In L. Cliffe and J. Saul (Eds.), *Socialism in Tanzania*, Vols I and II; Nairobi: East Africa Publishing House.

Conroy, W. G., Jr. (1979) Some historical effects of vocational education at the secondary level. *Phi delta kappar*, **61**, No. 4, 267–271.

Court, D. (1972) *Village polytechnic leavers: The Maseno Story*; Nairobi: University of Nairobi, Institute of Development Studies, Working Paper No. 70.

Diyasena, W. (1976) *Pre-vocational education in Sri Lanka*; Paris: UNESCO.

Dore, R. (1975) *The diploma disease*; London: Allen and Unwin.

Evans, D.R. and Schimmel, G.L. (1970) *The impact of a diversified educational program on career goals at Tororo Girls High School in the context of girls' education in Uganda*; Amherst: centre for International Education, University of Massachusetts.

Figueroa, M., Prieto, R. and Gutierrez, F. (1974) *The basic secondary school in the country: An educational innovation in Cuba*. Paris: prepared for the IBE.

Foster, P. J. (1965) The vocational school fallacy in development planning. In C. A. Anderson and Mary J. Bowman (Eds.) *Education and economic development*; Chicago: Aldine.

278 *George Psacharopoulos*

Godfrey, M. (1977) Education, productivity and income: A Kenyan case study. *Comparative education review*, **21** (1).
Grubb, W. (1979) The phoenix of vocational education: Implications for evaluation. In *The planning papers for the vocational education study* (195–215). Washington, DC: National Institute of Education.
King, K. (1978) *Education and self-employment*; Paris: UNESCO/IIEP.
Klingelhofer, E. (1967) Occupational preference of Tanzanian secondary school pupils; *Journal of social psychology*. **72**, No. 2, (pp. 149–159).
Lema, A. A. (1978) *Education for self-reliance: a brief survey of self-reliance activities in some Tanzanian schools and colleges*: Dar-es-Salaam: Institute of Education, University of Dar es Salaam.
Lillis, K. and Hogan, D. (1983) Dilemmas of diversification: Problems associated with vocational education in developing countries; *Comparative education*, **19** (1).
Lourie, S. (1978) *Production schools and rural employment in Panama*; UNESCO Paris.
Nyerere, J. K. (1967) *Education for self-reliance*; Dar-es-Salaam: Government Printer.
Orata, P. T. (1972) *Self-help barrio high schools: The story of 250,000 students, earning their education and preparing themselves for life*; Singapore: Eastern Universities Press for Seameo Regional Center for Educational Technology.
Oxtoby, R. (1977) Vocational education and development planning: Emerging issues in the Commonwealth Caribbean. *Comparative education*, **13** (3).
Price, R. F. (1973) The part-work principle in Chinese education. *Current scene*, **11** (9).
Psacharopoulos, G. (1981) Returns to education: An updated international comparison; *Comparative education* **17** (3) (pp. 331–341).
Psacharopoulos, G. (1983) Education and private versus public sector pay. *Labour and society*, **8** (2).
Psacharopoulos, G. and Hinchliffe, K. (1983) Tracer study Guidelines. Washington DC: World Bank Education Department.
Psacharopoulos, G. and Loxley, W. (1984) *Diversified secondary curriculum study (DiSCus)— Survey instruments*; Washington DC: Education Department, The World Bank.
Psacharopoulos, G. and Loxley, W. (1985) *Diversified secondary education and development*; Baltimore: Johns Hopkins University Press.
Psacharopoulos, G. and Zabalza, A. (1984) *The destination and early career performance of secondary school graduates in Colombia*: Findings from the 1978 cohort; Washington D.C.: Education Department, The World Bank, Staff Working Paper No. 653.
Ruddell, D. (1979) Vocationalising Ghana's schools: Purpose and product; Unpublished Ph.D Thesis, Faculty of Commerce, University of Birmingham.
Sato, Kuniu (1974) *An alternative approach to vocational education*. Bangkok: ILO, Asian Regional Team for Employment Promotion.
Schiefelbein, E. (1979) *Education and employment in Latin America*; Paris: Report Studies.
Silvey, J. (1972) Unwillingly to school: The occupational attitudes of secondary school leavers in Uganda. In Jolly (Ed.), *Education in Africa*; Nairobi: East African Publishing House.
Tchen, Y. (1977) Education and productive work in China; *Prospects*, **7** (3).
Unger, J. (1980) Bending the school ladder: The failure of Chinese education reform in the 1960's. *Comparative education review*, **24** (2).
Van Rensburg, P. (1974) *Report from Swaneng Hill: Education and employment in an African country*; Stockholm: The Dag Hammarskjöld Foundation.
Vulliamy, G. (1980) *SSCEP and high school outstations. A case study*. Port Moresby: ERU Research Report No. 33, University of Papua New Guinea.
Weeks, S. (1978) *The Foster fallacy in educational planning*. Port Moresby: ERU Research Report No. 32, University of Papua New Guinea.

CHAPTER 16

Evaluating the Context of Diversified Secondary Education in Tanzania

KENNETH KING

University of Edinburgh

THIS chapter will center on Tanzania and its history and experience of diversification. The intention is to relate some of these comments to the analysis carried out by Psacharopoulos and Loxley, with the collaboration in Tanzania of Omari. Their book, *Diversified Secondary Education and Development (1985)*, is a very useful account of the evaluation of this experience both in Tanzania and Colombia. By putting their results so openly into the public domain (unlike much agency-supported evaluation which remains quite inaccessible), they have made a very valuable contribution to the diversification debate. This chapter explores somewhat further the context of Tanzanian diversification, and takes some of the data made available by the study to help illustrate these contextual factors.

One of the most fundamental problems in assessing what at first sight looks like another version of IDA[1]-diversification is that there are a series of other diversifications which were intended to impact on Tanzanian secondary school students during this period. The first of these, reaching back to the Arusha Declaration and Education for Self-Reliance, but reinforced by the Musoma Declaration of 1974, underlined the diversification away from the purely academic, not just for pedagogical reasons, nor to help cover the recurrent costs of education, but to encourage socialist attitudes to work:

> A socialist is a worker. Therefore by introducing work in schools we are building socialist habits among the students. A student who refuses to sweep his room, for example, or wash his plate after a meal, puts himself in a class of people who live on the work of others, which is incompatible with socialism. (Musoma Declaration, 1976, p. 13)

So quite apart from the formal diversified curriculum with its four special subjects, there was, out of school hours, a set of powerful pressures on schools to engage in productive work. This tendency towards actual produc-

---

[1] Schools funded through the International Development Association, an affiliate of the World Bank.

tion in schools, for a variety of socialist, economic and pedagogical reasons, was further reinforced in 1976 (a year or two before this 1981 sample joined Form 1) by the establishment in the Ministry of Education of a special cell on productive education, and a series of grants to schools for mini-enterprises (Court and King, 1978, p. 31). This meant that there were in many secondary schools two different traditions of diversification running side by side; one of these had usually emphasized the importance of *orientation* to work, and the *educational* value of industrial and agricultural work; the other was quite explicitly concerned with production and the need for students to experience real work:

> As a nation, we have no excuse whatsoever for failing to give a chance to the thousands of able-bodied young men and women to participate fully in the production process, particularly those who are in secondary schools and other institutions of higher learning. We have not given them an opportunity to combine theory with practice, and in so doing we have made our students believe that they have a right not to work. (Musoma Declaration, 1976, p. 3.)

Virtually no research has been undertaken on the interplay of these two different traditions of diversification. But quite apart from the agenda of socialist formation, and of reducing the Ministry's contribution to recurrent expenditure, it must have been plain to many students in the most productive schools as the 1970s wore on, and the economic crisis deepened, that the school maize fields, chicken batteries, coffee plantations (and even vineyards) were at least protecting the nutritional standards of the boarding schools from being further eroded. Since the Ministry never put into operation its original intention of reducing its grants to schools as they became more profitable, this particular diversification-towards-production actually gave headquarters budgetary flexibility. In theory, this school-based production would be in addition to whatever work in agriculture, technology, commerce or domestic science was being pursued in the formal diversified curriculum. In practice, headteachers, especially those in schools with large farms, would need to make some very careful judgments about trade-offs between food production and results in the national Form 4 examinations. For most schools in Tanzania, little is known about the negotiations at the school level on educational production; equally little is known about the technologies of production or the use of hired labor as opposed to student labor. But the indications are that there must have been a very considerable range of experience in agriculture alone between the immensely productive Cuban-aided agricultural schools, the schools in rich cash-crop areas, the schools in arid regions, by contrast, where twice as much work might bring in half the result, and the schools where agriculture is only a cosmetic bias. In the various school-level compromises between IDA-diversification and what might be termed ESR[1]-diversification there are likely to have been some major differences in exposure to practical agriculture skill acquisition, as well as to the knowledge base for the "science and practice of agriculture" syllabus.

I shall return in a moment to look at whether the research of Psacharopoulos and Loxley casts any light on this very complex set of agricultural initiatives in schools, but first it is important to point to a further crucial diversification that was set in motion throughout the secondary school system just a couple of years before this 1981 sample of Form 4 students managed to enter Form 1. This might be termed the diversification of the traditional selection and assessment procedures to include work experience, work attitudes, community orientation, etc.

> The National Executive Committee, therefore, direct that the excessive emphasis now placed on written examinations must be reduced, and that the student's progress in the classroom plus his performance of other functions and the work which he will do as part of his education must all be continually assessed and the combined result is what should constitute his success or failure. (Musoma Declaration, 1976, p. 4)

These measures included an attempt to de-link university entrance from a reliance on cognitive achievement alone, as well as the introduction of non-academic aspects of school performance. A detailed discussion of these matters exists elsewhere, (Court and King, 1978), but for our present purpose it is worth stressing that this third diversification (away from the exclusively academic) should potentially have reinforced the thrust of the first two traditions of diversification.

The attempt to reduce the diploma disease, or perhaps, more accurately, to broaden the scope of the disease to include non-conventional selection through work, should have helped schools to "sell" the bias subjects to their student bodies. Again, it is in fact very difficult to know at the school level how much leverage these non-academic assessment measures actually exerted on student attitudes to work, and particularly on the practical sides of the diversified syllabuses, and on ESR-diversification. The organizational complexities of assessment through work experience (both in school and after school) are obviously enormous, and in many cases the students probably concluded that they should continue to concentrate on the written examination. They were often correct to do so, as this note on the practical side of the agricultural bias examination makes clear:

---

[1] Education for self-reliance.

Notes on practical work.

Only questions pertaining to Laboratory and Workshop work shall be asked. Otherwise for the purpose of examinations, field practicals and or project work will be continuously assessed or locally examined, so that cumulative marks gained are finally averaged by the appropriate Examinations Council Authorities. (Ministry of National Education, n.d., p. 154)

However, given the intention of the Government to emphasize the value of work commitment and manual skill in any overall assessment procedure, it will be worth seeing if the World Bank data set can shed any light, directly or indirectly, on this.

There is, still, a fourth level of diversification which needs to be noted before looking at the data, and that concerns the diversification towards rural and self-employment of the secondary school graduate, who had long been accustomed to think of him-/her-self as a unit of high-level manpower headed for the formal urban sector, and virtually guaranteed a wage job.

In one of the very first Ministry papers relating to diversification, back in 1971, this emphasis was already present, even though there were only just over 5000 boys and 1000 girls in the government-supported Form 4 classes at that time. It is instructive to reproduce this comment since in one form or another it remains a constant over the next 10 or 15 years:

It is hoped that when this program is complete, the future secondary school leaver will be a handy as well as a brainy product who will be able to find himself a useful occupation as a self-employed person or as a productive member of any of our "ujamaa" institutions. He should be productive while in school and also immediately he leaves school. It is a departure from the former practice where school leavers have to go in for preparatory training before they are expected to be productive members of the society. The aim is not only to give them such skills as would help secondary school leavers find useful occupations on completing their formal education but also to make them productive even while in school. They are expected to learn as they produce and produce as they learn. This is what "Education for Self Reliance" advocates. Schools may not be and need not be the proper centers for intensive technical training. But they ought to be the initiators of human resource development. They must be able to offer the initial training required in a modern economy, a basic vocational training beneficial to those who proceed no further after Form 4, but at the same time giving a useful background for those who join industry or craft and technical instructions and training. A secondary school leaver going to his village or joining an "ujamaa" village should be of immediate use to the latter too. And, so on. In other words, "the education provided by Tanzania for the students of Tanzania must serve the purposes of Tanzania". There is a great need—yet unassessed—for people with a practical orientation in ujamaa villages. Our education system is bent on fulfilling that need. (Directorate of Planning and Development, Ministry of National Development, 1971, p. 2)

This notion of secondary education for self-employment would become more marked in the mid to late 1970s as planners began to explore the concept of village manpower development, and by implication began to emphasize the contradiction between a secondary school system whose size was defined by formal sector requirements and a village development strategy whose needs for more educated and committed people were enormous (Court and King, 1978). Despite this clear rationale, the size of government-supported Form 1 in 1980 was virtually identical to Form 1 in 1977, at 8800 just 2000 more than it had been in 1970. Thus, within the government sector at any rate, the diversification of the old manpower philosophy of the secondary schools took place against a background of stability, or even rigidity in the size of the government school places. If government secondary school students were somewhat less protected in their search for urban jobs in the late 1970s, it was less because of a rural diversification policy with its implications for dramatic school expansion, than because of a quiet mushrooming of private secondary schools competing for the same urban employment.

These several patterns of diversification (IDA;ESR;in assessment; and to rural employment) have all played upon either the policy-makers, the teachers or the students, or all three, over the period of the 1970s. They may perhaps be reconceptualized in the following way. One pattern of diversification takes for granted that the secondary school student will take a leadership role in the public or parastatal sectors of the economy, and in this case the apparatus of diversification is expected to make him or her socially responsible to the majority who have not received the privileges and the duties of post-primary education in a poor country. To this end, there is the participation in productive labor, the assessment of commitment to the school and the larger community, and finally, after school, the exposure to work experience and national service. Although we have characterized these measures as diversifications of conventional academic schooling, they are all part of the attempt to socialize the intellectual elite to the responsibilities of leadership. In other words, a diversification away from purely individual goals towards a series of national and community obligations. The other pattern of diversification fits those who do not continue with further formal education or training after Form 4, but who enter the labor market, either as employees or on their own account. They share with the first group the experience of productive labor, and the assessment of their non-academic achievements. But they do not receive the socialization through national service or work experience. As they are not proceeding with further academic work, it is possible that the exposure to a particular bias in a more technical field may prove useful either directly or indirectly.

It will of course always be possible to argue that for a poor country to seek to offer some form of pre-vocational exposure across the ability range in a highly selective school system is a luxury it can ill afford. By definition many of the recipients of the IDA-diversification will never use it in a narrow sense. It will however be much harder to judge whether they have profited from what we have called ESR-diversification, intended to build some sense of solidarity with productive labor. And it might be even harder to estimate, for those destined for university, the extent to which attitudes laid down in the secondary school are reinforced by the years of pre-university work experience and national service[1]. These kinds of issues remain pertinent, for as Tanzania gears up in the late 1980s for what has to be a very low-cost version of secondary expansion, it may well seem that these earlier measures for the socialization of the fortunate few of the 1970s were remarkably generous and even a little indulgent.

Psacharopoulos and Loxley's (1985) study in Tanzania is principally concerned to pinpoint the possible advantages that might accrue to diversified school students (in the IDA sense) over against students from schools that have not undertaken diversification. Students were originally selected from all four biases (agricultural, commercial, technical and domestic science), though the last was dropped as there were too few schools involved and it had not been thoroughly implemented. The control group was provided by a set of schools that had not adopted a bias at the time of the research. The sample was drawn from both public and private schools in the proportion of approximately three public to one private. However, the actual proportions between public and private school samples in the different biases differ quite significantly from the overall ratio. Allowing for some small deviation in the rounding up from the percentages, the division between public and private students in the sample is as shown in Table 1.

TABLE 1. *Evaluating the Context of Diversified Secondary Education in Tanzania*

Curriculum bias	Public	Private	Total	No. of schools
Academic	710	309	1019	13
Agricultural	1158	221	1379	18
Commercial	748	539	1287	19
Technical	405	87	492	7

Source: Psacharopoulos and Loxley (1985, Tables 6.2 and 6.51).

[1] There have recently been significant changes in the amount of time laid down between secondary school graduation and university entrance.

Since a good deal of the argumentation in the Tanzania case study relates to comparisons of cognitive achievement, it would be important to know as much as possible about the composition of these four crucial curriculum categories. Some examples may make this clearer. The category of "academic" is strictly speaking not a bias at all, but in a school system where there had been strong pressure since the very beginning of the 1970s to allocate one of the four biases (including domestic science) to all secondary schools, those which still did not have this at the time of sampling in 1981 would in some sense have to be regarded as a residual category. It would have been difficult for one of the well-known rural schools to have resisted taking on a bias for almost 10 years. The tendency, therefore, might be for the academic category to be composed perhaps largely of urban schools, who could justify not having agriculture because of their situation and not having technical education because of expense. Alternatively, they could also be day schools, or relatively recent foundations. Since traditionally in Tanzania the distinction between day and boarding has been very important, and has coincided, until recently, with an urban/rural division, it could well be that the academic category in the research is composed largely of urban day schools.

One of the surprising results of the research project is, of course, that the no-bias (academic) group of schools appear to do almost as well on the special vocational achievement test as do the schools with the biases Psacharopoulos and Loxley, 1985, (Table 6-9). The latter test was composed of some 80 items (20 for each of the biases, including domestic science), and, thus, the academic group could be expected to be at some considerable disadvantage, since there was no cluster of items for which they had a head start. Nevertheless, they would appear to have done as well as the commercial and technical bias schools on the agricultural test items, better than the agricultural and technical bias schools on the commercial test items, and better or as well as the agricultural and commercial streams on the technical test items. Overall it could be said of these special vocational tests that each separate set of bias schools did slightly better than other biases (or the academic schools) on the test items aimed at their special bias, but there was little difference when it came to answering items on the other bias fields. Which suggests there is little transferability of principles learnt in the different biases to other curriculum areas, and that the commonsense of the academic schools managed to do as well as the bias schools in areas that were outside the latters' speciality.

In point of fact it is impossible to tell from the normalized mean used in the published tables what the actual performance was like on the original tests. From earlier papers, however, it can be seen that, in general, performance was very mediocre in all vocational achievement tests. Thus in commerce the mean scores (out of 20) were in general around five points; in agriculture around six, and in technical around seven (Omari, 1982 p. 14). It is important to put these perhaps surprisingly low scores into the wider context of competence in English and Tanzanian secondary schools all of which have maintained English as a medium. Diversified bias teaching—and all the test items—are in English, but evidence from a very recent study suggests that achievement is extremely low:

> While the number of non-readers and those able to read only very simple picture books has halved by mid way through Form IV the number getting within reach of being able to read easy unsimplified texts is less than 10 per cent. It is extremely worrying to find that nearly 1/3 of all pupils are still at the picture book reading level after four years of official English medium education. These results are a clear indication that *throughout their secondary school career little or no other subject information is getting across to about 50 per cent of the pupils in our sample. Only about 10 per cent of Form 4s are at a level at which one might expect English medium education to begin.* [Emphasis added] (Criper and Dodd, 1984, p. 34)

Without looking more carefully at the original test questions, it would be difficult to make a judgment, but it would seem not impossible, in the light of the language situation above, that the vocational test items were to some extent testing English comprehension as well as specialized knowledge. And that therefore the academic schools, with their extra 16–20 periods to distribute on the basic subjects, were able to keep up by virtue of their English comprehension. To take these kinds of issue further, it would be important to know more about the academic group of schools.

Similarly, with the technical bias schools. These would appear to do much better in their own subject area than do the other biases, which suggests that their bias gives them more of an advantage in their own field than do the others. Again, to get behind these interesting results, it is important to "unpackage" the technical bias schools. It is soon clear that the technical bias is somehow more special in Tanzania than is commercial or agricultural. Only a handful of government schools have been allowed to take on the technical bias, and all of these are included in the World Bank sample of seven. Of the government technical schools, several were much older foundations with a very strong craft/trade school emphasis before their conversion, and the remainder were more recent. It is also plain that the external agencies have played an important role in cautioning against diversifying more technical schools than there would be external support to maintain. To a greater extent therefore than with commerce or with agriculture, there do not appear to be minimally diversified technical schools in the government sector. The donor anxiety that technical schools either be properly equipped or not started at all may be part of the explanation for the relatively better achievement in technical bias. However, there are additional reasons which can be deduced partly from the World Bank data set and partly from knowledge of the technical school context.

First, the Bank's data in general makes plain that government schools perform better than private, in general, and that boys outperform girls. In the sample, the technical schools are dominated by the government schools, and within these by boys over girls. There is, however, a further factor which is an extension of these. In Tanzania, there are in fact quite a large group of private (community) technical schools, organized by the successor organization to the Tanganyika African Parents Association (TAPA) (United Republic of Tanzania, 1978, p. 62). These 20 private technical schools are in general equipped very meagerly, and their academic reputation nationally is far from established. Had a number of these foundations been added to the technical bias sample, it is certain that the apparent advantage of this specialization would have been eliminated rather rapidly. Equally, the cost of the technical specialization would have been slashed, since *Wazazi* (TAPA) schools are run with an absolute minimum of equipment.

The reason for raising this issue is not principally to question the sampling, but rather to explore whether the data are able to offer us an insight into diversification-in-practice. There is no doubt that there are some interesting questions to be raised in the bias schools about the relationships between achievement in the academic subjects and the amount of time dedicated officially to diversification. But because of the links between what we have called IDA-diversification and ESR-diversification (with the latter's emphasis on productive labor, food production and income generation), it becomes important to gain some measure of the practical skill acquisition associated with the bias, and not only some of its academic content. In much of the existing literature on Tanzanian diversification, including the Bank's case study, it is very difficult to get a sense of these practical dimensions of diversification, and particularly in what way the obligations to pursue productive labor do or do not intertwine with the school's practical bias.

For instance, do the government technical bias schools seek to reinforce the lessons of diversification through productive activities in building, subcontracting, metal trades, etc? Or do they have to "diversify" from the technical work into agricultural labor in order to secure additional food and income? In what ways do the commercial bias schools (which would appear to be largely situated in towns, and be day schools rather than boarding) carry out practical income-generating activities? Do they run typing pools, for example, or run mini-companies that sell food on the roadside? We have already alluded to the extraordinary range of agricultural practice, from the half-day "Cuban" schools, to the relatively high technology Nordic-aided community school, to the cash crop schools with their vines and coffee. Even though the government schools have in general far from reached the goal of covering 25 percent of their recurrent costs (excluding teacher salaries), can it be suggested that diversification contributes to the quite remarkable productivity of certain agriculture bias schools? Finally, it must be remembered that in one sense all schools must have a bias towards self-reliant activities and income generation. So that even the "academic" schools in the Bank sample will be obliged to pursue some ESR-diversification, and this might well be in agriculture, depending on their location.

There is clearly no easy way to handle the acquisition of practical skills through the bias program. It would be possible to look at the number of students from technical schools who successfully sat for the Grade Three Trade Test, though that national certificate might be thought more appropriate to the vocational schools than to the technical schools. It would have been possible to look at the national examination results at the end of Form 4, to see what indication there might be from the practical parts of the practical subjects. Or again, it might have been feasible to look at the reaction of local employers to such technical leavers. This latter would have been particularly worth doing in two or three urban centers such as Tanga (and now also Moshi) since there exist in these not only a biased secondary school but also a very well equipped vocational training center. In this local context, it would perhaps have been possible to locate the difference between the vocational impulse with the emphasis on education, and the vocational impulse with the emphasis on training (King,1985). Finally, some indication of technical capacity might have been gained from the scale and complexity of the income-generating activities undertaken by the school. None of these would have been conclusive, and some could have been frustrated by the larger economic crisis, affecting imported materials, spare parts, and even local supplies of wood, cement and bricks, etc. In a number of workshops, doubtless, under-capacity and under-utilization of practical skills could be attributed to such factors. The present data set, however, can give no feel for whether the machine tools are standing idle in Ifunda, Moshi or Tanga, or whether groups of students with their instructors are running profitable automobile repair workshops outside the back door of the school, or taking lucrative contracts for domestic furniture. Such operations are in one way much easier to organize in developing countries, but their "success" is sometimes very much to the disadvantage of the small independent contractors in the neighborhood.

Remembering, however, the two populations that are going through the diversified schools (those who are being socialized through work for their later leadership roles, and those who may directly enter the labor market), it is also very complicated to make a judgment about attitude change, political commitment to the school and the larger community. The Bank study acknowledges, at the very end of the Tanzania case, that diversification "may still be considered worthwhile if the political objectives for which it was adopted are being realized" (Psacharopoulos and Loxley, 1985, p. 209). Perhaps quite properly, there was no attempt by this externally-funded study to make a comment on this dimension of diversification. In passing, however, it may be noted that the sampled students appear to regard auto-mechanics as more important to Tanzania than party workers or youth leaders. On the more positive side, they also seem to regard primary schoolteachers as much more important than either secondary or university teachers. (Psacharopoulos and Loxley, 1985, Table 6.22.).

If both the practical and political dimensions of diversification are difficult to assess from the research project, the local dynamic and current tensions within the whole bias movement are also hard to assess from this data set. In effect the Bank study was undertaken at a very crucial time in the history of Tanzanian education. A Presidential Commission had just the year before begun to review some of the most sensitive issues in Tanzanian educational policy, and would report by 1982. The dimensions of the private secondary school explosion were beginning to become clear, and particularly the impossibility of imposing a strict system of biases upon their curricula. Equally, in a large number of both government and private schools, including schools with special biases, there had grown up a practice of allowing separate fee paying academic streams to develop. Organized under the offices of the resident tutors of adult education, these particular streams of adults turned out to be the same age as the other students in the schools. They followed the same curriculum in the afternoons/evenings as did the regular students. The only difference was that they did not need to follow the diversified subjects. What had emerged quite silently was indeed a series of "academic control groups" within some of the diversified schools.[1] Finally, as the bulge of the UPE entrants of 1977 moved through the primary schools, the pressure for secondary school expansion broke through, and a whole series of new initiatives by districts, communities, educational foundations and the local churches began to take shape. As many of these were predicated upon community financing, and often made use of available buildings rather than custom-built facilities of the sort that were erected for diversification, it would seem highly probable that the Government will be unlikely to impose the precondition of a bias.

Nyerere has said as recently as 1984 that "whenever and wherever we do create secondary schools, they must be Secondary–Technical schools, with many of them being biased to agriculture and other science subjects" (Nyerere, 1984, p. 9). However, the speed with which self-help movements in secondary education have proceeded, makes it rather unlikely that there will be, even initially, much beyond a cosmetic diversification. In an interesting change of direction on the older manpower policy of the secondary schools, Nyerere has justified this techno–scientific emphasis as follows:

> A person with an agriculture or science based secondary school education can be trained to be an administrator if necessary. We have a

[1] See further K. King, The end of education for self-reliance, Occasional Paper No. 1, Centre of African Studies, Edinburgh, Jan. 1984.

number of departmental heads in different ministries who are trained professionals of one kind or another, but an administrator cannot do the job of an Agricultural Officer or an Engineer. I could not, for example, do the job of an Engineer, but an engineer can decide to become a teacher or a politician. (Nyerere, 1984, p. 9)

What will be the results of these expansionary pressures upon the traditional emphasis upon diversification? One possibility is that as the competition for Form 5 and university entrance intensifies, the schools that are currently allocating a third or more of their curriculum time to the biases will be forced dramatically to reduce this proportion, so as to remain competitive with schools spending no time on these areas. This scenario will emphasize one of the continuing paradoxes of diversified education: that the best diversified facilities are often located in the parts of the secondary school system which are least interested in exploiting them. The schools with the weakest financial base will find themselves pursuing the narrowest of academic curricula, and preparing their students for national "O"-level type exams which many will fail. At the upper end of the range of well-endowed schools, there will increasingly be pressure to under-utilize the technical and agricultural facilities—and to reduce the bias from 16 periods to an elective three or four.

It is common in situations of very rapid educational change for the preoccupation with the new initiatives to proceed with very little understanding and awareness of the value of the old. It must be one of the regrets of the first phase of diversification in Tanzania during the 1970s that almost no research was conducted at the school level to illuminate the achievements and failures of diversification. What were the mechanisms that allowed some of the highest scoring schools in Tanzania to combine this with very remarkable agricultural productivity? Is there an enduring legacy of the realization by teachers and students that productive labor can bring in millions of shillings into the school's recurrent budget? It is not too late for some research to look at some of these questions, and the possibility of doing so has greatly been assisted by the ground that has been broken by the World Bank study. A number of items in such a research agenda have recently been laid out in the University of Dar es Salaam's *Papers in Education and Development,* No. 10 (see King and Komba, 1985, pp. 8–24).

In concluding, it might be useful to add to that research agenda just one of a whole series of research tasks suggested by the World Bank's Tanzania case study. This consists of the fascinating evidence that of the rather small number of Form 4 graduates who had actually joined the labor market within a year of leaving school, no less than 121 of those who were traced admitted to being self-employed (Psacharopoulos and Loxley, 1985, pp. 191, 207). What was surprising about this small group was that they claimed to be getting just exactly twice the amount of money that their employed colleagues in the public and private sector were getting. Since a significant number of these were working on their own farms or on family farms and in petty commerce, it might just be relevant to look in a little more detail at the relations if any between their school experience and the rigors and rewards of self-employment.

I wish to end by raising some questions about the implications and consequences of this particular critique of vocationalism. Has it really altered the diversification policy of the Tanzanian government? Has it managed to change policies towards technical and vocational education and training within the Bank itself? These are of course both part of a larger and more troublesome question: what is likely to be the impact on government of a research study?

Over the last 20 years, there has been no shortage of academic studies criticizing the vocational orientation or the vocational impulse in schooling. Arguably, there are few articles more quoted than Philip Foster's "Vocational school fallacy in development planning," and there have been many more that have pursued different aspects of the same general debate (see King, 1971, 1977). And yet, it would appear that such writing has been much more influential amongst the academic community and amongst students of development studies than it has amongst members of the policy community. In the eyes of the latter, as they face the problems of youth unemployment on a larger and larger scale, there are few options available, and one of the commonest initiatives continues to be some form of vocational orientation for the academic school. In 1987 alone, the Ministers of Education of the Commonwealth countries have selected as their main theme for their triennial conference the importance of "vocationally-oriented schooling;" Britain has decided to extend a diversified type of schooling into every secondary school in the country; and even the World Bank, in recognition of the fact that the Education Programme spends more on technical and vocational schools than any other type of schooling has decided to launch a major policy study on the topic. The vocational school paradigm may be dead in the view of many academics and researchers, but in the world of politics it still seems to have a good deal of life in it, both in the poorer developing countries and in the richer industrialized nations of Europe and America.

References

Court, D. and King, K. (1978) *Education and production needs in the rural community: Issues in the search for a national system.* Paris: IIEP Working Paper.

Criper, C. and Dodd, W. A. (1984) Report on the teaching of the English language and its use as a medium in education in Tanzania. July–Aug. 1984.

Directorate of Planning and Development, Ministry of National Education (1971) Diversification/vocationalisation of secondary education: draft paper, July. (Mimeo.)

King, K. J. (1971) *Pan-Africanism and education.* Oxford University Press.

King, K. (1977) *The African artisan.* London: Heinemann.

King, K. (1985) *The planning of technical and vocational education and training*. Paris: IIEP Occasional Paper.

King, K. and Komba, D. (1985) Analytical comments on presented research reports and discussion trends. In *Papers in education and development*, No. 10, special issue on educational research in Tanzania. Dar es Salaam: Department of Education, University of Dar es Salaam.

Ministry of National Education (n.d.) *"The science and practice of agriculture syllabus" for agricultural biased secondary schools in Tanzania.*

Musoma Declaration (1976) Directive on the implementation of "education for self-reliance". Reproduced in *Papers in education and development*, No. 3, Department of Education, University of Dar es Salaam.

Nyerere, J. (1984) Speech to the Education Seminar, Arusha, Oct. 1984.

Omari, I. M. (1982) Diversification of secondary school curriculum and learning outcomes: some preliminary results. Paper at Arusha Workshop of Decentralisation of Research and Evaluation Capacities in Tanzania, 13–17 Dec. 1982. (Mimeo.)

Psacharopoulos, G. and Loxley, W. (1985) *Diversified secondary education and development: Evidence from Colombia and Tanzania*. Baltimore: John Hopkins University Press.

United Republic of Tanzania (1978) *Vocational training and technical education in Tanzania*. Joint SIDA, GTZ, DANIDA mission to Tanzania.

CHAPTER 17

Vocational Secondary Education in Trinidad and Tobago and Related Evaluation Results

MAURICE CHIN-ALEONG

Ministry of Education, Trinidad and Tobago

OVER the past two decades vocational secondary education has become an exceptionally outstanding educational reform movement. This has been so in both developed and developing countries. However, the thrust in vocational secondary education has been more pronounced in the developing countries. A relatively recent path leading towards the vocationalization of secondary education is the Diversified Secondary School Curriculum Programme.

The protagonists of the movement for the diversification of the secondary school curriculum have been crusading for some time now. Their obvious reason was, and still is, to vocationalize education. These crusaders contend that general secondary education has a poor track record for preparing students for the world of work. They argue that by using various models and orientations, the objectives of vocational education could be accomplished. Among these models are:

(i) an information exchange between school and the world of work;
(ii) an alternation between school and work, including an exchange of personnel; and
(iii) an integration of school and work.

This chapter attempts to point out the origins and rationale for vocationalization in Trinidad and Tobago. It also seeks to examine the proposed models for future vocationalizing and points out that various components of these models have been tried elsewhere before. Third, it examines some related evaluation studies. These studies, given their limitations, tend to show that diversification has not had the type of success or impact that was expected. The chapter then touches on an alternative model which would ensure that vocational education is pursued as a complement to general education. Finally, the need for more comprehensive evaluation studies is urged and the conclusion drawn that whatever are the strengths and/or weaknesses of secondary vocational education, it will be with us for the foreseeable future.

Origins, Rationale and Delivery Systems

The call for vocational education in the British Caribbean is by no means new. Throughout the 20th century political leaders and educators have contended that vocationalizing education was the correct means of promoting national development. The general argument runs that in the past, academic education failed to encourage people who did not gain white-collar employment, to lead productive lives. That it gave people false aspirations and created contempt for trades, crafts, manual and agricultural work. The solution therefore was a reorientation of the curriculum (Williams, 1968).

Attempts to vocationalize secondary education in Trinidad and Tobago came in three waves. The first phase occurred in the late 1950s and early 1960s, through the establishment of secondary modern schools. The idea behind these schools was to move away from the orientation of the fully loaded academic program and to offer such practical subjects as typing, home economics, woodwork, etc. The second phase took place in the 1960s and early 1970s. This period witnessed the development of a 15-year education plan (1968–1983). This plan proposed a two-tier secondary structure comprising junior secondary (Forms 1–3, in which industrial arts and home economics were compulsory) and senior secondary (Forms 4–5 or 6) schools. At the senior secondary level, it was proposed to offer "basic disciplines and scientific education on the basis of which the employer would build his specific job training rather than the specific training at school" (Government of Trinidad and Tobago, 1974, p. 37). Students who did not qualify for the second cycle of secondary education would go to trade and farm schools and youth camps. The third phase or great thrust started in 1975 with modifications to the 1968–83 education plan, by way of new proposals by the then Prime Minister. These modifications demanded the implementation of a Diversified Secondary School Curriculum (Government of Trinidad and Tobago, 1975).

The principal rationale for the great thrust into technical/vocational education, in Trinidad and Tobago, rests on the notion that the kinds of job necessary for modern development, and created by high technology, require specialized skills. Furthermore, these specialized skills can best be taught and delivered to the labor market by way of formal programs developed and pursued at secondary and post-secondary schools. This view holds, that vocational education, in addition to being beneficial to the individual (in the form of enhanced employment prospects and earnings) also develops the country as a whole. This development is realized through a more productive work-force and therefore a higher Gross National Product.

Technical/vocational education had been advocated as the vehicle through which the manpower requirements of the country could be attained. That is to say, that it was, and to a large extent still is, considered as the solution to the dual problem of unemployment (mainly among the young and unskilled) and the projected occupational structure of the labor force necessary for industrialization.

In 1975, in an address to the Caribbean Union College, the Prime Minister sought to show the need for more technical/vocational graduates and therefore a new type of school. He noted that a comparison of 1968 manpower estimates and 1973 targets showed a shortfall in the professional, technical and craftsmen areas but a surplus of applicants in the clerical and sales areas. He further noted that those shortfalls would have been exacerbated by the demands of industrialization around the planned petroleum-based heavy industries (Williams, 1975). The response to this situation was the proposal that both academic and vocational courses (specialized training) be pursued under one roof and under common management (diversified curriculum comprehensive schools). Three models for the delivery of vocational education therefore now exist. These fit into what have been identified as "non-formal," "parallel vocationalized" and "components of a core curriculum" systems (Lillis and Hogan, 1983).

In drawing up the rationale and guidelines for a system of diversified curriculum for secondary education in Trinidad and Tobago, the Prime Minister emphasized that

> it must be realized and accepted that any Education plan for Trinidad and Tobago must have (as) one of its prime goals, the preparation of our citizens for suitable employment opportunities. The majority of citizens leaving the Secondary Education system seek either immediate employment or further education at some higher level. The majority belong to the former group.

Whereas in the past and certainly during the preparation of the draft Education Plan, the opportunities that were available were not very clearly defined and a general sort of education in the traditional sense was as good as any other, circumstances in Trinidad and Tobago have changed and a clearer picture is now emerging. Various studies have shown that for any country involved in heavy industrial development, the requirements for personnel can be broken down, generally, into the following categories:

10–15% professional;
15–20% sub-professionals and technicians;
60–70% persons with general training but with definite exposure to the sciences;
10–15% skilled craftsmen. (Government of Trinidad and Tobago, 1975, p. 5)

In particular the following proposals were made:

(i) That the norm for secondary education be a period of at least five years.

(ii) That the three-year Junior Secondary School program remain an integral part of the Education Plan.

(iii) That the concept of programs in specialized craft training done in isolation in Government controlled vocational schools be rejected.

(iv) That technology in all its aspects be given a priority position in any modification of the Education Plan.

(v) That an integrated comprehensive program embracing the traditional academic, pre-technician, commercial, general industrial, and limited specialized craft-training utilizing common "facilities" and with common management be adopted as the national model for 14-plus education. This model should be a basis for the planning of all future facilities.

(vi) That the denominational organizations be accepted as having a critical and important role in the education system particularly at the secondary level. In accepting this as a matter of policy however, these organizations should be requested to adopt the national model as identified at (v) and to prepare a plan leading to the implementation within their own programs of this policy within the shortest possible time and certainly within five years. The denominational participation hereafter should be based on the rejection of the old formula of cost sharing, with the public sector assuming full responsibility for all costs of education structured along the lines of the national model.

(vii) Denominational Boards which accepted the National Model would be funded 100 percent for construction and equipment costs in conforming with the National Model (Government of Trinidad and Tobago, 1975, pp. 10–11).

Thus the national model for secondary education in Trinidad and Tobago was the diversified curriculum model in which the planners, after some time, sought to implement a parallel vocationalized system. That is, a technical/vocational track which runs parallel to the dominant academic model—all under one roof. It must be pointed out here that when the senior comprehensives were first designed, it was explicitly stated that there should be three definite tracks, viz. (a) an academic track; (b) a pre-technician track; and (c) a specialized craft stream. The academic track was to make provision for students who would be interested in furthering their academic education or gaining employment that would require such skills. The pre-technician stream, like the academic track, would cater for students desirous of becoming professionals or sub-professionals but at the same time would cater for a majority of students who would wish to enter the labor market immediately upon leaving school—hopefully, some of these at the inter-mediate level. However, the specialized craft stream was to concentrate on crafts training with some limited basic general education (see Appendix 1 for details on periods allotted to curriculum tracks). The diversified model, as claimed elsewhere, was directed towards the creation of manpower for socio-economic growth. Important additional objectives were: to stem the tide of too much growth in the interest of academic work, and to develop intermediate skills that would allow entry into the skilled labor force. It would appear that the parallel vocationalized system is based on the assumption that general and technical/vocational education are substitutes for each other. It fails to understand that vocational studies are built on and around bodies of theories. Therefore, vocational studies are best taught on a proper foundation of general education (Blaug, 1974; Blaug and Rumber-ger, 1984).

An examination of the various systems of vocational education shows that one might speak of pre-vocational secondary education, secondary voca-tional and post-secondary vocational education. The first normally refers to an orientation and information about "skills clusters," generally industrial arts and home economics. The second refers to courses provided in second-ary schools for the development and certification of particular skills which will afford young people direct entry into the labor market. The third refers to development and certification of particular skills at ordinary and advanced levels. These skills are learned, however, on the foundation of a general secondary education and on a body of theory.

No one has any quarrel whatsoever with the first or third. It is generally the second, i.e., secondary vocational education, which provides the arena for contention. The argument is: schools are simply not equipped to fit people neatly into jobs that require specialized skills or to assist in alleviating the unemployment problems by creating self-employment (Blaug, 1973). In particular, secondary vocational education requires each student at an early age (14+), to select a craft subject which the student will pursue as his/her vocation. It has been argued by many that one ought not to propose the selection of a "vocational" subject at secondary school without due con-sideration to vocational maturity. It was in addressing the matter of early specialization, among other things, that in 1982, the Cabinet appointed a Committee to examine the content, organization and administration of technical/vocational education in secondary schools.

The Committee submitted its report in 1984. It emphasized that it was not in support of early specialization in skill training for direct entry to the labor market. The Committee recommended the teaching of a set of skills related to a particular job (skills clusters), strongly supported by the normal general academic program. That is to say, the "Components of a core curriculum" model, was advocated. This model recommends pre-vocational work rather than the production of job skills for direct entry into the labor market.

Pre-vocational work, therefore, becomes a compulsory component among the other components of the curriculum. In the absence of a cost–benefit/effectiveness analysis the Committee looked at the comparative costs of salaries for the upkeep of the technical/vocational and academic tracks. The cost of salaries for vocational education was found to be extraordinarily high (Report, 1984). This is partly due to the wide range of vocational subjects offered at the comprehensive schools but mainly so, because of the small sizes of classes for vocational subjects. At present more than 25 vocational subjects are offered at senior comprehensives. These are included in the following which were generally supposed to be offered by all senior comprehensives (the general model of the comprehensive is the 1564 enrollment):

General courses (offered at the junior secondary school)

1. Industrial arts
2. Home economics
3. Agricultural science

Specialized crafts (offered at the senior secondary comprehensive schools)

1. Automechanics
2. Machine shop
3. Electrical installation
4. Welding
5. Masonry
6. Construction, carpentry
7. Nurse's aide
8. Plumbing
9. Air conditioning
10. Domestic electronics
11. Dressmaking and design
12. Tailoring
13. Food preparation
14. Clerk/typist
15. Shorthand/typist
16. Housekeepers' craft
17. Agricultural craft
18. Beauty culture

Pre-technician courses (offered at the senior secondary comprehensive schools)

1. General electricity
2. Metalwork/metals
3. Principles of accounts
4. Food and nutrition
5. Fashion and fabrics
6. Typewriting
7. Office procedures
8. General draughting
9. Woods/woodwork
10. Principles of business
11. Clothing and textiles
12. Surveying
13. Shorthand
14. Agricultural science

(See Appendix 1 for further details.)

However, there appears to be sustained interest in the vocationalization of education in Trinidad and Tobago. In this context though, a more rational approach of training in "skills clusters" is recommended. Also, the approach to a more judicial mix of academic and vocational studies is now being considered. The draft plan for education development in the country (1985–1990) is dominated by technical/vocational education and training with some new orientations and models. These orientations embrace programs ranging from diversifying the curriculum to on-the-job training schemes, sandwich courses and life-long education programs, in collaboration with employers. It is useful to note that such plans include payment to firms in one form or the other.

The statistics on public secondary education show that out of a secondary school population of 92,000, 61,000 attend schools with diversified curricula. That is to say that two-thirds of public secondary school students attend schools in which vocational education is taught. The education plan (1985–1990) proposes that over the five-year period schools which do not now have vocational subjects on their curriculum, should begin to offer suitable vocational subjects, that is, subjects appropriate to their structure and location. The plan itself has implicitly stated its orientations to vocationalizing.

Methods of Vocationalizing

An examination of the Plan for Educational Development in Trinidad and Tobago (1985–1990) reveals three basic orientations or methods for vocationalizing. These might be identified as: an information exchange; an alternation between work and school (including an exchange of personnel) and an integration of school and work (Government of Trinidad and Tobago, 1985).

Information Exchanges

The central idea of this orientation is that there should be a mutual exchange of information between schoolchildren, would-be workers and industry. This is based on the premise that given available jobs in the labor market, people will make their skills available to capture returns for these skills if they know all about the job skill requirements and the demands of the communities. Teachers too, will need to understand how things are done in industries. On the other hand, industries must be informed of school programs and approaches.

The problem with the information exchange method is that the situation is dynamic and the lead time necessary for the acquisition of skills makes it necessary that rapid and timely information be always available. The danger of narrow specialization becomes evident.

Upon successful completion of training programs the demand for certain skills could be drastically altered. Since narrow specialization is more likely to suffer from employment with shifts in the employment pattern, the argument for training in "skills clusters" is now much in vogue. Indeed, there is much truth in the proposition that general education tends to make people trainable, whereas specialized training develops a person trained in a specific area. Moreover, information normally gained from labor market studies generally indicates supply and demand. They hardly ever indicate the intricacies involved in the intermediate steps between training for a job, actually obtaining a job and promotion. The strength of the information orientation is that it will tend to eliminate wastage and over-supply of particular skills.

It is evident that an information exchange program will call for strong communication links between industry and the education system, and the maintenance of a data base. This would obviously necessitate additional expenditure, thereby making the present vocationalizing programs more expensive. Already secondary vocational schools require greater capital and recurrent expenditure than traditional secondary schools because of the types of building and equipment and sizes of class required for conducting practical (vocational) subjects.

Alternation between Work and School

The argument here is that students are not learning how to work. That in order to train students properly for work, it is necessary to cooperate with industry. Since employers know best what they want, then they should assist in the direction and formulation of programs. This system is best implemented by an exchange of personnel between education and firms. For example, people from industry will be requested to do some lecturing or teaching and/or assist in the setting up of programs/courses, while teachers will be asked to spend some time in industries to become acquainted with their actual schedules.

In this system sandwich courses should be a common feature. Courses will be pursued by day releases or block release systems. Moreover, it is anticipated that firms will be requested to provide short- or medium-term on-the-job training and apprenticeship programs. It is further proposed that firms will be paid by tax rebates or otherwise for expenses incurred in the training of students and apprentices. The plan summarizes this situation as:

> An adequate and stable source of funds is necessary to implement a comprehensive National Training Plan. Direct or indirect funding is necessary to elicit the participation of industry as partners in the training enterprises. Financing is also necessary to provide the support services such as monitoring the performance of the system, data

collection and management and materials development, among others. The portion of the unemployment levy that was intended for training should be utilized to support this training plan. Financial arrangements such as those which have been successfully implemented in other countries can be explored.

Tax rebate policies and duty free and tax relief concessions can form an overall package of incentives for firms to participate in the national training enterprise. In some circumstances, however, it may be necessary for the government to provide direct funding to private firms through a sub contracting arrangement so that the facilities of these firms can be used to provide up-to-date on site training. A variety of other cost-sharing arrangements can be explored; but the end result is that firms will see it as beneficial to participate in the training system. (Government of Trinidad and Tobago, 1985, pp. 147–148)

No doubt firms would see this as beneficial to them. Most economists have already pointed out that in such situations firms are doubly paid. In the first instance trainees are paid less than their productivity in the long run and secondly the very firms receive monetary compensation for offering general training or employing trainees (Becker, 1964; Ziderman, 1978). In fact, many claim that firms often indulge in on-the-job training programs to obtain cheap unskilled and semi-skilled labor in the process of training. Such training, it is argued, is seldom done in a formal setting in the firm, but rather learners are attached to experienced workers as helpers. The firm is even happier when it is paid for this.

There are benefits to be derived from the "alternation" model. It would provide practical approaches to work skills and actual work while still at school. But work and productivity are very much connected with the cognitive and affective domains and not merely psychomotor skills and labor. These aspects, cognitive characteristics and affective traits, all agree, have as much to do with output as skills themselves (Blaug, 1974).

The technical aspect of the "alternation" method is to define the correct mix of school and work. Moreover, if the program is to be sustained it must be backed by a strategy for generating employment.

Integration of School and Work

In this model there is no distinction between school and work. The work-place is simulated in school. The introduction of such programs are justified under the rhetoric of rationale for all similar programs: (i) to develop proper work attitudes; (ii) to remove the distinction between mental and manual work; and (iii) to stress the importance of punctuality and regularity, etc.

Also in this model, school programs are organized along the lines of the firm. They produce goods and services for sale and the funds thereby gained are used for the upkeep of the program. Therefore the greater the productivity of the school the more resources will be ploughed back into and made available to the school (although the school will still be maintained by the Government).

The idea of the integration between school and work has already been put to the test, generally by command economies and developing countries. Varying degrees of success and failure have been reported. Arnove (1977), reporting on the China case, observed that the Chinese citizens saw the program as a "mobility trap." In the British Caribbean itself, Jennings-Wray and Teape (1982) noted that the program conducted in Jamaica, did not particularly enhance the job prospects of its graduates, though students could benefit from such programs. Moreover, since most of the programs have been attempted by socialist countries it ought to be noted that private employers may not necessarily require the identical traits and characteristics from workers as do governments. All this must be seen against the arguments:

(i)   that most jobs in a modern economy do not really require as much specialized skills as those formulated in formal school syllabi. And even where this is so, a great deal of these skills could be acquired on the job in a relatively short period;

(ii) employment and productivity are not necessarily related to the distribution of resources.

But if all that is done at work is to be done at school, the argument will present an omnibus for subjects to be included in the school curriculum. Very strong cases could be made for inclusion of almost any subject in the school curriculum, e.g., driving. Furthermore, if the school is to replicate all that is actually done at work, there is the risk of the school becoming boring (e.g., student alienation) and lacking in spirit and ideals. These are supposed to be the exact opposites of the ideals of schooling. Schooling stresses the development of citizens who are not only influenced by the profit motive but those who serve the good of the community and their country.

Finally, the idea of an integration between school and work is the basis for lifelong education. It is contended that workers are in constant need of having to upgrade their skills and very often to reorient their skills to new situations mainly because of rapidly changing technology. Workers should therefore return to school every so often. But what better place could one upgrade one's skills than on the job? What is obvious is, any system which must simulate the workplace, and train and retrain people is expensive (income forgone, etc.). Such a system would require policymakers to develop methods and methodologies for analysis of costs, benefits and effectiveness.

Two aspects of the "integrated" model need to be examined. First, could the school really simulate the rhythm of the workplace? Second, like the alternation model the integration model would need the support of a strategy for creating employment. Could the education system acting on its own do this?

Classroom Orientations

With respect to skills acquired in school, the plan proposes to allow students to pursue both specialized craft and academic programs at secondary school graduation level. That is to say, students would be encouraged to offer simultaneously an examination which would certify them as being competent craftsmen (National Examination Council Craft Certificate) and the normal GCE or GXC "O" level examinations. Already some concerned have predicted tragedy in this move, since they have pointed out that the failure rates of the National Examinations Council Craft Certificate are already alarmingly high. They claim that, to now add general academic-oriented courses to this workload, would spread the ability and efforts of the students too thinly. The idea behind this proposition, however, is to enable the student to pursue both technical/vocational and academic studies as he/she pursues a career path.

It has been strongly contended that the mix of academic and vocational programs leads to the development of a "general" curriculum (belonging to neither vocational nor academic) and wherever this type of curriculum has been established the results are notorious (Grubb and Lazerson, 1975). A second approach is to pursue a group or cluster of related skills to provide basic knowledge in predetermined skills clusters, and a program of technology studies as part of the general curriculum to promote the technological literacy of students. Somehow these propositions appear to be intuitively correct. Only evaluation studies will tell whether intuition should be the guiding light. Indeed, there has been much concern in recent times, about the type of evaluation studies that are suitable for testing the efficacy of educational programs. In this context, the human capital approach with its rates of return technique has been very much criticized. Many have proposed that tracer type studies to ascertain the effectiveness of programs in enhancing employment prospects and wages would be a better approach. The ideal study would be a combination of cost analysis and tracer types with indices of labor market performance.

Use of Cost Analysis

Because resources are scarce and decision-makers must make choices between alternative ways of achieving given ends, they must examine the strengths, weaknesses and costs of programs before making proper decisions. It is in attempting to do this that cost analysis in education proves to be a ready and useful tool. Two types of cost analyses have figured prominently in the education industry—Cost–benefit analysis (CBA) and Cost effectiveness analysis (CEA).

Given the limitations and arguments against the use of CBA or rate of return analysis, such as: (i) CBA indicates past trends between supply and demand and not future events, or (ii) CBA tells us where to invest but not in what quantity, etc., CBA in conjunction with other indicators is extremely useful. Its main strength is that it combines in a convenient form, information on the costs of different kinds of education, together with information about the balance between supply and demand for different types of education and the relative wages for different types of skills. One general argument is that while CBA does not tell us about future conditions and likelihood of profitability it does indicate whether we have been right in the past. On the other hand, CEA has many attributes. Its efficacy in the education sector lies in its appropriateness for programs with multiple objectives, all of which need not be expressed in a single unit or monetary terms (Blaug, 1968).

The use of cost analysis becomes even more urgent when one considers that the education plan (1985–1990) recommends diversification of the entire system. Any comprehensive evaluation of the diversification programs will have to include both types of analysis. In this manner the evaluation exercises will examine both external and internal efficiencies. But even so, studies to indicate much more than streams of enhanced earnings and employment will be required.

There is a need for indicators relating to increases in cognitive areas, development of entrepreneurial skills (if this is possible), changes in attitudes with respect to employment, ability to market skills, tendency towards acquiring more knowledge (schooling), teachers' ability, elimination of sexual stereotyping of jobs, job satisfaction, vocational maturity, etc. Most of all there is always a need to evaluate alternative means for achieving intermediate and long-range objectives. Having noted the value of cost analysis and other evaluation studies we now look at the results of some previous studies and also some work on costs of these programs.

Some Results of Related Studies

Statistics on the outcomes of two labor market follow-up studies of secondary school graduates are quite pertinent. The more recent of the two studies was done by the Division of Technical/Vocational Education and Training, National Training Board, Ministry of Education, in 1982–1983. The study might well be described as an intra-sector study since its objective was to measure labor market performance within a single sector of the secondary school system, namely, the senior comprehensive (diversified curriculum) schools. The principal objective of this study was to determine if there were marked differences in the labor market performances and perceptions of school-leavers which could be attributed to the curriculum of the stream pursued (Ministry of Education, 1983). The second related study was conducted by the Central Statistical Office, and dealt with the graduates of primary and secondary schools and institutions. It might very well be described as an inter-system analysis. That is to say, it looked at the job performance of 1977 graduates from the entire secondary system—the diversified curriculum schools and the traditional secondary schools and technical institutes (control schools) (Central Statistical Office, 1979).

Follow-up Study of Senior Comprehensive (Diversified Curriculum) Graduates: Intra-sector Analysis

The ideal study would have been one in which students were identified while in school and their progress recorded. Then after a given time, following graduation, say 12 months, their labor market performance could be reported. However in this case, records from school files as could be found, along with files kept by the Training Board, were used to obtain a sample of 901 graduates.

Of this initial target sample, 615 graduates responded. Of these responses, 607 were usable questionnaires—a yield of 67 percent. Table 1 gives a breakdown of the sample.

TABLE 1. *Summary of Respondents by Stream and Sex*

Sex	Pre-technical		Academic		Specialized crafts		All cases	
	No.	%	No.	%	No.	%	No.	%
Male	93	48.7	49	32.9	212	79.4	354	58.3
Female	98	51.3	100	67.1	55	20.6	253	41.7
Total	191	100.0	149	100.0	267	100.0	607	100.0

Among the objectives of the work was to focus on graduates of the specialized crafts programs. The concerns were:
(1) Were they finding jobs which were related to their training?
(2) Were they more quickly absorbed into the labor market?
(3) Were they better disposed than other graduates to find work?
(4) Did they command higher initial salaries?
(5) Were they satisfied with their jobs?
Against this background, a major concern was whether streaming (tracking) made a statistically significant difference in the outcomes outlined above (Ministry of Education, 1983).

In judging the results of the study it would be most useful to look at the five main areas from among the several which were used to characterize labor market performance: time taken to find first full-time job, job satisfaction, job preparation, wages and relatedness of school training to first job obtained. The study showed that specialized craft graduates fared better than the other graduates in all areas but the fifth (see Tables 2–6 below). However, in all such cases the statistical differences were not significant.

TABLE 2. *Time Taken (in months) to find the First Full-Time Job (by Stream)*

Stream	Mean	SD	N
Pre-technician	12.5	9.1	123
Academic	9.6	8.2	71
Specialized crafts	7.9	8.4	208
All cases	9.6	8.8	402

TABLE 3. *Mean Job Satisfaction* by Stream*

Stream	Mean	SD	N
Pre-technician	2.37	0.88	119
Academic	2.26	0.75	71
Specialized crafts	2.07	0.85	203
All streams	2.20	0.85	393

* Scale: 1 = very satisfied; 2 = satisfied; 3 = dissatisfied; 4 = very dissatisfied.

TABLE 4. *Mean Preparedness* by Stream*

Stream	Mean	SD	N
Pre-technician	2.63	0.89	114
Academic	2.64	0.91	70
Specialized crafts	2.37	0.93	199
All streams	2.50	0.92	383

* Scale: 1 = excellent preparation; 2 = good preparation; 3 = fair preparation; 4 = poor preparation.

TABLE 5. *Average Monthly Salaries of Graduates by Sex and Stream (in TT Dollars)*

Stream	Sex								
	Male			Female			All cases		
	Mean	SD	N	Mean	SD	N	Mean	SD	N
Pre-technician	687	364	63	547	261	51	624	328	114
Academic	605	299	27	620	371	40	614	341	67
Specialized crafts	644	419	165	577	264	31	634	399	196

Source: Ministry of Education (1983).

TABLE 6. *Relatedness of First Job to Training Received at School*

Relatedness	Pre-technician						Specialized crafts						All cases					
	Male		Female		Total		Male		Female		Total		Male		Female		Total	
	N	%	N	%	N	%	N	%	N	%	N	%	N	%	N	%	N	%
Same as area of training	9	12.9	9	18.4	18	15.1	67	39.0	8	25.0	75	36.8	76	38.9	17	21.0	93	28.8
Highly related	15	21.4	10	10.4	25	21.0	29	16.9	4	12.5	33	16.2	44	16.9	14	17.3	58	17.9
Slightly	18	25.7	12	24.5	30	25.2	24	13.9	6	18.8	30	14.7	42	14.0	18	22.2	60	18.6
Not at all	28	40.0	18	36.7	46	38.7	52	30.2	14	43.7	66	32.3	80	30.2	32	39.5	112	34.7
Total	70	100.0	49	100.0	119	100.0	172	100.0	32	100.0	204	100.0	242	100.0	81	100.0	323	100.0

Table 2 shows that the specialized craft graduate took slightly less time, on the average, to obtain his/her first job. However, the mean time for the academic graduate was the same as the overall mean for all tracks. In terms of job satisfaction, Table 3 shows that again on the average the specialized craft graduate was more satisfied with his job. But, then again, the mean grading for all streams was very close to that of the academic and not far off from the pre-technician. When preparation for work is examined the craft graduate is noted to be better prepared for work (Table 4). However, as in all other cases the other groups approximate the mean. The very important statistics on average monthly earnings of graduates reveal that there is no significant difference between earnings of different groups. Table 5 shows that graduates who had gained specialized skills had a mean monthly earnings of $634. For the academics it was $614 and for the pre-technicians $624. Noteworthy though, is the report that 62.5 percent of females and 46.3 percent of the males of specialized crafts graduates felt that their school training bore little or no relationship to their first jobs (see Table 6).

A major finding of this work also is that in the specialized craft area, employers were not concerned about credentials. This is questionable if only for one reason—the time of the survey. Two major caveats are important in analyzing the data:

(i) at the time of survey the responding graduates would have been reflecting the events of a boom period (1974–1981); and

(ii) there is the assumption that all students of the senior comprehensives are the same in intelligence and attainment. However, students attend these schools on the basis of the Common Entrance Examination and range from approximately the 16th to 75th percentile in performance at this examination.

It is known that Trinidad and Tobago enjoyed a boom period (1974–1981) with the increase in petroleum prices in 1973. During that period it was reported that labor and materials were in excessive demand and that the construction industry, which caters for most craftsmen, could not cope with the demand. It is not strange, therefore, that with the great demand for skilled craftsmen, employers would have turned a blind eye to certification and experience. What is surprising is that the performance of the specialized crafts graduate was not better.

However, recent figures and general indications of the labor market indicate new trends. With the recent decline in petroleum prices there is now rising unemployment. The unemployment rate is now 15 percent, and the 15–18 age group accounts for 55 percent of all unemployment (news bulletin). The wages of skilled craftsmen and tradesmen have fallen within recent times, while that of the white-collar worker (academic graduate) have remained the same over the identical period. This changing trend is depicted by Appendices 2 and 3. These tables are part of a survey conducted by the Central Statistical Office. They deal in the main with employment by sex, employment status and occupational and educational status. Appendix 2 shows that for the first half of 1984, unemployment was lowest for people with secondary school certificates and university degrees. Appendix 3 shows that in the same period unemployment was higher for craftsmen and construction workers than for clerical workers. (Central Statistical Office, 1985).

TABLE 7. *Cost per Successful Technical/Vocational Secondary School Student*

Technical/vocational program	Total cost ($)	No. of passes	Cost per student ($)
National Examinations Councils			
1. Pre-technician level	612,670.00	28 (197)	21,881.07
2. Specialized craft	8,201,070.00	95 (2,527)	83,684.38 (3,233)
External Examinations			
1. GCE 'O' level	53,274,300.00	3765 (17,130)	14,149.88 (3,110)
Regional Examinations pre-technician level			
1. General	28,123,730.00	9043 (2,217)	12,685.48
2. Basic	16,766,010.00	1938 (5,391)	8,651.19

Parentheses around a number indicate number examined and cost per number examined.
Regional examinations refer to the Caribbean Examination Council (CXC). They are structured along the lines of the British 'O' levels and CSE.
Source: Max Richard's Report.

But even accepting the results of the study, a different flavor is added when it is studied in relation to costs. When these results are seen in relation to work done by the Cabinet-appointed Committee in 1982 (Report, 1984), to look into secondary vocational education, new light is thrown on the matter. Table 7 reinforces the notion that technical/vocational education is expensive. Its very nature includes heavy capital and substantial recurring costs. According to Table 7 the costs in terms of teachers' salaries (using 1982 figures) for training a technical/vocational student is $3233 while that for an academic student is $3110. Moreover, the cost of producing a successful specialized craft graduate is $83,684 while that of a successful "O" level (full certificate) graduate is $14,150. A glance at the costs, in terms of teachers' salaries and initial salaries of graduates, casts doubt on the profitability of "specialized skills" graduates. Clearly, while the teachers' recurrent cost in producing a successful specialized craft student is over five times as much as that of producing a successful general secondary student, the starting salaries of both sets of graduates are approximately the same (the salary of the craft graduate actually being 1.016 times that of the academic graduate).

What is obvious is that the marginal gains or advantages held by the specialized craft graduates in all areas cannot justify implementation of the diversified program, even when only an intra-system study is made. This point is reinforced even further when one considers that over the years less than 5 percent of the students of the diversified curriculum schools have been able to gain a full certificate at the GCE/CXC "O" levels and the National Examination Council (Craftsmen Diploma). On the other hand, over 50 percent of the students from control schools are successful at their examinations—an indication that the traditional secondary schools are more productive in the area of imparting cognitive skills.

A final comment on this study is in order. It is most important to note that the stipulation for responses from graduates was that they should have been in the labor market for at least one year. The obvious difficulty with this stipulation is that it allowed different cohort groups with different characteristics to participate simultaneously. The results, therefore, must be somewhat "blurred." They should, however, still be addressed, but it is now more than evident that similar work using a single cohort would be useful.

Survey of Graduates from All Secondary Schools: Inter-sector Analysis

We now turn to the inter-sector analysis. In looking at the job performance of all post-primary (excluding university and teachers' colleges) graduates, it ought to be mentioned that the Central Statistical Office has attempted to trace three cohort groups, namely the 1977, 1979 and 1985 graduates. So far work has been fully completed only on the 1977 cohort. With respect to the 1979 cohort only Phase I (students' expectations and characteristics) have been completed while Phase II (actual job performance) is now being collated. The follow-up questionnaires for Phase II of the 1985 cohort are now being distributed. I will therefore look at some of the results of the 1977 and 1979 cohort groups.

The three most useful categories of information about the 1977 graduates are: the status of graduates 12 months after graduation; distribution of graduates who did not seek employment by reasons; and graduates with jobs and job satisfaction.

Tables 8–10 show that in all areas, the traditional secondary (control) schools outperformed the senior comprehensive (diversified curriculum) schools. Table 8 shows that a greater percentage of traditional school graduates (47.8 per cent) sought jobs in comparison to that of the diversified curriculum graduates (44.2 per cent). In terms of gaining employment, again

TABLE 8. *Status of Graduates 12 months after Leaving School by Educational Level*

Educational level	No. of respondents	Sought jobs (%)	Did not seek jobs (%)	Not stated (%)	Working (%)	Not working (%)	Not stated (%)
All levels	3,784	48.6	50.6	0.8	28.2	71.0	0.8
Primary	412	21.6	74.8	3.6	11.4	84.5	4.1
Junior secondary	554	4.7	95.3	—	1.4	98.6	—
Government and assisted secondary	1,248	47.8	51.8	0.4	28.5	71.0	0.5
Private secondary	411	56.2	43.6	0.2	25.3	74.2	0.5
Senior comprehensive	251	44.2	55.8	—	23.5	76.5	—
Technical and vocational	354	89.3	10.4	0.3	70.6	29.4	—
Commercial	116	76.7	21.6	1.7	39.7	59.5	0.9
Youth camp	225	87.6	11.1	1.3	36.9	61.8	1.3
Trade centre	199	85.4	12.1	2.5	51.8	47.7	0.5
Hotel school	14	85.7	14.3	—	85.7	14.3	—

Source: Central Statistical Office, Republic of Trinidad and Tobago.

TABLE 9. *Percentage Distribution of Graduates who did not Seek Work by Reasons for not Seeking Work and Educational Level*

Graduate level	Reasons for not seeking work				
	Was not interested	Did not have the right training	Decided to go back to school	Other*	Not stated
All levels	1.8	13.6	46.1	37.3	1.2
Primary	4.2	12.3	56.2	24.7	2.6
Junior secondary	1.5	1.5	4.0	93.0	—
Government and assisted secondary	1.2	14.7	71.0	12.1	0.9
Private secondary	1.1	32.4	60.3	5.0	1.1
Senior comprehensive	—	35.7	50.7	13.6	—
Technical and vocational	8.1	5.4	35.1	48.6	2.7
Commercial	—	20.0	56.0	8.0	16.0
Youth camp	—	12.0	48.0	32.0	8.0
Trade centre	—	4.2	50.0	45.8	—
Hotel school	—	—	—	100.0	—

* Included here are students who had to continue their education at senior secondary level.
Source: Central Statistical Office, Republic of Trinidad and Tobago.

TABLE 10. *Graduates with Jobs by Educational Level and Job Satisfaction/Dissatisfaction*

	Number of graduates with jobs	Graduates who are satisfied with present job	%	Graduates who are not satisfied with present job	%	Not stated	%
All levels	1,068	458	42.9	578	54.1	32	3.0
Primary	47	25	53.2	20	42.6	2	4.3
Junior secondary	8	2	25.0	5	62.5	1	12.5
Government and assisted secondary	356	155	43.5	198	55.6	3	0.8
Private secondary	104	52	50.0	50	48.1	2	1.9
Senior comprehensive	59	19	32.2	40	67.8	—	—
Technical and vocational	250	122	48.8	122	48.8	6	2.4
Commercial	46	15	32.6	27	58.7	4	8.7
Youth camp	83	22	26.5	56	67.5	5	6.0
Trade centre	103	42	40.8	52	50.5	9	8.7
Hotel school	12	4	33.3	8	66.7	—	—

Source: Central Statistical Office, Republic of Trinidad and Tobago.

more of the traditional secondary graduates gained employment, 28.5 per cent as compared to 23.5 per cent of the diversified curriculum graduates. In terms of having the right training of employment, again the traditional graduate had a superior performance; whereas 35.7 per cent of the senior comprehensive graduates thought they did *not* have the right training, less than a half of this number (14.7 per cent) from the traditional schools had similar thoughts. The story is the same for job satisfaction/dissatisfaction. Actually, 43.5 per cent of the traditional school graduates reported that they were satisfied with their jobs while only 32.2 percent of the senior comprehensive graduates reported likewise. What is most significant in this study is that the graduates of the technical and vocational institutes (a sector of the traditional approach or control group), did very much better than the secondary schools in all areas.

For instance, 89.3 percent of graduates from technical institutes sought jobs of which 70.6 percent were successful. Furthermore, a meager 5.4 percent reported that they did not believe that they had the right training while 48.8 percent indicated that they were satisfied with their jobs. Given their superior success rate in examinations (National Craftsman Certificate) in comparison to the senior comprehensives it could be easily deduced that the technical institutes do a better job than senior comprehensives in imparting vocational skills.

Recalling that among the objectives of the diversified curriculum program were those lessening certain types of white-collar job expectations among school-leavers, and encouraging middle-level technicians and craftsmen, it is now obvious that these objectives have not been achieved. Tables 11 and 12 show that more 1979 comprehensives graduates than traditional secondary expect to join the professional and related class in employment. Similarly, the comprehensive students hope to earn greater wages than the traditional graduates. But, as noted above, present trends do not point in this direction. They indicate a fall in the job prospects for crafts and related graduates.

But what of costs? Although the study does not show wage earnings, yet costs of producing graduates will be useful statistics. In dealing with capital costs it needs to be pointed out that since 1972 only diversification curriculum schools have been built. The last of the traditional schools were completed in the mid-1960s. Recent statistics on building costs indicate that in 1982 it cost $22 million to construct a senior comprehensive while the figure was $20 million for junior secondary (1440 enrollment model).[1] In the mid-1960s it cost less than $1 million to build a modern secondary school

---

[1] The Claxton Bay Senior Comprehensive (enrollment—554) and El Dorado Junior Secondary schools were opened in 1983.

TABLE 11. *Percentage Distribution of School Graduates by Choice of Occupation and Type of School*

Type of school	Choice of occupation								
	Professional, technical and related workers	Administrative and managerial workers	Clerical and related workers	Sales workers	Service workers	Agricultural workers	Production related workers	Don't know	Not stated/ not applicable
All schools	23.2	0.3	17.7	0.5	5.3	0.2	11.2	23.5	17.9
Primary	6.8	—	1.5	0.4	1.9	—	32.6	33.3	23.5
Junior secondary	11.9	—	2.9	0.2	2.6	—	5.5	4.2	72.6
Private secondary	28.0	0.3	29.1	0.4	4.6	0.2	2.7	19.1	15.6
Government and assisted secondary	27.8	0.5	14.9	0.9	4.3	0.1	4.2	32.7	14.7
Senior comprehensive	29.4	0.2	19.2	0.2	8.7	0.3	9.0	25.8	7.1
Commercial	3.0	—	69.6	0.7	1.9	—	0.4	13.7	10.7
Technical and vocational	19.0	—	30.5	—	2.4	—	33.7	11.3	3.1
Trade centre	1.0	0.3	—	—	3.3	—	80.3	8.0	7.0
Youth camp	5.6	—	8.4	—	18.0	—	59.8	6.8	1.5
Hotel school	5.6	8.3	16.7	—	47.2	—	—	19.4	2.8
Farm school	27.3	—	—	—	—	72.7	—	—	—

TABLE 12. *Percentage Distribution of School Graduates by Expected Monthly Income and Type of School*

Type of school	Expected monthly income							
	Under $300	$300–$699	$700–$1,099	$1,100–$1,499	$1,500–$1,899	$1,900 and more	Don't know	Not stated/not applicable
All schools	2.5	23.1	29.7	10.6	5.2	6.0	2.1	20.8
Primary	25.4	11.0	5.3	0.4	0.4	—	15.2	42.4
Junior secondary	0.4	4.8	8.4	6.4	3.9	4.9	—	71.2
Private secondary	2.0	32.7	29.4	7.6	2.5	4.4	2.0	19.4
Government and assisted secondary	1.9	22.7	30.7	10.9	6.1	7.0	2.9	17.7
Senior comprehensive	1.3	20.8	33.2	16.1	7.8	8.8	0.2	11.8
Commercial	1.1	47.0	33.3	1.5	0.4	—	2.6	14.1
Technical and vocational	1.2	23.6	56.5	13.9	3.8	0.5	—	0.5
Trade center	7.0	33.0	26.0	15.3	6.7	8.7	2.0	1.3
Youth camp	4.3	33.4	41.2	8.7	5.3	4.0	0.6	2.5
Hotel school	2.8	13.9	66.7	11.1	2.8	—	—	2.8
Farm school	—	—	90.9	9.1	—	—	—	—

(including additions).[1] This school has a sixth form and offers some limited practical subjects. Capital costs for these schools therefore amount to $490,516, $445,924 and $22,296 per annum respectively. Even if the latter figure (for the traditional sector) is adjusted for inflation it would stand at $169,968[2] which is still less than half of that for the diversified school. This means an annual capital cost per student of $885 per senior comprehensive, $309 for junior secondary (single shift) and $212 for traditional schools over a 50-year period. That is to say, for a five-year period capital cost per student for the diversified curriculum program would $(3 \times 309) + (2 \times 885)$, i.e., $2697, while for the traditional schools it would be $1060. Obviously the capital cost per student in the diversified program is two-and-a-half times as much as that of the traditional schools. However this additional expenditure is not compensated for by salaries of vocational graduates.

Moreover the trend of increasing costs for the maintenance of diversified school programs is obvious when compared with other schools. Statistics on salaries for secondary schools in the year 1985 indicate that a normal senior comprehensive is almost twice as expensive as a traditional grammar school of similar size. (Table 13 gives relevant details). An analysis of these figures reveals that cost per student per annum at a senior comprehensive is $3870, at the junior secondary the sum is $2019, while at the traditional grammar type school it is $2562. That is to say that the teacher cost at the senior comprehensive is 150 percent that of the traditional secondary school. Viewed from another perspective, a student moving through the new sector—senior comprehensive via junior secondary would utilize a teacher cost of $2804 in comparison to that of $2562 for a student progressing through a traditional grammar type school. This means to say that implementation of the diversified curriculum sector implies a 10 percent increase on teacher cost per student over the traditional sector.

Statistics relating to the implementation of vocational programs in traditional schools are also *not* encouraging. According to Table 13 the teacher cost for such schools turn out to be the highest—$3225. This is certainly not a healthy indication, costwise, for those who advocate that all schools should offer vocational programs.

But even within the comprehensive school sector a unit analysis shows that technical vocational education is expensive not only in terms of capital costs but also in terms of recurrent costs. Table 14 shows that technical/vocational subjects cost twice as much per unit as academic subjects.

---

[1] The San Fernando Modern Secondary, which has a sixth form and an enrollment of 800, came on stream in 1962.

[2] The capital costs were annualized using $r \times 6$ percent interest rates offered on bonds by Central Bank and also using a building life span of 50 years as stated in architects' briefs. The figure (of $1 million generously used) is adjusted based on inflation rates as given by an *"Assessment of the Plan for Educational Development in Trinidad and Tobago (1968–83)."*

TABLE 13. *Comparison of Teachers' Salaries of Four Schools, 1985*

School type	No. of staff	Enrollment	Salaries
Senior comprehensive	100	1,363	5,274,096
Junior secondary	63	1,672	3,376,774
Traditional secondary (in which some vocational education is offered)	44	742	2,393,329
Traditional grammar school	58	1,111	2,846,921

In spite of the high costs of vocational education and failure of these programs, granted, for a host of reasons: lack of competent teachers, lack of social acceptance of vocational education, inertia of the education system, etc., yet over the past two decades there has been a great thrust in diversified secondary curriculum schooling.

Surely there must be reasons for this great thrust and insistence on its implementation in the face of works which point to its inertia (Psacharopoulos, 1985). Perhaps the reasons might be summed up in three words—faith, politics and intuition.

People the world over, and more so in developing countries, continue to have great faith in education. Education is seen as the great equalizer. Citizens do believe that programs developed in schools which certify their competencies in various areas will lead them to well-paid jobs. In the second instance political leaders find it very appealing, in the face of rising unemployment, to tell the masses that their children will be exposed to curricula designed to suit the varying aptitudes, abilities and interests of all students. Each student in such a scheme must find his niche. In this approach also the problem of unemployment because of unemployability of graduates (mismatch between job openings and skills of graduates) will be alleviated. Thus education, the great equalizer, will even things out. Finally, intuitively it seems correct that offering a diversified curriculum will provide all students with relevant training geared to needs of the community, so that even graduates who fail to secure jobs with firms can create their own employment. But, as has been said by others before, vocational education might be intuitively correct but so far it has been shown to be empirically wrong.

Recent evaluation studies in Colombia and Tanzania confirm this (Psacharopoulos, 1985). At this point in time it must be assumed that everyone is eagerly awaiting the results of some study which will show successful labor market results and cost-effectiveness of the diversified curriculum program in a particular country. Towards this end cost analyses and other evaluation projects should be continued. While it is difficult to witness a return to traditional academic secondary schooling, traditional secondary school programs with broad workshop courses should not be too difficult to implement. The key to proper school programs would be in defining the proper input mix of the different types of subjects.

Alternative Model

Few will oppose the inclusion of pre-vocational or "skill cluster" approaches. Comprehensive schools could be arranged without being dominated by the notions of manpower requirements and at the same time vocational education could be treated ordinarily. That is to say that alongside the academic subjects there could be broad workshop courses. To ensure an appropriate secondary education for all, a core curriculum of not less than 24 subjects with no more than nine electives for workshop (craft) courses is suggested. This means a maximum of nine periods for specialized crafts which could be grouped in clusters. This mix should ensure that students are able to continue general programs with an orientation to workshop courses for those who are so inclined.

Conclusion

Technical/vocational education is a recurrent theme. Somehow during the 1970s it was in low profile. This is most likely because it was then travelling in the guise of *diversification*. Diversification has been recognized for what it is and is now open to question. The majority, if not all, developing countries, have implemented programs of diversification of secondary school curricula. The reasons and objectives for the establishment of diversification have been generally the same throughout the developing world. Among these are:

(1) to bridge the gap between school and work;
(2) to develop an egalitarian society by educating all under one roof;
(3) to produce the skills needed by industry for development;
(4) to implement curricula suitable to aptitudes, ages and abilities of the various young citizens, etc.

These notions are by no means new. They were expressed by economists and educators before and immediately after independence. Research work on technical/vocational education and employment in developing countries have highlighted the fact that education is often given a role which, by itself, could do little in terms of employment and national development (Jennings-Wray and Teape, 1982).

The diversification program has now been in train for over 20 years. It now spans the African and Asian continents, America and the Caribbean. In particular, the program has been implemented in Trinidad and Tobago since 1975 and its graduates now have had several years' exposure to the labor market and society in general.

TABLE 14. *Unit Analysis of Composite and Two-tier System: Teacher Cost per Pupil per Subject and Teachers' Workloads*

| Subject | 1,200 Enrollment 'all age' | | | | 1,440 Enrollment junior secondary followed by 1,564 enrollment (not comprehensive (for O levels)) | | | | | | For a 5 year course in the two tier system i.e. 3×(8) + 2×(11) | For a 5 year course in the single tier i.e. 5×(4) |
| | | | | | Junior secondary level | | | Senior secondary level | | | | |
	Number of students participating in subject	Number of teachers required	Teacher cost per pupil per annum	Teacher's workload —number of teach periods per week	Number of students taking subject	Number of teachers required	Teacher cost per pupil	Number of students taking part in subject	Number of teachers required	Teacher cost per pupil		
1. English Language and Literature	1,200	6	114.11	27.3	1,440	6	93.00	1,344	7 (29)	118.86	516.72	570.55
2. Mathematics	1,200	6	114.11	26	1,440	6	93.00	1,344	7 (30)	118.86	516.72	570.55
3. General Science	720	3	95.09	24	1,440	5	77.50	—	—	—	—	—
4. Chemistry	480	2	95.09	16	—	—	—	1,344	9 (18)	76.41	385.32	475.45
5. Physics	480	2	95.09	19	—	—	—	1,344	9 (18)	76.41	385.32	475.45
6. Biology	256	2	178.09	16	—	—	—	896	3 (27.3)	—	385.32	523.51
7. Social studies	720	3	95.09	24	1,440	5	77.50	—	—	—	—	—
8. History	480	2	95.09	22	—	—	—	1,344	4 (27)	67.92	368.34	475.45
9. Geography	480	2	95.09	16	—	—	—	1,344	4 (23.5)	67.92	368.34	475.45
10. Spanish	1,200	4	76.07	28.5	1,440	4	62.00	1,344	6 (29)	101.88	389.96	380.35
11. Agriculture	816	5	139.06	24.8	1,440	6	93.00	160	3 (26.6)	427.73	1,134.46	695.30
12. Business studies	64	2	688.88	30	—	—	—	160	5 (29.6)	688.88	1,377.76	1,377.76 (only 2 yr course)
13. Home economics	456	5	135.07	28.4	1,440	3	62.00	192	6 (28.6)	826.65	1,829.30	1,785.35
14. Art and craft	752	2	60.70	19	1,440	3	46.50	96	1 (12)	137.76	149.33	316.95

15. Music	752	2	60.70	19	1,440	3	46.50	32	1 (12)	118.44	376.38	303.50
16. Industrial arts	360	2	122.46	27	1,440	4	62.00	—	—	—	—	
17. Construction technology	32	2	1,377.75	20.5	—	—	—	192	2 (21)	229.63	645.26	3,122.75*
18. Mechanical technology	32	2	1,377.75	20.5	—	—	—	64	2 (21)	688.88	1,563.76	3,122.75
19. Machine shop	32	2	1,377.75	18	—	—	—	32	1 (30)	688.88	1,563.76	3,122.75
20. Auto mechanics	32	2	1,377.75	18	—	—	—	32	1 (30)	688.88	1,563.76	3,122.75
21. Carpentry	32	2	1,377.75	18	—	—	—	32	1 (30)	688.88	1,563.76	3,122.75
22. Electrical installation	32	2	1,377.75	18	—	—	—	32	1 (30)	688.88	1,563.76	3,122.75
23. Plumbing					—	—	—	32	1 (30)	688.88	1,563.76	
24. Welding		Not offered			—	—	—	32	1 (30)	688.88	1,563.76	
25. Air conditioning					—	—	—	32	1 (30)	688.88	1,563.76	
26. Surveying					—	—	—	32	1 (30)	688.88	1,563.76	
27. Electronics					—	—	—	64	1 (20)	688.88	1,563.76	
28. Drafting					—	—	—	640	4 (27.5)	323.77	1,563.76	

Parentheses indicate period per week per teacher.   * Includes industrial arts and junior secondary level.

Source: Educational Planning Division, Ministry of Education, Trinidad and Tobago, Classification/Compensation Plan 1981–87; Civil Service estimates. The average salary of special teachers = $1568, technical/vocational = $1837, and graduates = $2069 per month. Technical/vocational teachers IV are equivalent to graduates.

That there is sustained interest in technical/vocational education in Trinidad and Tobago is evident. The draft plan for education development in Trinidad and Tobago highlights this interest. Moreover, influential people still talk of the great necessity for technical/vocational education to produce the necessary linkages within the labor force. Close scrutiny of this plan identifies three models which are to be pursued: (i) an informational exchange between industry and school; (ii) an alternation between school and work; and (iii) an integration of work and school. These models are not new. They have been proposed before and some have been tried elsewhere. For example, Stafford *et al.* (1982) state:

> The argument for introducing a broad vocational orientation into the school curriculum is not new; but despite repeated exhortations to bridge the gap between school and employment, relatively little has been achieved.
>
> This is partly due to the lack of knowledge about the needs of industry among teachers who may never have worked in the industry themselves. Therefore, a first step towards introducing a broad vocational orientation into schools is to make information about industry more readily available to teachers.

In other literature on the subject we have been told of the attempts to integrate school and work (Figuero *et al.*, 1974). It has been reported that since the death of Mao in 1976 the integrated work and school program has given way to emphasis on academic work (Arnove, 1984).

However, whatever the failures or limited successes reported this should in no way discourage further evaluation.

Attempts so far, to determine the efficacy of the diversification of the secondary curriculum in Trinidad and Tobago tend to show that the program after all, might not be cost-effective. The sum total objectives are far from being attained.

There seems to be a very distinct pattern in the development of technical/vocational education. It would appear that in times of low demand for vocational skills industries are left to themselves to provide these. However, in times of economic boom and rapid industrial development schools are called upon to provide these required skills. In Trinidad and Tobago, in 1968, when the first education plan was proposed (and the GNP was low), it was suggested that a general orientation to vocational skills would be attempted in the secondary schools. In 1975 when the GNP was high and the Government had proposed a program of industrial and agricultural development, the schools were assigned the task of providing the necessary skills required. Now in the latter half of the 1980s, with falling oil prices and a slowing down of the economy, it is proposed again, that there should be cooperation between industry and school. In 1967 the GNP was $1,1912 million, in 1968 it was $1,394.8 million, and in 1975 was $4,645.9 million with the promise of steep and steady economic growth.

But there is still the sociological aspect of vocational education. It would still seem that most people have a high regard for academic (general) secondary education and low esteem for technical/vocational education. In Trinidad and Tobago, for instance, pupils are assigned to secondary schools on the basis of a National Common Entrance Examination at eleven plus. Pupils are allowed four choices of school which they would like to attend, based on merit. It is well known that the top 15 percent of these students opt for and attend grammar schools. This is so because of the citizens' perception of education.

It would be of the utmost importance to recognize recent works that have been done on workers' attitudes/characteristics in connection with the education/training–employment nexus. Much evidence now seems to point to the direction that while cognitive knowledge and skills are indeed important for economic development and employment, yet it is a bundle of characteristics which includes much of the traits from the affective domain, that figure so prominently in the education/training–employment relationship (Bowles and Gintis, 1976; Blaug, 1984). Indeed we have come to observe that as societies grow more advanced, there is an increased need for technology and a flexible labor force. What this means is that the actual skills imparted in schools (apart from advanced literacy and numeracy) may be less important than the creation of attitudes and cognitive abilities which enable individuals to adjust to frequently changing job situations (Fägerlind and Saha, 1983: Blaug, 1984).

Indeed, what has now been noted, is that workers with low levels of schooling and those with work experience limited to a specific skill are at a disadvantage in the labor market when they are displaced. The point is, that technology changes are rapidly taking place, and it would seem that learning periods for specific trades are becoming shorter while the *modus operandi* of various technology generally has the tendency to lessen skills required for contemporary jobs (Blaug and Rumberger, 1984).

With respect to the literature concerning the successes and failures of vocational education in enhancing employment prospects of secondary graduates, a review would show strong cases put forward by both proponents and opponents of secondary vocational education. Recently many have argued that failures in vocational education at the secondary level lie in the comprehensive school system (Bottoms and Copa, 1983; Weisberg, 1983). They argue that specialized vocational education schools (generally post-secondary) schools always do better. In particular, with special reference to the United States, Weisberg (1983) has argued that the most widely accepted labor market studies project the most rapid growth in service, finance and trade, the majority of new jobs created are expected to be in the areas of health services, computers, repair of business and industrial machines, banking, secretarial services and recreation. Employers in these areas will need strong general skills, not job specific skills. Moreover, such job specific skills, when taught in a classroom are best taught at post-secondary level and not in comprehensive high schools. Although it may be aruged that this deals with the United States situation, the situation for Trinidad and Tobago need not be far off this mark.

Much could be said for the diversified secondary curriculum. Indeed, there is more than a semblance of truth in the notion that school and work are related. However, there are good reasons to doubt whether the diversification program will ever be effective in enhancing school output, in solving unemployment, under-employment and workers' dissatisfaction. Charges that unemployment is mainly due to a mismatch between worker skills and job requirements, because of school output, are simply false prosecutions. Experience has shown that investment in education expansion does not create jobs except those directly connected with the education system, e.g., teachers, laboratory assistants, etc. On the other hand, it is economic expansion that enhances employment. While schools might be able to assist in training, schools by themselves cannot create jobs. The failure of the system is probably not in vocational orientations but in the fundamental education function of teaching the young to read, write, compute, think analytically and act responsibly as workers, neighbors and community-oriented citizens.

Most employers are willing to point out that the problems faced in work situations are not technical (Grubb and Lazerson, 1975; O'Toole, 1979). Rather these problems are complex, interdependent and have more to do with whether or not people are able to work with each other co-operatively and ethically. School principals have reported that this is the identical feedback they normally get from employers in Trinidad and Tobago.

Finally, however the drive for vocationalizing education is linked with national economic problems, and to what extent there is hope for solutions, it seems that the vocationalizing trend will be around for a long time. At this point in time it is difficult to imagine what events, changes and ideologies can alter this course.

References

Arnove, R. E. (1984) Educational policy in China and India: The problems of overcoming the work/study dichotomy. *Phi delta kappan*, March.

Becker, G. S. (1964) *Human capital: A theoretical and empirical analysis*. New York: National Bureau of Economic Research.

Blaug, M. (1968) Cost benefit and cost effectiveness analysis. In *Budgeting programme analysis and cost effectiveness analysis in educational planning*. Paris: OECD.

Blaug, M. (1973) *Education and the employment problem in developing countries*. Geneva: ILO.

Blaug, M. (1974) Educational policy and the economics of education: Some practical lessons for educational planners in developing countries. In *Education and development reconsidered, The Bellagio conference papers*. New York: Praeger.

Blaug, M. (1984) *Where are we now in the economics of education*. London: University of London.

Blaug, M. and Rumberger, R. W. (1984) The growing imbalance between education and work. New York: *Phi delta kappan*, Jan.

Bottoms, G. and Copa, P. (1983) A perspective on vocational education today. *Phi delta kappan*, **64** (5).

Bowles, S. and Gintis, H. (1976) *Schooling in capitalist America*. New York: Basic Books.

Central Statistical Office, Trinidad and Tobago (1979) A survey of school graduates 1977, Report on Phase II.

Central Statistical Office (1985) Trinidad and Tobago, Continuous sample survey of population.

Fägerlind, I. and Saha, L. (1983) *Education and national development: A comparative perspective*. Oxford: Pergamon Press.

Figuera, M., Prieto, I. and Gutierrez, E. (1974) *The basic secondary school in the country: An educational innovation in Cuba*. Paris: IBE/UNESCO.

Government of Trinidad and Tobago (1974). *Draft plan for educational development in Trinidad and Tobago* (1968–1983). Trinidad and Tobago: Government Printer.

Government of Trinidad and Tobago (1975) *Prime Minister's proposals to Cabinet on education*. Trinidad and Tobago: Government Printer.

Government of Trinidad and Tobago (1985) *Plan for educational development in Trinidad and Tobago* (1985–1990). Government of Trinidad and Tobago.

Grubb, M. W. and Lazerson, M. (1975) Rally round the workplace: Continuities and fallacies in career education. *Harvard educational review*, **45** (4).

Jennings-Wray, Z. P. and Teape, V. E. (1982) Jamaica's work experience programme. *Prospects*, **12** (4).

Lillis, K. and Hogan, D. (1983) The dilemmas of diversification: Problems associated with vocational education in developing countries. *Comparative education*, **19** (1).

Ministry of Education (1983) A summary report of Project Concern, a Follow-up study of graduates of the senior comprehensive schools and the on-the-job training programmes. Division of Technical/Vocational Education and Training, Ministry of Education, Trinidad and Tobago.

O'Toole, J. (1979) Education is education, and work is work—Shall ever the twain meet? *Teachers' record*, Fall.

Psacharopoulos, G. (1985) Curriculum diversification in Colombia and Tanzania. *Comparative education*, **29** (4).

Report (1984) *Report of the Cabinet appointed Committee to examine the content, organization and administration of technical/vocational education in secondary schools*. Port of Spain, Trinidad and Tobago.

Stafford, E. *et al.* (1982) School and work: A Technique to help bridge the gap. *Educational research*, 243–248.

Weisberg, A. (1983) What research has to say about vocational education and the high school. *Phi delta kappan*, **64** (5).

Williams, E. (1968) *Education in the British West Indies*. New York: University Place Book Place.

Williams, E. (1975) *Education and decolonisation, an address to the Caribbean Union College*. Trinidad and Tobago.

Ziderman, A. (1978) *Manpower training: Theory and practice*. Basingstoke: Macmillan.

APPENDIX 1

TABLE A1. *Specialized Craft Courses: Weekly Periods per Student/Class of 16*

Branches and courses		Weekly periods per course, per student per class																Roll form 4	
		Technology		Business studies		Home economics		Garment construction		Beauty culture		Total						No. of classes	Class size
		4	5	4	5	4	5	4	5	4	5	4	5	T					
A. Industrial crafts																			
1. Carpentry:	Theory	3	3									3	3	6				1	16
	Workshop	12	12									12	12	24					
	Drawing	3	3									3	3	6					
2. Masonry:	Theory	3	3									3	3	6				1	16
	Workshop	12	12									12	12	24					
	Drawing	3	3									3	3	6					
3. Electrical installation:	Theory	3	3									3	3	6				1	16
	Workshop	12	12									12	12	24					
	Drawing	3	3									3	3	6					
4. Air conditioning:	Theory	3	3									3	3	6				1	16
	Workshop	12	12									12	12	24					
	Drawing	3	3									3	3	6					
5. Plumbing:	Theory	3	3									3	3	6				1	16
	Workshop	12	12									12	12	24					
	Drawing	3	3									3	3	6					
6. Welding:	Theory	3	3									3	3	6				1	16
	Workshop	12	12									12	12	24					
	Drawing	3	3									3	3	6					

7. Machine shop:	Theory	3 3	3 3 6		
	Workshop	12 12	12 12 24	1	16
	Drawing	3 3	3 3 6		
8. Auto mechanics:	Theory	3 3	3 3 6		
	Workshop	12 12	12 12 24	1	16
	Drawing	3 3	3 3 6		
B. *Business studies*					
Typing and office practice:	Theory	6 6	6 6 12	2	16
	Practical	12 12	12 12 24		
C. *Home economics*					
(i) Food and nutrition:	Theory	2 2	2 2 4		
	Practical	8 8	8 8 16		
(ii) Clothing and textiles:	Theory	2 2	2 2 4	2	16
	Practical	2 2	2 2 4		
(iii) House craft:	Theory	2 2	2 2 4		
	Practical	2 2	2 2 4		
D. *Garment construction*	Theory	6 6	6 6 12	1	16
	Practical	12 12	12 12 24		
E. *Beauty culture*	Theory	6 6	6 6 12	1	16
	Practical	12 12	12 12 24		

Similar enrollment for Form 5.

TABLE A2. *Allocation of Electives in Pre-Technician Courses*

(In the second column, No. (i) relates to students whose emphasis is on pre-technician courses and No. (ii) relates to students whose emphasis is on academic courses.)

Elective branches and subjects		Weekly periods per subject					Roll		Type of teaching accommodation
		Technology (4 5)	Agriculture (4 5)	Business studies (4 5)	Home economics (4 5)	Creative arts (4 5)	No. of classes (4 5)	Size of class (4 5)	
1. Technology									
(a) Const.*		4					5 5	16 16	Workshops
(b) Mechanical†	(i)	4 4					} (5 5)	(16 16)	
(c) Technical drawing w.r.t. (a&b)	(i)	4							Draughting rooms
	(ii)	2 2					1 1	16 16	
1A. Drafting‡	(i)	12 12					— 1‡	— 16‡	Draughting
	(ii)	2 2					— 1‡	— 16‡	
1B. Surveying§	(i)	12 12					1 —	16 —§	Specialized rooms
	(ii)	2 2					1 —	16 —§	
1C. Electronics	(i)	12 12					1 1	16 16	Specialized rooms
	(ii)	2 2					1 1	16 16	Specialized rooms
2. Agriculture									
(a) Agricultural science	(i)		4 4				3 3	16 16	Laboratory and field classroom
(b) Theory	(i)		4 4						Workshop and field
(c) Mechanics	(i)		2 2						
	(ii)						2 2	16 16	
3. Business studies									
(a) Typing	(i)			4 4			3 3	16 16	Specialized room
(b) Shorthand				4 4					
(c) Office practice				4 4					
(d) Commerce									
(e) Principles of accounts	(ii)			2 2			1 1	16 16	

					Specialized rooms and classrooms
4. Home economics					
(a) Food and nutrition		4 4			⎱
(b) Clothing and textiles	(i)	4 4	4 4	16 16	
(c) Home management	(ii)	4 4 2 2	1 1	16 16	
5. Creative arts					
(a) Art and craft	(i)	4 4			Art and craft room
(b) Music and movement		4 4	1 1	16 16	Music room
(c) Physical education		4 4	1 1	16 16	Multipurpose area courts and field
(a) Art and craft	(ii)	2 2	1 1	16 16	Art and craft room
(b) Music and movement	(ii)	2 2	1 1	16 16	Music room
(c) Physical education	(ii)	2 2	1 1	16 16	Multipurpose area courts and field
Pre-technician groups (i)			18 18	16 16	
Academic groups (ii)			10 10	16 16	

* Wood, electrical, masonry.
† Machine, metal, welding and foundry.
‡ Biennial intake starting in year of opening.
§ Biennial intake starting one year after opening.

NOTE: Excepting Branches IA, IB and IC each pre-technician student (i.e., at No. 6 in each branch) should choose three components of any of the courses.

APPENDIX 2

TABLE A3. Labor Force by Sex, Employment Status and Educational Attainment

Both sexes *

Educational attainment	Six months ended	Total labor force (2)+(3) (1)	Persons with jobs (2)	Total unemployed (4)+(5) (3)	Persons without jobs and seeking work (4)	Other unemployed (5)	Unemployed as a % of labor force (6)	Persons with jobs plus persons without jobs and seeking work (7)	Persons without jobs and seeking work as a % of col. (7) (8)	Labor force (9)	Persons with jobs (10)	Persons with jobs plus persons without jobs and seeking work (11)	Total unemployed (12)	Persons without jobs and seeking work (13)
Total all education	38 30.12.82	447,000	404,400	42,700	22,400	20,300	10	426,700	5	100	100	100	100	100
	39 30. 6.83	442,400	393,300	49,100	27,300	21,800	11	420,600	6	100	100	100	100	100
	40 31.12.83	456,400	405,500	50,900	32,100	18,800	11	437,600	7	100	100	100	100	100
	41 30. 6.84	470,900	410,600	60,400	37,300	23,000	13	447,900	8	100	100	100	100	100
No education	38 31.12.82	7,900	6,700	1,200	500	700	15	7,200	7	2	2	2	3	2
	39 30. 6.83	7,600	7,400	300	200	100	3	7,500	2	2	2	2	1	1
	40 31.12.83	6,000	5,700	300	100	300	6	5,800	1	1	1	1	1	—
	41 30. 6.84	8,100	7,800	300	200	200	4	8,000	2	2	2	2	1	—
Kindergarten	38 31.12.82	1,800	1,400	400	200	200	23	1,700	15	—	—	—	1	1
	39 30. 6.83	2,300	2,200	100	100	—	4	2,300	4	1	1	1	—	—
	40 31.12.83	3,000	2,900	100	100	—	3	3,000	3	1	1	1	1	—
	41 30. 6.84	2,800	2,600	200	200	—	6	2,800	6	1	1	1	1	—
Standard 1–2	38 31.12.82	10,200	9,600	600	200	400	6	9,800	2	2	2	2	1	2
	39 30. 6.83	9,000	7,900	1,000	600	400	11	8,500	7	2	2	2	2	2
	40 31.12.83	10,200	8,900	1,300	1,300	100	13	10,100	12	2	2	2	3	4
	41 30. 6.84	13,100	11,400	1,700	1,100	600	13	12,500	9	3	3	3	3	3

Each educational attainment as a proportion of total all education

Standard 3–5	38	31.12.82	68,900	61,500	7,400	3,400	4,000	11	64,900	5	15	15	15	17	15
	39	30. 6.83	71,600	63,300	8,300	5,600	2,700	12	68,900	8	16	16	16	17	20
	40	31.12.83	71,500	63,900	7,600	4,400	3,300	11	68,300	6	16	16	16	15	14
	41	30. 6.84	65,900	57,900	8,000	5,000	2,900	12	63,000	8	14	14	14	13	13
Standard 6–7	38	30.12.82	175,800	159,800	16,000	8,800	7,100	9	168,700	5	39	40	40	37	40
	39	30. 6.83	171,500	152,300	19,200	10,800	8,400	11	163,100	7	39	39	39	39	40
	40	31.12.83	171,000	152,300	18,300	11,700	6,500	11	164,100	7	37	38	37	36	37
	41	30. 6.84	176,700	154,300	22,400	13,600	8,800	13	167,900	8	38	38	37	37	36
Secondary (School Certificate not obtained)	38	31.12.82	124,300	108,700	15,700	7,900	7,800	13	116,500	7	28	27	27	37	35
	39	30. 6.83	125,900	107,500	18,400	8,900	10,000	15	116,400	8	28	27	28	38	32
	40	31.12.83	140,500	119,800	20,700	13,300	7,400	15	133,200	10	31	30	30	41	42
	41	30. 6.84	152,100	127,600	24,500	15,000	9,500	16	142,600	11	32	31	32	41	40
Secondary (School Certificate obtained)*	38	31.12.82	42,700	41,600	1,100	1,000	100	3	42,600	2	10	10	10	3	4
	39	30. 6.83	39,200	37,900	1,300	900	300	3	38,800	2	9	10	9	3	3
	40	31.12.83	39,900	37,900	2,000	900	1,100	5	38,800	2	9	9	9	4	3
	41	30. 6.84	39,000	36,500	2,400	1,400	1,000	6	38,000	4	8	9	8	4	4
University	38	31.12.82	11,800	11,500	300	200	100	3	11,700	2	3	3	3	1	1
	39	30. 6.83	12,400	12,300	200	200	—	1	12,400	1	3	3	3	—	1
	40	31.12.83	12,200	11,900	300	300	100	3	12,200	2	3	3	3	1	1
	41	30. 6.84	11,700	10,900	800	700	100	6	11,600	6	2	3	3	1	2
Educated in a foreign country	38	31.12.82	700	700	—	—	—	—	700	—	—	—	—	—	—
	39	30. 6.83	1,100	900	200	—	200	15	900	—	—	—	—	—	—
	40	31.12.83	1,200	1,000	200	100	100	14	1,100	8	—	—	—	—	—
	41	30. 6.84	900	800	200	200	—	18	900	18	—	—	—	—	—
Other	41	30. 6.84	500	500	—	—	—	—	500	—	—	—	—	—	—
Not stated	41	30. 6.84	300	300	—	—	—	—	300	—	—	—	—	—	—

* Includes Higher School Certificate and G.C.E. 'A' level (any number).

TABLE A4. *Unit Analysis of Composite and Two-tier System: Teacher Cost per Pupil per Subject and Teachers' Workloads*

Subject	1,200 Enrollment 'all age'				1,440 Enrollment junior secondary followed by 1,564 enrollment (not comprehensive (for O levels))							
	Number of students participating in subject	Number of teachers required	Teacher cost per pupil per annum	Teacher's workload —number of teach periods per week	Junior secondary level			Senior secondary level			For a 5 year course in the two tier system i.e. $3\times(8) + 2\times(11)$	For a 5 year course in the single tier i.e. $5\times(4)$
					Number of students taking subject	Number of teachers required	Teacher cost per pupil	Number of students taking part in subject	Number of teachers required	Teacher cost per pupil		
1. English Language and Literature	1,200	6	114.11	27.3	1,440	6	93.00	1,344	7 (29)	118.86	516.72	570.55
2. Mathematics	1,200	6	114.11	26	1,440	6	93.00	1,344	7 (30)	118.86	516.72	570.55
3. General Science	720	3	95.09	24	1,440	5	77.50	—	—	—	—	—
4. Chemistry	480	2	95.09	16	—	—	—	1,344	9 (18)	76.41	385.32	475.45
5. Physics	480	2	95.09	19	—	—	—	1,344	9 (18)	76.41	385.32	475.45
6. Biology	256	2	178.09	16	—	—	—	896	3 (27.3)	—	385.32	523.51
7. Social studies	720	3	95.09	24	1,440	5	77.50	—	—	—	—	—
8. History	480	2	95.09	22	—	—	—	1,344	4 (27)	67.92	368.34	475.45
9. Geography	480	2	95.09	16	—	—	—	1,344	4 (23.5)	67.92	368.34	475.45
10. Spanish	1,200	4	76.07	28.5	1,440	4	62.00	1,344	6 (29)	101.88	389.96	380.35
11. Agriculture	816	5	139.06	24.8	1,440	6	93.00	160	3 (26.6)	427.73	1,134.46	695.30
12. Business studies	64	2	688.88	30	—	—	—	160	5 (29.6)	688.88	1,377.76	1,377.76 (only 2 yr course)
13. Home economics	456	5	135.07	28.4	1,440	3	62.00	192	6 (28.6)	826.65	1,829.30	1,785.35
14. Art and craft	752	2	60.70	19	1,440	3	46.50	96	1 (12)	137.76	149.33	316.95

15. Music	752	2	60.70	19	1,440	3	46.50	32	1 (12)	118.44	376.38	303.50
16. Industrial arts	360	2	122.46	27	1,440	4	62.00	—	—	—	—	—
17. Construction technology	32	2	1,377.75	20.5	—	—	—	192	2 (21)	229.63	645.26	3,122.75*
18. Mechanical technology	32	2	1,377.75	20.5	—	—	—	64	2 (21)	688.88	1,563.76	3,122.75
19. Machine shop	32	2	1,377.75	18	—	—	—	32	1 (30)	688.88	1,563.76	3,122.75
20. Auto mechanics	32	2	1,377.75	18	—	—	—	32	1 (30)	688.88	1,563.76	3,122.75
21. Carpentry	32	2	1,377.75	18	—	—	—	32	1 (30)	688.88	1,563.76	3,122.75
22. Electrical installation	32	2	1,377.75	18	—	—	—	32	1 (30)	688.88	1,563.76	3,122.75
23. Plumbing	Not offered							32	1 (30)	688.88	1,563.76	
24. Welding	Not offered							32	1 (30)	688.88	1,563.76	
25. Air conditioning	Not offered							32	1 (30)	688.88	1,563.76	
26. Surveying	Not offered							32	1 (30)	688.88	1,563.76	
27. Electronics	Not offered							64	1 (20)	688.88	1,563.76	
28. Drafting	Not offered							640	4 (27.5)	323.77	1,563.76	

Parentheses indicate period per week per teacher.   * Includes industrial arts and junior secondary level.
Source: Educational Planning Division, Ministry of Education, Trinidad and Tobago, Classification/Compensation Plan 1981–87; Civil Service estimates. The average salary of special teachers = $1568, technical/vocational = $1837, and graduates = $2069 per month. Technical/vocational teachers IV are equivalent to graduates.

Index